But it is much more than that. Ewell shows us how to get unstuck, how to begin from the ground up, how to "prolong the incarnation." This is a wondrously insightful and compelling vision for faith communities seeking to be a life-giving presence in their communities.

—Paul Sparks, coauthor of *The New Parish*

Sam's integrity glows through the pages of his "outsider-insider reflections. As he draws on the words and witness of Illich and develops his thinking to explore human flourishing, we discover afresh the power of incarnational mission in community with others. I'm grateful for this deep thinking from a deep soul.

—Heather Cracknell
Head of Development for Fresh Expressions, The Church of England

This is a thought-provoking exploration of how we live as people of a missionary God in the very peculiar contexts of today. Sam's deep reflection on his own journey will cause you to reflect too on what it might look like for you and your church to live out an abundant spirituality. Like gardening demonstration plots, our churches are to be spaces that offer love, care, and companionship (and good food) to the places and people they are in the midst of. *Faith Seeking Conviviality* will inspire you to do just that.

—Dr. Ruth Valerio
Global Advocacy and Influencing Director, Tearfund

Sam brings fresh insight into cross-cultural mission as he draws on the life of the late Catholic priest and philosopher Ivan Illich. Sam's book brings together deep theological thinking with the many engaging stories from both Ilich's and his own faith journey as missionaries in Central and South America.

The practical theology approach that he takes gives him a lens that locates the theology of the missionary among the people where they find themselves. Sam highlights some essential arguments and identifies the dangers of assimilating or exporting our own culture into the mission field.

In this book Sam brings a much-appreciated vulnerability into his own learning as he allows Illich's life to help him reflect on his identity as an American missionary. The book explores the conflicts within himself as he finds his identity being caught between two cultures. Not just American but not fully Brazilian either, he discovers a way of co-breathing and being surprised by the other.

>—Simon Jay
>CEO of The Haven Community Project
>West Midlands Area Coordinator for Urban Expression, Birmingham

Sam Ewell writes with clarity and conviction because he knows what he has lived. The wisdom of these pages comes from an unwavering commitment to "begin in the middle" and to discover there the life-giving truth of convivial friendship. This book jumped to the top of my reading list, because it is the work of a rare theologian whose uncompromising pursuit of Jesus inspires and helps us remember what theology is for. I am deeply grateful for it.

>—Chanon Ross, PhD
>Program Director, Lilly Endowment, Inc.

Sam Ewell's theology is the most "earthed" theology I have ever encountered. He lives what he writes and he writes what he lives, and both his life and his writing draw their energy, through roots that go deep, from the worm-enriched soil—humus—that we humans share together, and share with a multitude of other-than-human life. Never has there been a more critical moment for us humans to intensely inhabit one of Sam's central mottos: "Treat the earth as if your life depends on it." Never has there been a more urgent need for those of us who are part of churches and societies scarred historically, culturally, and politically by "the colonial wound" to pursue the possibility of tending and cultivating our edges in ways that enhance life rather than entrench divisions. In a world still largely captivated by "throwaway culture," Sam invites us, by beginning anew with "a preferential option for the discarded," to open ourselves in radical receptivity to "God's in-breaking economy of abundance." Put down your roots and drink deeply of the wisdom of this book. It is rich soil indeed.

>—Rev. Dr. Al Barrett
>Rector, Hodge Hill Church

Ewell's book is an exciting contribution that crosses so many unfortunate boundaries in theological thought and action. Historically, he engages with a key theological figure, Ivan Illich, whose thought and actions continue to instruct us given the diversity of our present world. Missiologically, he reminds us of the need for authenticity in mission and for the constant critique of our tendencies to make the "other" into our image and likeness. In terms of ethics, he challenges us to take our living together seriously, accepting each other as gift and not threat. With regard to theology generally, he challenges our approaches to methodology, reminding us of the necessity to constantly theologize out of the messy entanglements of life.

—Rev. Dr. Carlton Turner
Tutor, Queen's Foundation for Theological Education, Birmingham

Faith Seeking Conviviality is a joyful blend of musicality, theological reflection, horticulture, and missiology; as an act of practical theology, it is a gift. Sam's commitment to bringing his whole self to the theological task allows for an easy flow between the diverse themes and creates coherence, encompassing Sam's journey in mission and the thought of Ivan Illich. This book is a helpful introduction to Illich's thought and practice, but it also offers a worked example, with full disclosure, of the impact of his categories of "gratuity" and "conviviality" on missional practice in Brazil and in the UK. We need more stories like this. Navigating difference and embodying the solidarity and justice of the kingdom of God is the call of the church in this time; and here Sam Ewell offers an account of what happens when we seek to live this calling in communities. As with any personal story, its gift lies not in "telling how to" but in offering moments of resonance, that we might attend to the contours of our own stories more deeply and be helped to notice God at work in them.

—Dr. Anna Ruddick
Community Engagement Associate, Livability

As this decade seems destined to mark the intensification of inequality worldwide, it is hard to imagine a time when radical responses to injustice by Christians were more necessary. In this book, Sam Ewell offers us a host of tools for addressing this crisis of compassion. While the work of Ivan Illich lies in the foreground, particularly his incarnational Christianity and social critique, the book is also richly interwoven with biographical narrative and personal reflections on the practice of intercultural life and ministry. Ewell offers us a close look at the *viradas* or forms of "turning" that stand as waypoints on this journey into faith seeking conviviality. The book is eminently readable, yet at the same time engages with cutting-edge theological scholarship. For anyone seeking to make their ministry and theology relevant in an increasingly pluralistic world, Ewell's book should be required reading!

—Jeremy Kidwell
Senior Lecturer in Christian Ethics, University of Birmingham

In this deeply engaging volume, Samuel Ewell offers his readers several gifts. He opens a window onto the too-little-known life and work of Ivan Illich. At the same time, he carries out a deeply Illichian experiment, telling his own story of dislocation and relocation, and the process of working out his "mission" with fear and trembling. Indeed, readers will find themselves invited into a form of conviviality as they read. Those doing the work of theology will find a final gift as well: Ewell both describes and models a form of theology that resists the myth of detached "objectivity" and that is, rather, always unapologetically situated in its own time, place, and story. Rooted in the Incarnation, it embraces particularity wholeheartedly. What a breath of fresh air!

—Dr. Holly Taylor Coolman
Assistant Professor of Theology, Providence College

This fine and fascinating text has the capacity to kick-start a renewed reflection on mission, on Christian discernment, on how to truly engage with the worlds we find ourselves in so as to draw all these diverse and separate moments into a communal experience that we can rightly call convivial.

To work this transformation the author travels from the US to Brazil and since on to the UK. He learns to inhabit and play the rhythms of samba and to indwell wonderfully different modes of community. As a result his original clear ideas of mission and church are blown open and gradually reconfigured. Throughout this journey of mind and heart, Samuel, like Dante with his Virgil in the *Divine Comedy*, has the companionship of his own muse, Ivan Illich, to help him bring together the past and present into a new open-ended synthesis. His attentive and creative re-reading of Illich would be reason enough to celebrate this text. But like the subtle rhythms of salsa it's just one of the many rich currents that flow into this convivial theology.

This is a work of charm and encouragement but also of disturbing insights that provoke and transform. It challenges deeply held presuppositions, prizes them open and reconfigures their parts. The author is sharing his own deeply pondered journey of change. It is a gift for those willing to receive it. It calls into question our theological, missional, and pastoral positions and pushes them till they break open. He then takes the insights that emerge and reads them, alongside the Scriptures and the experiences of the groups with which he works, with the same subtlety he brings to playing percussion in his band where the individual musicians both play their piece and yet adapt to the unique playing of their fellows. The outcome is fresh, life-enhancing, and convivial models of living the Christian way. Throughout he speaks not as a pedagogue but as one whose own presuppositions are still being ruptured and creatively reconfigured under the inspiration of the divine Spirit he encounters on the streets in the slums, in the making of music, in the building of a wormery, and in the creating of a communal garden on waste land.

The text is subversive; it reveals the ever-present possibility of bringing to birth a more communitarian, convivial way of life for all. May it be so.

—David McLoughlin
Emeritus Fellow of Christian Theology,
Newman University, Birmingham

Faith Seeking Conviviality

Faith Seeking Conviviality

Reflections on Ivan Illich, Christian Mission, and the Promise of Life Together

SAMUEL E. EWELL III

Foreword by WILLIE JAMES JENNINGS

CASCADE Books • Eugene, Oregon

FAITH SEEKING CONVIVIALITY
Reflections on Ivan Illich, Christian Mission, and the Promise of Life Together

Copyright © 2020 Samuel E. Ewell III. All rights reserved. Except for brief quotation in critical publications or reviews, no part of this book may be reproduced in any manner without prior written permission from the publisher. Write: Permissions, Wipf and Stock Publishers, 199 W. 8th Ave., Suite 3, Eugene, OR 97401.

Cascade Publications
An Imprint of Wipf and Stock Publishers
199 W. 8th Ave., Suite 3
Eugene, OR 97401

www.wipfandstock.com

PAPERBACK ISBN: 978-1-5326-1461-3
HARDCOVER ISBN: 978-1-5326-1463-7
EBOOK ISBN: 978-1-5326-1462-0

Cataloguing-in-Publication data:

Names: Ewell, Samuel E., III, author. | Jennings, Willie James, 1961–, foreword.

Title: Faith seeking conviality : reflections on Ivan Illich, Christian mission, and the promise of life together / Samuel E. Ewell III ; foreword by Willie James Jennings.

Description: Eugene, OR : Cascade Books, 2020 | Includes bibliographical references and index(es).

Identifiers: ISBN 978-1-5326-1461-3 (paperback) | ISBN 978-1-5326-1463-7 (hardcover) | ISBN 978-1-5326-1462-0 (ebook)

Subjects: LCSH: Illich Ivan—1926-2002. | Missions. | Missions Theory. | Marginality, Social Religious aspects Christianity.

Classification: BV2061.3 E97 2020 (print) | BV2061.3 E97 (ebook)

Manufactured in the U.S.A.   DECEMBER 26, 2019

Scripture quotations are from New Revised Standard Version Bible, copyright © 1989 National Council of Churches of Christ in the United States of America. Used by permission. All rights reserved worldwide.

A summary of the material in this book was previously published as chapter 19 in *Challenging Tradition: Innovation in Advance Theological Education*, edited by Perry Shaw and Havilah Dharamraj, Carlisle: Langham Global Library, 2018. Used by permission. www.langhampublishing.org.

Excerpts from chapter 9 were previously published in chapters 13 and 15 in *Mission in Marginal Places: The Praxis*, edited by Paul Cloke and Mike Pears, Milton Keynes: Paternoster, 2016. Used by permission. www.authenticmedia.co.uk

I dedicate this work to my friend and *irmão mais velho*, Claudio Oliver, who has inspired me and countless others with his friendship and his "preferential option for the possible."

Contents

Foreword by Willie James Jennings xix
Acknowledgments xxi

Introduction: Beginning in the Middle—
   Doing Theology from the Land of Samba 1

PART ONE—Itinerary: Prolonging the Incarnation

V̲i̲r̲a̲d̲a̲ (P̲a̲r̲t̲ O̲n̲e̲): B̲e̲i̲n̲g̲ T̲u̲r̲n̲e̲d̲ t̲o̲w̲a̲r̲d̲ B̲r̲a̲z̲i̲l̲ 29
   Being Joined and Sent 29
   Being Immersed 31
   Being in Between: Becoming *Brasicano* 32

Chapter 1: Theology Taking the Illich Turn 35
   Ivan Illich: On and Off the Radar of Theology 35
   Biography as Theology: Approaching Ivan Illich 38
   The Pilgrimage of Ivan Illich 40

Chapter 2: Following Illich in the Americas 43
   Questioning Americanization as Assimilation 43
   Questioning Alliances for Progress 49
   Questioning "the Seamy Side of Charity" 53

Chapter 3: Following the Naked Christ 58
   Attending to Theodrama: The Shape of the Journey 59
   Discerning Act 3: The Incarnation and the Center of the Journey 64
   Inhabiting Act 4: A Question of Witness 68

INTERLUDE: OVERHEARING THE GOSPEL ACCORDING TO SAMBA (PART ONE): MISSIONARY ADOPTION AND THE NEW "WE" 81
    Following 82
    Participating 83
    Joining 85

PART TWO—Detours: Navigating (Dis)Order and Progress

Virada (Part Two): Being Turned toward the Seminary, Sanctuary, and Street 91
    Seminary 92
    Sanctuary 94
    Street 97

Chapter 4: Ivan Illich in Conversation 105
    Table Talk (Part One): The Theologians, the Other Storytellers, and the Longing for the Particular 106
    Table Talk (Part Two): Framing the Detours: Human (In)dignity and the Rise of the "Technological Ethos" 113
    Table Talk (Part Three): Historicizing "(Dis)Order and Progress" 120
    Conclusion: Questioning Certainties—Attending to "(Dis)Order and Progress" 126

Chapter 5: Ivan Illich and the Prophetic Imagination 132
    Ritualizing Consumption 133
    Demythologizing the Promethean Enterprise 142
    Toward the Politics of Conviviality 150

Chapter 6: The Corruption of the Best Is the Worst: Ivan Illich and Christian Mission after (Dis)Order and Progress 161
    Revisiting the Gospel according to Truman: Development as "Economic Peace" 162
    Revisiting "the Corruption of the Best Is the Worst": Good and Bad Samaritans 171
    Recontextualizing Human Dignity 174
    Conclusion: Whose Image? Which Flourishing? Discerning Two Rival Versions of Inclusion 184

INTERLUDE: OVERHEARING THE GOSPEL ACCORDING TO SAMBA (PART TWO): MISSIONARY POVERTY AND THE "TRUE WELCOME" 190
    O Passo: Learning to Hear the Eloquence of Rhythm 192
    The Pedagogy of the *Roda*: Enacting the "True Welcome" 194

PART THREE—Re-turn: Taking the Convivial Turn

Virada (Part Three): Being Turned by Friendship 199
    Snapshot #1: Claudio's Wormery 201
    Snapshot #2: The Sisters' Nursery Garden 202
    Snapshot #3: Dona Raquel's *Quintal* 203

Chapter 7: Back to the Future:
   Or, the Re-turn of Hope as a Social Force 208
    The Ambiguity of *Esperando*: On Waiting and Hoping 210
    The Long Revolution 212
    Reimagining Response-ability: Accounting for the Hope within Us 215

Chapter 8: Convivial Recovery as Improvisation 223
    Reimagining Mission as Improvisation 223
    Ilich on Convivial Recovery 228
    Lessons from New Social Movements Taking
      the Convivial Turn 231

Chapter 9: Another World Happens—a View from Casa da Videira 236
    A Preferential Option for the Possible 236
    Vida Paraoikiana (1): "Subversive Habitation" and the Reincorporation of "Life around Homes" 242
    Vida Paraoikiana (2): Re-inhabiting the "Parish" as a Demonstration Plot for Abundant Life 249

INTERLUDE: OVERHEARING THE GOSPEL ACCORDING TO SAMBA (PART THREE): BECOMING ALIVE AND THE ABUNDANT COMMUNITY 257
    Manifesting Abundance 257
    Cultivating Conspiracy 259

Conclusion: Beginning Again in the Middle—
    Doing Theology from Someone Else's Garden 264
        Why Are You Entering Someone Else's Garden? *Faith* Seeking
            Conviviality 267
        How Do You Enter Someone Else's Garden? Faith *Seeking*
            Conviviality 269
        What Do You Do in Someone Else's Garden? Faith Seeking
            Conviviality 273
        What Happens in Your Own Garden? Cultivating the Edges 281

Bibliography 287
Name/Subject Index 297
Scripture Index 304

Foreword

EVERYONE APPRECIATES THE FAITHFUL friend, the one who over time emerges as a gift of consistent presence. They are embodied grace. Such a person is a pearl of great price that cost us nothing, unless we too wish to be such a friend. Then the cost increases dramatically, pulling an entire life into the work of being a consistent presence. Consistent presence is at the heart of the gospel message that we Christians proclaim. In truth, this is the theme that holds together the disparate stories of Scripture, the many cardinal doctrines of the faith, and the lives of the faithful—divine presence, consistent presence. Yet this presence very rarely points to itself, is infrequently loud, and often episodic in theophanic display. But it is obvious, even palpable, for those whose senses have been trained to discern the endless moment of visitation.

Such discerning is the inheritance of the followers of God and the lovers of Jesus, but we who would claim these titles continue to squander this heritage. To be formed to discern divine presence would also move us toward leading lives of consistent presence as we follow Jesus into the places and to the people that are sites of divine love and desire. Sam Ewell understands this, and on the occasion of reflecting on the life and intellectual legacy of Ivan Illich, he puts this crucial insight to work in offering us a corrective vision of missions. There is much that needs correcting in prevailing thinking about missions, most centrally the vision of a Western world that will "develop" the rest of the world toward national and capitalistic existence. Developmental vision grew out of Christian vision turned malignant and made the sick soil of modern colonialism. Illich sought to exorcise the development demons from the soul of a Christianity that had strayed from the life of Jesus and the communal realities constituted in and through his life.

Illich's prescient work anticipated our current decolonial moment in which so many peoples in the world, especially nonwhite Christians, are challenging the epistemological regimes of the Global North and resisting the horrors of Western development with its growing economic disparities, widespread ecological damage, and increases in violence against women. His work also pointed to the imperative of joining and life together as a way of life that refuses both evangelistic technique and Western technology as the central preoccupations of would-be do-gooders or missionaries. Yet Ewell enhances the power and beauty of Illich's ideas by articulating them through his own ideas and his spot-on sense of the current obstacles facing us in forming seriously Christian community.

Sam Ewell is the right person to present Ivan Illich to new audiences because he lives against the old dualisms of thought and action, life and career, profession of faith and professional vocation. Memoir and testimony merge in Ewell's writing and become a compelling framework for the serious analytical work he carries out in this text. It is a challenge to write in this way without becoming personally overindulgent or lifelessly wooden, but he avoids these pitfalls while astutely placing his own life journey next to the life and intellectual journey of Illich. In so doing, Ewell marks a path for us to contemplate if we want a faith that gives witness to presence.

Christianity lives by how well it gives witness to presence, and in this regard we often live in either feast or famine. We enter famine when Christian intellectuals lose sight of their work as a practice of presence and allow developmental logics to drive their vision of life together. Yet a feast always waits for us when we do our work cognizant of a God made flesh and who by the Spirit is drawing flesh together in a conviviality that challenges death. This is the feast that God has prepared for us and that Sam Ewell gives us a foretaste of in this book.

—WILLIE JAMES JENNINGS

Acknowledgments

I would like to express to my gratitude to the following for their support and friendship during the writing of this book:

Friends at Casa da Videira (Brazil) for their vision, inspiration, and commitment, for receiving me and sending me away as their "reverse missionary";

Irmã Francisca, for spiritual direction and for being an *amiga-no-caminho*;

Friends at Queen's Foundation for being the "village" that welcomed us, especially upstairs neighbors, Helen Stanton and Dede Tyndall;

Companions for Hope, for "being neighbors on purpose" in Summerfield/B16;

Parishioners at St. Patrick's Catholic Church, for showing up and showing how in a parish as diverse as ours, every Sunday can be Pentecost;

My parents and mother-in-law, whose prayers, emails, and conversations (even if long distance) have encouraged me along the way;

Meus amores, Rosalee, James, Isabella, and Katharine: my immediate family who have shown such love, patience, and good humor along the way (. . . *não há palavras para dizer obrigado*);

To God, who is good all the time. Especially today . . .

Introduction

Beginning in the Middle—
Doing Theology from the Land of Samba

> We do not learn from experience; we learn from reflection upon experience.
>
> —Trevor Hudson

Even though I have studied and "done" theology for the last twenty years, identifying myself as a *theologian* is not something that rolls off my tongue easily or naturally. Given the landscape of contemporary theology, one of the challenges of claiming to be a theologian is that theology—as an academic discipline—has become so professionalized. While this trend is not unique to the field of theology, this means that theologians tend to get socialized and herded into evermore specialized intellectual silos with like-minded specialists: systematic theologians, biblical studies, church historians, and so on. Herein lies both the difficulty and opportunity of identifying myself as a *practical* theologian, and this book as a work of *practical* theology.

One misreading of that claim to do practical theology (especially given the theological landscape that I just mentioned) would be simply to brand practical theology as another discipline in the wide field of theology. On that misreading, practical theology is just another silo alongside others. But as Terry Veling has pointed out, practical theology does not refer to another branch or discipline; rather it "is an attempt to heal this fragmentation of theology, such that it resists being slotted into another theological specialty."[1] In fact, Veling goes on to suggest that practical theology seeks "a certain reintegration of theology into the weave and fabric of human living, in which theology becomes a 'practice' or a way of life."[2] In other words, practical theology is not another "type" of theology defined by its particular content. Rather, practical theology is more like a verb, an integrated activity "that attempts to honor the great learnings of theological wisdom with the desires of God and the coming of God's kingdom 'on earth, as it is in heaven.'"[3]

BECOMING AN AMATEUR THEOLOGIAN

If one of the marks of practical theology is a sensibility to integrate and therefore transgress disciplinary boundaries, then it follows that practical theologians will see themselves less as professionals in a disciplinary field and more as amateurs practicing a craft. I owe this distinction between professionals and amateurs to Wendell Berry and his insights regarding how we tend to value knowledge in the contemporary "knowledge economy." As Berry observes, professionals operate as experts in a field of knowledge; the professional's authority comes from the status of being recognized as an expert by other experts. The amateur, however, does not operate as an expert or specialist in one defined field. Rather, taking a cue from the etymology of the term *amateur*, Berry points out that the amateur is the one who acts and thinks out of love (*amor*).

To be clear, professional and amateur do not refer to degrees of knowledge but rather to two different sensibilities for acquiring and sharing knowledge. The amateur is not necessarily less knowledgeable than the professional, and, of course, there are professionals who actually love what they know. Berry makes this distinction neither to discredit the knowledge of professionals nor to romanticize "amateur status" but to value the integrated forms of knowledge that amateurs can share. His fundamental point is that to live well, we cannot reduce knowledge to professionalized disciplines, because the forms of knowledge that these disciplines produce are too fragmented to live by. We will have to have the courage to transgress disciplinary boundaries; we will have to learn

---

1. Veling, *Practical Theology*, 3.
2. Veling, *Practical Theology*, 3.
3. Veling, *Practical Theology*, 3.

to operate as amateurs whose love and knowledge of what is true, good, and beautiful compel us to cross disciplinary lines.

So, it is in this spirit of doing practical theology as an amateur that I have written this book. I am not a professional theologian, nor do I claim to be an expert in Latin American history or in Christian mission. Therefore, I am a generalist with no ascribed authority or expertise in those disciplinary fields. I have written, nonetheless, because my love for the place and people of Brazil compelled me to reflect theologically on my experience there—and to do so even as an amateur.

For me, the shift in mindset for reimagining what it might mean to do theology as an amateur theologian (and not just study it as an academic field) has everything to do with the quote with which I began this introduction: "We do not learn from experience; we learn from reflection upon experience."[4] I first came across this insight in Trevor Hudson's book *A Mile in My Shoes: Cultivating Compassion*, in which he shares how a mentor passed this wisdom on to him at an early stage in his ministry, leading to his awareness that "only when we stop to reflect upon [our] experiences and extract their hidden insights do we open ourselves to the possibilities of real change."[5]

In *A Mile in My Shoes*, Hudson also shares openly about the challenge of integrating this insight into his journey of faith as a congregational minister. This journey led Hudson to ask the question, What does it look like to hold together a call to ministry of compassion and proclamation of Jesus' kingdom as good news to the poor, while serving as a white pastor of a largely white, middle-class congregation out of touch with the violence and racialized oppression in apartheid South Africa? He knew that there was an "experience/encounter gap" between his congregation and those suffering most under apartheid, and in his desire to bridge that gap with compassion, he heard this call to action: "Take members of your congregation with you to where their brothers and sisters are suffering."[6]

This call in turn led Hudson to launch what he called a Pilgrimage of Pain and Hope, a weeklong immersion experience that created the conditions for direct contact with the struggles and joys of suffering neighbors. Over the subsequent years of facilitating such pilgrimages, Hudson distilled a pedagogical core with three primary components:

---

4. Hudson, *A Mile in My Shoes*, 57.
5. Hudson, *A Mile in My Shoes*, 58.
6. Hudson, *A Mile in My Shoes*, 17.

- encounter—as personal engagement with the pain of a shattered and fragmented society, as well as stories of living hope emerging from the brokenness;
- reflection—as regular periods of personal journaling, group discussion as well as daily meditation on Scripture, other readings, and personal experience;
- transformation—not as a programmed outcome but rather as a process of growing in "Christlikeness" by remaining open to the Holy Spirit who transforms "hearts of stone into hearts of flesh."[7]

Inspired by the ethos of Hudson's local Pilgrimage of Pain and Hope, a partnership emerged between the Methodist Church in South Africa (led by Peter and Elizabeth Storey) and the Office of Black Church Studies at Duke Divinity School in North Carolina in order to facilitate the Pilgrimage of Pain and Hope experience for US pilgrims in South Africa. That experience for international pilgrims would later expand to Brazil, where my wife, Rosalee, and I were privileged to serve on a team of facilitators for the pilgrimages in 2006 and 2008.

It would be difficult to exaggerate the impact that those two pilgrimages had on me as a US national living in Brazil. On the first pilgrimage in 2006, like my fellow US pilgrims, I was exposed to a Brazil that most tourists—or even many residents—do not choose to see up close. I experienced that pilgrimage not as a short-term mission trip but as a deeper immersion into everyday Brazilian realities. During the second pilgrimage, in 2008, I experienced the learning cycle of encounter/reflection/transformation as both familiar and strange, both encouraging and disturbing. I knew that I wanted reflection and transformation to catch up with the experience of my encounters. By the end, I knew that I wanted to become—to use Hudson's phrase—a "pilgrim in daily life."[8]

Fortunately, then, my understanding of theology (in general) and academic research (in particular) would change as a result of my journey into the land of samba. For the pilgrimage experiences and its pedagogy eventually led me to pursue doctoral research, and it was that research, in turn, that sowed the seeds for this book. What I discovered in Brazil was a way of doing theology that was not equivalent with the desire to become an academic professional (i.e., doing research on other people's research).

---

7. Hudson, *A Mile in My Shoes*, 22.
8. Hudson, *A Mile in My Shoes*, 22.

Rather, I discovered a way of doing theology that emerged directly out of the desire to make sense of my intercultural experience as a US national married to a Brazilian and living as a missionary in Brazil from 2003 to 2010. At a formal level, my doctoral research explored cultural, political, and ethical questions related to Christian mission by reappropriating the life and thought of the Roman Catholic priest and intellectual Ivan Illich. Yet, at the most fundamental level, my experience as a missionary served as the narrative matrix and interpretive lens for the entire research agenda.

To use a bit of methodological jargon, there is a "hermeneutical spiral" in play throughout this book—which is a fancy way of saying:

- I interpret Illich through my experience (with attention to the "live questions" provoked through encounters); and
- I interpret my experience through the life and thought of Illich (with attention to his "responses" to my questions).

My approach includes autobiography, but it is not a spiritual memoir. My approach also includes theological commentary on a Christian intellectual, but it is not a "theology of Ivan Illich," either. Rather, my approach emerges out of the space created *between* my direct personal encounters in Brazil (and beyond) and my encounter with Ivan Illich. Given that I have taken this methodological route, I would like to highlight three reasons why I integrated personal experience into the task of doing theology and why I have written *this* book in *this* way.

LEARNING TO DRINK FROM OUR OWN WELLS

In so much theological research, the person of the researcher may appear (if at all) at the beginning and the end, but otherwise disappears off the page. This so-called "objective" approach isolates the "object" being researched from the "subjective" researcher. This, however, is problematic for both practical and theological reasons. Why? Because every researcher is always already bringing personal experience into the research process. Therefore, while the voice of the researcher as a person can be *muted*, it cannot be simply "turned off"—nor should it be. But it is as if the process of being formed in an academic environment conditions theologians to see personal experience as burdensome "baggage" to "get rid of" instead of as a kind of hidden treasure worthy to be researched and shared with others.

My own introduction to academic theology and research began when I was a seminary student at Duke Divinity School in the late 1990s. As a seminarian, I was fortunate to become friends with and learn from a number of doctoral students—including the one that I married!—whose reading knowledge and academic rigor seems to leave us seminarians behind. Unfortunately, my impression of doctoral research at that time was less about learning to reflect deeply and theologically about one's lived experience and social location, and more of an elite group of professionalized specialists who wrote texts on each others' texts. I did not go into a doctoral program straight after seminary precisely because I thought it meant spending four to six years researching something that only eight other people in the world might read! So, I left seminary highly motivated to live out the theology that I learned in seminary but totally unmotivated to do academic research on it.

Yet, as I mentioned earlier, my understanding of doing theology and research changed because of my journey into Brazil. Over time, I realized that I did not need to keep doing theology in order to stay up to date with other professionals in an academic field; I needed to do theology to survive—to make sense of what was happening around me and inside of me as a missionary in Brazil. Over time, I realized that I could not afford *not* to do theology if I wanted to integrate and give voice to my experience. That is what led me to reimagine what research could be for.

As a researcher, I was fascinated not so much with answering questions about Illich (my newfound theological guide) but rather with the way that Illich responded to and even reshaped my personal questions. Therefore, I was not drawn toward writing a "theology of Ivan Illich" type thesis and establishing myself as a scholar in Illich studies, nor was I drawn toward writing a mere spiritual memoir. I was drawn toward doing theology in the space emerging between Illich's life and thought and my own. And yet, it was not at all clear to me how to move from gathering research to "writing up."

Full disclosure: for the first couple of years of my doctoral program, I struggled to find a form for my thesis that fit the function that I needed. I knew that I had to meet the formal requirements for a doctoral thesis, yet I also intuited that the energy for the research came from attending and responding to my personal questions. The breakthrough came when I submitted a draft chapter using personal narrative as a way to frame the question, Why Illich? My supervisor responded enthusiastically, in effect saying, "You have just written the first chapter of your thesis. The shape of your personal narrative and journey in Brazil gives you a form for presenting your scholarship on Illich in a compelling way."

Looking back on my experience as a doctoral student at a major research university, I realize now how fortunate I was to swim against the current of a dominant yet debilitating tendency in theological research: namely, the tendency to objectify knowledge as something to be found and studied in isolation from lived experience. This tendency isolates a researching "subject" from a researched "object" based on the assumption "that a person's background, identity, personality, experience and worldview needed to be subjugated to the need for a scientific kind of method."[9] This assumption, while still dominant, has been called into question on the grounds that the subject/object dichotomy is a false one.[10]

A growing number of researchers (and practitioners) recognize that locating oneself in the activity of research is not a liability at all. Rather, it is a more reflective, authentic way of "showing one's work," and where one takes a stand.[11] Indeed, if "knowledge is formed through the encounter, that is . . . in the space between the self and the other,"[12] then the question is, Wouldn't advanced theological researchers want to locate those encounters and give voice to lived experiences out of which theological imagination emerges?

Alongside my experience of pilgrimage in Brazil, my rereading of Gustavo Gutiérrez's *We Drink from Our Own Wells* provoked me to integrate my experience into my theological reflection. Whereas Hudson offered a pedagogy of pilgrimage for individuals and groups integrating experience into common journey, Gutiérrez embraced experience as the starting point for a holistic theological method and spirituality. In the introduction to *We Drink from Our Own Wells*, Gutiérrez writes, "A Christian is defined as a follower of Jesus, and reflection on the experience of following constitutes the central theme of any solid theology."[13]

---

9. Cloke and Pears, *Mission in Marginal Places*, 3.

10. Ward and Burns, *War*, 52.

11. For a broad range of contributors who advocate for the integration of lived experience into advanced research, see the essays in Cloke and Pears, *Mission in Marginal Places: The Praxis*, as well as those in Scharen and Vigen, *Ethnography as Christian Theology and Ethics*.

12. Cloke and Pears, *Mission in Marginal Places*, 18.

13. Gutiérrez, *We Drink from Our Own Wells*, 1.

As a Latin American liberation theologian writing in the 1980s, Gutiérrez articulated the spiritual experience of the poor in Latin America and the commitment to the process of liberation in that context. Paradoxically, Gutiérrez's emphasis on contextualized or situated experience is precisely what enables his theology to resound beyond his own contextual horizon in Latin American.

Henri Nouwen points out (reflecting on his own experience in Latin America with Gutiérrez), "I am increasingly struck by the thought that what is happening in the Christian communities of Latin America is part of God's ways of calling us in the North to conversion."[14] Like Nouwen, I too had embarked on a spiritual journey from the North to the South; like Nouwen, I was challenged and inspired by Gutiérrez's conviction—following St. Bernard of Clairvaux—that every Christian spirituality involves followers of Jesus learning how to "drink from their own well."[15]

RESPONDING TO WORD AND WOUNDS

A key part of what it meant for me to learn to "drink from my own well" was learning to get my head around one of the most intensely debated issues within contemporary theology: the issue of how social location shapes the doing of theology. In recent years, the issue has become even more central in the light of an increasingly globalized economy, the unprecedented fluidity of social mobility and forced migrations, as well as the shift of Christianity's numerical center from the North Atlantic to the global South in an era of so-called world Christianity.[16] Thus a critical, yet constructive, appreciation of the contextual character of theology has become unavoidable.

Of course, what is at stake here is more than one's address. It is an awareness not only of where one is located, but also in relation to whom one is located, even to ask the question, To whom do you belong? One of the threads that runs through my own theological reflection, and a subtext for what follows, has to do with responding to that question from more than one place: I am a US national and a permanent resident of Brazil, currently living in Birmingham, UK. The set of questions that I bring into this work, therefore, arises out of an experience of place and

---

14. Nouwen, "Foreword," in Gutiérrez, *We Drink from Our Own Wells*, xxi.
15. Gutiérrez, *We Drink from Our Own Wells*, 5.
16. See Ott and Netland, *Globalizing Theology*.

sense of Christian identity that has not evolved around a more or less fixed location but rather around multiple places, or even as a movement between them.

Argentinian theologian Nancy Bedford develops a similar line of questioning in her essay "To Speak of God from More than One Place." She examines the issue of the limitations and merits of place by focusing on the experience of Latin Americans becoming identified as migrants in a global context. The question Bedford raises is, "What might it mean for theology when—as a result of transnational migration—we begin to speak of God 'from more than one place'?"[17] By focusing on migration, both as a more generalized experience of Latin Americans in the US context, as well as her own journey from Buenos Aires to the Chicago area, Bedford attends to how the dynamics of migration tend to destabilize established categories, expectations, and assumptions related to the question of identity. One of the theological insights that Bedford's argument suggests is that migratory existence and the Christian life share the "ambiguous yet promising possibilit[y]" of a movement that does not annul what comes before, but rather destabilizes a previous social location and frame of reference for the sake of something new.

While Bedford clearly highlights the idea that migratory existence can entail oppressive and dehumanizing forms of destabilization, she also wants to make clear how destabilization can be understood as a positive influence for theologians. As she extends the analogy between migratory existence and the Christian life as a "Way," she offers a compelling insight regarding what migrants and theologians might have in common:

> The experience of migrants is precisely that of a series of epistemological ruptures; time and time again migrants are exposed to "others" in new ways. This opens up possibilities for discovering and rediscovering the gospel (and themselves) in new ways as well. When theologians think as migrants and migrants as theologians, epistemological rupture and renewal are almost unavoidable.[18]

I find Bedford's comments compelling because she eloquently articulates something that I had intuited as a missionary in Brazil. Reading Bedford, I recognized that like migratory existence, missionary existence could also require an ability "to speak of God from more than one place."

---

17. Bedford, "To Speak of God," 98.
18. Bedford, "To Speak of God," 11.

Like becoming a migrant, becoming a missionary can entail a journey from rupture to renewal.

I would, therefore, reword Bedford's statement as follows: *When theologians think as missionaries and missionaries as theologians, epistemological rupture and renewal are almost unavoidable.* This highlights my contention that my research arises not simply out of a generic experience; more precisely, it arises in the light of how the experience of becoming an intercultural missionary was one of rupture and renewal. Thus, I present an extended instance of reflective practice that examines the dynamic of rupture and renewal and what it has to offer to contemporary theology.

Methodologically, this means that while all theologians inevitably draw upon past traditions, when theologians think as missionaries and missionaries as theologians, then it becomes clear that the task of theology cannot be reduced merely to the transmission of a theological heritage. To use a musical motif of "call and response," theology always emerges as a call to respond faithfully to ongoing encounter with both the Word and wounds.

The Word is God's call to Adam and Eve in Genesis 3: "Where are you?"—the ultimate contextual question. The Word is God incarnate in Jesus, the eternal Son of the Father; it is the word spoken through the prophets, the Word for whom John the Baptist prepared the way. It is the whisper of the Spirit and the words of Scripture—not just about how we read them but how they read us. To hear Scripture as God's Word is to hear it as a Word that always calls forth a response.

Consider the end of the gospel of John, chapter 6. Jesus has spoken to the crowds, to the Pharisees and to the disciples, many of whom leave him—they cannot respond to him. And Jesus turns to the disciples and asks, Aren't you going to leave also? Peter responds, Where else could we go? You have the words of eternal life. That is response to the Word.

That said, doing theology at the intersection of intercultural mission is not just about responding to the Word; it is also about holding together the power of the Word and the wounds of the world that also call for a response. I borrow this notion of wounds from Mary McClintock Fulkerson and her reflection on the urgency of enabling theological reflection to emerge as responses to the wounds of the world. Speaking about theological method in the context of feminism, she writes,

> Wounds generate new thinking. Disjunctions birth invention—
> from a disjuncture in logic, where reasoning is compelled to
> find new connections in thought, to brokenness in existence,

> where creativity is compelled to search for possibilities of reconciliation. Like a wound, theological thinking is generated by a sometimes inchoate sense that something *must* be addressed.[19]

In other words, wounds interrupt our thinking; they disrupt patterns and expose cracks in the systems. Wounds demand an urgent response: the death of biodiversity, child trafficking, gang violence, hunger . . . you can name any number of wounds that shape your theological reflection and that provide the context for your missiology. In his encyclical *Laudato Si'*, Pope Francis makes clear that to respond to the social and ecological wounds of our time, we must hear "*both the cry of the earth and the cry of the poor.*"[20] We have to listen to the wounds, to see and hear these situations and to ask, What does good news look like here? What does good news look like for Christian women in Syria? What does good news look like for flood-ravaged Kerala? What does good news look like in my inner-city neighborhood?

And since Jesus—the Word made flesh (John 1:14)—came to suture and heal the wounds of the world, it makes sense that theology must offer responses that hold Word and wounds together. If we focus on responding only to the wounds, there is the danger that mission studies will become merely an ideology, a critical framework for whatever context or situation has been observed. Without the Word we can attempt to respond to the wound without the power and wisdom of God, possibly deepening, instead of healing, the wound. If we focus on responding only to the Word, our theology or missiology can become insular, having a conversation with itself without the urgency of actually asking, What does good news look like in this context? For this place? With these people?

As grateful as I am for my seminary training, my formation still shaped me to think we first sort out our theology in Scripture or a doctrinal tradition and then, in a second move, we apply that to a particular situation. What I am suggesting, along with McClintock Fulkerson, is that doing theology cannot be reduced to the reproduction and transmission of past concepts applied to contemporary contexts; but it is also not reducible to new concepts or theologies only for contemporary situations. It is responding to Word and wound together and asking, What is God's Spirit doing here? Theology arises out of dilemmas—out of

---

19. Fulkerson, *Places of Redemption*, quoted in Scharen and Vigen, *Ethnography as Christian Theology and Ethics*, 66.

20. Pope Francis, *Laudato Si'*, 27. Italics in original.

situations that matter—and asking, What does good news look like here?, with all the complexity and creativity that the gospel demands.

Take the narratives of Acts 10–15 and Peter's encounter with Cornelius. Peter thought he knew what it meant to embody God's word and to be faithful to Jesus's call to follow. He had mission down. He preached powerful sermons, he healed, he attended to the wounds of the poor, he organized the church to serve the widows and orphans, and he spoke truth to power and endured persecution.

It would seem that Peter's theology was "sorted," but then it took a vision, a trance and the Spirit's very compelling power to open Peter's eyes to a new wound that demanded a response of which he did not know how to make sense. That wound was the Gentile asking to enter, and it hit him like a ton of bricks. His response in both preaching and staying at Cornelius's home was at the same time a response to God's Spirit coming upon those who were completely other and "outside."

Put yourself in Peter's place, in the shoes of those leaders of the church in Jerusalem who had to hear Peter's report about what happened at the home of Cornelius the Gentile. The church leaders had a theology of the Word, and they knew how to respond to the Word. It took the disruption, the wound caused by Gentile inclusion, for them to see something new about God's Word and about their response to it. They could not just respond to the Word in the abstract; they had to respond to the Word in the wound. For God's Word had come to those "unclean" people in ways those leaders could never have anticipated and for which they never prayed. Doing theology, then, has to be about holding Word and wound together and being prepared to be surprised.

In order to hold together experiences of reflecting on Word and wound (or, as Bedford puts it, the epistemological ruptures that can lead from rupture to renewal), I think of these transitions in terms of the Portuguese word for "turning point"—*virada*. *Virada* is not an explicitly religious term, for in *futebol* you might speak of how an important play or goal *virou o jogo* (changed the game) or *deu uma virada* (turned the game around), but you can also speak of a *virada na sua vida* (a turning point in one's life). It is in this more general but stronger sense that I am using the term. In using it I refer to an encounter or event that leads to enduring change in one's perceptions, attitudes, and way of life. In the Christian tradition, conversion is a way of talking of the ongoing movement of being changed and turned toward life in and with God. *Viradas*, then, are a way of talking about significant episodes within that movement of "being turned." There were many *viradas* during my seven years in Brazil, and I will narrate some of these *viradas* throughout the book. The decisive *virada* that I want to mention here was encountering the witness of Ivan Illich.

BECOMING A WITNESS

The third reason for writing this book in this way has to do with integrating personal experience and theological research into a form of witness. To put matters this way is another way of transgressing the subject/object dichotomy I mentioned earlier. In doing theology as a form of witness, I am not investigating a topic "out there" divorced from my relationship with it; nor is it a private affair of introspective navel-gazing and trying to sort things out just for my own sake. Rather, doing theology is an ongoing process of discovery that moves from personal experience to a new sense of awareness to sharing knowledge with others by taking a stand. In other words, what I offer here is a way of giving testimony—being a witness by showing and telling what one has discovered by experience.

In the preface to *Witnessing: Prophecy, Politics, and Wisdom*, Maria Clara Bingemer and Peter Casarella highlight how the term *witnessing* functions as a contested yet vital theological concept. On the one hand, *witnessing* can smack of proselytism to our contemporary ears; on the other hand, the biblical term *martyresthai* (from which we get the English word *martyr*) is much richer. The latter includes but goes beyond the legal connotations of witnessing as giving a testimony in court. Bingemer and Casarella synthesize the overlapping meanings of witnessing in this way:

> Witnessing illuminates a path that can be followed. One stands in the company of the poor of Jesus Christ, and their example of sanctity and justice marks out the direction of the journey. The texts that record the act and the words and deeds archived into memory come back to life when the follower recognizes that these fixed deposits of experience suggest both crisis and renewal in one's own way of life. Christians call this path discipleship and enter it wholeheartedly in spite of the known cost.[21]

Following Bingemer and Casarella's lead, I am interested in showing why witnessing matters in theological reflection for three main reasons:

---

21. Bingemer and Casarella, *Witnessing*, ix.

- First, witnessing directs our attention not only to the past but also to the future. Therefore, doing theology can never be reduced to mere rehearsal or retrieval of past moves. Rather, it is a remembering of the past that guides our steps into the future.
- Second, witnessing functions to renew theological imagination. In fact, what they say about "fixed deposits of experience" leading to "crisis and renewal in one's own way of life" suggests that "witnessing opens up new horizons for theological reflection."[22]
- Third, witnessing "fits" within the contemporary turn from speculative theology to narrative theology (read: from the abstract to the particular) in which, "at present, there is also a growing emphasis on the importance of doing theology not only from texts but also from witnesses."[23] While theology has always drawn from the lives of saints and the testimony of "the great cloud of witnesses" (Heb 12:1), Bingemer and Casarella argue that there is renewed appetite for stories of lived experience that witnessing offers.

In light of this renewed appreciation for witnessing, I offer an initial snapshot of my encounter with the witness of Ivan Illich. What follows is a summary of that encounter, and how that encounter happened in the most Illichian way—that is, in the context of friendship.

In November 2007, I was introduced through a mutual friend to a Brazilian named Claudio Oliver. Claudio would become not only my closest friend in Brazil but also an older brother figure. During my first visit to his home in the city of Curitiba, what I recall most was Claudio's enthusiastic description of his postgraduate research in education on Paulo Freire, Leo Tolstoy, and Ivan Illich. I had read a lot of Freire and some Tolstoy, but I had never heard of Ivan Illich. I left that visit with two takeaways:

- a cultural critique and meditation from Claudio on Matthew 10:16 ("You Americans get the part about being 'innocent as doves,' but what about being 'wise as serpents'?"); and

---

22. Bingemer and Casarella, *Witnessing*, xi.
23. Bingemer and Casarella, *Witnessing*, 12.

- a printed copy of Illich's 1968 address to North American short-term missionaries in Latin America, entitled "To Hell With Good Intentions."

Simply from reading the title and having Claudio's recommendation, I recognized immediately that Illich was going to be an important thinker for me. By the time I arrived at home and read the text thoroughly, I knew I had found a guide clearing a path and pointing beyond the fallout of "good intentions."

In order to understand the message of that 1968 talk, it is helpful to situate it against the backdrop of the story that Illich tells his audience of young, short-term North American missionaries in Mexico—a story in which Illich weaves four narrative threads together. First, Illich lays out the idea that the US struggle to maintain the "American way of life" has led to a crusade to spread its particular form of freedom and democracy around the world under the banner of development. Second, the story clarifies that the battle lines for this struggle to bring about assimilation into this way of life have been drawn on three fronts: the Vietnam war in Asia; within the US itself, especially in urban centers; and the declared "war on poverty" in Latin America. Third, in 1961, the US government initiated a new relationship with Latin American nations through the Alliance for Progress, coupled with the missionary zeal of the Peace Corps. Fourth, in response to the influx of "secular missionaries" through the Peace Corps, the Roman Catholic Church intensified its own missionary efforts from the North with the formation of the Papal Volunteers for Latin America, with the expressed goal of "tithing people" as missionaries to the South.[24]

In Illich's view, this amounted to nothing less than a "benevolent invasion of Mexico"[25] and other Latin American countries. That Illich likened the missionary efforts of both church and state to military strategy is not accidental. For Illich, Christian volunteer movements such as the Papal Corps, as well as government-sponsored efforts such as the Peace Corps, ended up, despite their good intentions, being enlisted in a quasi-religious crusade to sustain the American way of life. Their service to

---

24. The initiative known as the PAVLA, in fact, called on Catholic communities in the United States and Canada to send 10 percent (i.e., a tithe) of all its priests and nuns to Latin America. Illich describes the intention and the reality of this initiative in his *Celebration of Awareness*, 53–68.

25. Illich, "To Hell with Good Intentions," 1.

God or country, Illich tells us, was fundamentally misplaced, and therefore their zeal to serve ended up creating or aligning itself with the "ideal conditions for military dictatorship" and "help[ing] the underdog accept his destiny"[26] in the emerging order of Cold War geopolitics. Addressing those who had come to serve in Mexico, primarily short-term North American volunteers, he sums up his message as follows:

> Today, the existence of organizations like yours is offensive to Mexico. I wanted to make this statement in order to explain why I feel sick about it all and in order to make you aware that good intentions have not much to do with what we are discussing here. To hell with good intentions. This is a theological statement. You will not help anybody by your good intentions. There is an Irish saying that the road to hell is paved with good intentions; this sums up the same theological insight.[27]

Illich's 1968 address no doubt intended to challenge the adequacy of "good intentions," but it went beyond merely pointing out how good intentions can lead to harmful outcomes.[28] Rather, his more fundamental insight had to do with the recovery of a deeper sense of missionary awareness, which entails both (*a*) the recognition of the arena in which our actions of service and mission take place, and (*b*) the capacity to renounce "good intentions" in order truly to act for the sake of what is good, what is right, or what is fitting. Illich concludes with a remark that is at once a modest yet subversive proposal for missionary formation and presence: "I am here to entreat you to use your money, your status, and your education to travel in Latin America. Come to look, come to climb our mountains, to enjoy our flowers. Come to study. But *do not come to help.*"[29]

Thus, while the 1960s peace movement protested against the war in Vietnam, Illich spoke out as a different kind of peace activist, one who campaigned tirelessly against the massive influx of "do-gooders" promoting *pax Americana* and for "the voluntary withdrawal of all North American voluntary armies from Latin America."[30] "To Hell with Good

---

26. Illich, "To Hell with Good Intentions," 3.
27. Illich, "To Hell with Good Intentions," 2.
28. For recent accounts of how the "good intentions" of mission can lead to harmful (even if unintended) consequences, see Lupton, *Toxic Charity*, and Corbett and Fikkert, *When Helping Hurts*.
29. Illich, "To Hell with Good Intentions," 5; italics mine.
30. Illich, "To Hell with Good Intentions," 1.

Intentions" can be read as a marker that flags how a series of issues regarding US domestic and foreign policies gave shape to the discourse and practice of Christian mission in Latin America by the late 1960s, namely, the crusade to sustain the American way of life, the ramifications of white privilege in a racialized US homeland, and the possible co-opting of Christian mission in the Americas inside the development paradigm.

As a US national serving as a missionary in Brazil, I found Illich's talk to be a jolt to the system, to say the least. Although written nearly forty years before I first read it, his message for do-gooders pricked the insular, missionary bubble that had slowly formed around me. Over the next few days, I mulled over "To Hell with Good Intentions" many times, always hovering over the last lines: *Come to enjoy our flowers, come . . . but please do not come to help.*

I knew that I had not gone to Brazil out of a sense of duty to help needy people; I knew that I didn't even need to leave Durham, North Carolina, for that. I went because I was married to a Brazilian, and I believed in the promises of our marriage vows that "her people had become my people." I went because I sensed a growing desire to become part of this people, to become immersed in their way of life. I went because, as a couple, we were responding to a growing desire and a call to *be there*, not primarily to go as helpers.

But somewhere along the way, "being there" got hijacked by "good intentions." Somewhere along the way, planning projects led me to stray from the path of personal presence. Suddenly, Illich's proposal, "Come, but not cast in the role of helper," led me to reflect back upon what being sent to Brazil *could* mean.

Fundamentally, the insight of Illich's message challenged my burdensome temptation to "fix" all that was wrong with Brazil by playing the role of "do-gooder." At the same time, the more I read Illich, the more I realized he was not letting "do-gooders" like me off the hook. Reading him closely, I understood that he was not advocating disengagement as the antidote to "do-gooderism" but rather a different kind of presence—a more aware, more subversive presence. I realized that if I were going take Illich as my guide, I was going to have to question not only my intentions and actions but also the arena in which Christian witness has unfolded in Brazil. More generally, I realized that by taking Illich as my guide, I would have to question the certainties and assumptions that shape the way Christians imagine their place and role in relation to God's good intentions for the whole world.

More than anyone else, then, Illich has influenced me by naming the air I breathed as a missionary, by navigating a similar path in the Americas that I was to embark upon as a disciple, and by inspiring me to embrace both the truth that comes to us in Jesus (Eph 4:21) and "the world that has come upon us."[31] More than anyone else, Illich offered me a way of not suppressing the questions and "epistemological ruptures"[32] that came with becoming a missionary and integrating them as a way toward the renewal of my own theological imagination (see Rom 12:1–2). In other words, I encountered Illich as someone who was not just *informing* me about the air that I breathed and its effect on me (as a doctor might inform a patient) but as someone who was *witnessing* to me (as a friend guiding and accompanying another on a journey) while enabling me to become a witness myself. I have written this book, then, as a form of witness, an extended testimony that is at the same time an exercise in doing theology with and after Ivan Illich.

Here, I will simply highlight a point about my method by borrowing a phrase from Rowan Williams: "The theologian *is* always beginning in the middle of things."[33] This means that the theologian neither begins at the beginning, in the sense of starting from scratch, nor does she begin at the end by securing a standpoint that provides a complete and totalizing overview. Rather, the theologian is always already "placed" within history and therefore works from "a practice of common life and language already there, a practice that defines a specific shared way of interpreting human life as lived in relation to God."[34] To paraphrase, we access knowledge through encounters—by facing and responding to a lived experience with other people, places, and even written texts. The question then is, How does theological research and writing "show the work" of growing in knowledge-through-encounter?

Illich has enabled me to "begin in the middle," which is simply shorthand for the methodological approach by which I show my work of

---

31. Jennings, *Christian Imagination*, 290.

32. Bedford, "To Speak of God," 113.

33. Williams, *On Christian Theology*, xii. Williams makes this reference to "beginning in the middle" in the prologue to his collection of essays *On Christian Theology*. Although he makes no direct reference to Dietrich Bonhoeffer here, this trope of "beginning in the middle" can be found in Bonhoeffer, *Creation and Fall*, 30.

34. Williams, *On Christian Theology*, xii.

- reflecting theologically upon my own social location (involving both "movement" and "placement"); and
- challenging the split between researching "subject" and researched "object" by placing myself and making my own reflection-upon-location visible in the research and writing itself.

In putting the matter in this way, I am suggesting that my approach of "beginning in the middle" allows the notes of theological reflection to resound in an *ethnographic* key. In pointing to the ethnographic character of the research, however, I am not referring primarily to the use of particular ethnographic techniques. After all, I did not move to Brazil to do fieldwork. I did not live in Brazil for seven years as a participant observer but rather as a spouse, as a father of Brazilian children, and as a permanent resident. Therefore, I am referring to ethnographic research not as a set of *techniques* but as a research *process*:

> In contrast to quantitative research, ethnography primarily uses an inductive method, which means that rather than apply a broad principle to a concrete situation, it seeks to discover what truth or valuable insight is found within specific locations—discovered in communal and individual stories, cultures, practices, and experiences. Ethnographic methods provide a path *by which* truth emerges, rather than a way to apply truth.[35]

Clearly, my research on Illich is also quantitative and bibliographical, yet my journey as an "outsider-insider" in Brazil required the same dispositions and habits of a good ethnographer. Situating this book within the nascent ethnographic turn in theology and ethics is useful. Recent edited volumes such as *Ethnography as Christian Theology and Ethics* and *Mission in Marginal Places: The Praxis* make a compelling case for placing the voice and located experience of the researcher in the activity of theological writing and research. This is because it is precisely ethnographic dimensions such as (1) embodied knowing, (2) the integration of human experience and (theological) tradition, and (3) critical self-reflection that allow theological truth to emerge.[36]

As I continued to turn my understanding of Illich and my own experience toward one another, I was able to frame the answers I found through my scholarship on Illich as a response to the two basic questions that gripped my imagination as a missionary "beginning in the middle":

---

35. Scharen and Vigen, *Ethnography as Christian Theology and Ethics*, 16–17.
36. Scharen and Vigen, *Ethnography as Christian Theology and Ethics*, 61–62.

- First, given the history of Christian missionary expansion in its colonial and neocolonial forms, and the fallout of that expansion—what Eduardo Galeano poignantly termed "the open veins of Latin America"[37]—on what *basis* do we go on fulfilling the "Great Commission" (Matt 28:16–20) as Christ's disciples?

- A second question, intimately related to the first, is this: What makes it possible to embody a distinctively Christian presence that is *missionary* without being *manipulative*?

In reappropriating Illich for contemporary theology, I make two overarching moves. First, I bring his explicitly theological commentary, focused on the Incarnation, together with his earlier social criticism, focused on conviviality, arguing that they operate in tandem as complementary expressions of his "Incarnational Christianity."[38] Second, I show that he offers a compelling contribution to the practice of Christian mission. Illich's threefold contribution, I argue, relates to

- his understanding of the incarnational basis of mission;
- his diagnosis of the social conditions that undermine and even corrupt this incarnational logic; and
- his insights for regenerating an incarnational pattern for mission and the cultivation of life together as responses to wider social concerns, such as economic and ecological crises.

This book is not just a reappropriation of Ivan Illich; it is an exercise in doing theology with and after Illich. As such, there is a distinct logic to the form of the book. The form fits the function of integrating reflection on the life and thought of Ivan Illich with my own personal experience. One could say the book follows a narrative arc that bears a musical (rather than merely a linear) logic that moves from beginning to end by

- introducing the theme of a journey (itinerary) in Part One;
- developing a set of dissonant variations on that theme (detours) in Part Two; and
- resolving those variations in relation to the original theme (return) in Part Three.

---

37. See Galeano, *Open Veins*.
38. Cayley and Illich, *Rivers North of the Future*, 41.

In Part One, I offer a theological reading of Illich's life in terms of the motif of journey, or *itinerarium*, that is, his understanding of the Christian life as a form of pilgrimage. I explore how Illich's own witness embodies the logic of discipleship and mission, and how I perceive that witness illuminating the contours of the journey of discipleship as a missionary in Brazil. Finally, I focus on how Illich's life and theological imagination contribute to a contemporary understanding of incarnational mission.[39]

In Part Two, I explore the dissonance between this notion of journey (or *itinerarium*) and modern *detours* (or "turnings away") from an original trajectory for human flourishing. More specifically, I examine the conflict between the incarnational ethos of Christian mission and another ethos, which I refer to as a "technological ethos." I show that in Illich's view, the detour of the "technological ethos" is inextricably linked to a fundamental misperception of human dignity. I go on to discuss this false trajectory via Illich's identification of a Promethean drive characterized by a dominant but false idealization of independent individuals, coupled with a dominant but also false dependence upon technological artifacts. By contrast, Illich encourages us to discern how progress and development generate a novel social space, which he calls a technological milieu, and which not only eclipses and even corrupts the human self-image but also undermines and corrupts the incarnational logic of Christian mission itself.

In Part Three, I engage with the extended metaphor of this thesis—journey—by exploring the motif of re-turning in three overlapping ways:

- re-turning relates to the way Illich avoids retreating nostalgically into the past, but rather emphasizes re-turning to the "mirror of the past" in order to live fully and to be alive in the present;

---

39. One of the notable trends in contemporary theology and missiology has been a focus on incarnational mission, emphasizing how Jesus's own life shows a pattern of vulnerable embodiment that his followers are called to imitate.

It is also worth noting that critics of incarnational mission have pointed out that some accounts of incarnational mission have not adequately accounted for the whole life of Jesus Christ (life, death, and resurrection), nor have they accounted for the overall Trinitarian shape of mission. In referring to incarnational mission in this book, I am not concerned with defining or defending it as a school of thought; rather, I simply acknowledge it as a contemporary discourse (i.e., extended conversation) that gives some doctrinal precision to Illich's trope of "prolonging the Incarnation." For recent accounts of incarnational mission, see Wells, *A Nazareth Manifesto*, and Ruddick, "From the Ground Up: Creating Community through Incarnational Mission."

- re-turning to the Way is not a straightforward movement from "problem to solution"; rather, it represents a movement from diagnosis of alienation to responses—or, imagining possible ways to go forward; and
- re-turning resonates with the Christian notion of repentance, a "turning around" or "turning back" to the (path)way, linked to a renewed mindset of imagination (Rom 12:2).

In terms of discipleship and mission, I argue that making a "convivial turn"—a preferential option for freedom in interdependence—is, in fact, a theological turn. In other words, the cultivation of conviviality enables us to reclaim the freedom of living in hope and enacting Christian mission in authentic and faithful ways.

In addition to the way that the theme of journey functions as a hinge concept across the narrative arc of the entire book, there is also a "call and response" dynamic within each of the three parts. Each part begins with a personal narrative that introduces a question (the call); the middle chapters offer an extended commentary on Illich in relation to the question raised (the response); the final section returns to a personal narrative that integrates the call and the response.

In this way, the very form of the book allows me *to reflect on my experiences of "turning points" on a journey of intercultural mission and to follow Illich's lead as a theological guide*. It is also my intention that the form of blending personal narrative and theological reflection will engage both amateurs and theological professionals on a journey of integrating and living out one's convictions.

Finally, a note about some of the keywords in this book.

First, *Incarnation*. In taking Ivan Illich as a theological guide, I follow his lead in placing an accent on the incarnational logic of the Christian life. While this emphasis is not an estoreric aspect of Illich's theology nor of his Catholic Christian faith, in discussing this theme with friends and colleagues over the years, a few of them (especially my Barthian friends) have pushed back, highlighting the risk of using language like "prolonging the Incarnation." They say, "Aren't you diminishing the uniqueness of the Incarnation? Aren't you inflating and distortion the vocation of the church when you say it is called to 'prolong the Incarnation'?"

I hear the concern, and I agree that there is a risk. But I would add that there is also a risk is settling for less. True, we are not the Messiah; we are not the Incarnation of the Word. And yet: if we cannot say theologically that we are called to share and participate in the life of Christ as the "body of Christ," then we risk turning the person of Jesus Christ into an abstract Ideal, a moral exemplar who might inspire us but who does not actually create the conditions for his followers to share in his life as members of the *totus Christus*. Ironically, then, if we drive a theological wedge between the Incarnation (as Christ's embodiment of the Word) and our incorporation into the body of Christ (as our embodiment in the church) then we fall right into the lap of the Protestant liberals whom Karl Barth railed against as he sought to amplify the uniqueness of the Incarnation! So yes, there is a risk in affirming the call to "prolong the Incarnation," but again, I would add—and I hope to show—that it is a risk worth taking.

I acknowledge that the Incarnation is a singular, unsubstitutable event by which the Word of God became flesh (John 1:14). I also acknowledge that as the Messiah, Jesus Christ makes possible a "new humanity" (Eph 2:15)—a new social possibility in which previous ethnic, racial, and cultural markers are no longer borders that permit or deny access for belonging together as the people of God. Rather, with the coming of the Incarnate Messiah, those borders are made permeable and transformed into new forms of belonging (Gal 3:27–28).

Therefore, without in any way diminishing the uniqueness of Jesus Christ as the Incarnation, I want to amplify his uniqueness. To do so, I do not focus on the doctrinal articulations of the mystery of the Incarnation (i.e., one person in two natures; fully human, fully divine). I assume these doctrines as articles of faith in order to explore how the logic of the Incarnation both interrupts and transforms contemporary forms of belonging in order that we might share in Christ's work of making a "new humanity."

Putting the matter this way brings me to a second keyword: *mission*. There was a time (even in my lifetime) when mission was considered by many to be a specialist activity for an elite group of God's people. I can still remember how once a year there would be a "Lottie Moon Christmas Offering" to memorialize the pioneering Baptist missionary to China and to support those who followed in her footsteps. But the fact that we only talked about Christian mission once a year and highlighted missionary activity on the other side of world only reinforced the notion that Christian mission is an activity for a select few—and the further away from home, the better! A shift has taken place in the practice and theology of Christiam mission, however, and this shift radically challenges the notion that Christian mission is reducible to exotic, overseas activity carried out by a select few. In practice, "staying put" has become just as vocational as going overseas, and attending to the quality of local relationships in our neighborhood, or parish, has become just as intentional as forging collective responses to global concerns for our common home. In theory, the shift entails a double affirmation: Christian mission begins with God who is missionary; and derivatively, the church is "missionary by its very nature."[40] In reality, this means that the church "must also share and continue in God's healing, fulfilling, challenging and redemptive work."[41] This also means that Christian mission is a not a specialist enterprise for a few good men and women but a "single but complex reality"[42] for the whole people of God.

Paradoxically, it was only by embarking on an overseas journey as a missionary to Brazil that I discovered a more holistic understanding of Christian mission as our active participation in God's purpose as God's people, beginning from wherever we are placed. That said, in what follows, I am less concerned with defining what counts (or not) as mission as I am with the process of becoming the kind of people who actively seek to share in God's mission to renew the world out of love (John 3:16). Said a bit differently, I am interested in examining how mission and spirituality belong together and naturally lead to what Pope Francis has aptly called "missionary discipleship."[43]

Finally, while *Incarnation* and *mission* are commonplace terms in Christian theology, my third keyword, *conviviality*, is certainly less common. There is no *doctrine* of conviviality, as such. So it is worth remembering that throughout the history of Christian theology, Christian theologians and intellectuals have always borrowed terms of their contemporaries and used them for theological purposes. For example, *perichoresis*, originally a concept used to describe interlocking movements of choreographed dance, became in the hands of the Cappodocian fathers a useful term for imagining the mutual indwelling or "unity-in-difference" of God's triune life. The Latin root for conviviality, *con-viver*,

---

40. Bevans and Schroeder, *Prophetic Dialogue*, 1. This phrase is a taken from *Ad Gentes*, Vatican Council II, Decree on the Church's Missionary Activity.

41. Bevans and Schroeder, *Prophetic Dialogue*, 1.

42. Bevans and Schroeder, *Prophetic Dialogue*, 1. Bevans and Schroeder develop the notion of Christian mission as a "complex reality" by highlighting six elements or "constants" of mission (64–71).

43. See Pope Francis, *Evangelii Gaudium*.

simply means "living with" or "life together." The noun form, *convivium*, refers more specifically to common life around a table or a feast. For Illich, then, conviviality marries the Latin overtones of enjoyment with a positive notion of self-limitation and discipline.

Conviviality is always personal but never individualistic. It is "individual freedom realized in personal interdependence." Moreover, cultivating a convivial way of life enables us to delink mission from the lure of techniques in order to receive and to share the peace of Christ relationally. The phrase *faith seeking conviviality* is my shorthand for seeking, finding, and sharing the promise of abundant life together (John 10:10). This is not a technical problem to be "fixed" but a relational possibility to be shared.

PART 1—ITINERARY

Prolonging the Incarnation

VIRADA (PART ONE): BEING TURNED TOWARD BRAZIL

BEING JOINED AND SENT

THE STORY OF HOW our family ended up in Brazil begins on May 29, 1999, when I married Rosalee Velloso da Silva, a Brazilian-American who was born and raised in São Paulo, Brazil. We took our wedding vows from the book of Ruth, recognizing and celebrating the idea that through our life together, somehow our people's lives would be joined as well. In the light of those vows, there is a real sense in which our journey to Brazil was a Ruth narrative in reverse. In our case, *her* people would become *his* people, too.

In 2000, at about the time that our first child, James, was born, we received an invitation to serve as theological educators at Faculdade Teológica Sul Americana, a theological seminary in Londrina, Paraná, Brazil. At that time, Rosalee was in the middle of her PhD studies at Duke Divinity School, so there was no rush toward an imminent move. Nonetheless, after a subsequent visit to Londrina and the seminary, we sensed that the invitation to come was an "open door" (Rev 3:8) for us, so we began to pray and discern with others about a possible move to Brazil.

Many of the key figures in the discernment process were members of our local church, Mount Level Missionary Baptist Church, historically an African-American congregation in Durham, North Carolina. The congregation was founded in 1864 by former slaves who were emancipated from the plantations that covered the landscape of North Durham at the time. Mount Level was decisive in our discernment regarding Brazil, for just as the congregants made it possible for us to cross the "color line" by being joined to their worship and life together, they also recognized and strengthened our call to cross a different kind of threshold—that of being sent to Brazil as their missionaries. By late spring of 2003, Rosalee (great with child) successfully defended her PhD dissertation, and in the early summer of 2003, Isabella was born. Within a three-month window, Rosalee became Dr. Rosalee and our second child was born. Less than a month later, Mount Level commissioned us to serve as missionaries in Brazil. We were riding a wave of newness, even as we prepared for another season of newness in Brazil.

The text for the commissioning service sermon came from the sending narrative at the end of the Gospel of John.

> When it was evening on that day, the first day of the week, and the doors of the house where the disciples had met were locked for fear of the Jews, Jesus came and stood among them and said, "Peace be with you." After he said this, he showed them his hands and side. Then the disciples rejoiced when they saw the Lord. Jesus said to them again, "Peace be with you. As the Father has sent me, so I send you." When he had said this, he breathed on them and said to them, "Receive the Holy Spirit." (John 20:19–22)

Pastor Turner's sermon that Sunday was entitled "Breaking Out of the Huddle." He illustrated how in the same way that in American football the huddle happens before the players are sent out to execute the play, so too does our gathering represent a moment of coming together for the sake of being sent, or "breaking out." In football, the function is not to stay in the huddle, for the huddle exists for the sake of the play that follows. In the same way, the function of the church gathering together cannot be limited to a kind of "holy huddle," as he put it. Rather, while the church today, like the church described in John 20, may be tempted to remain in the insularity of its holy huddle, out of fear of what lies beyond its doors, the alternative lies precisely in receiving and sharing Christ's peace and being led by his Spirit that he breathes on us. By the time Rev. Turner finished, his sermon had developed, nuanced, and even exploded the analogy between the "holy huddle" and the gathered church. The question before us was not so much "Has our 'huddling' given us an effective game plan or strategy for what we are going to do after being sent?," but rather, "Are we willing to submit to the One around whom we gather?"

During that service, we were commissioned by being encircled, and during the Altar Prayer, the church reenacted the scene of John 20 where the circle of disciples took shape around Jesus, the one who occupied the center of the circle. The church prayed for us, blessed us, anointed us, and even breathed on us, just as Jesus breathed his Spirit on the gathered disciples. As we were being encircled, I recalled how we had been drawn to Mount Level five years earlier. It all began with a simple visit to the church where my professor pastored. Yet, during that visit we found ourselves encircled during the passing of the peace by those who could not have had any other reason to embrace us except the conviction that Christ had made peace between us (Eph 2:14). We had been "caught" by this peace extended to us by our African-American brothers and sisters, and now they were commissioning us to share that same peace in Brazil.

In July 2003, therefore, we arrived in Brazil not only with the prospect of being theological educators, but with a wider frame of orientation and purpose: we arrived as those who had been sent there. For Rosalee, having been raised in Brazil, there was a sense in which this was a return trip. For even though we were not in the same city or state where she had been born and raised, she spoke Portuguese, and more significantly, she was, in fact, a Brazilian citizen. My arrival in Brazil was slightly different—and bumpier. Suddenly, I was no longer just an English-speaking American but also a *gringo* who could hardly string together a complete sentence in Portuguese.

BEING IMMERSED

My arrival in Brazil was an immersion into a whole new world. The more I thought about it, the more I perceived in this cultural-linguistic immersion a kind of parable of another immersion at the heart of the Christian life: baptism. In the early Christian context, baptism meant "to be immersed." For the early Christians, baptism also signified being immersed into a person—the person of Jesus Christ: "Do you not know that all of us who have been [immersed] into Christ Jesus were [immersed] into his death? Therefore we have been buried with him by [immersion] into death, so that, just as Christ was raised from the dead by the glory of the Father, so we too might walk in newness of life" (Rom 6:3–4).

In fact, the key insight that became my compass of orientation during my first two years in Brazil was to connect baptismal living (in general) and intercultural-missionary living (in particular) as realities of immersion. Learning a language and cultural cues by immersion happens through direct contact with another linguistic world, field, and way of life. It takes time, often six to eight months, to become conversational; it is dynamic, with days when you feel like you could write poetry and others when you cannot manage a simple phone call; and it is challenging, with the ever-present temptation to resort to the effortlessness of expressing yourself in your "first" language. Like learning a language, learning the gospel by immersion into Christ and the kingdom he inaugurates also takes time, is dynamic, and is challenging. In fact, it takes a lifetime. Even after being "transferred [and immersed] into the kingdom" (Col 1:13), we will be tempted to return to a way of speaking and living that does not depend on the power of God.

As an immersed language learner of Brazilian Portuguese, I was learning what anyone who has become fluent in a second language through immersion will tell you: learning to speak another language goes far beyond learning to say foreign words. Someone who is fluent in Portuguese can tell you that a *churrasco* is much more than "having a barbeque," although that is how a *churrasco* might appear to someone visiting Brazil. Likewise, *futebol* may translate into English as the sport that Americans call soccer, but Brazilians would tell you that *futebol* is not just a sport primarily played with your feet. Rather, *futebol* refers to a quasi-religious phenomenon whose own "liturgical season" comes to a climax every four years with the World Cup. On another, deeper level, as a language learner I became acutely aware of how becoming fluent in another language involves becoming immersed in another way of life.

BEING IN BETWEEN: BECOMING *BRASICANO*

By the end of our first two years in Brazil, I came to appreciate a distinction made by Brazilian social anthropologist Roberto DaMatta between "brasil" and "Brasil." Whereas "brasil" names a more or less static and statistical entity that you might encounter through a Wikipedia entry, "Brasil" refers to the complex but distinctive identity of "a people, a nation, a set of values, choices, and ideas about life."[1] For DaMatta, answering the question, "What makes brasil, Brasil"?[2] is not a matter of isolating a timeless essence of Brazilian-ness but rather of attending to how certain

---

1. DaMatta, *O que faz o brasil, Brasil?*, 11.
2. DaMatta, *O que faz o brasil, Brasil?*, 11.

historical factors, such as Portuguese colonization, geography, and even climate, have given rise to a distinctive Brazilian identity and cultural "way of doing things" [*jeito... de fazer coisas*].³ In describing this distinctively Brazilian way of doing things, DaMatta invents and then contrasts the identities of "José da Silva" and "William Smith," in order to highlight certain realities of Brazilian culture and identity:

> I know, then, that I am Brazilian and not North American, because I like to eat *feijoada* [a typical Brazilian dish of beans and pork] and not hamburgers ... because I speak Portuguese and not English; because, listening to *música popular* [traditional Brazilian music], I can immediately tell the difference between a *frevo* and a *samba* [two Brazilian rhythms]; because *futebol* is, for me, a game that is played with one's feet, not with one's hands.⁴

In contrast to this hard distinction between "José" and "William," I had come to share something in common with each of them. Why? Because although I grew up eating hamburgers, I now liked eating *feijoada* as well; because I could speak English *and* Portuguese; because I could also tell the difference between a *frevo* and a *samba*; and because football became, for me, a game played with one's feet, not with one's hands.

I recognized that I was somehow in between José and William; I was on my way to becoming what missiologist Paul Hiebert describes as an "outsider-insider."⁵ I was married to a Brazilian, the father (by 2006) of three Brazilian citizens, a permanent resident of Brazil, a fluent and comfortable speaker of Portuguese (accent included, of course), as well as a convert to *futebol* and Brazilian percussion. How then could I be just a foreign outsider or another *gringo*? I was no William Smith. Yet I knew I would never speak Portuguese like my children, nor "get Brazil" like a Brazilian. I knew somehow that I would never become Brazilian, nor become José.

Perhaps even more unsettling than recognizing that I would never become Brazilian was accepting that I could never just "reset" my previous identity and sense of belonging as an American. By 2007, I had internalized a range of Brazilian cultural cues, gestures, and perceptions in the midst of being estranged from certain features of my "United States

---

3. DaMatta, *O que faz o brasil, Brasil?*, 16.
4. DaMatta, *O que faz o brasil, Brasil?*, 16.
5. Hiebert, "Missionary as Mediator," 300.

of American-ness." I was traversing two distinct yet overlapping linguistic and cultural fields, and I found myself in a space of "in-between-ness," that of an outsider-insider. From that space, I began to question: Is this "in-between-ness" simply about being fated to a kind of no man's land, a cultural black hole whose gravity holds me suspended between "never-going-back-to-being-just-American" and "never-fully-arriving-as-Brazilian"? Or, might this "in-between-ness," with all of the change and newness it brought, be a sign of transformation for myself as well as good news for those Brazilians around me?

1

Theology Taking the Illich Turn

IN THE *VIRADA* WITH which I began Part One, I set up how I became an "outsider-insider" as North American missionary in Brazil. That experience, in turn, has become the prism through which I glimpsed a way forward for discipleship and mission—a path illumined by Ivan Illich. To shift the metaphor slightly, his life and thought offered a mirror by which I was able to observe more truthfully my own journey from the US to Brazil. How I managed to finish all my formal seminary studies without even hearing of Illich is a question that I still ask myself. I did eventually encounter Illich, and arguably at just the right time. For if I had encountered his theology without my missionary experience in Brazil, it is likely that the light reflected in the mirror would have shone too brightly for me to see anything with it. At any rate, my personal theology (in particular) ended up taking a decisive "Illich turn," and in this chapter I begin to make the case for why contemporary theology (in general) should do the same.

IVAN ILLICH: ON AND OFF THE RADAR OF THEOLOGY

In 2007, the CIA released a declassified intelligence report from 1969 entitled "The Committed Church and Change in Latin America."[1] The central claim of that document was that an underlying ecclesial shift had taken place: the Catholic Church in Latin America was no longer

1. See CIA, "The Committed Church."

primarily an institutional "chaplain" for the maintenance of the status quo. It had become, at least in part, "a force for change."[2] More specifically, the report characterized three different stances within the Catholic Church regarding social change: the Reactionaries (anti-Vatican II and *pro status quo*); the Uncommitted (the majority of clergy and laity, those open to gradual change without radicalism); and the Committed. In the CIA's typology, this last group was further subdivided into "Progressives" and "Radicals," as those who shared a common commitment to catalyze structural change as well as "an antipathy towards the established order as precluding social justice."[3] The document is striking, not only in the fact that the CIA paid its staff to do research on the church but also in its basic tone and message: "Watch out for certain groups in the Latin American Catholic Church, especially those who are progressives and radicals!" Included in its list of radicals was a priest named Ivan Illich.

Even before his death on 2 December 2002, Ivan Illich had been described by Eric Utne as "the greatest social critic of the twentieth century." An Illich obituary in *The Times* also described him as "one of the most radical thinkers of the late 20th century."[4] Clearly, a wider audience had recognized what the CIA research analyst described as Illich's "charismatic appeal, intellectual brilliance, and zest for controversy."[5] It is notable, however, that Ivan Illich, arguably one of the greatest Christian intellectuals of the twentieth century, has remained largely and curiously "off the radar" in contemporary theology.

This seems curious because, as Illich's friends and interpreters such as Lee Hoinacki and David Cayley have pointed out, Illich's whole corpus can be read as a set of theologically inflected investigations into modernity's dominant certainties, institutions, and systems.[6] If that is the case, then perhaps it is not so puzzling that the CIA not only carefully researched Illich as a "radical" but even planted a mole inside his learning center in Cuernavaca, Mexico. More puzzling, however, is why contemporary theology has not taken Ivan Illich as seriously as the CIA.[7]

2. CIA, "Committed Church," 56.
3. CIA, "Committed Church," 32.
4. Quoted in Hoinacki, "Trajectory of Ivan Illich," 383.
5. CIA, "Committed Church," 32.
6. See Hoinacki, "Trajectory of Ivan Illich," 383; Cayley, "Introduction," in *Rivers North of the Future*, 1–44.
7. A notable exception to my observation about Illich being overlooked in the contemporary field of theology is Todd Hartch's recent monograph, *The Prophet of*

In this chapter, I suggest that the time has come for theology and Illich to be turned more compellingly toward one another. While one of my aims is to reappropriate Ivan Illich's significance for Christian theology, I do not intend to provide Illich's intellectual biography, a comprehensive survey of his work, or indeed a "theology of Ivan Illich." I am not interested in a mere retrieval of Ivan Illich; I propose instead to do theology *with* and *after* Illich.

In this chapter, I will follow the trajectory of Illich's life so that it might engage the discourse of theology as both an important challenge and as a largely untapped yet constructive resource. To do so, I will follow Illich's *itinerarium* and focus on the theological imagination that is at the heart of Illich's life and theology, specifically:

- the Incarnation as a new horizon of love and knowledge that we are called to prolong; and

- his conviction that the Incarnation cannot ultimately be managed or controlled but only followed, thereby providing the basis for a shift from mission as expansion to mission as encounter.[8]

In this way, I explore how Illich's own witness embodies the logic of discipleship and mission as a response to the vocation to "prolong the Incarnation"[9] and how his witness illumines the contours of my journey of discipleship as a missionary in Brazil by reframing it in relation to the difference that Incarnation makes.

Cuernavaca: Ivan Illich and the Crisis of the West. Hartch's work is an incredibly detailed and scholarly contribution to the study of mission in Latin American and to "Illich studies," and I have learned immensely from his scholarship. That said, whereas Hartch offers a more forensic reading of Illich as a historian who locates Illich in the field of mission and world Christianity in Latin America, I offer a personal reading as a missionary/practitioner doing theology with and after Illich. Also, whereas the overall tone of Hartch's reading tends to position Illich as anti-missionary, I read Illich as someone who was against what he saw as the *corruption* of Christian mission, not Christian mission per se. Therefore, while I do think that Illich's criticisms of mission can be severe and even hyperbolic, I still read him as someone who engaged Christian mission in Latin American with a double-edged sword: offering both critical and constructive insight for authentic missionary activity.

8. See Bevans and Schroeder, *Prophetic Dialogue.*
9. Cayley and Illich, *Rivers North of the Future*, 207.

BIOGRAPHY AS THEOLOGY: APPROACHING IVAN ILLICH

In this chapter, I want to tell a story not just about Illich, but also through him. My reading of Illich in this chapter turns on the claim that his witness operates from and points to the Incarnation as its center. With this in mind, I want to spell out and examine what is at stake in doing "biography as theology."[10] In other words, I am suggesting that we not fixate on the "finger" of Illich's biography, but rather at that reality to which the "finger" is pointing: the Incarnation. With this in mind, I want to spell out and examine what is at stake in telling the story this way.

Writing in the 1960s and early 1970s, North American theologian Jim McClendon developed a methodological emphasis on doing theology through life stories as a way of healing the untenable divorce between doctrine and ethics, between Christian belief and action. In terms of ethics, McClendon's approach was influenced by the recovery of an ethics of character as a response to the decidedly utilitarian cast of Christian ethics then predominant in the North American context. In terms of doctrinal theology, McClendon sought to move beyond what he called "propositional theology," that is, the tendency to reduce theology to the act of retrieving, cataloguing, and transmitting doctrinal propositions as abstract concepts, separated from the lives and character of the great "cloud of witnesses" (Heb 12:1). Biography as theology represented McClendon's method of integrating doctrine and ethics, incorporating both the "turn to character" (i.e., the character of persons-in-community) and the "narrative turn" into the heart of theological discourse.

As a way of summarizing the logic of this method, McClendon offers two statements about the complementarity of biography and theology. First, he states that Christian doctrine involves more than the isolation and coverage of correct propositions: it deals with "living convictions which give shape to actual lives and actual communities." Therefore, we must attend to Christian lives, and "theology must be at least biography."[11] Second, because our attention to these lives enables us to challenge, refine, or even deepen "our own theologies," then "biography at its best will be theology."[12] McClendon's point is that for theology to be adequate, it must attend to particular lives that are representative of

---

10. See McClendon, *Biography as Theology*.
11. McClendon, *Biography as Theology*, 37.
12. McClendon, *Biography as Theology*, 37–38.

the Christian faith and community. Furthermore, he argued that certain lives have a "compelling quality" to them, something that "strikes" us. Biography as theology, therefore, is about "understand[ing] this compelling quality theologically."[13]

McClendon elucidates this further by making it clear what biography as theology is not. He writes,

> [The] intention cannot be to discover what X believed religiously, and then argue that we should believe the same thing. *That is not what biography as theology means.* . . . It is not that you must think as they think, or say what they say. It is rather that your theology *must be adequate to lives such as these lives.*[14]

In what way, then, am I seeking to approach Ivan Illich's life story as a way of doing biography as theology? In this chapter, I am seeking to tell a story about and through Illich, one that does not merely rehearse the significance of Illich's ideas, but more fundamentally displays the compelling quality of his witness as a Christian intellectual while providing a theological argument that is adequate to his life. While I am deeply interested in what Illich thought and wrote, my aim is not to recruit more "Illichians" who merely subscribe to what he thought or to believe as he did. What is compelling about Illich's witness is the clarity of vision and depth of character with which he lives into the difference that the Incarnation makes. Both in the shape of his living and in his theological commentary, Illich attends to this incarnational difference, that is, how the lives of all Christians are called to bear a "Christic" form, precisely because the Christian life is a participation in the life of Christ.[15]

As Lee Hoinacki has pointed out, Illich lived first and foremost as a Christian witness. To approach him as a witness is not only to see him (and his "life story") but also to look with him at what he sees, including the breadth of the theological horizon that frames his thinking and orders the trajectory of his life journey as life in Christ.[16] In Illich's own terms, what fascinates me is the way he seeks and embraces "the one thing that matters in the Gospel sense, namely, the *itinerarium nostrae vitae in Deum* [journey of our life in God]."[17]

13. McClendon, *Biography as Theology*, 190.
14. McClendon, *Biography as Theology*, 40.
15. See McClendon, *Biography as Theology*, 201.
16. Hoinacki, "Reading Ivan Illich," 1–5.
17. Illich, "Philosophy . . . Artifacts . . . Friendship," 1.

I suggest, then, that biography as theology provides an appropriate methodological lens for interpreting Illich as a Christian witness and for addressing the problem of how to provide a theological interpretation of a person whose relationship to the field of theology, and to the church, is not only neglected but also quite ambiguous.

I am not suggesting that references to Illich are unheard of in contemporary theology. Rather, I would argue that theologians have not engaged seriously with his life and thought since Illich's notable ascent as a public intellectual in the 1970s. This is not altogether surprising, for Illich's wide-ranging thought traversed multiple disciplines (for example, theology, history, education, economics, technology), and he did not write primarily in a theological idiom. The link, therefore, between Illich's writing and his theologically imbued imagination is not always self-evident. But as Cayley's description of Illich makes clear, there is a sense in which Illich's corpus is deeply, though often only latently, theological, and written in such a way that seems to demand further theological analysis:

> As a thinker, Illich is impossible to classify in conventional categories. He is a man neither of the left nor the right, as little a romantic as he is a conservative, no more an anti-modernist than he is a post-modernist. He might be called an anarchist, but only insofar as he believes the refusal of power to be at the heart of the Christian gospel, not because he subscribed to the political tenets of anarchism. The most that can be said, I think, is that he shows how revolutionary a faith Christianity is.[18]

THE PILGRIMAGE OF IVAN ILLICH

As a way of turning toward Illich, I can think of no better place to start than Cayley's *Ivan Illich in Conversation*, a collection of edited transcripts from interview sessions between Cayley and Illich. Although Cayley originally organized these sessions to accompany a commentary on Illich's writings, the result is something much richer: an extended conversation between friends on a constellation of themes that emerge in Illich's writings, including theology, the church, modern institutions, development, education, technology, energy, medicine, work, gender, and urban planning. These transcripts show that, although Illich repeatedly

---

18. Cayley, "Introduction," in Cayley and Illich, *Ivan Illich in Conversation*, 54.

offers insightful commentary on his *oeuvre*, it is clear from his comments that he is not interested in merely quoting himself or recycling past insights. Instead, he traces the contours of the pilgrimage of his life and thought as a Christian intellectual.

Illich's philosophical and theological trajectory was indeed very much that of a pilgrim, a twentieth-century itinerant intellectual.[19] Born in what was then Dalmatia in 1926, he came from the "Old World" of pre–World War II Europe, a world in which identity and imagination were still strongly linked to one's place and family of origin. Illich's early life, however, was uprooted from that world when war and genocide forced his half-Jewish family into an unsettled, and more or less covert, migration from Vienna to Florence and later to Rome. Toward the end of his life, Illich referred to his "destiny as a wandering Jew and Christian pilgrim."[20] Responding to a question by Cayley about his background, Illich describes his pilgrimage in this way: "Since I left [as a child] the old house on the island in Dalmatia, I have never had a place which I called home. I have always lived in a tent like the one in which you are sitting at this moment."[21]

This understanding echoes that of the author of the book of Hebrews, where all those who see themselves as Abraham's children must embrace an ambiguity, that of being from a place while also belonging to a people who "confessed that they were strangers and foreigners on the earth . . . desir[ing] a better country" (Heb 11:13–16). In Illich's case, being "a naturalized United States citizen of part Spanish, part German, part Yugoslav, part Catholic, part Jewish descent,"[22] his Abrahamic faith illumined his critical engagement not only of particular sites on his sojourn, but also his reading of the disordered contours of the post–World War II landscape in the West. In a poignant response to Cayley, Illich describes his understanding of this ambiguity in the following way:

> I can't do without tradition, but I have to recognize that its institutionalization is the root of an evil deeper than any evil I could have known with my unaided eyes and mind. This is what I would call the West. By studying and accepting the West as the

---

19. David Cayley has also provided extended introductions to Illich's biography and thought in his two collaborative works with Illich. See Cayley and Illich, *Ivan Illich in Conversation*, 1–57; and Cayley and Illich, *Rivers North of the Future*, 1–44.

20. Cayley and Illich, *Rivers North of the Future*, 147.

21. Cayley and Illich, *Ivan Illich in Conversation*, 80.

22. Gray, *Divine Disobedience*, 233.

perversion of Revelation, I become increasingly tentative, but also more curious and totally engaged in searching for its origin, which is the voice of him who speaks. It's as simple as that . . . childish, if you want, childlike, I hope.[23]

What undergirds and permeates Illich's activity as a Christian intellectual, then, is this sense of Abrahamic dispossession, and the commitment to live in faith as a response to God's Word—"the voice of him who speaks."

This metaphor of pilgrimage also highlights my own struggle as a missionary pilgrim struggling to embrace becoming a *brasicano* (see *Virada* Part One). For, on the one hand, that *virada* describes my own missionary desire to follow, to respond to a call that is as personal and particular as the one made to Abraham. On the other hand, if Illich's references to "institutionalization" and "perversion" are brought together with his criticisms of the missionary idealism of "good intentions," then we can appreciate how easily missionary desire can become entangled and perverted by the illusion and inadequacies of imagining missionary existence as "being in control," even for the sake of the well-being of others. Consequently, I suggest and will develop throughout Part One how the Illichian orientation toward pilgrimage and Abrahamic dispossession reframes the missionary endeavor. Dispossession means the abandonment of forms of social control that are de-incarnational, that is, ways of encounter that distort the I-Thou embodied relationality that is at the heart of the Christian social imagination. As the next chapter will illustrate, Illich's own pilgrimage led him into new lands in which intercultural mission came into direct conflict with (de-incarnational) projects of assimilation that encounter the other by attempting to re-create them in one's own image. In order to explore these encounters, we turn to his journey into and across the Americas.

23. Cayley and Illich, *Ivan Illich in Conversation*, 243.

2

Following Illich in the Americas

QUESTIONING AMERICANIZATION AS ASSIMILATION

In 1951, Illich arrived in the United States as a priest and postdoctoral student at Princeton University. In Illich's narration of his own immigration, he recalls that the decision to move to the US was a matter of mixed motives. In part, he came in response to the challenges of his priestly colleagues who said that he could not succeed in the States. In part, he came to avoid becoming a papal bureaucrat, a position for which he was highly qualified and most likely being prepared.[1] Opting for postdoctoral studies became Illich's route to America.

Upon arrival in New York, however, Illich's plans took a turn away from the world of the university and toward parish life. During those first days, and in the home of his hosts, Illich found himself overhearing repeated references to the "new immigrants," the Puerto Ricans. After spending a few days on the streets of the *barrios* in Upper Manhattan, Illich sensed a desire to serve as priest among these new immigrants. It took only a short visit to the office of Cardinal Spellman, then archbishop of the diocese of New York City, to facilitate his assignment to Incarnation Parish in Washington Heights, a predominantly Irish neighborhood that was in the process of being reshaped by a massive influx of Puerto Ricans.

Out of his own experience of immigration, Illich began to question one of the dominant certainties of American life, indeed, one of the

1. Cayley and Illich, *Ivan Illich in Conversation*, 84.

pillars of the American social experiment, that of Americanization as the goal of immigrant assimilation.[2] The formula for this social experiment was simple: add any immigrant group and transform them into Americans. In other words, Americanization was another word for a process of cultural conversion in which immigrants were stripped of the markers of their cultural identity and heritage in order to be clothed in the common garb of American citizenship. It was the necessity of this alchemy of assimilation that Illich questioned. By challenging the logic of assimilation, he also raised the following question for Americans, particularly American Catholics: Instead of seeing the Puerto Rican migration as social burden that demands a helping hand toward assimilation, is it possible to welcome their presence as a gift, namely, a culturally distinct Catholic faith, to be received and embraced?

These questions reflect Illich's own journey as an immigrant, a journey that traversed significant social and cultural distance from both priestly colleagues as well as the parishioners he felt called to serve. As Francine du Plessix-Gray points out in her biographical profile, Illich, like the Puerto Ricans, also arrived in New York as someone whose background did not make it easy for him to "pass" as American or to "fit in" in an obvious way in his new setting. Unlike the Irish priests among whom Illich would serve, he could not claim to come from a recognized immigrant population.

Another aspect of Illich's background that caused him to stand out in Washington Heights was not so much being Eastern European, but rather his upbringing as an Eastern European aristocrat. Illich's Catholic father had been a wealthy landowner from Dalmatia, and subsequent to his father's death, Illich's family lived in several places in Europe, allowing Illich to learn to speak multiple languages and to develop a cosmopolitan sensibility. His family's circle of friends included intellectuals such as Rudolf Steiner and Rainer Maria Rilke.[3]

At the age of twenty-four, Illich had master's degrees in theology and philosophy from the Gregorian University in Rome, and by the time he arrived in the United States, he had completed a doctorate in the philosophy of history from the University of Salzburg, writing on Arnold Toynbee. Unlike his priestly colleagues who came from working-class Irish backgrounds, Illich was socialized as a highly educated aristocrat.

---

2. Illich, *Celebration of Awareness*, 32.
3. Gray, *Divine Disobedience*, 242.

This was sometimes problematic. For example, upon meeting the newly arrived priest, the pastor of Incarnation Parish, Monsignor Casey, probed Illich:

> "Ivan Illich? What kind of name is that to go around with?"
>
> "Ivan is Johann, Jean, John," the young priest answered affably, always enjoying his control of many languages.
>
> "Ivan sounds Communist," said his superior, "we'll call you Johnny."[4]

On another occasion, Illich remarked to Father Conolly, "I wish like you I had been a slaughterhouse butcher, because I could be closer to the other priests." In response to Illich's comment about his background, Conolly replied, "You were not cast for the role of shepherd . . . but for empire."[5]

The irony is that the distance that Illich felt between himself and his fellow priests is precisely what made it possible for him to excel as a parish priest among the Puerto Ricans. From his aristocratic, cosmopolitan upbringing, Illich cultivated his gift for languages and openness to others. Thus, while his Irish colleagues tended not to embrace the task of learning Spanish and struggled to speak it fluently, Illich immersed himself in the life-world of Puerto Ricans and mastered Spanish in a matter of months. His competence and ease of interaction with the Puerto Rican community, as well as his devotion as a priest, would eventually gain the respect of the Irish clergy with whom he served. But, as du Plessix Gray insightfully summarizes Illich's experience as a parish priest in New York, "Illich was to learn everything about the American clergy except how to be one of them."[6]

This "difference-in-similarity," which marked Illich's way of relating with the priestly cohort, was nowhere more apparent than in the relationship between Illich and Cardinal Spellman. Despite their many differences, both Cardinal Spellman and Illich took the Puerto Rican "Great Migration" seriously, though for different reasons. As the archbishop of the New York diocese, the apparent challenge for Spellman was how to assimilate the Puerto Rican constituency, then a quarter of the Catholic population of the archdiocese, into the mainstream of American

---

4. Gray, *Divine Disobedience*, 241.
5. Gray, *Divine Disobedience*, 241.
6. Gray, *Divine Disobedience*, 244.

Catholicism.⁷ From the archbishop's perspective, the burning issue was how to both help and integrate the new immigrants.

For Illich, this myopic focus on helping and integrating Puerto Ricans into the mainstream could also lead to a subtly condescending sidestepping of authentic encounter. The question for Illich was, In what way does the Puerto Rican presence offer both a challenge and a gift to American Catholicism? In Illich's view, the question of "How can we help them fit in?" both misinterpreted the challenge and squandered the gift. Indeed, he thought that the most adequate way to respond began by recognizing that "what they need is not more help but less categorization according to previous schemes, and more understanding."⁸

Through his experiences and relationships within the Puerto Rican immigrant community in New York City, as well as from his trips to the island of Puerto Rico, Illich was able to draw some crucial insights regarding their background and their ways of adapting to life on the US mainland. In effect, Illich asked the question, How can Puerto Ricans tell and live out their story as immigrants as an alternative to the dominant story of "before, we were immigrants, but now we have become Americans"?

In an early essay entitled "Not Foreigners, Yet Foreign," Illich makes the case that Puerto Ricans are not only relative newcomers, but more significantly, "a new type of immigrant: not a European who had left home for good and strove to become an American, but an American citizen"⁹ who is immigrating, perhaps temporarily, from an island to the mainland. More specifically, Illich identifies a seeming paradox related to the Puerto Rican presence, namely, that "these Puerto Ricans are not foreigners, and yet they are more foreign than most of the immigrants who proceeded them."¹⁰ This paradox, Illich suggests, requires closer attention, because understood stereotypically, it tends either toward xenophobia, that is, "These newcomers could never be like us," or toward the "sameness fallacy" of "These newcomers are just like us, immigrants who became Americans."

Illich is responding here to how Americanization creates a stage upon which all immigrant identities gain a new *telos*. All lives that enter

---

7. Gray, *Divine Disobedience*, 241.
8. Illich, *Celebration of Awareness*, 40.
9. Illich, *Celebration of Awareness*, 34.
10. Illich, *Celebration of Awareness*, 31.

upon this stage must be assimilated into the new "we" of American citizenship, a process in which immigrants are stripped of cultural heritage and identities as primary markers, in order to be reborn as Americans clothed with the badge of citizenship. It is, in fact, a corrupted conversion narrative, one in which the immigrant subjectivities are not so much transformed as they are dissolved and lost within the contours of Americanization with its grand narrative about the remaking of immigrants into the image of a given idealized American.

It is important to recognize that within the alchemic process of immigrant transformation, two crucial marks identified immigrants who "passed" as Americans: the ability to pass as white[11] and the ability to speak English. In this way, one's perceived racial identity and spoken tongue become decisive agents in the alchemy of Americanization, the rite of passage by which immigrants or the "American-yet-other" lose one set of identity markers in order to find themselves as fully American.

To appreciate the fullness of Illich's cultural commentary is to recognize how it cuts as a double-edged sword. Illich challenges a veil of cultural stereotypes in order to cast new light on the Puerto Rican paradox: while their "history is more foreign to Europe than to America,"[12] they are yet perceived as the immigrants who are the most foreign of all. Illich, then, focuses on the Puerto Ricans in order for American citizens, especially those of immigrant nationalities and cultural heritages, to see the Puerto Ricans differently, or less differently, as the case may be, and to recognize the contribution their presence brings.[13] In this I would suggest that Illich offers his commentary on the challenge and gift of the Puerto Rican presence as a kind of mirror in which Americans might see themselves. In other words, inside of his plea for "less categorization" and "more understanding," Illich cuts deeply against the grain of Americanization as the blessed destiny of every immigrant, thereby challenging it as a desirable certainty.

Illich, himself an immigrant, both does and does not submit to this process of stripping and being clothed. He does learn to submit to his

---

11. Jacobson, *Whiteness of a Different Color*, 8: "The European immigrants' experience was decisively shaped by their entering an arena where European—that is to say, whiteness—was among the most important possessions one could lay claim to. It was their *whiteness*, not any kind of New World magnanimity, that opened the Golden Door."

12. Illich, *Celebration of Awareness*, 35.

13. Illich, *Celebration of Awareness*, 40.

clerical role and priestly work in the church, just as he submits to the work of language learning: crucially, he navigates in English and learns Spanish, the language of the new immigrant.

Within the Puerto Rican community, Illich embraces not only their language but also their festivals and the shape of their everyday life. He learns how to embody the inflections of their speech as well as the rhythm of their silences.[14] He learns the nuances of their way of being Catholic. He does not fetishize their differences from the distance of a tolerant, proto-multiculturalist observer, but rather he celebrates them and their heritage. In short, his witness among them, for them, and against the alchemy of Americanization celebrates a different kind of newness and change. It is not a stripping in order to become culturally naked before the dominant cultural other, but a kind of becoming that offers a gift to the other and to Catholicism in America.

Thus, Illich's response to the "Great Migration" and his relationship with the Puerto Rican people demonstrated his desire to chart a "third way" (still largely uncharted in the US context) between mere cultural assimilation and mere tolerance. Arguably, the most profound and obvious example of this took place when Illich unfolded the newness of Puerto Rican outsider immigrant status into a ritualized celebration in which they could participate as insiders. He organized a Puerto Rican Catholic *folk fiesta*, an event that exceeded all expectations:

> In 1955, [Illich] organized a Fiesta de San Juan [at Fordham University] to serve as a day for Puerto Rican Catholics to celebrate their religious and cultural heritage. Naming the event after the patron saint of Puerto Rico, Illich conceived of the celebration on the model of traditional *fiestas patronales*, which freely mixed religious processions and a solemn high mass with picknicking, card playing, music, dance, and theatre. . . . On June 23, the eve of the feast, the police estimated they would need officers to control a crowd of about 5,000; the next day, 35,000 people descended on Fordham for a celebration of ethnic cultural identity unprecedented in postwar America.[15]

In this way, long before Christian missiologists advocated for a politics of receptivity to minority (especially immigrant) voices in the midst, Illich's "politics of carnival" created the conditions for some of those (immigrant) voices to be heard. He did this not by becoming "the voice

---

14. Illich, *Celebration of Awareness*, 41–51.
15. Shannon, "Ivan Illich's Politics of Carnival."

of the voiceless," but rather by playfully yet intentionally co-designing a performance in which the celebration of minority voices took center stage, while those usually at the center found themselves offstage or in the audience.

QUESTIONING ALLIANCES FOR PROGRESS

Not long after the record-breaking festal crowd gathered for the San Juan Mass at Fordham University, Illich moved from serving the Puerto Rican community in New York City to serving them on the island itself. At the request of Cardinal Spellman, Illich was appointed as both a monsignor and the vice-rector of the Catholic University of Puerto Rico, where he served from 1956 to 1960. As part of the pastoral work of this appointment, Illich administered a learning center where "Yankees" (as he often described them) could come not only to learn Spanish but also to undergo an immersion experience in Puerto Rican culture, and to enter into what he described as "the spirit of poverty."[16]

Illich's time in Puerto Rico, however, was shorter than he expected. Although he was well suited for his administrative and pastoral duties and at ease with life on the island, by October 1960 the conflict between Illich and the Catholic hierarchy had come to a breaking point over Illich's criticisms of the Catholic Church's political lobbying. In late 1960, Illich left Puerto Rico to establish a new learning center. After a four-month pilgrimage from Santiago, Chile, to Caracas, Venezuela, Illich continued his journey northward, arriving in Mexico. By the spring of 1961, Illich had settled outside Mexico City, in Cuernavaca, where he established his new operation base.

In this alternative learning center on the outskirts of Mexico City, Illich was not retreating from the prophetic stance he established in New York City and Puerto Rico. Rather, Illich was repositioning himself to subvert another dominant certainty that had emerged in tandem with Americanization: the certainty that "alliances for progress," whether the US government-sponsored Peace Corps or the ecclesiastically sponsored Papal Corps, were compatible with the incarnational logic of Christian mission in the Americas.

Here it is important to frame the significance of Illich's social location in relation to North-South relations, and his vehement critique

16. Illich, *Celebration of Awareness*, 42.

of alliances for progress, against the backdrop of the shifting geopolitical landscape at the beginnings of the 1960s. By 1961, this landscape was configured around "Cold War" polarities: the capitalist democracies of the West, following the lead of the United States, and the communist regimes of the East, following the Soviet Union. Within such a configuration, the Latin American continent found itself positioned not only as the South or as part of the "Third World," but also center stage, as the strategic zone upon which these superpowers, "West" and "East," desired to extend their alliances, their markets, and their power.

Shortly after taking office as US president in 1960, John F. Kennedy launched an ambitious international relations program known as the Alliance for Progress. This alliance was, in effect, a repeat performance of the post–World War II Marshall Plan for rebuilding an allied Europe. This time the US would be building alliances with southern neighbors, pledging $20 billion dollars in US investment between 1961 and 1969. To give this strategic alliance a face and to sustain its "relational heartbeat," Kennedy also established the Peace Corps, a voluntary army of young men and women who were prepared to serve the cause of progressive democracy, not as officers in the US military but as patriotic ambassadors of American goodwill and benevolence. These were America's "secular missionaries" responding to Kennedy's famous clarion call to service: "Ask not what your country can do for you—ask what you can do for your country."[17]

What is less well known is that just before Kennedy enlisted the Peace Corps to fight the so-called war on poverty in the Third World, Pope John XXIII issued another call for service in the South. Illich describes this call in the following way:

> In 1960 Pope John XXIII enjoined all United States and Canadian religious superiors to send, within ten years, 10 per cent of their effective strength in priests and nuns to Latin America. This papal request was interpreted by most United States Catholics as a call to help modernize the Latin American Church along the lines of the North American model. The continent on which half of all Catholics live had to be saved from "Castro-Communism."[18]

---

17. This clarion call, "Ask not what your country can do for you—ask what you can do for your country," was delivered by President John F. Kennedy at his inauguration in Washington on January 20, 1961.

18. Illich, *Celebration of Awareness*, 53.

Thus, in 1960 the pope called upon religious superiors in North America to tithe people instead of money, directing the Catholic Church in North America to send 10 percent of its priests and those with religious vocations as an offering for service in "defense" of the Latin American Catholic Church. In this way, the Catholic Church established its own volunteer army, not a Peace Corps, but the Papal Corps.

At the same time that the pope was mobilizing the Papal Corps in the North, Illich was establishing not one but two learning centers: the Centro de Investigaciones Culturales (CIC), in Cuernavaca, and a "sister organization," founded in collaboration with Brazilian colleagues such as Dom Helder Câmara, the Centro de Formação Intercultural (CEN-FI), in Petrópolis, Brazil.[19] Both centers were linked to the Center for Intercultural Formation (CIF), a Catholic missions and research center based at Fordham University in New York. This linkage back to American Catholicism is not incidental to Illich's purposes: he founded CIC, later renamed Centro Intercultural de Documentación (CIDOC), as an alternative learning center for North American priests and missioners coming to serve in Latin America. In other words, he was preparing a place to receive the "invasion" of the Papal Corps. Illich did not try to block the missionary invasion, which he knew was impossible, nor did he simply accept the cultural imperialism and sense of American exceptionalism that infected the Papal Corps. Rather, he created a center that provided intercultural missionary formation while subverting the imposition of dominant American cultural values that undermine missionary presence.[20]

While committed to the work of theological formation, CIDOC was less a conventional seminary and more of a free university that combined language training, library research, seminary-based reflection, and a small publishing house. Rather than focusing on doctrinal teaching, the focus at CIDOC was on cultivating a certain kind of awareness by submerging a Christian theological vision into the realities of sociopolitical change in Latin America: poverty, schooling, transportation, modes of production, and energy consumption, to name a few. Mexican priest and CIDOC collaborator Julio Torres described CIDOC's aims as "provid[ing] a pastoral method more deeply rooted in the cultural tradition of Latin America, and to combat the prevailing trend of developing

---

19. Zaldívar and Uceda, "Ivan Illich and the Conflict with the Vatican," 3.
20. See Hartch, *Prophet of Cuernavaca*, especially chapter 7.

countries imposing their solutions on underdeveloped countries."[21] Illich said something similar, summarizing the ethos at CIDOC as follows: "I would like to help people smile . . . smile the social system apart. Here at CIDOC we smile violence apart. It is a place where violent people can come and learn a *respeto para la vida* [respect for life]."[22] One of Illich's favorite quotes came from Ché Guevara: "One must toughen up without losing one's tenderness."[23]

In many ways, Illich's CIDOC was to Latin America in the 1960s what Dietrich Bonhoeffer's Finkenwalde experiment was to Germany in the 1930s.[24] Both Finkenwalde and CIDOC were founded by visionary Christian leaders who positioned themselves on the margins of established ecclesial structures; both were committed to catalyzing an authentically Christian counter-witness to the distortions of culturally dominant forms of Christianity. Bonhoeffer's experiment attempted to reformulate and delink Christian witness from its captivity within the emerging social imagination of the German nation and the *Volk*-theology that emerged and solidified between World War I and World War II. Illich's experiment attempted to examine and delink Christian missionary activity from its corruption within emerging alliances for progress that inextricably linked the Americas in the post–World War II era. At the heart of both experiments was an emphasis upon cultural *kenosis* as a process of guiding participants in "self-emptying" or unlearning the dominant habits of social division.

Strikingly, in his resettlement and his agenda with these learning centers, Illich managed to position himself and his centers inside official Catholic missionary structures in order to question them. Officially, CIDOC existed to provide intercultural missionary training, a process of formation that embedded rigorous language study with immersion into the cultural nuances of peoples and places. Unofficially, CIDOC existed to question the Papal Corps as an alliance for progress.[25] More precisely, what Illich questioned, and attempted to subvert, was not missionary activity per se but the co-optation of Catholic missionary presence inside another missionary endeavor. In Illich's view, the work of the Papal Corps

21. Gray, *Divine Disobedience*, 276–77.
22. Gray, *Divine Disobedience*, 274.
23. Gray, *Divine Disobedience*, 282.
24. See Bonhoeffer, *Life Together*.
25. Illich, *Celebration of Awareness*, 57.

was taking place on the stage of the Alliance for Progress in such a way that the Christian gospel was being cloaked inside the missionary expansion of the "American way of life."[26] Illich argued, like many radicals in Latin America, that the Alliance for Progress was, in effect, "an alliance for the progress of the middle classes."[27] As such, the missionary campaign of the Catholic Church, to the extent that it was aligned with such an alliance, would end up training and sending "pawns of United States cultural imperialism."[28]

QUESTIONING "THE SEAMY SIDE OF CHARITY"

By the mid-1960s, in the light of less-than-desirable numbers on the ground in Latin America, the North American church was struggling to maintain enthusiasm for the missionary effort directed from the US homeland. In order to galvanize support and funds for the "Help Save Latin America" cause,[29] a large conference was planned for both Catholic and Protestant representatives from the United States and Latin America in Boston in 1967.

In January 1967, just days before the conference, Illich published his criticisms of North American missionary efforts in the Jesuit magazine *America*, calling for a reexamination of the entire missionary enterprise in an essay entitled "The Seamy Side of Charity." Illich's essay seems to state the obvious: that from a numerical perspective, the Papal Corps could hardly be called a success. After five years, the project had offered less than one-tenth of the "relational tithe," with only 1,622 responding to the "call for 20,000."[30] At another level, Illich tried to move the debate away from questions of missionary strategy, or means, to the unaddressed but vital questions of missionary purpose, or ends. He also turned the spotlight away from the numbers game and intended outcomes and toward the reality of the unintended or unwanted side effects of missionary intervention. Thus, Illich's basic question was, "Why not, for once, consider the seamy side of charity; weigh the inevitable burdens foreign

---

26. Illich, *Celebration of Awareness*, 22.
27. Illich, *Celebration of Awareness*, 253.
28. Illich, *Celebration of Awareness*, 253.
29. Illich, *Celebration of Awareness*, 57.
30. Illich, *Celebration of Awareness*, 57.

help imposes on the South American Church; taste the bitterness of the damage done by our sacrifices?"[31]

By returning to Illich's attention to the seamy side of charity, clarification is needed regarding what he is and is not saying about missionary presence. First, he is not condemning all missionary efforts. He is not questioning whether such missionary ventures can do good or lead to any positive change. Nor is he trying to undermine "the unquestionable joys of giving and the fruits of receiving."[32] But he is saying that such projects cannot rest on "uncritical imagination and sentimental judgment," that is, on ways of thinking and acting that swallow "Latin America needs you" and "Red danger" as unquestionably authentic calls for Christian mission. By referring to the Papal Corps itself as "a peculiar alliance for the progress of the Latin American Church,"[33] Illich argues that the church must attend to the way in which its presence can be fused into, and therefore confused with, "the many-faceted effort to keep Latin America within the ideologies of the West."[34] Put more strongly: "Men and money sent with missionary motivation carry a foreign Christian message, a foreign pastoral approach and a foreign political message. They also bear the mark of North American capitalism of the 1950s."[35] Illich is saying that the motivation driving "well-intentioned missionary ventures"[36] is not the most important issue at stake. Rather, he wants to draw our attention to the arena in which those intentions come to life, as well as their potentially undesirable consequences:

> We must acknowledge that missioners can be pawns in a world ideological struggle and that is it is blasphemous to use the gospel to prop up any social or political system. When men and money are sent into a society within the framework of a program, they bring ideas that live after them. It has been pointed out, in the case of the Peace Corps, that the cultural mutation catalyzed by a small foreign group might be more effective than all the immediate services it renders. The same can be true of the North American missioner—close to home, having great means at his disposal, frequently on a short-term assignment—who

31. Illich, *Celebration of Awareness*, 58.
32. Illich, *Celebration of Awareness*, 59.
33. Illich, *Celebration of Awareness*, 57.
34. Illich, *Celebration of Awareness*, 58.
35. Illich, *Celebration of Awareness*, 58.
36. Illich, *Celebration of Awareness*, 58.

> moves into an area of intense United States cultural and economic colonization. He is part of this sphere of influence, and, at times, intrigue. Through the United States missioner, the United States shadows and colors the public image of the Church. The influx of United States missioners coincides with the Alliance for Progress, Camelot, and CIA projects and looks like a baptism of all three. The Alliance appears directed by Christian justice and is not seen for what it is: a deception designed to maintain the status quo, albeit variously motivated.... Within these realities, the United States missioner tends to fulfill the traditional role of a colonial power's lackey chaplain.[37]

The fundamental issue for Illich is not whether the church's primary motivation for investing heavily in social projects and facilitating significant funds "for the poor" was, in fact, to "contain Castroism and assure its institutional respectability."[38] Perhaps those two realities cannot be neatly separated from one another. Nevertheless, what remains clear for Illich is this:

> By becoming an "official" agency of one kind of progress, the Church ceases to speak for the underdog who is outside all agencies but who is an ever-growing majority. By accepting the power to help, the Church necessarily must denounce a Camilo Torres, who symbolizes the power of renunciation. Money thus builds the Church a "pastoral" structure beyond its means and makes it a political power.[39]

Speaking as a voice within the Latin American church, Illich attributes the negative result of this inter-American alliance to the false dependence it generates upon the North American church. In his analysis, it is precisely "this kind of foreign generosity [that] has enticed the Latin American Church into becoming a satellite to North Atlantic cultural phenomena and policy.... The Latin American Church flowers anew by returning to what the Conquest stamped her: a colonial plant that blooms because of foreign cultivation."[40] Without attending to the seamy side of this partnership, the result is a double blindness: the North American church does not have to "face the painful side of generosity: the burden

---

37. Illich, *Celebration of Awareness*, 65–66.
38. Illich, *Celebration of Awareness*, 61.
39. Illich, *Celebration of Awareness*, 61.
40. Illich, *Celebration of Awareness*, 59.

that a life gratuitously offered imposes on the recipient,"[41] while the Latin American church does not see beyond the horizon of this disabling dependence on foreign exports.

Illich diagnoses this surplus of North American clergy, as well as other debilitating aspects of this "foreign transfusion," as symptoms of denial on the part of the American church to "face up to the sociopolitical consequences involved in their well-intentioned missionary ventures."[42] At a deeper level, Illich writes to expose and repair a wound caused by ecclesial failure. Specifically, there is the failure that results from "the underdeveloped ecclesiology of United States clerics who direct the 'sale' of American good intentions."[43] More generally, however, there is the failure that comes from fear of becoming open to new ecclesial forms of life:

> Exporting Church employees to Latin America masks a universal and unconscious fear of a new Church. North and South American authorities, differently motivated but equally fearful, become accomplices in maintaining a clerical and irrelevant Church. Sacralizing employees and property, this Church becomes progressively more blind to the possibilities of sacralizing person and community. . . . In fear, we plan *our* Church with statistics, rather than trustingly search for the living Church which is right among us.[44]

The issue Illich raises is: What kind of church are we prepared to imagine and inhabit?

I will return to this question later, but at this point I want to highlight how Illich's pilgrimage in the Americas both anticipates and illumines the *viradas* of my own journey. Observing Illich's arrival in the United States and his relationship with the Puerto Rican community, there is a resonance between the dynamics of his "being sent" as a missionary priest in the United States and our "being sent" from there. In the same way that he was "caught" and drawn into the Puerto Rican community in New York City, so too were we "caught" by the presence of the African-American church in Durham, North Carolina. Just as Illich "crossed over" in order to join in their ways of worship, we also found ourselves "crossing over" into a social and ecclesial space that challenged the two

---

41. Illich, *Celebration of Awareness*, 65.
42. Illich, *Celebration of Awareness*, 58.
43. Illich, *Celebration of Awareness*, 68.
44. Illich, *Celebration of Awareness*, 64, 68.

dominant modes of relationality generated around the "color line": the drive toward assimilation, or "passing" and becoming the same as the other; and the drive toward multicultural tolerance, or maintaining a tolerant yet detached relation to the other. We experienced a "third way"—a new form of belonging that transgressed the "color line"—and it was precisely that newness of belonging that Illich sought to cultivate.

Following the arc of Illich's journey southward into Puerto Rico and Mexico also illumines the difficulties and possibilities of delinking an authentic missionary encounter from the "good intentions." He asserts that paternalistic forms of missionary service are hidden inside other "narratives of inclusion," in this case, the implicit narrative of American exceptionalism. Indeed, one can read Illich's critique of the Papal Corps as an "alliance for progress" as a more expansive critique of the subtle dynamics of missionary idealism that I experienced as a US missionary in Brazil. I am referring now to that subtle form of control that understands mission as diagnosing and meeting needs (even by imposition), rather than responding to encounters. Thus, I am suggesting that both in the United States and across the Americas, Illich's witness illumines and deepens the questionings of my own intercultural missionary experience. He does so by discerning and questioning missionary encounters of assimilation that are de-incarnational. With this in mind, I turn more closely to the center of his theological imagination, the Incarnation.

3

Following the Naked Christ

IN THIS CHAPTER I want to shift the focus of attention from the arc of Illich's journey into and across the Americas, and toward the center of his own Christian imagination. Here, the Incarnation and the incarnational logic of Christian life must be attended to. At the same time, I want to take seriously a certain ambiguity surrounding Illich's legacy, particularly as it relates to Christian theology. Close readers and friends of Illich have appreciated Illich's "humanist radicalism,"[1] whether they read him primarily as a Christian intellectual, a social critic, a "critical traditionalist,"[2] or simply as a post-development thinker who was ahead of his time. Nonetheless, readers less familiar with the overall shape of Illich's life and *corpus*, or less generous in their reading of it, may ask, What distinguishes Illich's stance from that of being just a clever social critic or historian?

To be clear, the ambiguity surrounding Illich's legacy tends not to be *ad hominem*. It is not concerned with whether Illich was an authentic Christian, since no one appears to doubt his character or his abiding Christian faith.[3] Rather, a lingering question around Illich's witness seems to be this: To what extent are Illich's iconoclastic engagements with the dominant certainties of modernity, such as Americanization and alliances for progress, related to his theological convictions as a Christian

---

1. See Fromm, in Illich, *Celebration of Awareness*, 7–10.
2. Schroyer, *Beyond Western Economics*, 9.
3. See Sbert, *Epimeteo, Iván Illich y el sendero de la sabiduría*.

intellectual? What, if anything, provides the legitimacy for reading Illich's social criticism as theologically imbued investigation? Put another way, the question is, How decisive is Jesus Christ for Illich's personal witness, the art of his living, and the art of his writing? Looking at Illich's better known social criticism, especially from the 1970s, it is not at all clear that the person of Jesus Christ is decisive for his intellectual project. Most of what he published in the 1970s and until the late 1980s contains no explicit christological references. Yet, I would argue that in the light of Illich's early writings until the late 1960s,[4] as well as the later books of interviews with David Cayley,[5] it can be seen just how decisive the person of Jesus Christ is for Illich's stance.

To be clear, my aim is not to demonstrate, as Lee Hoinacki has done, that Illich was "doing theology in a new way."[6] While Hoinacki's nuanced reading of Illich is convincing, I am arguing a slightly different point. I aim to show that Illich's witness is imbued by a theological center: the Incarnation. Therefore, in this chapter I shift the focus of attention from Illich's stance against dominant certainties toward Illich's stance as an intellectual who operates from and points to a "center," that is, toward Illich's stance for the Incarnation as a personal reality in which Christians are called to participate (1 John 4:9). To do so, I will attend to the way that Illich imagines the Christian life unfolding inside a theodramatic horizon.

ATTENDING TO THEODRAMA: THE SHAPE OF THE JOURNEY

In *Theology and the Drama of History*, Ben Quash develops a theodramatic account of history, which he distinguishes from a "theology of history" and characterizes as "a heuristic for thinking theologically about history."[7] As distinct from a dramatic conception of history, nondramatic accounts tend to fall into one of two categories: either the "epic," which emphasizes an objective, or overarching coherence to history, or

---

4. See especially Illich, *Celebration of Awareness*; Illich, *The Church, Change and Development*.

5. Cayley and Illich, *Ivan Illich in Conversation*; also Cayley and Illich, *The Rivers North of the Future*.

6. Hoinacki, quoted in *Ivan Illich in Conversation*, 54. See Hoinacki, "The Trajectory of Ivan Illich."

7. Quash, *Theology and the Drama of History*, 9.

the "lyric," which highlights the subjective, the contingent, self-involving, and indeterminate character of historicity.[8] According to Quash, the problem with non-dramatic accounts of history and human action is the inherent tendency to make either subjects (the lyric account) or structures (the epic account) the key to interpreting how we live and act within history.[9] Both the epic and lyric dimensions have their place. When taken alone, however, each is insufficient, either absolutizing a contingent structural configuration to the detriment of subjects (the epic alone), or isolating human subjectivity or agencies in abstraction from its necessarily social, or structured, context (the lyric alone). In relation to Illich's journey into and across the Americas, one can read Americanization and the alliances for progress as an overly epic process of assimilation.

A theodramatic approach, Quash argues, is especially suited for attending to the complex nuances of theology's subject matter as well as avoiding certain nagging tendencies, such as an inability or unwillingness to "take history seriously." While history does matter to theology, given the intellectual trajectory of the West, and more specifically the shaping of academic disciplines within that trajectory, history's place within theology cannot be taken for granted. As Quash points out, theology does not differ from other disciplines of inquiry because it is concerned with a different history than they are; rather, theology is concerned with a different way of reading history, namely, an eschatological account that reads "history as having an origin and end in God's purposes."[10] A theodramatic approach, then, encourages and enables theological reflection that holds together history and eschatology.

In the light of Quash's insights, I suggest that Illich's own pilgrimage illumines the theodramatic shape of the Christian faith. Illich expresses the lyric dimension in terms of the early Christian notion of *revolutio*, or *reformare*, that is, "self-renewal, the renewal of the person, which God will perform, as the major *social* task of a Christian community."[11] He expresses the epic as the perception of living within a providentially

---

8. Quash, *Theology and the Drama of History*, 35–39.
9. Quash, *Theology and the Drama of History*, 2–3.
10. Quash, *Theology and the Drama of History*, 6.
11. Cayley and Illich, *Ivan Illich in Conversation*, 211.

ordered cosmos, "a world in the hands of God."[12] Moreover, what Illich calls "the journey of our life in God"[13] holds the lyric and the epic together.

In an interview with David Cayley, Illich explicitly addresses the ambiguity of his witness:

> Again and again during the last forty years I have been asked the question, "Where do you stand?" I have usually, at the beginning of any major lecture series, told my audience that I stand within the Christian faith, in order that they should be aware that my prejudices may differ from theirs.[14]

In many ways, this conversation continues another conversation with Cayley, one in which Illich interprets his own life in terms of a medieval motto: "*nudum christum nudus sequere*, [which means] nakedly following the naked Christ."[15] While Illich has very little to say directly about the concept of discipleship, his motto "following the naked Christ" offers a medieval gloss on Christian discipleship, as well as an interpretive lens for approaching Illich's life and thought. Although not self-interpreting, the simplicity of the phrase does suggest a certain shape and logic to the Christian life. First, following is an action; it is what disciples do. It is their response to the call of Jesus to "follow me." Second, that response must be given in relation to the One who calls, something that sets up the turn to the naked Christ, the Savior who renounced the worldly power of Caesar and Pilate. It is through the naked One that we are called to enact "courageous, disciplined, self-critical renunciation accomplished in community."[16] Finally, that Christ is followed "nakedly" suggests that the Incarnation is more than a key doctrinal locus; it means that all other claims on our lives are de-centered and re-centered by the authority of this person through whom we are called to live (Gal 2:20; 1 John 4:9). The motto serves as an interpretive clue or key that points to the Incarnate Christ as the center of Illich's vision of the Christian life.

Another of Illich's friends, Domencio Farias, sheds further light on Illich's stance in his essay "In the Shadow of Jerome," where he also interprets Illich's life in comparison with fifth-century scholar St. Jerome.

---

12. Cayley and Illich, *Rivers North of the Future*, 64–70.
13. Illich, "Philosophy . . . Artifacts . . . Friendship," 1.
14. Cayley and Illich, *Rivers North of the Future*, 146.
15. Cayley and Illich, *Ivan Illich in Conversation*, 283.
16. Cayley and Illich, *Rivers North of the Future*, 44.

Farias's essay is an extended commentary on Illich's motto, also attributed to St. Jerome.[17] Like St. Jerome, Illich was both a Dalmatian and "a wandering, homeless man, but one nevertheless rooted in a tradition that is itself tied to a particular land and history."[18] In his reading of Illich, Farias highlights how Illich's witness embodies the paradox of "nomadic rootedness," a condition eloquently described as follows:

> Jerome's call, *nudum* Christum *sequere*, follows an Abrahamic dispossession: "Get thee out of thy country!" (Gen. 12:1). He is in the great tradition of the Exodus, of the individual and of a people who experience a God different from the other gods, those with fixed abodes in certain sites, of a God who passes over the earth and can be known only by someone disposed to see his back as he passes by—and to follow him.[19]

Interpreting Illich's witness through the lens of the motto *nudum Christum sequere* involves what Farias calls a "hermeneutic leap."[20] Such a leap requires attention to a pattern that emerges from the act of following, a pattern grounded in hearing and responding to a call in obedient trust. Seen in this light, Farias suggests that the tagline, "following the naked Christ," serves as the interpretive key by which "to grasp the essential unity of [Illich's life]—the unity of a way of living that saves itself by appearing to lose itself."[21]

Farias's interpretation of Illich asserts that the latter's life exemplifies the "storied witness"[22] of the people of God, a people who do not "live, move, and have their being" (Acts 17:28) in themselves, but rather who fully receive and become themselves through following Another. More precisely, they become themselves through a relationship of call and response "with the voice of [the One] who speaks."[23] Only the Creator, Farias writes, is "the Major Transcendence," but "there are the minor reciprocal transcendences of the souls who in the pilgrim church, live not only an apophatic theology, but also an apophatic anthropology."[24]

---

17. Farias, "In the Shadow of Jerome," 59–70.
18. Mitcham, "Challenges of This Collection," 11.
19. Farias, "In the Shadow of Jerome," 61–62.
20. Farias, "In the Shadow of Jerome," 59.
21. Farias, "In the Shadow of Jerome," 59.
22. McClendon, *Witness*, 350.
23. Illich, *Ivan Illich in Conversation*, 243.
24. Farias, "In the Shadow of Jerome," 68.

Hoinacki throws light on this in his essay "The Trajectory of Ivan Illich," where he addresses the ambiguity of Illich's legacy with the following insight:

> I do not think that one can characterize Illich with any conventional label, whether that be of an academic discipline, such as sociologist, or a descriptive adjective, such as conservative. But I do think one can examine Illich's life and work in terms of certain thematic threads, for his Christian faith, his practice of friendship, his relationship to words and Word, readiness for surprise, attention to the other, and so on. It is my contention that, given the trajectory of his life, his bio or curriculum vitae, the principal analytical concept giving intelligibility to the way he lived, to what he said and wrote, is his apophatic theological stance.[25]

Without this interpretive key, Hoinacki insists, Illich's interlocutors may end up with superficial or misleading readings that reduce him to a priest-theologian turned social critic, while in fact, Illich's whole corpus may be read as way of "doing theology in a new way."[26] On Hoinacki's reading, before 1971 Illich addressed audiences inside and outside the church, speaking openly as a "churchman" and "Catholic believer."[27] However, from 1971 on, beginning with *Deschooling Society*, Illich adopted an apophatic perspective, producing a series of books that were "apophatic explorations about God, the Church, and the believer's movement towards God."[28]

In following Hoinacki's and Farias's interpretation of Illich's apophatic stance, it must be noted that, within theology, the concept of *apophasis* is a multivalent one, used variously to denote God's transcendence, or otherness or hiddenness; a theological method also referred to as the *via negativa*; and as a way of conceptualizing the iconic dimension of creation and, more precisely, of the human being as created in the image of God.[29] While one could argue that Illich's use of *apophasis* overlaps with each of these three senses, I want to highlight how Illich's apophatic expression is not reducible to sheer negation, that is, "not this," but rather

---

25. Hoinacki, "Trajectory of Ivan Illich," 384.
26. Hoinacki, quoted in Cayley and Illich, *Ivan Illich in Conversation*, 54.
27. Hoinacki, "Trajectory of Ivan Illich," 385.
28. Hoinacki, "Trajectory of Ivan Illich," 385.
29. On apophatic theology, see McFarland, *Difference & Identity*, 14–29; Jennings, "'He Became Truly Human,'" 252–53; Nellas, *Deification in Christ*, 21–104.

is a form of iconoclasm for the sake of the truly iconic that comes to us through the Incarnation of the Word (Col 1:15; 2 Cor 4:4). Illich engages "what is but should not be," and in doing so, he "clears the way for surprise and mystery."[30]

To summarize, Illich's life is expressed apophatically to the extent that it enacts an Abrahamic dispossession—a quality of creaturely freedom, a self-transcendence that is not self-referential but rather "ec-centric"—established in relation in the Incarnation as its "center." To describe Illich's stance as apophatic is to say that the shape is hidden within the act of responding to a call (Col 3:3). This is because the fullness of his life, the "more than" of being "in Christ" (Rom 5:9–10, 15, 17; 11:12) cannot be isolated in terms of the context of the following itself, whether that be Dalmatia, Austria, Italy, New York, Puerto Rico, Cuernavaca, or Bremen. Illich would call that "misplaced concreteness."[31] Instead, such ec-centric fullness originates from the One who is followed: Christ, the "image of God" (Col 1:15; 2 Cor 4:4) through whom our creaturely *imago* is being renewed (Col 3:10).

DISCERNING ACT 3: THE INCARNATION AND THE CENTER OF THE JOURNEY

In order to develop this line of thought, I want to turn to *Improvisation: The Drama of Christian Ethics*, in which Sam Wells offers an account of the dramatic shape of the Christian story that complements Quash's insights. More specifically, Wells explores how the Christian theodrama as a five-act play might be approached:[32]

- Act 1: Creation
- Act 2: Israel
- Act 3: Jesus
- Act 4: Church
- Act 5: Eschaton

---

30. Cayley and Illich, *Ivan Illich in Conversation*, 242.

31. Cayley and Illich, *Ivan Illich in Conversation*, 287.

32. The notion of the five-act play is not original to Wells; rather, his account amends Tom Wright's proposal. See Wells, *Improvisation*, 51–53.

Wells describes the relationship of acts and our being "placed" in Act 4 within the theodrama as follows:

> This is a truly theo-dramatic model.... The principles and the narrative of the first act continue through the three that follow; the covenant of the second act is alive and significant in the third and fourth; the theme of the third is the key to understanding all the others; and the character of the fourth ("the holy city") is at least partly preserved, though transformed, in the fifth. The role of the fourth balances the need for a genuinely human dimension to the drama with the need for a genuinely divine shape. If the fifth act is explored too fully the drama becomes too epic; if it is ignored, the drama becomes too lyric. It is in preserving the delicate balance of this fivefold shape that the genuine theodrama of the five-act play unfolds.[33]

To say that the Incarnation is the center of Illich's faith is also to recognize how the Incarnation "contextualizes" us within the theodrama between the climax (Act 3) and the end (Act 5). Illich offers his most explicit account of the Incarnation as an historical turning point in his commentary on the parable of the Good Samaritan, which might be read as his "gospel in brief." While Illich never produced a systematic reflection on this parable, his reflections on it are woven throughout the text of *The Rivers North of the Future: The Testament of Ivan Illich*, especially in the sections entitled "Gospel" and "*Mysterium*."

Framing his reflections on the Good Samaritan, Illich makes two observations regarding the surprise and newness that the Incarnation makes possible. First, it "explodes certain universal assumptions about the conditions under which love is possible."[34] The Incarnation, Illich argues, establishes a new basis or condition for human relationality, interrupting "the traditional basis for ethics, which is always an *ethnos*, an historically given 'we' which precedes another pronunciation of the word 'I.'"[35] The *ethos*, or a collective way of living, is circumscribed within a prior *ethnos*, a "we" given through birth and/or place, such as the way both Plato's and Aristotle's accounts of ethics turned on their conception of the ethnic "we" of Athenian citizenship.

The logic of the Incarnation, however, cannot be contained ethnically, or within a prior "we." In manifesting God's love to the ethnic other

---

33. Wells, *Improvisation*, 53.
34. Cayley and Illich, *Rivers North of the Future*, 47.
35. Cayley and Illich, *Rivers North of the Future*, 47.

and in announcing that "whomever loves another loves [Jesus himself] in the person of that other,"[36] the Incarnate Savior transgressed the boundaries of the ethnic "we." The Syro-Phoenician woman can respond to Israel's Messiah in faith: "Have mercy on me, Lord, Son of David; my daughter is tormented by a demon" (Matt 15:22). Peter can cross over into Gentile territory to share a meal with the uncircumcised, receiving their food as clean and receiving Cornelius's household as co-members in God's family (Acts 10:1—11:18). The Jewish-Gentile difference, the threshold that distinguished the people of God from "the nations," can be crossed in faith. This threshold has not been destroyed but has become porous through the opening of incarnational difference. Now there is "one new humanity in place of the two" (Eph 2:15). The Incarnation, it could be argued, created a new "we" that is no longer defined in terms "of blood or of the will of the flesh or of the will of man" (John 1:13). The new "we" is established solely in relation to a person, the Incarnate Savior.

Second, Illich observes that in transgressing such a boundary and unleashing "a new dimension of love [that is] . . . highly ambiguous," the Incarnation introduces a danger. He identifies the danger as a movement from incarnation to institutionalization: "a temptation to try to manage and, eventually, to legislate this new love, to create an institution that will guarantee it, insure it, and protect it by criminalizing its opposite."[37] There are at least two senses, then, in which the Incarnation is a scandal:

- as the irruption of a novel freedom and a renewed relationality in which the only determinative border is one's relation to the "Word made flesh" (John 1:14); and

- as the emergence of "an entirely new kind of power, the power of those who organize Christianity and use this vocation to claim their superiority as social institutions."[38]

To illustrate the force of this twofold scandal, Illich turns back to the parable of the Good Samaritan. As Illich points out, the question that Jesus is answering with this parable is not, "How should I behave toward my neighbor?," but rather, "Who is my neighbor?" And yet, Illich's research on the history of the interpretation of this parable suggests that there is a modern bias away from reading the parable in terms of

---

36. Cayley and Illich, *Rivers North of the Future*, 47.
37. Cayley and Illich, *Rivers North of the Future*, 47.
38. Cayley and Illich, *Rivers North of the Future*, 47.

the freedom and permission to embrace and be embraced by the other who is encountered. Illich suggests that the modern reading focuses on the normative obligation or duty to love anyone who is needy. There is an interpretive shift in which attention to the other is displaced from the "ought" that arises from embodied relatedness to the "ought" that conforms to a codified norm. This displacement or interpretative slippage signals the corruption of the incarnational threshold that generates a new "we." Illich's reading of the parable seeks to recover the scandalous new "we" made possible through encountering the other who previously remained outside and untouchable. Illich explains:

> This is an act which prolongs the Incarnation. Just as God became flesh and in the flesh relates to each one of us, so you are capable of relating in the flesh, as one who says ego, and when he says ego, points to an experience which is entirely sensual, incarnate, this-worldly, to that other man who has been beaten up. Take away the fleshy, bodily, carnal, dense, humoural experience of self, and therefore of the Thou, from the story of the Samaritan and you have a nice liberal fantasy, which is something horrible. You have the basis on which one might feel responsible for bombing the neighbour for his own good. This use of power is what I call the *corruptio optimi quae est pessima* [the corruption of the best is the worst].[39]

From Illich's reading, the Samaritan's response prolongs the Incarnation precisely because it "liberates from the ethnic boundary without destroying it."[40] His comments on the significance of this surprising encounter, an encounter in which a "Thou" brings out my vocation to neighborliness, are summarized in this passage:

> Our contemporary perception of self, of human relationship, so-called inter-personal relationship, has been deeply corrupted. When norms are brought into the "ought" . . . the glorious side of the encounter between the Palestinian and the Jew is hidden. What the Lord told the Pharisee with this story is this: it is open to anyone who walks down the road to move away from the road and establish a relationship, a fit, a tie, with the man who is beaten up. To do so corresponds to the nature of two human beings and permits this nature its full flowering. The Samaritan

39. Cayley and Illich, *Rivers North of the Future*, 207. I will return to Illich's understanding of how institutionalization corrupts the Samaritan's freedom later, in chapter 6, when I develop Illich's notion that "the corruption of the best is the worst."

40. Cayley and Illich, *Rivers North of the Future*, 199.

has the possibility of establishing a proportion, a relatedness to the other man which is entirely free and conditioned only by his hope that the beaten-up Jew will respond to it by accepting his relationship. . . . Any attempt to explain this "ought" as corresponding to a norm takes out the mysterious greatness of this free act.[41]

In terms of Wells's five-act model, Act 3 is climax precisely because the Incarnation is "the point to which the creation of the world pointed forward, and [it] is the point to which the end of the world, as final conclusion and as purposeful *telos*, points back."[42] Because "all things have been created through him and for him" (Col 1:16), the coming of Christ in Act 3 points back to the mysterious truth announced in Act 1: that creation is "a world in the hands of God."[43] Similarly, Act 3 establishes the difference and the continuity between Acts 2 and 4. It fulfills the promise of Gentile inclusion into the people of God, the promise made to Abraham at the beginning of Act 2. It makes possible, with the descent of the Holy Spirit at Pentecost, the sending of the church as the "body in Christ" in Act 4. And ultimately, Christ's promise to return orientates us in hope, in anticipation of the fullness of the *eschaton* in Act 5.

INHABITING ACT 4: A QUESTION OF WITNESS

Here, I want to develop how Illich's own journey relates to his reading of the parable of the Good Samaritan—particularly how he navigated the tension between the vocation to "prolong the Incarnation" and the institutionalization of that vocation. To do so, I want to return to an interpretation of Illich offered by Francine du Plessix Gray in her book *Divine Disobedience: Profiles in Catholic Radicalism*, on which I drew earlier. In this work, du Plessix Gray explores the emergence in the 1960s of a new Catholic radicalism, a stance characterized by the tension between gospel obedience and the dictates of the institutional church.[44] By utilizing anecdotal and interview materials, her biographical sketch of Illich portrays him as a priest and intellectual who manifests Catholic dissidence while remaining radically orthodox. To borrow a phrase from Robert Inchausti,

---

41. Cayley and Illich, *Rivers North of the Future*, 206–7.
42. Wells, *Improvisation*, 52.
43. See Cayley and Illich, *Rivers North of the Future*, 64–70.
44. Gray, *Divine Disobedience*, ix.

what makes Illich's stance so challenging, and so threatening, is the fact that his is a "subversive orthodoxy."[45]

As du Plessix Gray points out, from early on in his career, Illich took the work of criticism seriously, understanding it as "a work of love." Because Illich understood the priestly role preeminently as an office of unity, his early criticisms of the American church were written pseudonymously, under the pen name Peter Canon. "A critical attitude," Illich would insist, "is precisely one of the areas in which Christian love for the Church can develop.... Criticism is the fruit of hard work and prayer."[46] Later, writing in the 1960s from his learning center in Cuernavaca, Mexico, during times that moved to a strong revolutionary beat, Illich pressed on with the work of criticism. While friends with notable figures of the first generation of Latin American liberation theology, such as Brazilian Archbishop Dom Hélder Câmara, Peruvian theologian Gustavo Gutiérrez, and Brazilian educator Paulo Freire, Illich's stance did not map neatly onto a left-right political spectrum. Indeed, one could say that he stood outside the left-right encampments, or, better, he stood between them. This is not because he was anti-revolutionary, but rather because he insisted on being revolutionary in a correct way:

> I am attacked by both the left and the right because I insist on rigorously correct behavior. I am profoundly opposed to the Underground Church because it is counter-revolutionary. You reform by staying within the system. I believe in good manners, in playing the rules of the game. If you don't like the rules of chess, stop playing but do not try to reform the rules of chess.[47]

Thus, the left attacked his "good manners," while the right attacked his "subversive mannerliness." As an experiment in cultivating a deeply Christian account of revolution, Illich would insist the "CIDOC is in its deepest sense a contemplative place... and this is scandalous to both the left and the right."[48]

I began chapter 1 by referring to the declassified CIA report that identified Illich as a radical, a marginal voice, but one that managed to attract the attention of the US government. To describe him as a radical

---

45. See Inchausti, *Subversive Orthodoxy*.
46. Gray, *Divine Disobedience*, 244.
47. Gray, *Divine Disobedience*, 274–75.
48. Gray, *Divine Disobedience*, 275.

or as a revolutionary also raises the question, How was Illich's stance perceived and treated by the Catholic Church?

Of course, Illich's activities—including his criticism of the church—did not happen in an ecclesial vacuum. As I mentioned earlier, one of the keys to Illich's witness in Latin America was his ability to assess and use his status as a priest and monsignor, forging tactical alliances within the Catholic hierarchy. On the northern front, the strong bond between Illich and Cardinal Spellman in New York left Illich practically untouchable by the forces that opposed him. In the South, the key to the operational success of CIC/CIDOC was the friendship between Illich and Father Méndez Arceo, bishop of Cuernavaca, Mexico.

The Illich-Arceo tandem, however, eventually provoked much protest from conservative Catholics in Mexico, most notably from the Comité pro Reindivicación de la Iglesia Católica en Cuernavaca (Committee for the Recovery of the Catholic Church in Cuernavaca). In formal complaints to Catholic officials, this committee described Illich in the following way:

> That strange, devious, and slippery personage, crawling with indefinable nationalities, who is called, or claims to be called, Ivan Illich.[49]

By late 1967, this same committee eventually entered a plea to the Conference of Mexican Bishops to close CIDOC and to have Illich removed from Mexico. At first, he appealed to Spellman for support and to gain time. However, after a stage of declining health, Spellman died in early December 1967, leaving Illich without the protection of his American archbishop. Within the same month, Spellman's successor, John McGuire, wrote to Illich, communicating that a Vatican directive had called for Illich's return to the New York diocese by 12 January 1968.[50] After a series of Vatican reports produced for the cardinals of the Holy Office, Illich was eventually summoned to appear by 25 June 1968 before the Congregation for the Doctrine of the Faith at the Vatican.

On 18 June 1968, Illich appeared at the Vatican for interrogation regarding his political and doctrinal views. In the presence of Monsignor Casoria and Cardinal Seper, of Illich's native Yugoslavia, Illich received

---

49. Gray, *Divine Disobedience*, 269. The original Spanish reads as follows: "Eso personaje extraño y sinuoso, escurrizido y reptante de nacionalidad indefinible, que se llama, o dice llamarse, Ivan Illich."

50. Zaldívar and Uceda, "Conflict with the Vatican (1966–1969)," 7.

an elaborate questionnaire grouped under headings such as "Dangerous Doctrinal Opinions," "Erroneous Ideas Against the Church," "Bizarre Conceptions Concerning the Clergy," and "Subversive Interpretations Concerning the Liturgy and Ecclesiastical Discipline." Cayley chronicles Illich's impression of the interrogation as follows:

> The questions, as Illich said later, were of the "When did you stop beating your wife?" variety; to have answered at all would have required him to accept numerous unacceptable premises. "What would you answer," he was asked, "to those who say that you are petulant, adventurous, imprudent, fanatical . . . hypnotizing, [and] a rebel to all authority . . . ?"[51]

This explains, in large part, Illich's response to the inquisitorial procedure in the form of a letter:

> Let me start by saying that, faced with the authoritative procedures which, at least in my opinion, are so very questionable in both substance and style, I am left—as a Christian and a priest—with a single, clearcut choice.
>
> I can, on the one hand, simply withold any defense of myself, without claiming my most reasonable rights or advancing my most lawful defense. Or, on the other hand, I can (not for my sake but for the sake of defending the divine constitution of the Church and the honorable status of its ecclesiastical institutions) set myself systematically in opposition to everything which I recognize as a distortion of the Gospel, contrary to the divine principles which govern the Church, contrary to what has been decided by the Councils, and even contrary to the most recent and repeated statements of the highest ecclesiastical authorities.
>
> Eminence, I must acknowledge to you that I have decisively opted for the first way, and that I have resolved to take as my watchword, "If a man asks you to lend him your coat, then give him your shirt as well" (Matt 5:45).[52]

Illich later described the surprising conclusion to this inquisition as follows:

> As we parted [Cardinal Seper] gave me an *embrazo* [hug], most affectionately. And then a most extraordinary thing happened. We were speaking in Croatian, and as the Cardinal led me to the door his last words to me were "*Hadjite, hadjite, nemojete*

---

51. Cayley and Illich, *Rivers North of the Future*, 9.
52. Illich, quoted in Gray, *Divine Disobedience*, 239.

se vratiti!" which means "Get going, get going, and never come back!" In other words, "Beat it!" It wasn't until I was going down the stairs from his office . . . that it struck me that he was quoting from the Inquisitor's last words to the prisoner in Dostoyevsky's story of the Grand Inquisitor.[53]

In response to this conflict with the Vatican, Illich took two additional direct actions. He first wrote to Cardinal Terence Cooke communicating his decision to renounce all clerical duties and privileges and to live as a layman. Although formally renouncing the clerical responsibilities of an active priest, Illich asked to renew two commitments common to all priests: the daily practice of praying the breviary and the condition of celibacy, both of which he embraced as a personal vocation instead of as institutional requirements. Illich then went public with the details of the interrogation in the Mexican newspaper *Excelsior* and in *The New York Times*, achieving the desired effect of shaming the Roman Curia and persuading them to leave him alone.

Later, Illich would describe his criticisms of the church as "a question of witness."[54] In fact, he states explicitly that his criticism was "not an attempt to speak *against* the Church," but rather "an attempt to raise the fundamental issue of what a Church with this tradition represents in the world of today."[55] We miss his point—or better, what he is pointing to—if Illich's stance in New York, in Mexico, and at the Vatican is read as a series of anti-ecclesial rants. More generally, it should be noted that Illich does not witness against the church per se but rather against the dominant certainties, especially ones that both draw from and distort an ecclesial or Christian social imagination.

Here, it is important to recall that I am approaching Illich not only in terms of his discourse or ideas, but more adequately in terms of his "biography as theology." As a contrast to my approach, David Gabbard's *Silencing Ivan Illich* offers a Foucauldian discourse analysis of Illich's double "exclusion" from the field of education as well as from the Catholic Church. Gabbard's use of Foucault does offer insights for approaching Illich, particularly the connection between Illich's parallel critique of schooling and ecclesial power, and his parallel exclusion from the official discourses of both institutional forms. However, there are two

---

53. Illich, quoted in Gray, *Divine Disobedience*, 240.
54. Cayley and Illich, *Ivan Illich in Conversation*, 102.
55. Cayley and Illich, *Ivan Illich in Conversation*, 103.

key limitations to Gabbard's approach for my purposes. As it was written in the field of education, it therefore does not offer theological analysis; and, because written in the early 1990s, it preceded the publication of two books that shed light on the relationship between Illich's life and the development of his thought.

In those books, *Ivan Illich in Conversation* and *The Rivers North of the Future*, Illich makes two crucial moves. First, he makes explicit certain theological themes expressed previously in an apophatic mode.[56] Second, he reveals that his stance in relation to the Catholic Church, as well as to other academic discourses, was "a question of witness,"[57] or the voluntary embrace of a personal vocation and not merely a passively accepted exclusion at the hands of institutionalized power. While recognizing the contribution that Gabbard makes by reading Illich via discourse analysis, I suggest that it is worth going beyond that approach in order to integrate Illich's life in a way that is congruent with its underlying theological character, and in order to make sense of statements such as the following: "out of a deep respect for the corruption of the best which becomes, in a way, the worst, some of us might have the vocation of testifying to our love of the Church by making ourselves completely powerless outside its context."[58]

Ultimately, my reading of Illich as a witness is a theological attempt at agreeing with that CIA analyst who identified Illich as a radical. But, in a more biblical idiom, it is to hear him as a subversively prophetic voice, as "one crying out in the [industrialized] wilderness" (Isa 40:3) of post–World War II modernity.[59] It is to hear him as an itinerant prophet who exposes the myopias and excesses of American exceptionalism, as he traverses not only the East-West divide but the North-South axis as well. It is to hear him as a prophetic Christian pilgrim who, like a maturing jazz musician, struggles to find an idiom and form to articulate his art. It is to hear him working out a series of variations on one of the basic riffs of the prophet Jeremiah: "Stand at the crossroads and look; ask for the ancient paths, ask where the good way is, and walk in it, and you will find rest for your souls" (Jer 6:16). Like Jeremiah, who denounced the false prophets for proclaiming "'Peace, peace,' when there is no peace" (Jer

---

56. Hoinacki, "Trajectory of Ivan Illich," 385.
57. Cayley and Illich, *Ivan Illich in Conversation*, 102.
58. Cayley and Illich, *Ivan Illich in Conversation*, 104.
59. Prakash and Stuchaul, "Voice in the Wilderness," 511.

8:11), Illich denounced the false prophets of the North who, in the name of "order and progress," "benevolently" invaded neighboring countries and extended their empire for the sake of false peace.

To compare Illich with biblical prophets such as Jeremiah is also to recognize that Illich was more than a social critic. He was, according to friend and collaborator Carl Mitcham, an elegist, one who "witnesses to what is absent but might have been present, and in this witnessing, the act of thoughtful concern for the past . . . both asserts the loss and casts into the present a new kind of awareness."[60] Such awareness turns on the following insight: "It is not the Church's task to engineer [the future's shape]. She must resist the temptation. Otherwise she cannot celebrate the wondrous surprise of the coming, the advent."[61]

In this chapter, I have offered a theological reading of Illich's life in terms of the motif of journey, or *itinerarium*, that is, his understanding of the Christian life as a form of pilgrimage. More specifically, I have turned to Illich's journey as a pilgrimage into and across the Americas, as well as the sense in which his journey finds its center through the Incarnation. In concluding this chapter as well as Part One, I want to focus on how Illich's life and theological imagination might contribute to a contemporary understanding of incarnational mission. To do so, I turn to the work of the late Australian missiologist Ross Langmead, who develops a useful account of incarnational mission in terms of the three interrelated aspects of

1. following Jesus, or "seeing Jesus as the pattern for mission";
2. participating in Christ, or "experiencing the continuing presence of Christ in the church as the body of Christ"; and
3. joining God's incarnating mission, or "understanding the activity of God in a sacramental/incarnational framework."[62]

Here, I want to conclude by taking a closer look at these three aspects in order to appreciate Illich's contribution. Illich's motto—"following the

---

60. Mitcham, "Challenges of This Collection, 9.
61. Illich, *Celebration of Awareness*, 100.
62. Langmead, *Word Made Flesh*, 48.

naked Christ"—clearly highlights the first aspect of incarnational mission. For Illich, "seeing Jesus as the pattern" has to do fundamentally with Jesus's renunciation of worldly power, his refusal to align himself with the Caesars and Pilates of his day. Following, as noted earlier, has to do with a response of dispossession, an openness toward the vulnerability of love. That said, "Christianity is not primarily about the imitation of an outstanding founder; it is about the 'power of God for salvation' (Rom. 1:16)."[63] It is more than imitation at a distance; it is a following that includes participation in the life of another. Or, in the words of St. John, we follow Christ so that we might share his life, so that "we might live through him" (1 John 4:9). As the Incarnate Messiah, this One is the anointed One through whom a new "we"—indeed, a new humanity (Eph 2:15)—comes into being.

The second aspect of incarnational mission highlights ecclesial embodiment, or in Pauline terms, the church as the body of Christ. Taken in the strongest terms, this aspect understands "the church as the continuing incarnation."[64] This view represents the sacramental-incarnational ecclesiology prominent not only within Roman Catholicism, but also in Anglo-Catholic circles and in Eastern Orthodoxy.[65] In his early essays on ecclesiology, Illich clearly shares this view, insisting that "the mission of the Church is the social continuation of the Incarnation and Missiology is its study."[66]

As Langmead points out, this view has the advantage of highlighting the intrinsic link between the work of the Incarnation and God's ongoing work in the church, but there are at least two dangers, as well. First, to speak of the church as continuing the Incarnation can lead to a position where the church "will become unchallenged as the mystique of divine authority grows."[67] Thus, a thorough account of the church as the body of Christ needs to account for the history of ecclesial failure as well as God's promises to be present in the life and work of the church. I have already discussed how Illich's criticism of the Catholic Church clearly recognizes the danger of ecclesial hubris. It is equally important to acknowledge,

---

63. Langmead, *Word Made Flesh*, 52.
64. Langmead, *Word Made Flesh*, 53.
65. Langmead, *Word Made Flesh*, 53.
66. Illich, *Church, Change and Development*, 85.
67. Langmead, *Word Made Flesh*, 53.

however, Illich's appreciation of what ecclesial life, particularly liturgical life, makes possible.

In one of his last essays, entitled "The Cultivation of Conspiracy,"[68] Illich weaves together stories about *peace*, the one word that evokes what he most "cherished and tried to nourish."[69] In telling the stories, Illich reiterates his insight that peace is not an abstractly universal condition,[70] but rather it is "a very specific spirit to be relished in its particular, incommunicable uniqueness by each community."[71] This move toward historicizing the varieties of peace, which he calls "people's peace," sets up his commentary on the early Christian ritual of *conspiratio*, or "kiss of peace." As Illich tells us, the ritual action of the *conspiratio* lies at the origin of the peace he sought to cultivate, and which he describes as follows:

> The Eucharistic gathering in the very first Christian centuries explicitly claimed to establish a new "we," a new plural of the "I." This "we" was not of this world. It didn't belong to the world of politics in the Greek sense, or of citizenship in the *urbs*, in the Roman sense. These guys got together for a celebration which had two high points, one of them called *conspiratio*, and the other one *comestio*. . . . This *conspiratio* was expressed by the mouth-to-mouth kiss, *osculum*. . . . The Christians adopted this symbolism . . . to signify that each one of those present around the dining table contributed of his own spirit, or, if you want, the Holy Spirit, which was common to all, to a create a spiritual community, a community of one spirit. They then sat down and shared the same meal. . . . Slave and master, Jew and Greek, each contributed equally to making the community to which, through his contribution, he could then belong.[72]

As close readers of Illich have observed, ritual is a central concept in his social criticism (see chapter 5). Indeed, the contrast between what Illich calls the "ritualization of progress"[73] and the *conspiratio* as contrasting rituals of inclusion is noteworthy. The former operates as a ritual of inclusion that encloses participants within an "artificial" dependence

---

68. Illich, "The Cultivation of Conspiracy," 233–42.

69. Illich, "Cultivation of Conspiracy," 238.

70. For Illich's historical analysis of peace as an embodied concept versus an abstract ideal, see Illich, "The De-linking of Peace and Development," 15–26.

71. Illich, "Cultivation of Conspiracy," 239.

72. Cayley and Illich, *Rivers North of the Future*, 216–17.

73. See chapter 3 in Illich, *Deschooling Society*.

upon dominant institutions or service systems; the *conspiratio* embodies a reality of interdependence centered on a person. To return to the earlier discussion of the relationship between ethos and ethnos, it could be said that Illich highlights the *conspiratio* as a ritual action that embodies a shared ethos that originates from the new ethnos, the "new humanity" in Christ (Eph 2:15).

With his repeated use of terms like "atmosphere," "milieu," and "threshold," Illich explores how the Incarnation of the Word makes possible a reality of participation, a new "we" that belongs to the "I" of the Incarnation. The Incarnation makes possible an alternative social space, a new "inside" that we inhabit as "co-breathing . . . a conspiracy, a deliberate, mutual, somatic, and gratuitous gift to one another."[74]

Here, Illich describes the centripetal force of "co-breathing," yet for Illich there is always the counterpoint of openness, of "being surprised by the Other."[75] Here, he speaks of the second danger related to a strong view of the ecclesial mediation of incarnational mission, namely, a kind of ecclesiocentrism that collapses Christ's presence into the presence of the church. We find Illich's response to this danger in his discussion with David Cayley on the triadic shape of friendship:

> On the table, as you have noticed over the years, there is always a candle. Why? Because the text that shaped my understanding was *De Spirituali Amicitia*, a treatise on spiritual friendship by the twelfth-century Scottish abbot Aelred of Rievaulx. . . . [It] is in the form of a dialogue with a brother monk, and it begins with the words "Here we are, you and I, and, I hope, also a third who is Christ." If you consider his meaning carefully, you understand that it could be Christ in the form of Brother Michael. In other words, our conversation should always go on with the certainty that there is somebody else who will knock at the door, and the candle stands for him or her. It is a constant reminder that the community is never closed.[76]

These comments from Illich take us back to Illich's interpretation of the parable of the Good Samaritan, and more particularly, to the way in which the Incarnation provides a basis for an account of friendship that transgresses the "ethnic" boundary. It is inside this novel freedom, as opposed to the duty to be joined to others, that Illich seeks to place

74. Illich, "Cultivation of Conspiracy," 240–41.
75. Illich, *Celebration of Awareness*, 135.
76. Cayley and Illich, *Rivers North of the Future*, 150–51.

the missionary activity of the church. In other words, in the light of the Incarnation, mission entails the vocation toward "risky presence to the Other, together with the openness to an absent loved third, no matter how fleeting."[77]

Finally, the third aspect of incarnational mission highlights our "cooperating with God's 'incarnating' activity from creation, throughout history, climactically demonstrated in the Incarnation of Jesus Christ and continuing as the mission of God today."[78] Taken together with following Jesus and participating in Christ, this aspect of joining is the most encompassing aspect of incarnational mission. What is at stake is how the Incarnation provides the basis for holding together the relationship between creation and redemption, so that one is not pulled apart or isolated from the other.

On this point, Catholic theologian David Burrell has developed with doctrinal precision what Illich presumes yet mostly mentions in passing: God's act of creation establishes not only a context for our being creatures, but also creation establishes a relation between creatures and the Creator. This means that to be a creature is already to exist in relation to the Creator, and redemption, through the Incarnation of the Word, reveals and restores this relation. Burrell explores God's incarnating dynamic in relation to the creation/redemption dialectic:

> [The Incarnation] is the singular point where God and God's creation meet. . . . Jesus is the "Word made flesh," and the Word in question is the very One "through whom the world is made" . . . [Thus] the emanation of all things from God in the Word is in strict continuity with the generation of the Word from the Father, . . . [and] so creation and incarnation follow a parallel logic.[79]

Here, the important thing to notice is that Burrell does not collapse the distinction between creation and redemption, but rather he repositions the distinction in the light of the Incarnation as the decisive event in God's incarnational mission, of God's enfleshment. In a similar way, understanding the Creator/creation distinction in the light of the Incarnation does not abolish the distinction, but it does suggest a non-dualistic

---

77. Illich and Rahnema, "Twenty-Six Years Later," 106.
78. Langmead, *Word Made Flesh*, 55.
79. Burrell, "Incarnation and Creation," 213.

relationship, one perhaps best expressed metaphorically: "The universe is to its creator as the song on the breath of a singer."[80]

From this tight linkage of creation and redemption, this third dimension, which Langmead calls the "joining" of incarnational mission, three emphases follow.[81] Here, I simply want to highlight them, as I will return to these in the following chapters. First, "joining" means that incarnational mission affirms the goodness of creation. Illich expresses this insight when he writes that the Incarnation provides the basis for our developing "the ability to say one great 'Yes' to the experience of life."[82] Second, incarnational mission entails a kenotic or "self-emptying" dynamic.[83] Illich eloquently highlights this theme as well through the following:

> To communicate Himself perfectly to man God had to assume a nature which was not His, without ceasing to be what He was. Under this light the Incarnation is the infinite prototype of missionary activity, the communication of the Gospel to those who are "other," through Him who entered a World by nature not His own. The closer the pattern of a human life approximates this aspect of the "Kenosis" of the Word the more can that vocation be called a missionary one. . . . Just as the Word without ceasing to be what He is became man, Jew, Roman subject, member of a culture at a given moment in history, so any . . . missionar[y], without ever ceasing to be what he is, enters and becomes part of a "foreign" culture at the present moment in a given place.[84]

Closely related to this insight is the third emphasis that flows from "joining": namely, the Incarnation as the basis for inculturation, or "the two-way, critical, dynamic and in-depth interaction between gospel and culture."[85] Illich's critical engagements with American Catholic missionary efforts in New York and in Mexico represent this incarnational movement toward inculturation.

Later, I will return to Illich's nuanced understanding of inculturation. For now, the crucial point to recognize is that at the center of Illich's theological imagination is a person, the Incarnate Savior. By attending

80. Burrell, "Incarnation and Creation," 214.
81. Langmead, *Word Made Flesh*, 56–58.
82. Illich, *Celebration of Awareness*, 103.
83. Langmead, *Word Made Flesh*, 56–58.
84. Illich, *Church, Change and Development*, 113.
85. Langmead, *Word Made Flesh*, 57.

to the contours of Illich's own journey, what comes into view is how his witness, his stance in the world as a Christian, offers vital insights for imagining the incarnational logic of the Christian life.

To restate this within Quash's terms, what comes into view through Illich is a way of imagining how the Incarnation is a person who is at once the decisive agent of history's cast, who creates a stage, or context, for others to act, as well as the One who embodies the decisive action by which God's purpose for all of creation in history might be discerned.[86] What comes into focus is precisely how our lives fit with the decisively theodramatic logic of the incarnational mission, which is nothing less than our following, participating, and joining in the new "we" made possible through the Incarnation.

---

86. See Quash, *Theology and the Drama of History*.

Interlude

Overhearing the Gospel according to Samba (Part One): Missionary Adoption and the New "We"

At the beginning of Part One, I described being turned toward Brazil as a *virada*, or turning point. Marrying a Brazilian, moving to Brazil, and becoming an immersed learner of Brazilian Portuguese—these have all been important aspects of that personal journey into "her people becoming my people." Of course, it is likely that anyone who marries someone of another nationality, moves to a new country, and learns a new language as an adult will experience that journey as a transformative "turning point" in life. Yet, having lived through that and trying "to understand it backwards,"[1] I make sense of it all not by focusing on Brazil as such but by returning to a wider frame of orientation and purpose: we went to Brazil as those who had been *sent* there. We were commissioned with these words: "Peace be with you. As the Father sends me, so I send you. . . . Receive the Holy Spirit . . ." (John 20:19–22). Therefore, the as/so logic of John 20 is the theological frame inside of which I see the collage of images and experiences in Brazil.

By encountering Ivan Illich as a primary guide on that journey of sent-ness into Brazil, I came to understand the as/so logic of John 20 in terms of what Illich calls "prolonging the Incarnation." By taking Illich as my primary guide, I heard Jesus's words "As the Father sends me . . . so I send you" in a fresh way. I heard in them not only a command to be sent out but also an invitation to be included as his followers into a new "we" born from the "I" of the Incarnation. As I described earlier,

---

1. A reference to an adage attributed to Soren Kierkegaard: "The Christian life is something that you live forwards and understand backwards."

being turned toward Brazil and being sent as a missionary led to sense of "in-between-ness"—an acute awareness of "never-going-back-to-being-just-American" and yet "never-fully-arriving-as-Brazilian." Although I did not have the words to describe it then, I was looking for a way of imagining identity and belonging that was *more* than either American or Brazilian. In fact, I was undergoing what Illich calls "missionary adoption." I became the one who would forever be "a guest, marked by the strangeness of his birth," and yet forever "an adopted brother." I knew that I belonged, though I did not belong by birth but somehow through a "rebirth out of love into a new people."[2]

This belonging-with-difference provoked on ongoing question: How might this "in-between-ness," with all of the change and newness it brought, be a sign of transformation for myself as well as good news for those Brazilians around me? I did not hear the answer to that question as much as I *overheard* it. What I overheard did not happen in a church, nor in an overtly religious context, but rather in a samba circle (*roda de samba*). Here, I want to unpack how the *roda* became for me a parable for Christian witness by attending to three interrelated dynamics of incarnational mission: following, participating, and joining.

FOLLOWING

I found myself in the *roda* for the simple reason that Duda, the ensemble leader (*maestro*), invited me to join. More precisely, I was invited to join his *bloco*, an ensemble for playing Brazilian percussion, like the ones in carnival parades and street parties. Even though I had been playing music for all of my adult life, and was already playing percussion at our local church, I sensed it was time to learn more about playing Brazilian music, and I approached my friend Duda with the question, "What should I do in order to become a competent Brazilian percussionist?" His matter-of-fact response was along these lines: "There is only so much you can do on your own; to become competent, you need to spend time with a *bloco*, so why don't you join ours?"

Soon after Duda's invitation, I found myself spending every Monday night (and lots of spare time at the weekend) with Duda and other members of his *bloco*. What started off as a simple yes to an invitation to attend a workshop soon stirred up my latent desire to learn Brazilian

---

2. Illich, *Church, Change and Development*, 98.

percussion from Duda and his *bloco*. In the same way that I learned Brazilian Portuguese by immersing myself in the presence of competent speakers, I surrounded myself with these musicians to get insight into their technical ability and musical knowledge. I was playing "follow the leader" not just to copy their actions but to become like them as musicians. Before long, I was no longer a musical hobbyist; I was becoming a musical apprentice.

All the while, I could not stop making a comparison between the process of becoming a percussionist in an ensemble and the dynamics of Christian discipleship. From Dallas Willard I had a working definition of a disciple, or apprentice, as "simply someone who has decided to be with another person, under appropriate conditions, in order to become capable of doing what that person does or to become what that person is."[3] Based on this understanding of discipleship as apprenticeship, I knew that I had become Duda's disciple. How so? Precisely because I knew that I wanted to be with him in order to be able to play samba like him. Playing samba made it clearer that both musicianship and discipleship require an intentional process of formation, that no one just drifts into being a serious musician or disciple. By belonging to the group, I also recognized how both samba and discipleship make possible, and even require, a form of collective participation. Just as no one plays Brazilian percussion in a *bloco* as a solo performance, no one follows Jesus by playing solo either.

PARTICIPATING

Through the *bloco*, I came to new awareness of how formation and participation were at the core of both musicianship and discipleship. The more I struggled and grew as a percussionist, the more I came to recognize how the experience of joining the *bloco* served as a parable for the interpersonal process of formation and participation in Christ. The driving question at the heart of this experience of being included in the *roda* as a *gringo* was this: How might the experience of becoming a percussionist by being included in the *roda* shed light on the experience of following Jesus by being included in his circle of disciples?

Through the experience of being included in the *bloco*, I discovered a way of integrating the musical imagination of the *bloco* with a theological

---

3. Willard, *Divine Conspiracy*, 282.

imagination that was being increasingly shaped by my continuing encounter with Illich. In his early reflections on the intercultural formation of missionaries, Illich writes, "Preparation for the study of missiology . . . implies increased receptivity for the poetic, the historical, and the social aspects of reality."[4] My inclusion in the *roda de samba* was like a portal into a deeper cultural immersion, beyond the grammar, rhythm, and inflection of Brazilian Portuguese directly and more deeply into "the poetic, the historical, and the social aspects" of Brazilian reality.

The more I was drawn into the Brazilian cultural form, the more I began to imagine my experience of togetherness inside the *roda* as a parable for the incarnational logic of Christian discipleship and mission. While the *roda* offered an array of insights that could be developed theologically, I was caught not only by the contagious energy of the music, but even more so by the way the *roda* both required and enabled the inclusion of difference. For in the *roda*, different bodies and different gifts (i.e., instruments) come together not to be assimilated or tolerated but to contribute a unique voice in a dynamic ensemble—a new "we."

Put a bit differently, in the *roda* I discovered a parable of ecclesial belonging—the invitation to flourish together in the body of Christ through the inclusion and interdependence of different gifts (1 Cor 12). Just imagine the simple phrase of an *agogô*, a kind of cowbell that usually produces only two pitches or notes. Voiced, the phrase might sound like this: Ding . . . ding-dong . . . dong-ding . . . ding-ding-ding . . . dong-ding. This kind of phrase is not complicated, and by itself is musically uninteresting. But put the *agogô* part with the pulsating bass lines of the *surdos*, and you have bass and treble calling and responding. Add the *caixas*, or snares, and you can begin to feel the samba's groove, or swing. If you add the *repiques*, the *tambourins*, and the *rocars*, you then have all the *naipes*, or sections, working together, all playing different parts but as one group. Thus, different members are all playing simple parts that sound complex and incredibly beautiful *together*.

Within the musical space of the *roda*, therefore, the interdependent activity of making music actually creates the conditions for inclusion. Within this musical space, I am aware that I am playing a simple *agogô* line, but I am also aware of how my line fits with the ensemble. I no longer hear just a clanking cowbell sound; I hear the simultaneity of its voiced call-and-response with other instruments. In Illich's terms, the

---

4. Illich, *Church, Change and Development*, 87.

relationships in the *roda* embody not only complementarity but also conviviality, a term that for Illich refers to a sense of "individualized freedom in personal interdependence."[5]

JOINING

The more involved I became in the dynamics of the *roda*, the more I found myself thinking in terms of another circle, an image that comes from a fourth-century monk, Dorotheos of Gaza. For Dorotheos, the image of a circle portrays the inseparability of the Great Commandment to love God and neighbor (Matt 22:37–39).

> Imagine . . . that we have drawn a circle with a compass. God is at the center, where the point of the compass went. Now imagine that the outside of the circle is the world, and the lives of human beings are represented by many straight lines drawn from the outside to the center. Notice how as you follow a single line from the outside toward God, all the lines come closer together. This is the way human beings relate to God and to each other. . . .[6]

To elaborate this point, we can also say that Dorotheos's circle illustrates how a relationship with the center point of the circle (God) is inseparable from relationships with all of the other points (creatures) in the circle.

In this way, Dorotheos's circle offers a frame for superimposing my two other circles onto one another: circle #1 is the scriptural narrative of the circle of disciples gathering around the risen Christ in John 20; circle #2 is the experience of being included and participating in the *roda* gathered around Duda. For just as the samba circle includes a group of musicians gathered around their *maestro*, who stands in the center, so too does the sending narrative in John describe a group of participants, disciples, who are gathered around a person in the center, in order to follow, participate, and join in the "mission" that the One in the center makes possible.

In both the samba circle and the circle described in John 20, the person in the center of the circle must be followed. In the samba circle, following the *maestro* is what transforms the cacophony of the ensemble's instruments into the harmony of the *bloco*. In the circle of disciples, following the risen Christ—hearing and learning to put into practice his

---

5. Illich, *Tools for Conviviality*, 11.
6. Bondi, *To Pray and to Love*, 31–32.

words of life—is what transforms the scattered disciples living in fear into a new joining animated by love.

As I play the *agogô*, I am aware of being an apprentice within a community of apprentices who *interdepend* on one another to fully express themselves, just as I am aware that the *agogô*-ness of the *agogô* is most fully expressed in the *roda*. For it is in the *roda* that its distinctiveness—its unique voice—and its relatedness, or its capacity to build up other voices, can establish harmony and a sense of proportion. As I play the *agogô*, I am also most aware of my *gringo-ness*, as a foreigner surrounded and included by Brazilians within their *roda de samba*.

As a *gringo* being included in *roda*, I found myself returning to the logic of John's Gospel, particularly the "sending narrative": "As the Father has sent me, so I send you . . ." (20:19–22). As I recalled earlier, it was that text from our commissioning service at Mount Level Missionary Baptist Church that integrated my own experience of crossing the "color line" out of love. It was from that text that I made sense of being sent to Brazil as a way of being included in the "as/so" of Jesus's own mission from the Father. For that sending narrative is the conclusion to the prologue of the same gospel: that through the Incarnation of the Word, the Son's being-sent-from-the-Father brought something new into the world, a new human embodiment of God's fullness and grace (John 1:14). And therefore, according to the as/so logic of John's Gospel, this fullness makes possible a renewal of our humanity. Through the One, the many may become one "new humanity" (Eph 2:15)—God's *roda* with a diversity of gifts.

Seen in the light of this movement toward renewal through the Incarnation, I could now imagine how being turned toward Brazil did not have to create or lead into a cultural black hole of being suspended between "not just American" and "not yet Brazilian." It was neither something "to get out of" nor something to overcome; it was simply something new, a surprise that we might call becoming *brasicano*.

Therefore, another way of saying that the *roda* became a parable of incarnational inclusion is to say that the *roda* was where I overheard "the gospel according to samba." In the *roda*, I overheard (not through the sounds of speech but through the experience of the truth toward which Illich's finger pointed as guide),

> To communicate Himself perfectly to [humanity] God had to assume a nature which was not His, without ceasing to be what He was. Under this light the Incarnation is the prototype of

missionary activity, the communication of the Gospel to those who are "other," through Him who entered a World by nature not His own.... Just as the Word without ceasing to be what He is became man, Jew, Roman subject, member of a culture at a given moment in history, so any ... missionar[y], without ever ceasing to be what he is, enters and becomes part of a "foreign" culture at the present moment in a given place.[7]

Paradoxically, the *roda* became the site of encounter where I was most aware of my being *other* and being *included*, where I was simultaneously aware of my strangeness and my belonging as a *brasicano*. Yet, through being included in the *roda*, I gained a renewed identity. I no longer saw myself merely as a *gringo*, nor was I magically transformed into a Brazilian. Like the *agogô*, I had a distinct voice, yet a voice that belonged in the *roda*. I was "in between," but I knew that I was *in*, a *brasicano* who was a co-participant in the *roda*. As such, I knew that I would never be less than a *gringo* American, but at the same time, I knew that I was called to become *more*. This "more than" is what the Incarnation makes possible; this "more than" is what I discovered in the *roda*.

In the light of my experience in the *roda*, I began to imagine the experience of "missionary adoption" as a sign of the common Christian vocation to become "in-between." In one sense, this is a paraphrase for saying Christians are called to be "in the world, but not of it" (John 17:11ff.) But my more basic (if subtle) point is this: not all followers of Jesus are called to embark on an overseas immersion in intercultural mission, yet all followers of Jesus are called to belong to and manifest the "new humanity" (Eph 2:15) that the Incarnation makes possible. My experience of being included in the musical space of the *roda* is a parable because it points to and sheds light on another inclusion: inclusion in the body of Christ—the personal space created by the "Word made flesh" (John 1:14) that, Illich insists, Christians are called to inhabit and to "prolong."[8]

---

7. Illich, *Church, Change and Development*, 113.
8. Cayley and Illich, *Rivers North of the Future*, 207.

PART 2—DETOURS

Navigating (Dis)Order and Progress

VIRADA (PART TWO): BEING TURNED TOWARD THE SEMINARY, SANCTUARY, AND STREET

IN PART ONE, MY first *virada* described being turned toward Brazil. I described how the geographical journey to Brazil led to a theological journey of making sense of my experience as an intercultural missionary. In learning to follow the ways of the Brazilian people and culture into which I was immersed, I also learned to see that process inside of the vocation of prolonging the Incarnation.

As an intercultural missionary, I experienced what Illich calls a "missionary adoption"—a belonging based not on a natural or biological identity but rather on a renewed identity through "rebirth out of love into a new people."[1] In this way, I came to see (in retrospect) that my missionary adoption—first, through marriage, then through becoming a *brasicano* (neither just American nor Brazilian but a hybrid of the two)—echoed the same kind of adoption that all Gentile followers are called to undergo in order to share in the "new humanity" made possible through a Jewish Messiah. This belonging is a true belonging, yet it is a belonging that cannot be manipulated or forced. It is a belonging that recognizes—like an American in Brazil—that you are an outsider before you can even begin to see yourself or be seen as an insider. For as St. Paul describes it in the book of Ephesians, Gentile adoption into God's family is a re-membering that operates from the outside in:

> Remember that you [Gentiles by birth] were at that time without Christ, being aliens from the commonwealth of Israel, and strangers to the covenants of promise, having no hope and without God in the world. But now in Christ Jesus you who once

---

1. Illich, *Church, Change and Development*, 98.

were far off have been brought near by the blood of Christ. For he is our peace . . . (Eph 2:12–14)

All of which is to say: I do not take the journey of missionary adoption for granted. Reflecting upon that experience, I am aware that the more subtle and challenging struggle that I encountered as an American-missionary-becoming-a-*brasicano* was actually not negotiating a transcultural identity and a new cultural-linguistic framework. Learning to like *feijoda*, speak Portuguese, play *MPB* (Brazilian popular music) and *futebol* was simply a matter of time, plus effort and patience. The real struggle, that which led to the growing pains of what Bedford calls "epistemological rupture," came from trying to navigate the institutional matrix operating between the three *s*'s of seminary, sanctuary, and street.[2]

SEMINARY

During the first couple of years in Brazil—while I was still getting over the language barrier—one of the most important things I did was audit theology classes at the seminary where I would later teach. By the time that my "passive Portuguese" was good enough to follow along, I began to sense the strangeness not only of learning a new language, but of overhearing how others speak about God, and being Christian, in different dialects.

Sitting in those seminary classes, I recalled being a first-year seminary student at Duke Divinity School and my friendship with a Methodist pastor who had come to Duke from Liberia. We would sit next to one another in Stanley Hauerwas's introductory course to Christian ethics. About three weeks into the semester, as we were being disabused of the Protestant liberal narrative of "Christian ethics in America," my friend Nagbe finally turned to me and said, "Sam, I'm lost . . . just who is this Reinhold Niebuhr guy that Dr. Hauerwas keeps ranting against?! And why does Dr. Hauerwas keep saying that Niebuhr is the enemy of this class?!"

Later, in Brazil, I realized Nagbe had to overhear the gospel being told in another theological dialect. Nagbe was a Liberian who had spent the previous seven years as an exiled refugee in the Ivory Coast. From there he had come to the US on a student visa, but Nagbe was not

---

2. I borrow this triad from theological educator Ched Myers, which he develops in "Between the Seminary, the Sanctuary, and the Streets," 49–52.

anywhere close to being a "recovering Protestant liberal"—as Hauerwas described himself. Yet, Nagbe had to become theologically bilingual.

As a North American missionary living in Brazil, I had to commit myself to learning not only another tongue, Brazilian Portuguese, but also (like Nagbe) I had to become fluent in other theological dialects, including Latin American liberation theology and Brazilian-born forms of (neo)Pentecostalism.[3] At our seminary, however, the primary dialect, or better, the official language, for theological discourse was *missão integral*, or integral mission. Ever since the landmark Lausanne Conference on Evangelism and Mission in 1974, *missão integral* has been a watchword for many Latin American *evangélicos*. It was at this conference in 1974 that Latin American evangelical leaders, such as Samuel Escobar, René Padilla, as well as others, delivered a prophetic corrective to the dominant missionary ethos coming from the North Atlantic. The critical perspective of Latin American evangelicals highlighted the way the dominant (North Atlantic) ethos was largely characterized by an under-contextualized missionary practice, one in which the integral link between proclamation and Christian action had become tenuous, or even severed. One of the outcomes of that landmark conference, which launched the Lausanne Movement, was appending *integral* to *missão* as a conceptual marker that word and deed, or proclamation and costly service, are part and parcel of Christian mission.

At Faculdade Teológica Sul Americana, this conceptual marker occupied the center of theological discourse, and the task of doing theological education revolved around the phrase *missão integral*. The more I heard, learned, and read about *missão integral*, the more I realized that my concerns were not so much with the theological content of the concept, but rather the way the phrase was deployed and approached as unassailable. The discourse seemed to reflect *missão integral* as a static, already worked-out position that simply needed to be propagated. When I listened to colleagues talk or teach, I shared their sense of urgency around social transformation and how theology can and should inspire that. But I also sensed that they tended to use keywords such as "poverty" or "urban life" as social facts without questioning and probing them as historically conditioned realities. I also sensed a reticence to talk about other themes, such as race or gender.

---

3. See Barreto, *Facing the Poor in Brazil*; Longuini Neto, *O novo rosto da missão*.

I sensed that for many of my colleagues, theology effectively began in 1974. Or, to adapt Karl Barth's famous dictum, it seemed that theology was best done with "the Bible in one hand and the Lausanne Covenant in the other." What happened between the first-century Christians and 1974 did not seem to capture the imaginations of my colleagues. In spite of their discourse about pastors being agents of social transformation, not maintenance staff for insular local churches, I sensed that the notion of *ação social* (social action) was not integrated into the life of local ecclesial communities, but rather it seemed to be envisioned as something appended to "church-as-usual," as a programmatic annex. My own exposure to the concept of *missão integral* clearly offered an ethos of proclamation and social transformation, yet I also sensed a deep irony at work. For while my colleagues rightly criticized the manner in which North Atlantic theologies were disseminated in Latin America as theologies that were *acabadas* (worked out, finished), in approaching *missão integral* as unassailable, I sensed that they were no longer trying to do constructive theology but in fact had settled for their own *teologia acabada*—a "finished" theological product ready for export.

In the light of this, I began to see signs of the extent to which the contemporary theology in Brazil was undergoing its own rupture, its own dis-integration. The Brazilian struggle to face this reality would become part of my own struggle and my own disorientation. I suspected that the issues ran much deeper than the issues foregrounded by proponents of *missão integral*, but I also suspected that I was not seeing fully or clearly. Brazilians have a phrase for this: *o buraco está mais em baixo do que você imagina* ("the hole is deeper than you think"). I knew that I needed a wider frame of vision to see a bigger picture. I knew that "the hole was deeper," but I had no idea just how deep.

SANCTUARY

Although I have described seminary as a site of epistemological rupture or disorientation, it was in the sanctuary (the context of the gathered local church or congregation) that the sense of rupture would continue and intensify for me. My experience of sanctuary refers primarily to the five-year experience of helping to plant, serve, and become a pastor at the Igreja Batista Catuaí. While our local church was denominationally Baptist, we were located in what might be called the "Presbyterian belt" of southern Brazil. In this region, Baptists were a numerical minority among *evangélicos*. Perhaps more significant than the relative difference, or lack of difference, between Protestant ecclesial traditions, was the fact that our city of Londrina was considered to be one of the most "evangelized" cities in Brazil. I have heard Londrina compared with Colorado Springs in the US, as a medium-sized city that boasts a disproportionally large evangelical population, as well as being the home city for numerous faith-based NGOs and international mission agencies.

Generally speaking, there is a palpable sense of religiosity[4] that is woven into Brazilian culture: the expression *Deus é brasileiro* ("God is Brazilian") is at once playful and profoundly indicative of Brazilian religiosity. In Londrina, this religious sensibility was as much in the air as the scent of *café moído* (ground coffee), historically the main cash crop of the region.

What I found most disorientating about navigating the "sanctuary" in Londrina was that, despite the undeniably relational nature of Brazilian culture, what characterized the ecclesial culture was a severe dialectical tension between "religious individualism," on the one hand, and the church as "institutional provider of religious goods and services," on the other. This tension is not unique to southern Brazil, but what impressed me about this context was the intensity with which what Gerhard Lohfink calls "the heritage of individualism," and the conditions of a consumer society, gave rise to a vision of "a church which takes care of the individual, an institution which offers its wares to a group of individuals."[5]

Perhaps the most apt metaphor for this ecclesial sensibility is the notion of the church as the ark of salvation. Of course, this is a biblical image of the church that was readily incorporated by patristic writers—Cyprian, for example.[6] Nonetheless, in my Brazilian context, the church as ark was not so much the Cyprianic assertion that being incorporated into the church was a necessary condition for salvation, as that being inside the church protects or buffers us from the forces of the world, just as the ark protected its inhabitants from the adverse elements of rain and flood.[7] As an example, a common bumper sticker seen in Londrina reads, *Não estou em crise; estou em Cristo* ("I'm not in crisis; I'm in Christ"). The

---

4. Here, I am not using "religiosity" in a perjorative sense, but rather in a descriptive sense.

5. Lohfink, *Jesus and Community*, 4.

6. Cyprian, "Letter 69," 160–63.

7. Cyprian, "Letter 69," 161.

implicit theology of this slogan tended to suggest that authentic Christianity equals "struggle-free" Christianity.

There are, of course, exceptions to the tendency that I am describing. In fact, I can still hear my late father-in-law exhorting the members at our church to recognize that *Cristianismo não é uma guarda-chuva que te protege de qualquer e todo problema* ("Christianity is not an umbrella that protects you from any and every problem"). Nonetheless the dominant evangelistic strategy among the churches in Londrina was offering programs, or *campanhas* (campaigns), in order to attract and integrate outsiders into the membership of the local church. In this context, I found it hard to resist the impression that what churches were offering to their members and to outsiders was not only religious programs and services, but in fact a religious security system. The disabling consequence of this was not only the ubiquity of churches seeming to compete for religious clients to consume their goods and services, but also an ethos of ecclesial insularity.

After reading Rubem Alves's *Protestantism and Repression*, I sensed that the insularity that I was experiencing was, in fact, symptomatic of what Alves masterfully characterized as RDP, or "Right-Doctrine Protestantism." In his typology, Alves distinguished between "sacramental Protestantism," "Protestantism of the spirit," and RDP. What characterizes RDP is the way "it stresses *agreement with a series of doctrinal affirmations*, which are regarded as *expressions of the truth* and which must be affirmed *without any shadow of doubt*, as the precondition for participation in the ecclesial community."[8] While my ecclesial location was not repressive in any way recognizable within the Brazilian Presbyterianism through which Alves suffered in the 1970s, it was clearly recognizable as RDP.

One of the most obvious characteristics of RDP in my local ecclesial context was the understanding of Christian doctrine (or "right doctrine") as the secure foundation for Christian ethics (or "right living"). Here, the emphasis was not so much on the inseparability of doctrine and ethics as it was on the logical priority of establishing "right doctrine" as the condition for leading a regenerated life. In this scheme, "right doctrine" does not change; it is fixed, immutable, and, therefore, received as a certainty. Moreover, "right doctrine" provides the cognitive renewal that catalyzes personal (and social) change.

---

8. Alves, *Protestantism and Repression*, 8; emphasis in original.

Alves sums up the relationship between the personal and social ethic of RDP as follows: "Let the individual be converted and society will be transformed."⁹ Perhaps this motto would have been understandable during a time when *evangélicos* were a marginalized, and even persecuted, minority in Brazilian Christianity. But given that many *evangélicos* have entered the political arena and, as individuals, have been complicit in the corruption of the Brazilian political system, it is a difficult motto to maintain. Upon closer examination, the motto actually expresses an assumption regarding the priority of the individual above or over against social relations, something that is itself symptomatic of a rupture of the Christian imagination. Indeed, as one prominent Latin American Protestant theologian has pointed out, one of the deepest problems affecting Latin American Protestant churches "is not so much the absence of theology, nor its deviations . . . but rather its 'reductionism.'"¹⁰

STREET

Lastly, in this series of *s*'s is a *rua* (the street). Taken in its broadest sense, "street" refers here to everyday life, or in Portuguese, *o cotidiano*. My experience of the *cotidiano*, however, was framed and intensified by a set of experiences that took place in the *favelas* (slums or shantytowns). Once I had become more or less fluent in Portuguese, I began to visit ministries in the local *favelas*, as well as in *assentamentos* (squatters' settlements) around Londrina. Usually, I would be accompanied by a local pastor, and I would play guitar or lead a Bible study or prayer group.

In 2005, I arranged a short-term mission trip to Brazil with a close friend who was a youth worker for his Chicago-area youth group. We arranged for the group to be in São Paulo, where they would stay in the homes of young people from Morumbi Baptist Church. Together with the

---

9. Alves, *Protestantism and Repression*, 152.

10. Míguez Bonino, *Faces of Latin American Protestantism*, 111. Míguez Bonino describes this reductionism as follows: "The evangelical heritage of the Anglo-American 'awakenings,' whose fervor and impact we must not undervalue or lose, has resulted in a double reduction, Christological and soteriological. . . . This tendency, moreover, played into the individualistic, subjectivistic, and ahistorical character of the religious vision of modernity, ending up in some of the grave deformations our churches suffers. Thus, theology is practically swallowed up in Christology, and this in soteriology, and, even more, in a salvation which is characterized as an individual and subjective experience" (111–12).

youth from Morumbi, they would serve a local ministry in Vila Andrade, a *favela* on the periphery of the Morumbi *bairro*.

One of my clearest memories of the experience was the question my friend kept asking, almost like a mantra: "What does Vila Andrade have to do with Naperville?" The initial response of the group was a collective "Not much." After all, Naperville is one of the most exclusive suburban satellites in the West Chicago area; Vila Andrade is a *favela*. The force and shock value of the question, however, was an attempt to ask the participants to look beyond the obvious geographical distance and social gap between the two locations. The question was a way of asking the young people to move beyond the gaze of the tourist in order to pay attention to "whatever else" might be going on, to be surprised by what people from Naperville and Vila Andrade might have in common, and what they could possibly share together.

Several days into the trip, we, the group from Naperville and Morumbi, gathered together with the congregation from Vila Andrade for the Sunday *culto*, or worship service. The young people from Naperville, Morumbi, and Vila Andrade led the music; my friend preached, and I translated. The *culto* was joyful, yet intense. Afterward, I recall vividly how the Naperville young people responded to the question of the week: "What does Vila Andrade have to do with Naperville?" On one end of the spectrum, a young man seemed to position himself as a "spectator" of other people's struggle to be Christian: "*Their* lives are difficult. . . . I understand that *they* need Jesus, and that *they* worship so intensely, because for *them*, it's a matter of life and death. . . . *They* need him to survive." On the other end of the spectrum, some of the young people expressed indignation at the miserable living conditions of the Vila Andrade residents: "Why isn't *the church* in Morumbi doing more to change things? What can *we* do to help?"

What impressed me most about this experience was not so much what they said but rather the transparency of their responses, summed up in two phrases:

1. They are needy in a way that we are not; and
2. How do we meet their needs?

In their transparency, I also sensed that they were expressing what most visitors from the US, myself included, found themselves thinking when they were in a *favela*: *How do we meet their needs?* Like the majority of those young people, I wanted to respond. To be honest, I was not sure how. But the question about the contrast between Naperville and Vila Andrade stayed with me as a "live question," one that would not go away.

Nearly a year later, I returned to Vila Andrade with another group from the US, this time leading a pilgrimage organized by Duke Divinity School. During this second visit, I reconnected easily with the *mocidade* (youth group) from Vila Andrade and with Pastor Marcelo and his wife, Marisa. What I remember most about this return visit was an incident in one of the classrooms of the *crechê* (nursery). On one of the walls hung various framed paintings, mostly of outdoors scenes, and by each painting was a child's name. One of the pilgrims asked Marisa about this arrangement, and I reflected on her explanation in my journal:

> Many of the children who come to the crechê come from broken homes and from generally stressful situations. For many of them, their homes are not their place of refuge. Here, each child can adopt a painting, and that's why they have the names attached to the portrait. So when a child, say João, is having a particularly stressful day, we might say, "João, why don't you go spend some time with your portrait?" We have found that this practice of spending time being still and being quiet in front of the portrait helps the children to center themselves. It can be for them a kind of meditation. So, the portraits are not so much an escape, but a way to re-enter the present—a way to reframe how they respond to the noisiness and chaos around them. You don't take something away without putting something in its place. Our hope is that God is at work to replace the brokenness, and one small way that we choose to face and replace the chaos is by offering beauty instead.[11]

After Marisa had finished her explanation, I walked up to João's painting to have a closer look. At first, what I noticed was a simple landscape, something that was not particularly beautiful, and even a bit kitsch. All I saw was an unremarkable nature scene, a river, some rocks by its banks, and a few trees with autumn leaves. But I found myself lingering in front of it; I didn't want to leave without catching a glimpse of what little João was able to see. If this portrait had become for him a sort of "icon"—a window of vision into a wider, more beautiful, and more peaceful reality than he knew in Vila Andrade—then I wanted to be able to see it, too.

---

11. Journal entry, 27 May 2006.

As I looked again, I saw the same river continue to flow freely between its rocky banks. I saw the same trees releasing their colorful leaves to cover the ground below. I saw the same things as before, but as I saw them I remembered that the biblical narrative begins and ends with such a flowing river (Gen 2:10; Rev 22:1–2) and with a "tree of life" (Gen 2:9; Rev 22:2). Now, gazing on that tree and thinking about what it means to envision it, I remembered one of the last promises in Scripture: "To everyone who conquers, I will give permission to eat from the tree of life that is in the paradise of God" (Rev 2:7). Meditating on those fallen leaves, I recalled the familiar words that "the leaves of the tree [of life] are for the healing of the nations" (Rev 22:2), and suddenly I saw more than an unremarkable "nature scene." Because of João's determination to be still and to imagine the world differently, I was inspired to catch a glimpse of creation's destiny: a destiny that includes a renewed Vila Andrade and a renewed Naperville in God's new creation. I don't know what João thought about in front of that painting, but I do know what his relationship with that painting made me think: *Então, é assim que se faz escatologia a partir de uma favela* ("So, this is how one does eschatology from a *favela*").

I returned to Londrina ready to turn this eschatological imagination into action. Almost immediately I connected with Lu and Jorge, a couple new to our church, who were deeply committed to working with the women and children in João Turquino, a squatters' settlement recently turned *favela* on the periphery of Londrina. Through Lu's initiative, sense of humor, and contagious ability to connect, she had established good relationships. From this relational base, and through Bible studies, cooking classes, children's activities, and lots of *futsal*,[12] our church found ways to connect with the people of João Turquino.

Within months, the *Projeto João Turquino* was no longer just the work of a couple but had become the *projeto* of our local church. Over the next year or so, the *projeto* continued to gain momentum and visibility. There was more volunteer involvement from Igreja Batista Catuaí, and through our personal contacts, a few local churches from the US began sending volunteers and financial assistance.

Over time, however, while I felt that what we were doing in João Turquino was good, I had a growing sense that how we talked about and imagined it was actually one-sided. Again, it was our *projeto*, and

---

12. *Futsal* is short for *futebol-de-salão*, a small-sided version of *futebol* adapted to the smaller space and hard surfaces of urban areas.

they were *carentes* (needy). In retrospect, the very language of *projeto* and *programas* tended to veil the relational heartbeat driving what was actually happening, the sheer goodness of people doing things together with joy. Instead, perhaps even unintentionally so, we found ourselves doing *ação social* as something that "we" do for "them." We had connections with US churches, who were committed to what we were doing. These connections both facilitated the work and complicated the situation. Because, in effect, it became all too easy to allow social action to become a two-step exercise in (1) diagnosing the needs of others and (2) meeting those needs for them through US-funded *projetos*. In other words, it became all too easy for our presence in João Turquino to become a microcosm of the power game played out by the international aid and development industry.

In the late 1960s when my Brazilian father-in-law was finishing seminary in the US, he tried to recruit missionaries to Brazil by writing on the classroom board, "Brazil needs *you!*" He knew that his American peers were well trained and well resourced, and, understandably, he wanted to turn all that training and all those resources toward his home country of Brazil. When I visited churches in the US, I also wanted to turn my hearers' attention toward Brazil, but I tried a different pitch from that of my father-in-law's. My tagline was "Christians in Brazil and the US need *each other.*" I would talk about how we, Americans and Brazilians, need each other, just as Paul said that Christians in Macedonia and in Jerusalem needed each other (2 Cor 8:1—9:15). In fact, I was trying to extend Paul's thinking in order to imagine how Americans and Brazilians, people from Naperville, Vila Andrade, or João Turquino, might belong to a new "we." But the more I found myself playing the part of "bridge builder" and connector between our Brazilian church, João Turquino, and churches in the US, the more I sensed that the invitation to the possibility of a new "we" was becoming muted by the collective energy of the fund-raising and the intense desire not to "come and see" (John 1:39) but to "come and help" *them*.

The issue was not, as I had initially assumed, so much an unwillingness to express neighbor-love as it was a lack of imagination regarding what that love could look like. Our project in João Turquino was not a church-planting initiative—there were already church buildings on nearly every street—nor was it primarily relief or aid work, such as that done by World Vision. In fact, there was a fundamental and unresolved tension between cultivating friendships and running a project of *inclusão social* (social inclusion). The theme of inclusion is one that runs through my experience in Brazil and therefore through this book. For now, I want to make clear that the question that my experience in João Turquino raised was not, "Can social inclusion be a genuine Christian expression of neighbor-love?," but rather, "Into what do we imagine that we are including others through our acts of neighborly love?"

In retrospect, what I found disquieting about our *ação social* was the way we tended to imagine social inclusion primarily in terms of uplifting "them" to have the same privileges and access to goods and services that "we" have. Looking back, I can recognize how this assumption generated expectations from both sides, led to a disabling sense of dependence on the project, and, more subtly, involved an exercise of power that left the "helpers" invulnerable to the precariousness of life in João Turquino. Instead, I wish we had asked ourselves different and better questions, such as: What does João Turquino have to do with Igreja Batista Catuaí? What do the people in João Turquino and members of Igreja Batista Catuaí share in common? Or even: Into *what* are we all being included through Jesus's presence in our midst?

All the while, I tried to cling to the original sense of integration that came with being sent and arriving in Brazil: the "as/so" logic of the Incarnation, the peace of Christ, and the "inspiration" of the Spirit as an alternative to the insularity and fear of the "holy huddle" (John 20:19–23). Navigating between the seminary, the sanctuary, and the street, however, I gradually underwent a movement from initial orientation to disorientation. I could no longer envision—much less focus on—what I had glimpsed through João's painting.

As a missionary who had cast himself as a "bridge builder" or mission partner between institutions in Brazil and the US, I came to recognize that theological production and formation (seminary), visions for "being/doing church" (sanctuary), as well as the strategies and financial basis for social transformation (street) were, in large part, contained within a crippling binary: either institutional reproduction of or resistance to what came from the North. Even more disorientating, however, than the challenge of traversing the North-South barriers was the sense that much of what I was seeing, and even involved in, between these three *s*'s was counterproductive. That is, much of the institutional activity seemed to work against and even undermine the original intent. In the seminary, the work of facilitating theological learning and formation became locked into the production, dissemination, and defense of theological *certainties*; in the sanctuary, the ecclesial vocation to worship God and make disciples mutated into an emphasis on attracting and serving members as primarily passive religious consumers; and on the streets of places like João Turquino, neighbor-love with the marginalized ended up reinforcing a perception of "their" poverty as a social fact without challenging either the conditions that generated their poverty or our collective impoverishment.

In my experience as a missionary, a deeper challenge than becoming interculturally *brasicano* was the disorientation of becoming aware of the subtle forms of alienation. As I mentioned earlier, learning to speak Portuguese, to eat *feijoada*, to play *futebol*, to enjoy *MPB*—these were not my obstacles. My biggest obstacle came from the challenge of learning to live "in" and "out" of institutional realities without being "of" them. The tension for me was not between Christian identity and some other cultural identity (American or Brazilian), but discerning between the freedom of the Christian life and being conformed within the horizon of institutionalized expectations and performances.

By 2007, I found myself on the other side of an epistemological rupture. In Bedford's terms, a rupture had begun, and I was entering more deeply into a phase not so much of despair as of disorientation—not so much a "crisis of faith" as a "crisis of imagination". The more my missionary work was shifting toward the "street" pole in the triad of seminary/sanctuary/street, the more I simply could not make sense of much that was happening around me.

From an outsider's perspective, life in João Turquino seemed exceedingly precarious: the drugs; the number of children unsupervised on the streets, especially young girls vulnerable to prostitution rings; the under-resourced public services, not least in relation to schools and health clinics; and the difficulty of finding and maintaining regular employment. Nonetheless, many residents talked about the transformation of João Turquino from an *assentamento* (squatters' dwelling) into a municipal *bairro*: how the city "regularized" living conditions by bringing in lighting, paved streets, public services, and a public housing initiative. Many in João Turquino seemed to suggest that they had arrived in a better place. Many seemed content. Overall, people were not asking us for more; they were simply trying to "make do" with enough.

I wanted our church to engage in *ação social* in João Turquino, but I struggled to recognize what our presence there meant. From our side, there was a lot of giving, but little awareness of receiving. And what good were we doing by giving out *cestas básicas* (care packages) among families in which some of the children still walked the streets flaunting their MP3 players and brand-name sneakers? Granted, income disparity between those in our churches and the majority of residents in João Turquino was obvious enough, but not everyone in João Turquino was "cash poor." Nonetheless, much of our giving seemed to presuppose that the main problem was material poverty, that we understood how poverty worked, and that an adequate way to respond to the adversity of material poverty was primarily through the provision of more stuff. It seemed that in relation to both the partnerships between US and Brazilian churches, as well as the activities of Brazilian churches locally, the hard work of questioning conditions and discerning how to respond, how to be present, was suppressed or threatened by the desire to help. Although I didn't have the eyes to see or the words to describe what was happening around us, I knew that I was struggling to delink missionary presence from counterproductive "projects of intervention."[13] In other words, I was trying to delink my being there from being cast in the role of helper. I was trying to delink my presence from the inertia of "good intentions."

And yet, Brazil is a country of extremes. As many of my Brazilian friends have pointed out, it is not a poor country, bur rather *um país desigual*—a very rich country with a lot of poor, marginalized people. Through friends, like Lu, I had been welcomed into some of these people's homes. I had eaten meals with them. I had played *futsal* with their kids. I had studied the Bible and prayed with them. I had celebrated birthdays. I had become friends with some of them. In short, I had been encountered by them, and I knew that the answer to "not just being a helper" was not simply to turn away from these faces that I had encountered. I knew that while "good intentions" are not enough, knowing that is no excuse for following the path of the priest and Levite in Jesus's parable of the Good Samaritan—those who refuse encounter by "pass[ing] by on the other side" (Luke 10:31–32).

---

13. Rahnema, "Towards Post-Development," 397.

4

Ivan Illich in Conversation

THROUGHOUT PART ONE, I turned toward Illich by telling a story through his witness. Here in Part Two, I begin to shift the focus away from Illich's own story to his role as storyteller. Here, I explore the way in which Illich, and others, engage with the notion that "Christianity in the Western world lives and moves within a diseased social imagination."[1] In doing so, I weave together the voices of theologians as well as other contemporary intellectuals as a way of narrating the historical transformations in the West that decontextualize human dignity and the conditions for human flourishing.[2] In order to examine the missiological implications of these transformations, I explore how Illich and these other voices historicize progress and development as twin "project[s] of intervention"[3] inside a Western "universalist mission initiated in Europe."[4]

To return to my guiding metaphor of journey, or *itinerarium*, this chapter examines modern "detours"[5] from an original trajectory for human flourishing. More specifically, I examine the conflict between the incarnational ethos of Christian mission and another ethos, the

---

1. Jennings, *Christian Imagination*, 6.
2. See Soulen and Woodhead, *God and Human Dignity*.
3. Rahnema, "Towards Post-Development," 397.
4. Illich, *In the Mirror of the Past*, 93.
5. I am using the term *detour* in a sense that is fuller than the contemporary English usage of the term and closer to the original French, which means literally a "change of direction," or in the verbal form, *détourner*, to "turn away from."

"technological ethos."[6] In the light of Illich's analysis, we can see how the detour of the technological ethos is inextricably linked to a fundamental *mis*-perception, a false trajectory for the fullness of life. One could also describe this as a Promethean drive characterized by a dominant but false idealization of independent individuals coupled with a dominant but likewise false dependence upon technological artifacts. Illich thereby encourages us to discern how progress and development generate a novel social space, what he calls a technological milieu.[7] In turn, this technological milieu can corrupt the human self-image, even as it can also undermine and corrupt the incarnational logic of Christian mission itself.

It should be clear by now that this book does not focus on an "ideal" portrait of Christian mission. Rather, I "begin in the middle" by attending to particular performances, including my own, and with historical configurations along the North-South axis between the United States and its southern neighbors. In doing so, I want to focus on the tension between what the vocation to be missionary disciples makes possible and desirable, and how the responses to that vocation have led to faithful missionary encounters as well as to missionary distortions.

The *virada* that took place between the seminary, the sanctuary, and the streets, however, did not to lead to immediate answers or facile solutions; it simply led to the further questioning of my own certainties and enabled a return to my initial question, that which operates as the subtext of my research: What makes it possible to enact a distinctly Christian presence that is authentically missionary (sharable with others as "good news") instead of resorting to manipulative control or insular disengagement? With this *virada*, Illich challenged me to seek different questions and different responses. I was only able to grasp Illich's responses and formulate my own through extended conversations woven around Illich. It is to the shape of this conversation that I now turn.

TABLE TALK (PART ONE): THE THEOLOGIANS, THE OTHER STORYTELLERS, AND THE LONGING FOR THE PARTICULAR

To explain my reception of Illich, I want to offer an extended metaphor. Imagine a dinner party with two large but separate tables, between which I am mingling. At the first table, there is a group of theologians engaged

---

6. See Garrigós, "Hospitality Cannot Be a Challenge," 117.
7. Illich, "Philosophy . . . Artifacts . . . Friendship," 3.

in what I would describe broadly as a conversation in theological ethics, and specifically a conversation about the ethics and practice of Christian mission.

Table One: The Theologians

To help understand the conversation at Table One, the following typology presented by Sam Wells is helpful. Wells suggests that contemporary accounts of Christian ethics tend to fall into one of three camps, or strands of emphasis or orientations, which he identifies as universal, subversive, and ecclesial. By "universal," Wells has in mind an account of Christian ethics that is fundamentally concerned with engaging and communicating a useful, reasonable Christianity with a wider audience. Here, the emphasis falls upon Christianity's relevance and usefulness in relation to issues of public concern. The lingering problem with the universal position lies in the tendency to separate the universal significance of the gospel from the particularity of its revelation in Christ, thereby leaving Christian ethics as "ethics for anybody."[8] Alternatively, what marks the "subversive" is a certain suspicion of mainstream perspectives that allegedly universalize a minority, yet socially dominant, position, while suppressing alternative voices. This second strand valorizes the inclusion and empowerment of those excluded voices, whether suppressed for reasons of socioeconomic status, race, gender or geographical location. This is what Wells calls "ethics for the excluded."[9] Finally, the "ecclesial" strand aims to embody "a distinctively theological ethic."[10] With the subversive strand, it shares an emphasis on "the liberating power of Christianity."[11] Unlike the subversive strand, however, the ecclesial perspective understands that the generative source of this liberation lies less in the experience of various forms of exclusion and more in the appropriation of "the character and acts of God"[12] through the re-formation of identity through ecclesial practices. Similarly, it shares the universal position's concern to communicate and dialogue with other traditions or standpoints. But, unlike the universal account, the ecclesial strand privileges

8. Wells, *Improvisation*, 33.
9. Wells, *Improvisation*, 34.
10. Wells, *Improvisation*, 34.
11. Wells, *Improvisation*, 34.
12. Wells, *Improvisation*, 34.

Christian distinctiveness as a primary asset, not a burden. Here, the particularity of ecclesial practices and identity becomes the "door" through which Christians walk to encounter others, not a "wall" that they must overcome to reach others.

Wells advocates the ecclesial strand as the most promising way forward for contemporary Christian ethics. As with all typologies, Wells's account runs the risk of finding or illuminating general tendencies at the expense of losing or obscuring the nuance of particular positions that do not neatly fit into his typology. I am not offering a categorical defense of Wells, therefore. For my purposes, the importance of Wells's typology does not lie in its comprehensive accuracy, but rather in the way it identifies distinct voices in an existing conversation in contemporary Christian ethics.

Those who clearly identify with the ecclesial and the subversive strands share a common suspicion toward, and criticism of, false or abstracted universalisms; they differ, however, over how or where they locate the generative source of their particularity. Advocates of the ecclesial stance, most notably Stanley Hauerwas, insist that the church is the primary location for theological reflection and ethical enquiry; they insist that "the unit of ethics is neither the universal world nor the isolated individual but the particular church."[13] Advocates of the subversive stance, such as Ivan Petrella, identify two key elements at the heart of their position: (1) an epistemological break with the "standpoint of privilege" in order "to do theology from the standpoint of the oppressed,"[14] and (2) a practical commitment to structural and institutional change.[15]

The conversation among the ecclesial and subversive strands also remains split over where to locate the decisive forces of exclusion. In other words, there are those who insist on attending to the primacy of ecclesial context and the recovery of a distinctly ecclesial ethic; there are those who insist on attending to the primacy of contexts of exclusion, and specifically, to the particularity of "material context"[16] that generates economic oppression. Those on the subversive side of the table, such as Petrella, suggest that the ecclesial side is but another instance of the theological inability to deal with "material context," and that without making a turn toward the reality of material poverty and expansive "zones

---

13. Wells, *Improvisation*, 41.
14. Petrella, *Beyond Liberation Theology*, ix.
15. Petrella, *Beyond Liberation Theology*, 148.
16. Petrella, *Beyond Liberation Theology*, 3.

of social abandonment,"[17] theology becomes a reification of the wrong particulars and a mystification of the real challenge. Those at the ecclesial end of the table, such as Wells, respond that it is precisely by embracing an "ecclesial turn," and, therefore, the particularity of Christian practices, that we participate most fully in God's activity and purposes. This participation, in turn, enables an appropriately subversive stance in relation to the forces that distort God's purposes in the world, such as the sustained generation of material poverty.

There is, however, a group of missiologists at Table One whose perspectives do not conform easily to Wells's typology. They are concerned with the universality of the Christian gospel. What's more, their account of the universal scope of Christian mission turns on the particularity of the gospel, rather than an attempt to do "ethics for anybody." Similarly, they are concerned about ecclesial ethics, as well as being subversive of the forces that pull us away from the purposes of Christian mission. Furthermore, these writers insist that we must attend to the historical arena and configuration of Christian mission as a lens for approaching the dialectic of Christian missionary particularity and universal scope.

A key insight from the missiologists is that the story of Christian mission has been largely one-directional. Thus, it is vital to understand current theologies of mission, and practices, in the light of the history of Christian missionary movements and their relationship with the expansion of European civilizations in the West, in order to construct alternatives to missiology that flows "from the West to the rest." A key insight here is that all theologies are contextual, but that constructive theologies of mission must become aware of, and explicit about, their contextualization.

Deepening these more general insights regarding contextualization, Latin American missiologist Orlando Costas stands out as a significant voice at this table, because of the way he places this "contextual turn" in mission inside a christological turn: he argues that the Incarnation is the "coin" whose two sides are contextualization and mission. For Costas, the Incarnation makes contextualization not only possible but also imperative.[18] In terms of mission, then, the Incarnation is more than a means to

---

17. Petrella, *Beyond Liberation Theology*, 2.

18. Costas, *Christ Outside the Gate*, 6. In highlighting the biblical basis for this move, Costas writes, "As the Son of God, Jesus not only 'reflects the glory of God and bears the very stamp of his nature' (Heb 1:3), but has definitely, once and for all, made God contextual."

an end; the Incarnation is itself the very logic of mission and opens up concrete implications and connections, such as

- the experience of Incarnation as a continual reality and presence, especially among the oppressed;
- the evaluation of social experience, identity, and context "in light of the history of Jesus Christ";[19] and
- the commitment toward a "new order of life"[20] and toward the transformation of reality.

For Costas, this entails beginning with the Incarnation in order to explore the contradictions and historical consequences that have emerged in "a continent formed (and deformed) by Christianity."[21]

Given the history he explores, Costas's case for delinking missionary imagination and practice from the Christendom model resonates with the ecclesial and subversive strands at the table. Taking Costas as a representative of the missiologists at Table One, their focus is more nuanced and questioning of the particularity-universality dialectic that I described above. For Costas, the basis for why we share the gospel with others is neither ecclesial particularity nor the particularity of the excluded, but the particularity of the Incarnation, an insight that could not be more Illichian.

Table Two: The Other Storytellers

Gathered around my second table is a diverse group of contemporary intellectuals. They come from across the Americas, from Europe, and from different regions of Asia. Some are activists; others are academics. All of them are intellectuals committed to social change and cultural renewal. Some might consider themselves Christian, but no one at this table would identify as a theologian. That is what makes the conversation at Table Two different from that at Table One.

What these thinkers and activists share in common is an affinity with the thought of Ivan Illich. Some have collaborated closely with Illich, others have known Illich personally and have been influenced directly by him, still others have no direct personal link to Illich nor to his thought

---

19. Costas, *Christ Outside the Gate*, 15.
20. Costas, *Christ Outside the Gate*, 16.
21. Costas, *Christ Outside the Gate*, 35.

per se, but even for them the direction of their intellectual inquiry converges significantly with Illich's own. If, at Table One, we have a conversation among the theologians, then I would simply describe Table Two as a conversation among "other storytellers," those who are committed "to think[ing] more broadly about what is desirable and what is possible for the future of the multiple worlds that must coexist on this single planet."[22]

Going back to my metaphor of the dinner party with multiple conversations, what I am doing here is mingling between the tables and weaving their conversations together. Anyone sitting at Table Two can sense the legacy of Ivan Illich as a palpable presence. At Table One, Illich is either unknown or ignored, and therefore effectively absent. Thus, while my formal academic training locates me as a theologian at Table One, I prefer to mingle between both tables, because I find myself drawn to what each has to offer. Those at Table Two help me to grasp the clarity of Illich's social criticism of "the-world-as-it-is"; those at Table One help me to articulate the fullness of Illich's theological imagination regarding "the-world-as-it-should-be," or as Illich puts it, "a world in the hands of God."[23] Therefore, a primary reason for mingling between the tables is that the conversations at both tables keep turning me toward Illich.

Another reason for this method is that as I listen to both conversations, I notice that similar themes are being addressed, even if the questions are asked from radically different perspectives. One of these common questions has to do with the dialectic of universality and particularity. Broadly speaking, the conversations at both tables challenge the imposed dominance of universal ideals by which all should be measured and to which all should conform. Whether one identifies this as the "Westernization of the world,"[24] the "Global Project,"[25] the hegemony of neoliberal globalization,[26] or by some other descriptor, there is a common criticism of the dominance of a "false universal."

More specifically, the second conversation shares with the "subversive" strand of Table One an intense critique of forms of social exclusion, whether this is generated by the market system or by the sovereignty of nation-states, which eclipses the cultural logics of indigenous peoples. Like the "ecclesial" strand, many of the voices at Table Two advocate

22. Esteva, Babones, and Babcicky, *Future of Development*, x.
23. See Cayley and Illich, *Rivers North of the Future*, chapter 3.
24. See Latouche, *The Westernization of the World*.
25. Esteva and Prakash, *Grassroots Post-modernism*, 32.
26. See Santos, *The Rise of the Global Left*.

reclaiming and reasserting the particularity of traditions, that is, a return to the wisdom and traditions of the past in order to reimagine and inhabit a desirable future. They make this turn to the past, however, not out of a nostalgic longing for a golden age in the past; rather, they do so as an act of opposition to being "transmogrified into an inverted mirror of others' reality: a mirror that belittles them and sends them off to the end of the queue, a mirror that defines their identity, which is really that of a heterogenous and diverse majority, simply in the terms of a homogenizing and narrow minority."[27]

Of course, there are significant differences as well. At Table Two, the response to social exclusion is less a plea for inclusion into the machinations of state-market centrism or "the right to more" than it is a reclaiming of cultural autonomy and the liberty of "people's power" as vital expressions of radical democracy.[28] Similarly, when the voices at Table Two speak of exploring "community, communion, and re-membering"[29] as a way of imagining the future and inhabiting the future, they are not referring to ecclesial practices but rather to a diversity of cultural or communal practices.

What I overhear from the conversations at both tables is a profound desire to resist being assimilated, by cultivating or regenerating the conditions for "life together," which leads me to ask:

- What challenges (and insights) might the voices at Table Two bring to those whose advocacy of "ecclesial ethics," or the ecclesial turn, depends on the recovery and reasserting of "ecclesial difference"?[30]
- What insights might those at Table Two offer to those committed to coming to terms with Christianity's ecclesial failure and "diseased social imagination,"[31] as well as its promise for recalibrating and regenerating renewed forms of Christian "life together"?
- What might those in the ecclesia learn from, and possibly share with, these "other storytellers" who identify themselves and relate

---

27. Esteva, "Development," 7.
28. See Esteva and Prakash, *Grassroots Post-modernism*, chapter 5.
29. Esteva and Prakash, *Grassroots Post-modernism*, 55.
30. Hauerwas, *War and the American Difference*, 98–181.
31. Jennings, *Christian Imagination*, 6.

to others through their own cultural logics of "community, communion, and re-membering"?[32]

- Finally, how might turning to Illich offer a creative contribution and response to the voices at both tables?

TABLE TALK (PART TWO): FRAMING THE DETOURS: HUMAN (IN)DIGNITY AND THE RISE OF THE "TECHNOLOGICAL ETHOS"

In this section, I provide a frame for tracking lines of conversation at the two tables, following: (1) theological insights about the decontextualization of human dignity from the conversations at Table One, and (2) an interpretation of Illich, especially his criticism of the technological ethos,[33] from Table Two. As I mingle between these two conversations, I am also doing so as a way of situating Illich. As I suggested earlier, those seated around Table Two illuminate the clarity with which Illich perceived "the world as it is," especially in terms of his social criticism and perception of the world's *dis*-order; those seated around Table One illuminate the fullness of Illich's vision of a created order—"a world in the hands of God."[34]

Table One: (De)Contextualizing Human Dignity

The recent edited volume, *God and Human Dignity*, represents a collective theological attempt to address some contemporary debates about the dignity of being human. While the concept of human dignity is prominent in public discourse, the editors note a lingering problem, namely that "the pervasiveness of the discourse of human dignity in modern Western life masks the extent to which the meaning and substance of the terms has become vague and contested."[35] They contend, however, that abandoning the term "human dignity" and settling for a "lowest common denominator" is not the most promising way forward. Instead, they argue for the recovery of a thicker account of the concept itself, because

---

32. Esteva and Prakash, *Grassroots Post-modernism*, 55.
33. Garrigós, "Hospitality Cannot Be a Challenge," 113–26.
34. See Cayley and Illich, *Rivers North of the Future*, chapter 3.
35. Soulen and Woodhead, *God and Human Dignity*, 2.

the notion of human dignity is a primitive but neither self-explanatory nor self-sustaining term. Its meaningfulness is dependent on its being embedded within a broader and more comprehensive cultural, conceptual, and social framework. The contemporary crisis of human dignity results, we believe, from the fact that intersecting tendencies of modern culture and society have stripped the concept of a sustaining context, without supplying viable alternatives.[36]

In other words, human dignity must be re-embedded, or recontextualized, but doing so, they believe, entails examining how the early Christian tradition contextualized human dignity and how the terms have been appropriated and decontextualized within modernity.

The early Christian tradition, Soulen and Woodhead tell us, did not coin the concept of human dignity; rather, they borrowed it from its wider Greco-Roman use and shaped it for their own purposes. In antiquity, human *dignitas* was used to refer to either (*a*) an individual's position or social status, or (*b*) humanity's collective and distinctive position within the natural order. Emphasizing this second sense, the church fathers reconceived humanity's status in the light of God's works of creation, redemption, and eschatological consummation, thereby opening up a dynamic understanding of humanity's dignity in "the image of God" (Gen 1:26–28). Three points follow from this:

- Since creation is a gift from God, the creation, "being creaturely" means that our dignity is not self-ascribed, but rather that "*human dignity is conferred by God.*"[37]

- Since redemption is social and corporate and entails "an ecclesial rather than an individual horizon,"[38] it follows that "human dignity is achieved in relation, not in isolation."[39]

- Since eschatological consummation perfects the union of divinity and humanity, it follows that divine and human dignity are not competitive or at odds with one another. There is no sense in which "more of God" means "less of humanity." As St. Irenaeus puts it,

---

36. Soulen and Woodhead, *God and Human Dignity*, 2.
37. Soulen and Woodhead, *God and Human Dignity*, 5.
38. Soulen and Woodhead, *God and Human Dignity*, 6.
39. Soulen and Woodhead, *God and Human Dignity*, 7.

"The glory of God is a human being fully alive, and the life of humanity is the vision of God."[40]

What marks the emergence of the modern notion of human dignity, then, is precisely an attempt to decontextualize, or extricate, the concept from its prior theological matrix. The result is a novel, and fragile, conception of human dignity, one "placed on a purely *internal* basis (properties integral to 'human nature') rather than on an *external* basis (the God who creates and redeems humanity)."[41] Thus, instead of conceiving dignity as a derivative concept, grounded in God as source and giver, dignity becomes foundational, grounded self-referentially as a human property. In short, dignity ceases to be a gift; it becomes a "given."

For my purpose, I want simply to highlight two significant trajectories linked to this modern notion of human dignity. One trajectory, following Kant, grounds human dignity in the faculty of human reason. Here, our dignity is the natural expression of our rational freedom. As a normative principle, the concept of dignity also corresponds to and secures "specific rights inherent in and belonging to the human person."[42] Kant's notion of human dignity is decidedly elevated, and yet, fragile. The second trajectory, following Nietzsche, effectively dethrones the foundational position of human reason and, consequently, the Kantian basis for human dignity. In Nietzsche, reason is exposed as another name for "deeper instincts, prejudices, emotions, and strategies of control."[43] Human reason, understood in this way, is another name for will-to-power. Within this trajectory, human dignity is still embraced, not because it rests upon a rational foundation, but because it can be grounded "in the unfettered exercise of human freedom."[44]

To recognize, then, how human dignity has been decontextualized is to recognize how it has become destabilized as a fragile, deeply contested concept. Once extricated from the context of "being creaturely" in the image of God, the anthropological enterprise becomes, in effect, a battle over "the human image." When we invoke this notion of human dignity as a normative concept, we are left with the question, To whose image

---

40. Irenaeus, quoted in Soulen and Woodhead, *God and Human Dignity*, 7.
41. Soulen and Woodhead, *God and Human Dignity*, 10.
42. Soulen and Woodhead, *God and Human Dignity*, 10.
43. Soulen and Woodhead, *God and Human Dignity*, 11.
44. Soulen and Woodhead, *God and Human Dignity*, 12.

are we referring? I will return to this question later in Part Two when I develop Illich's contribution to the "program of recontextualization."[45]

Table Two: "We've Got the Whole World in Our Hands"—Hubris, History, and the Rise of the "Technological Ethos"

I turn now to a voice from the "other storytellers" at Table Two, voices that add some nuance to the theological account of the decontextualization of human dignity, while also providing a bridge to Illich and his array of historical investigations. Spanish intellectual Alfons Garrigós builds this bridge not by offering an explicitly theological reading of modernity but through a perceptive reading of Illich, one that historicizes the shifting perception of human dignity in relation to technology, and more specifically, "the arrogance of the technological ethos."[46]

What the theologians describe as the modern linkage between human dignity and human self-determination Garrigós characterizes in terms of "the logic of challenge."[47] As Garrigós rightly observes, we tend to speak of desirable social conditions as challenges, whether that be creating more jobs, better schools, more accessible and affordable health care, or more peaceful living conditions. We speak passionately about such challenges, and we even fight for them. Garrigós, however, sees a deeper problem related to the "challenge trap": "As long as we continue proposing the main issues of our time as challenges, offenses, or crises against which we have to test our strength, we will persist in making the same mistakes that gave rise to the problems in the first place."[48] For Garrigós, "the logic of challenge" is closely linked to "an ethos or ethical norm for which every problem, if not reality itself, is a challenge."[49] As the quintessential expression of this logic, Garrigós points to the modern turn to technology as a means of overcoming, and overreaching, any condition perceived as a limitation:

> It is not difficult for technology to follow the logic of challenge. Its great efficiency in shaping reality on a grand scale is admitted by all, but this very power tends to obstruct the ability to

---

45. Soulen and Woodhead, *God and Human Dignity*, 16.
46. Garrigós, "Hospitality Cannot Be a Challenge," 114.
47. Garrigós, "Hospitality Cannot Be a Challenge," 113.
48. Garrigós, "Hospitality Cannot Be a Challenge," 113.
49. Garrigós, "Hospitality Cannot Be a Challenge," 113.

recognize its limitations, to appreciate the point beyond which its transformations cease to promote habitable living space or truly human relations.[50]

While Garrigós's suspicion of "the logic of challenge" rests on a subtle interpretation of the term, what he is more fundamentally suspicious of is "the arrogance of the technological ethos" itself.[51] This way of speaking has everything to do with his reading of Illich, whose work he interprets broadly as "criticism of the predominance of the technological mode in Western culture."[52] Within the technological ethos, they both suggest, every limit represents a challenge to overcome, a limitation and a barrier "against which we must measure our strength."[53]

Thus, within the technological ethos every limit that we encounter ceases to be an opportunity and invitation to discern appropriate action, but rather becomes a provocation to act with hubris. Indeed, by working in Illich's shadow, Garrigós frames and synthesizes Illich's thought as it outlines the history of the West in terms of "the evolution of what the Greeks called 'hubris,'"[54] namely, a disposition toward unbounded presumption similar to what the Christian tradition calls "pride."

Furthermore, in suggesting that Illich's writings "recapitulate and interpret the history of the West,"[55] Garrigós expresses these transformations in terms of three epochs or stages:

- The first stage is the "classical-medieval," in which the cosmos, or beautiful order, provided the context, the sense of proportion and the appropriate "measure" for human action, such that to transgress this cosmic order is to commit an act of hubris within Greek thought or pride within Christian thought.[56]

- The second stage, or "modernity," arises "when the cosmos, in its ancient and medieval sense, disappears"; when humanity no longer derives reason from the cosmos or the Creator, but from itself; at this stage, therefore, "humans become the measure of themselves

---

50. Garrigós, "Hospitality Cannot Be a Challenge," 113.
51. Garrigós, "Hospitality Cannot Be a Challenge," 114.
52. Garrigós, "Hospitality Cannot Be a Challenge," 114.
53. Garrigós, "Hospitality Cannot Be a Challenge," 114.
54. Garrigós, "Hospitality Cannot Be a Challenge," 114.
55. Garrigós, "Hospitality Cannot Be a Challenge," 114.
56. Garrigós, "Hospitality Cannot Be a Challenge," 115.

and the world,"[57] leading to "a process of self-overcoming" that casts any sense of limit or constraint on human action in a negative light.[58]

- The third stage is a time characterized by a suspicion of reason's innocence, "the rejection of any common reason," and finally, the reduction of human freedom to "mere automatism—through history, the libido, or language."[59]

In his commentary on Illich, Garrigós summarizes the contours of these transformations in this way:

> We can say that in the West human beings found their measure first in the cosmos and then in God. In both cases, reason was ultimately subordinate to a trans-human norm indicating limitation to human action. . . . Under such conditions all limitations of reality are perceived as challenges. Surmounting them, the human subject transcends itself until, having questioned reason as a foundation and reduced it to nothing more than a method of calculation, humans find no other end for themselves than self-transcendence *per se* via extravagant self-indulgence. For people who seek to surpass themselves, reality cannot be anything other than a provocation. One sees, then, that a simplified synthesis of the Western ethos results in a unitary focus, a stance I call "technological."[60]

The rise of the technological ethos, then, corresponds to seismic historical shifts in human perception. Garrigós's reading of Illich suggests that we have quite simply misperceived our place in the world. What Garrigós calls the technological ethos is shorthand for a *modus operandi* that conforms to this misperception. Illich's way of framing this shift in perception is that "a world in the hands of God"[61] becomes "a cosmos contingent on [humanity]."[62] In fact, the latter perception could not arise without the former. This is because the medieval Christian perception of the universe turned on the notion of contingency, the perception that the world is neither necessary nor arbitrary, but rather exists as something gratuitous, "a pure gift"[63]—contingent on God as giver. However, "once

---

57. Garrigós, "Hospitality Cannot Be a Challenge," 116.
58. Garrigós, "Hospitality Cannot Be a Challenge," 117.
59. Garrigós, "Hospitality Cannot Be a Challenge," 117.
60. Garrigós, "Hospitality Cannot Be a Challenge," 117.
61. Cayley and Illich, *Rivers North of the Future*, 64.
62. Cayley and Illich, *Ivan Illich in Conversation*, 270.
63. Cayley and Illich, *Rivers North of the Future*, 65.

the universe is taken out of God's hands, it can be placed into the hands of people, and this couldn't have happened without nature having been put in God's hands in the first place."[64] Drawing Garrigós's stages into a Christian conception of a contingent universe, it is possible to argue that once the world that was a gift became a given, an object under our gaze and control, it became a challenge. Thus, the world as a gift bound to and held within the promise of a Giver, "a cosmos in the hand of God," became a threat, an object that must be subdued and overcome: in short, "a cosmos in the hands of [humanity]."[65]

Here, our turn to Garrigós (and through him to Illich) draws us more deeply, and more attentively, into the theological debate about human dignity. In mingling among these voices at the two tables, we are in a better position to observe the overlapping storylines that run between the modern decontextualization of human dignity, at Table One, and the rise of the technological ethos at Table Two. For in the same way that we take the world out of God's hands, so too we take dignity out of God's hands. In taking it into our own hands, dignity ceases to be a gift. Like the world in our hands, it has become a given and, subsequently, a challenge, in Garrigós's sense of the term.

In weaving these two conversations together, I suggest that we are in a better position to see that this modern notion of human dignity emerges as a particular conception of dignity, one that emerges from and in relation to other conceptions of the dignity of being human. More specifically, in the story I have been telling through and in relation to Illich, modernity only emerges out of the "colonial wound,"[66] the wound inflicted by the universalizing dominance of modern subjectivities as they emerge and exert themselves in relation to those "non-dominant" others. Seen not just in terms of modernity but in terms of modernity/colonialism, we are in a position to see more clearly how the modern notion of human dignity turns on a novel and provincial perception, a perception both recent and European, though later also reinforced by the US, and yet one that has been effectively universalized.

Thus, by recasting the debate about human dignity within terms of modernity/colonialism, it becomes clearer that we need to attend to more than the "modern" debate between the neo-Kantians and the neo-Nietzcheans. We need to attend to the way that both of these trajectories

---

64. Cayley and Illich, *Rivers North of the Future*, 70.
65. Cayley and Illich, *Ivan Illich in Conversation*, 252.
66. See Mignolo, *The Idea of Latin America*.

share the same detour, the same "turning away." In doing so, we need to recognize the way that this modern subject not only perceives its dignity as either a secure, foundational possession, as in Kant, or as a fragile yet attainable condition that it confers on itself through its exercise of freedom *qua* self-determination, as in Nietzsche. And, to discern the missiological implications of these transformations, we need to go further: we need to attend to the way this dominant subject, acting with hubris, assumes the godlike position in relation to the other: evaluating, measuring, and conferring dignity upon "less dignified" human subjects by encountering them and refashioning them in the self-image of the dominant subject.

TABLE TALK (PART THREE): HISTORICIZING "(DIS)ORDER AND PROGRESS"

This third round of "table talk" focuses exclusively on Table Two, and I want to frame what I hear at Table Two in terms of the disorientation that I described in the second *virada* at the beginning of Part Two. In that *virada*, I linked my experience of disintegration to a growing suspicion that much of the missionary activity happening around me, whether in seminary, sanctuary, or street, was in fact counterproductive. More specifically, the more I observed and became involved in projects of social inclusion that were framed in terms of "meeting the needs" of the excluded and marginalized, the more I asked the fundamental question, Into what are we and others being included?

Intuitively, I realized that to answer that question, I needed more insight into the social space or arena in which "meeting needs" and "sharing the gospel" were happening. I needed a wider narration of the Christian social imagination into which I was immersed in Brazil, in the land of "Order and Progress." Those two keywords are obvious to anyone who sees the Brazilian flag, but in my case, it took an encounter with Illich to enable me to see them not just as a nineteenth-century slogan but as a religiously performed ideal, even as a "gospel-in-disguise."

The Idea of Progress

American sociologist Robert Nisbet contends that "no single idea has been more important than . . . the Idea of Progress in Western civilization for three thousand years."[67] While "faith in progress" may be recognized as a definitive mark of the period known as modernity, Nisbet's basic argument supports Illich's historiography: belief in progress is not so much a modern invention as it is an ancient Western invention. In Illich's terms, what is modern about progress is its status as a certainty, its power to explain, but even more its power to persuade and direct not only the lives of intellectuals but of the masses as well.

This raises the question, How does progress offer a comprehensive explanation of the order of things? According to Russian sociologist Teodor Shanin, in order to come to terms with the impact of progress, especially its "darker side," one must first come to terms with its power as an idea.[68] In Shanin's discourse, the explanatory power of progress emerged gradually from the seventeenth to the nineteenth centuries, together with the rise of the social sciences. With this shift, there was a decisive transformation of the medieval worldview that understood history, and the ordering of natural processes or events, in terms of God's creative purpose. In effect, the idea of progress displaced medieval understanding by "offer[ing] a powerful and pervasive supra-theory that ordered and interpreted everything within the life of humanity, past, present and future."[69] Shanin unpacks the force of this progressive vision as follows:

> The core of the concept, and its derivations and the images attached to it, have been overwhelmingly simple and straightforward. With a few temporary deviations, all societies are advancing naturally and consistently "up," on a route from poverty, barbarism, despotism and ignorance to riches, civilization, democracy and rationality, the highest expression of which is science. This is also an irreversible movement from an endless diversity of particularities, wasteful of human energies and economic resources, to a world unified and simplified into the most rational arrangement. It is therefore a movement from badness to goodness and from mindlessness to knowledge, which gave the message its ethical promise, its optimism and its reformist "punch."[70]

Here, in its modern instantiation, the idea of progress takes on its air of irresistibility and inevitability. This is because progress offers "an

67. Nisbet, quoted in Sedlacek, *Economics of Good and Evil*, 233.
68. See Shanin, "The Idea of Progress."
69. Shanin, "Idea of Progress," 65.
70. Shanin, "Idea of Progress," 65.

ambiguous and yet, to its authors and consumers, remarkably satisfying solution to two major riddles the Europeans faced at the dawn of what the later came to be called 'modernity.'"[71] First, there was the question of the diversity of cultures and human experience. With the so-called age of discovery, the "discoverers" found themselves captivated with the challenge of making sense of the newness they encountered. In the face of "new lands, new people and new ways,"[72] the first question was, How do we explain all this diversity and newness? The second question, intimately related to the first, concerned the perception of time. Whereas the ancient model of history was characterized by "the myth of eternal return," and the cyclical pattern of birth, growth, and death, the modern shift turned on "a linear perception of time and shift into an as yet uncharted future."[73] As Shanin relates, the idea of progress explained this shifting perception of "the other," as well as the new perception of time, by linking the two, thereby answering the two questions at once:

> What produced diversity? The different stages of development of different societies. What was social change? The necessary advance through the different social forms that existed. What is the task of social theory? To provide an understanding of the natural sequence of stages from past to future. What is the duty of an enlightened ruler? To put to use the findings of scholars and to speed up the necessary "advance," fighting off regressive forces which try to stop it.[74]

Thus conceived, modern progress provided a powerful, and scientifically "objective," explanation for the complexity of the human world and the human condition. The "advanced" peoples, Europeans, were leading the way through time. The "advanced" could move forward with the expectation that the "backward" could and should arrive, because this advance was necessary and natural. Progress, therefore, meant that linear time was on everybody's side. The task of the "advanced" was not to change the direction of time, but rather to speed it up:

> The new orientation within the complex world of human endeavours carried the immense promise and optimism of the belief that, once understood, the human world could be reformed

---

71. Shanin, "Idea of Progress," 66.
72. Shanin, "Idea of Progress," 66.
73. Shanin, "Idea of Progress," 66.
74. Shanin, "Idea of Progress," 67–68.

scientifically, that is, by taking into account knowledge of the necessary and the objective.[75]

Converging with the Industrial Revolution and the forces of urbanization at home and colonialism abroad, the idea of progress seemed at once inevitable and irresistible, precisely because it brought into focus "an image of the unilinear and the necessary which was also the universally right and positive in the unfolding of human history."[76] Thus, while it remained debatable whether the driving force of progress was human reason or the forces of production, the general direction of history as one of progress remained a certainty, comparable to a law of nature itself.

As Shanin observes, it is precisely its undisputed status as a certainty that enabled the idea of progress to exert its impact not only as a comprehensive orientation and "tool of mobilization" but also as a dominant ideology, "a blinker on collective cognition."[77] In particular, the idea of progress and the rise of the modern state grew symbiotically, with the state as the primary instrument of progress, and progress as the state's primary justification. Here, Shanin clearly positions the twentieth century's ideological forces of progress as a self-fulfilling prophecy executed with religious zeal.[78]

Progress and the Making of "One World"

In his essay "One World" in *The Development Dictionary*, Wolfgang Sachs echoes Shanin's narration, highlighting the "shadow side" of progress by casting light on its incessant drive toward universalism. Here, universalism signals the movement from a planet of particulars to a "*uni*-verse" of enforced sameness. Therefore, for Sachs, as for many other post-development thinkers influenced by Illich, the story of progress cannot be told fully without telling it as a story of loss. This is not to say that progress offers no gains, but storytellers like Sachs turn our attention to what progress destroys, excludes, or makes absent. For within this progressive *uni*-verse, ecosystems are destroyed, biodiversity is diminished, the diversity of human languages dwindles, and with them, cultural

---

75. Shanin, "Idea of Progress," 68.
76. Shanin, "Idea of Progress," 68.
77. Shanin, "Idea of Progress," 69.
78. Shanin, "Idea of Progress," 70.

logics and "entire conceptions of what it means to be human"[79] are lost or made absent as well. Sachs summarizes the process thus: "Whichever way one looks at it, the homogenization of the world is in full swing. A global monoculture spreads like an oil slick over the entire planet."[80] For Sachs, then, a dominant thread in the storyline of progress is this universalizing vision of "one world," a rationally constructed and managed *uni*-verse identified by a range of synonymous buzzwords, such as "world society," "unified world market," or even "global responsibility."[81]

Indeed, out of the rubble of the Second World War, the United Nations announced the "gospel of progress" and proclaimed its vision of "one world" as a "global hope."[82] In Sachs's argument, what took place in the Fairmont Hotel on Union Square in San Francisco on 4 May 1945 marks a decisive event in this story:

> In Room 210, delegates from forty-six countries agreed on the text of the United Nations Charter. Hitler's Germany was finally defeated and time was running out for Japan. The Charter promulgated those principles which were designed to usher in a new era of peace. No wars any more and no national egoism. What counted was international understanding and the unity of mankind! After devastating conflicts the Charter held out the prospect of universal peace, echoing the pledge of the League of Nations in 1919, but pointing far beyond a mere security system.[83]

This reveals two significant and fundamental assumptions, the implications of which are important: first, violence arises when progress is impeded; second, enabling progress is the path to peace. Consequently, the Preamble to the Charter announces its vision: "to promote social progress and better standards of life in larger freedom . . . and to employ international machinery for the promotion of the economic and social advancement of all people."[84]

The point to be noticed here is how the United Nations' rhetoric established humanity, progress, and peace as pillars for making "one

---

79. Sachs, "One World," 111.
80. Sachs, "One World," 111.
81. Sachs, "One World," 112.
82. Sachs, "One World," 112.
83. Sachs, "One World," 112.
84. Sachs, "One World," 112.

world."[85] By universalizing the necessary link between progress and peace, this vision also universalizes an "idealized humanity," a vision of common humanity, "marching forward and upward along the road of progress."[86] At work is the same evolutionary bias that Shanin described, a global vision "for absorbing the differences in the world into an ahistorical and delocalized universalism of European origin."[87] The result is that by the mid-twentieth century, and through the auspices and oversight of the United Nations, a European ideal had expanded into a global faith.

Faith in Progress

A third voice at Table Two, the late Mexican intellectual José Sbert, corroborates what Shanin and Sachs have to say about progress, namely, its alleged explanatory power and the failure of its grand promises for global peace. Sbert also analyzes progress as a religiously performed concept, highlighting how "faith in progress" has operated as an illusory belief that "impelled people to become their own God and make their own history."[88] Like Shanin, he argues that progress offers a "modern destiny" toward "future perfection,"[89] while explaining history's imperfections or questions. Like Sachs, he points out how progress escalates the anthropocentric temptation to secure our own destiny through the work of our own hands, or as Sachs puts it, through the "rule of science, market and the state."[90] Read together, their analysis of "faith in progress" in terms of "one world" in which "[human]kind and peace realize themselves"[91] suggests that progress is less a rejection of a Christian vision for a "new humanity" (Eph 2:15) and "a new heaven and a new earth" (Rev 21:1) and more a parasitic corruption, or counterfeit, of those themes.

Of course, viewed from hindsight, from this side of two world wars, the Shoah, protracted violence, and continuing conflicts related to the necessary "march of progress" throughout the second half of the twentieth century, one could argue that the idea of progress has since lost

85. Sachs, "One World," 112.
86. Sachs, "One World," 112.
87. Sachs, "One World," 114.
88. Sbert, "Progress," 218.
89. Sbert, "Progress," 216.
90. Sachs, "One World," 113.
91. Sachs, "One World," 112.

its air of irresistibility and its explanatory power. "Faith in progress" as a historical project may indeed be on the decline, but this should not lead us to minimize the ways its legacy impinges upon the Christian social imagination and mission of the West.

I have turned to these voices as a way of examining more closely the historical unfolding of "order and progress," the motto on the Brazilian flag. I am suggesting that these voices expand Illich's insight regarding the centrality of progress in "the victory of a universalist mission initiated in Europe."[92] To develop how that European universalism transformed into "the adoption of the American way of life as a universal ideal,"[93] I turn to the emergence of the paradigm of "development" as an offspring of progress, and return to Illich directly in order to explore why he narrates "development . . . [as] the most pernicious of the West's missionary efforts."[94]

CONCLUSION: QUESTIONING CERTAINTIES— ATTENDING TO "(DIS)ORDER AND PROGRESS"

In this chapter, I have put Ivan Illich in conversation with theologians (Table One) and "other storytellers" (Table Two) in order to reenact the way that I began to hear and appreciate Illich's distinctive voice in the midst of the conversation. What kept drawing me toward Illich was not that he articulated his ideas with the doctrinal precision of my seminary professors, but rather that his theological vision covered the ground upon which I was sojourning in Brazil. Even though he did not primarily articulate that vision in a theological idiom, he held out a light that was bright enough to show the difference between the "narrow gate" of Jesus's way to life and the "wide road" of destruction (Matt 7:13–14)—the difference between the way and the detour.

Paradoxically, when I describe how encountering Illich set in motion a transformative series of *viradas* in my own journey, what I am referring to is not so much a turning toward new certainties, but rather a turning toward deeper questioning—or, in Illich's terms, the questioning of certainties. As a prime example of this, take the Brazilian flag and its motto. Brazil adopted the original version of the national flag in 1888, the

92. Illich, *In the Mirror of the Past*, 93.
93. Esteva, Babones, and Babcicky, *Future of Development*, 15.
94. Illich, *In the Mirror of the Past*, 95.

year it became a republic, and the year that it abolished slavery. Written across the flag is a motto, *Ordem e Progresso* ("Order and Progress"), which took its inspiration from the regnant positivism imported into Brazil in the late nineteenth century. The motto is a shorthand version formula for positivism extensively attributed to Auguste Comte: "Love as a principle and order as the basis; progress as the goal." While the principle of love did not make it onto the Brazilian flag, the flag effectively sacralizes the coupling of order and progress as two indubitable certainties that would guide Brazil on its way from being an empire to becoming a republic. Thus, in a world in which order and progress appear joined as inalienable truths, the story of Brazil can be told as a success story: the tale of a "sleeping giant" who awoke to emerge as a G8 nation. Thus goes the plot within the storyline of "order and progress."

From Illich's perspective, however, order and progress are not inalienable truths, and their status as certainties is as historically contingent as the fact that Brazilians speak Portuguese instead of Spanish, or prefer coffee instead of tea. In fact, at the same time that coffee, sugar, brazilwood, and gold became Brazil's most important exports, the European social vision of "progress as the goal" became one of Brazil's most precious imports. Thus, to borrow a term from Brazilian literary critic Roberto Schwarz, "order and progress" arrived in Brazil as a "misplaced idea."[95] Like a non-native plant that is introduced into a new habitat and manages to flourish, in the land of Brazil progress took root, grew, and naturalized into a formidable and unquestionable certainty.

In the light of Illich's historical investigations, the idea of progress remains significant, but also highly questionable. In Illich's view, progress is not only intricately woven into the history of the West, but more specifically and more subtly, it is woven into the way we imagine social inclusion as the expansion and provision of "Western needs."[96]

> Progress, the notion which has characterized the West for 2000 years and has determined its relations to outsiders since the decay of classical Rome, lies behind the belief in needs. Societies mirror themselves not only in their transcendent gods, but also in their image of the alien beyond their frontiers. The West exported a dichotomy between "us" and "them" unique to industrial society. This peculiar attitude towards self and others is

---

95. See Schwarz, *Misplaced Ideas*.
96. Illich, *In the Mirror of the Past*, 93.

now worldwide, constituting the victory of a *universalist mission initiated in Europe*.[97]

Illich argues that the social ideal of progress is arguably the West's oldest and most cherished ideal. While the ideal may predate Christian missionary expansion, by the time the western European church becomes a dominant social institution in late antiquity, Christian mission and progress operate in tandem: the outsider is no longer an alien whose presence evokes a barrier (the presence of the barbarian for the Roman); rather, "the alien [has] become someone in need, someone to be brought in."[98] Taken together, Illich insists, the idea of progress and the Christian practice of mission give rise to a view of the outsider as someone in need of help. Without this view, "what we call the West would not have come to be."[99]

For Illich *qua* historian, the task of historicizing and denaturalizing the link between progress and Christianity means attending to the way the image of the "them," or "alien," reciprocates and shifts in relation to the self-image of the dominant Western subject: how (1) the non-Roman barbarian becomes (2) the unbaptized pagan, who becomes (3) the infidel (who resists conversion to Christianity), who becomes (4) the one who resists the "civilizing" influence of the humanists, the "wild man," who, in turn, becomes (5) the native, toward whom the Europeans imputed needs, who finally gives rise to (6) the more recent outsider known as the "underdeveloped." Illich sums up this six-stage shift:

> Each time the West put a new mask on the alien, the old one was discarded because it was now recognized as a caricature of an abandoned self-image. The pagan with his naturally Christian soul had to give way to the stubborn infidel to allow Christendom to launch the Crusades. The wild man became necessary to justify the need for secular humanist education. The native was the crucial concept to promote self-righteous colonial rule. But by the time of the Marshall Plan, when multinational conglomerates were expanding and the ambitions of transnational pedagogues, therapists, and planners knew no bounds, the natives' limited need for goods and services thwarted growth

---

97. Illich, *In the Mirror of the Past*, 95.
98. Illich, *In the Mirror of the Past*, 95.
99. Illich, *In the Mirror of the Past*, 95.

and progress. They had to metamorphose into underdeveloped people, the sixth and present stage of the West's view of the outsider.[100]

From this historical perspective, it becomes clearer how the Brazilian sacralization of progress in the late nineteenth century fits within a "universalist mission initiated in Europe." It becomes clearer how, from the standpoint of the "missionaries of progress," the history of the republic of Brazil could be told as the conversion of a nation of "natives" into a "developed" nation. But Illich thinks from a different standpoint, and what he exposes is a sinister side of inclusion into this order and progress. He shows how becoming a developed nation demands from its citizens a kind of conversion: "the worldwide acceptance of the Western self-image of *homo economicus* in his most extreme form as *homo industrialis*, with all needs commodity-defined."[101] In Illich's view, the legacy of progress does not represent a linear advance through time, nor even a benign social vision, but rather a questionable ideal, one that leads to "development ... [as] the most pernicious of the West's missionary efforts."[102]

———

As I mentioned above, conversations at both tables kept turning me toward Illich, enabling me to recognize how, although Illich himself was at neither table, he belonged at both. Illich challenged me to seek different questions and different responses. I was only able to grasp Illich's responses and formulate my own through extended conversations woven around Illich, as well as a deep dive into not only Illich's work as a historian but also his work as a social critic of dominant institutions and technological forms.

For the task of holding the conversation together, however, I kept turning back to the conversations and voices of friends, especially Claudio Oliver, the friend who introduced me to Illich. It was primarily through Claudio and the Christian community of which he is pastor in Curitiba, Brazil, that I made the connections between Illich's voice, the voices at

---

100. Illich, *In the Mirror of the Past*, 94–95.
101. Illich, *In the Mirror of the Past*, 95.
102. Illich, *In the Mirror of the Past*, 95.

both tables, and the missional significance of cultivating a "subversive, communitarian expression of another way of life."[103]

In 2009, I worked closely with Claudio on *Relationality*, a booklet on relational responses to poverty. In it we distilled countless hours of conversation that took place in his garden, around his dinner table, and occasionally via Skype. In listening to, translating, and editing those conversations, I began to see clearly the polarity that Illich described in the late 1960s between "the manipulation of things and the relationship to persons."[104]

In *Relationality*, Claudio describes this tension as a conflict of agendas and promises—a conflict between the agenda of Truman-inspired economic development[105] as the panacea for poverty and a gospel-inspired agenda:

> Every time the church and her agencies try to promote development as defined by Truman, or try to overcome a specific definition of poverty that is based on income, home ownership and consumption capacity, or every time we try to include people in our unsustainable way of life or to give them access to the very lifestyle that has pulverized 30% of the earth's resources in the last sixty years, the question to be asked is: Who is setting the agenda?[106]

He continues by highlighting what happens when the biblical call to neighbor-love gets transmogrified by another agenda:

> The programs and solutions proposed by churches and agencies usually accept the economic and developmental definitions and standards uncritically. Even worse is when these attempts seek biblical, theological and spiritual justification in support of their efforts to help include "primitive," "underdeveloped," the "poor," the "jobless" into our standards of living. Such proposals are made to "educate" and "liberate" them from their traditional and sustainable lifestyles. As a result, money, professionals, and "good Samaritans" start swarming like bees to "help" . . .

103. Oliver, *Relationality*, 8.

104. Illich, *Celebration of Awareness*, 103.

105. While US president Harry Truman did not coin the term *development*, Illich and many other post-development thinkers highlight the way he resignified the term in his State of the Union address on 20 January 1949, effectively dividing the world into two groups: the "developed" and the "underdeveloped." I will return to the significance of Truman's development agenda in chapter 6.

106. Oliver, *Relationality*, 12.

> Don't get me wrong here. I'm not saying people are bad when they try to help. I believe it is quite the opposite; I believe the best and deepest desires in people's hearts have been put to work to try to overcome such problems. What I am saying is that all this good will and effort, all the energy and love at work may have been barking up the wrong tree.[107]

Here, Claudio's comments clearly echo Illich's critique of "good intentions." His comments also resonate with my intuition that the incarnational logic of mission can be *hijacked*. Claudio highlights the idea, as Illich had done before, that by raising the question of competing agendas, our missionary efforts can be turned away from God's original purposes and turned into a corruption of mission, a counterfeit. The theological task, therefore, lies in discerning the difference between the counterfeit and the original.

In Claudio's analysis, Truman's post–World War II development agenda promised a "better life" through the escalation of technical, institutional, and professional control over other people as well as the environment. Claudio observes, however, that Jesus's agenda does not turn on technical control, but rather on embodied presence. Indeed, to believe in the Incarnation is to believe that "Jesus is the incarnation of the most frequent promise in the Bible: God with us":[108]

> So we are encouraged to deal with [social problems, such as poverty] relationally because God has done so, because this has proved to be effective and real in history, and because we are not left alone. We have God, dwelling within us, among us, and most of all, present with us . . . through the others whom we encounter in the endeavor. I think this is a fair enough reason to risk the relational proposal of Jesus.[109]

Claudio's description serves as a lens contrasting two ways of approaching mission: either as a technical problem to be controlled, or a relational possibility to be shared. The next two chapters in Part Two continue to draw out the contrast between these two ways (one technique-based, the other relationally based). In other words, I follow the "detours" in order to juxtapose the conditions that corrupt this relational possibility with the invitation to "risk the relational proposal of Jesus."[110]

---

107. Oliver, *Relationality*, 13.
108. Oliver, *Relationality*, 20.
109. Oliver, *Relationality*, 20–21.
110. Oliver, *Relationality*, 21.

5

Ivan Illich and the Prophetic Imagination

IN THE LAST CHAPTER, I turned to Illich as a historian, reading him in conversation with theologians and "other storytellers" in order to gain a historic grasp of the "(dis)order and progress" that I encountered in Brazil. In this chapter I turn to Illich as a social critic, which is arguably the intellectual role for which he is most widely known and read. But even as I turn to his writings that focus on social criticism, I want to keep in view how these writings reflect Illich's "prophetic imagination." This is a term that I borrow from Walter Brueggemann in order to highlight the prophetic stance that permeates Illich's social criticism. In doing so, I am recognizing that Illich was more than a social critic, for like biblical prophets such as Jeremiah, he wrote as one seeking to respond to the voice of the God who speaks. In doing so, I am also making this less obvious point about the "prophetic imagination": what makes Illich comparable with the prophets is not that he says what they said (i.e., merely quoting or paraphrasing their commands) but that he does what they did:

- He *criticizes* the false consciousness of a dominant culture.
- He *energizes* others to seek an alternative vision of the future animated by the power of God's hope not human expectation.

As a biblical scholar, Walter Brueggemann clarifies how the work of the prophets is just this: "to nurture, nourish, and evoke a consciousness and perception alternative to the consciousness and perception of the dominant culture around us."¹ Brueggemann's shorthand for this dominant culture is "the American ethos of consumerism,"² and it is important to see that Illich's work criticizes the way in which this ethos has been exported and universalized in the West. Illich does this not by moralizing consumption as greed (an easy enough target); rather, he exposes its false expectations and inability to satisfy. That said, it is equally important to see how Illich's criticism is energized by the promise of a "better hope" (Heb 7:19). And it is precisely the juxtaposition between false expectations and the promise of hope that permeates Illich's imagination (in general) and this chapter (in particular).

RITUALIZING CONSUMPTION

In a revealing published conversation with longtime friend and colleague Majid Rahnema, Illich distinguishes between distinct stages in his approach to social criticism. In his first stage, begun during the 1950s, Illich "took as [his] model the pamphleteers of the Enlightenment . . . call[ing] on people to recognize the surreptitious injustices implicit in publicly financed professional organizations of teachers, social workers, and physicians."³ Illich goes on to describe his rhetorical turn from being discursively analytical to examining institutions such as compulsory schooling, transportation systems, and health care by "look[ing] at these fantasies as at a frightful Greek ogre, a fateful destiny in the pursuit of which all but some of the rich or protectively credentialed are highly likely to be ground up by the *rituals* created to reach it."⁴ In referring to these conditions as rituals, Illich draws attention to how the dominance of these institutions exercise the power to direct and hold captive our imaginations:

> These generate not just specific goals like "education" or "transportation," but a non-ethical state of mind. Inevitably, this wild-goose chase transforms the good into a value; it frustrates present satisfaction (in Latin, enough-ness) so that one always longs for something better that lies in the "not yet."⁵

1. Brueggemann, *Prophetic Imagination*, 13.
2. Brueggemann, *Prophetic Imagination*, 11.
3. Illich and Rahnema, "Twenty-Six Years Later," 107.
4. Illich and Rahnema, "Twenty-Six Years Later," 107.
5. Illich and Rahnema, "Twenty-Six Years Later," 104.

In this section, I examine Illich's social criticism of two prominent rituals in contemporary society in order to display what is at stake in Illich's attempt "to challenge a social system featuring obligatory 'health,' 'wealth,' and 'security.'"[6]

Deschooling Society: What It Is and Is Not About

With the publication of *Deschooling Society* in 1970, Illich unmistakably emerged as a leading voice in the arena of radical social criticism. Even today, it is arguably the book for which Illich is most recognized. In *Deschooling Society*, however, Illich is responding to a more general issue than schooling itself. He is questioning "the mutual definition of [human] nature and the nature of modern institutions."[7] More specifically, Illich is challenging the "institutionalization of values," a social process that transforms legitimate "nonmaterial needs [such as learning, knowledge, skills] into demands for commodities and rights to services."[8] As Illich points out, this particularly modern form of institutionalization must be challenged because it "leads inevitably to physical pollution, social polarization, and psychological impotence: three dimensions in a process of global degradation and modernized misery."[9]

Illich's account treats schooling as paradigmatic of "modern institutions" and as a primary mediating institution for the "ritualization of progress" and full participation in society.[10] In *Deschooling Society*, Illich works with the definition of school as "the age-specific, teacher-related process requiring full-time attendance at an obligatory curriculum."[11] Here, it is important to recognize that Illich was not advocating the abolition of schools as such, but the disestablishment of compulsory schooling, arguing that to the extent that schooling exercises a monopoly on learning, it then becomes economically unfeasible, pedagogically unsound, and socially divisive.

Doing social criticism from the perspective of a historian, he is also at pains to make clear the historical aberration that obligatory

6. Illich, *Deschooling Society*, 49.
7. Illich, *Deschooling Society*, 2.
8. Illich, *Deschooling Society*, 1.
9. Illich, *Deschooling Society*, 1.
10. Illich, *Deschooling Society*, 10.
11. Illich, *Deschooling Society*, 25–26.

schooling manifests. Historically, most learning happened "incident[ally] or informal[ly]." As an integral part of the quotidian patterns of living, "education did not compete for time with either work or leisure. Almost all education was complex, lifelong, and unplanned."[12] As Illich points out, with the advent of the industrial society, a significant break takes place that disrupts this porous interplay between living and learning. Borrowing from Philippe Aries's groundbreaking work on childhood, Illich relates to this modern division between living and learning as the emergence and "mass production of childhood" as a distinct phase of human development.[13] Thus, a first shift correlates schooling with industrialization and the institutional apparatus that promotes the "knowledge industry." A second shift corresponds with the post–World War II emergence of compulsory schooling as a dominant institution.

Here again, it is in relation to the way schooling becomes established (in the same sense that the church can be legally established) that Illich directs his critique not at the existence at schools as such but at obligatory schooling. Borrowing from Durkheim's insight that a mark of formal religion is its power to divide social reality into the two distinct realms of sacred and profane, Illich's "sociology of education" aims to expose the way in which "the very existence of obligatory schools divides any society into two realms: some time spans and processes are 'academic' or 'pedagogic,' and others are not. The power of school thus to divide social reality has no boundaries: education becomes unworldly and the world becomes noneducational."[14]

Illich goes beyond asking, What is a school? or, What happens or should happen in schooling?, in order to ask a deeper question: What does schooling do to us? Illich shifts the focus to attending to schooling's "hidden curriculum" under the rubric of ritual. For Illich, the two go hand in hand:

> The ritual of schooling itself constitutes such a hidden curriculum . . . [and] this hidden curriculum serves as a ritual of initiation into a growth-oriented consumer society for rich and poor alike.[15]

---

12. Illich, *Deschooling Society*, 22.
13. Illich, *Deschooling Society*, 26.
14. Illich, *Deschooling Society*, 24.
15. Illich, *Deschooling Society*, 33.

> School is a ritual of initiation which introduces the neophyte to the sacred race of progressive consumption, a ritual of propitiation whose academic priests mediate between the faithful and the gods of privilege and power, a ritual of expiation which sacrifices its dropouts, branding them as scapegoats of underdevelopment.[16]

From this perspective, schooling clearly initiates its participants into much more than what it promises through its explicit curriculum. And also much less, for its very efficiency at funneling students into "knowledge consumption" inhibits learning as a personal activity, thereby confusing inclusion within the curricular process with the sharing and acquisition of vital competencies.

But how does it do this? In answering this question, Illich puts his school/church analogy to work:

> The school system today performs the threefold function common to powerful churches throughout history. It is simultaneously the repository of society's myth, the institutionalization of that myth's contradictions, and the locus of the ritual which reproduces and veils the disparities between myth and reality.[17]

To explore the sense in which schooling performs as a "myth-making ritual," and, more precisely, as paradigmatic for what he calls the "ritualization of progress," Illich highlights four modern myths that schooling reposits, reproduces, and veils all at once:

- "The Myth of Institutionalized Values," which falsely equates process with the production of "value" and "demand." This is to confuse attendance with learning in the same way that it confuses church attendance with discipleship;[18]

- "The Myth of Measurement of Values," which grants false privilege to "the quantifiable," thereby "initiat[ing] young people into a world where everything can be measured, including their imagination, and indeed, [humanity itself]";[19]

- "The Myth of Packaging of Values" undergirds the "business" of schooling (pun intended) as "curriculum production" designed by

---

16. Illich, *Deschooling Society*, 44.
17. Illich, *Deschooling Society*, 37.
18. Illich, *Deschooling Society*, 38–39.
19. Illich, *Deschooling Society*, 40.

"educational engineers," funneled along the scholastic "assembly line," supplied by the "distributor-teacher," and consumed by the "consumer-pupil";[20]

- "The Myth of Self-Perpetuating Progress," which promotes "the value of escalation," a more-has-to-be-better attitude, linked to "open-ended consumption."[21]

In attending to the connection between schooling as a "myth-making ritual" and its "hidden curriculum," it is important to keep in mind the overall shape of Illich's argument. Illich is not concerned primarily with whether schooling can be improved, which is what distinguishes him from most reformers, even of the educational left. His concern is the way the ritual of schooling both assumes and conceals a false premise: namely, "that valuable knowledge is a commodity which under certain circumstances may be forced unto the consumer."[22] No doubt, this is how the ritual construes knowledge, but Illich wants to challenge this construal in order to recover knowledge as interpersonal *process* that is not reducible to an institutional *product*.

Thus, by taking schooling as a paradigm for the "ritualization of progress," Illich is, in effect, using schooling as a case study for his more general argument against a fallacy that undergirds the "consumer ethos"[23] of contemporary society. Illich's basic argument is that "substantive values," which he later refers to simply as "the good,"[24] cannot be produced, controlled, and manipulated according to a planned process. In short, the "good life" cannot be institutionalized and consumed "as the result of services or 'treatments.'"[25]

Energy and Equity: Why Energy Consumption Is a Justice Issue

Following the release of *Deschooling Society*, Illich broadened his critique of dominant institutions into a more general critique of the monopoly

---

20. Illich, *Deschooling Society*, 41.
21. Illich, *Deschooling Society*, 42–43.
22. Illich, *Deschooling Society*, 50.
23. Illich, *Deschooling Society*, 114.
24. Cayley and Illich, *Ivan Illich in Conversation*, 159–61.
25. Illich, *Deschooling Society*, 1.

of the industrial mode of production, doing so in *Tools for Conviviality*. Shortly thereafter, Illich extended his critique of the radical monopoly of industry, publishing an article in *Le Monde* that was later released in English as "Energy and Equity." The opening lines to Illich's essay read as follows:

> It has recently become fashionable to insist on an impending energy crisis. The euphemistic term conceals a contradiction and consecrates an illusion. It masks the contradiction implicit in the joint pursuit of equity and industrial growth. It safeguards the illusion that machine power can indefinitely take the place of manpower. To resolve this contradiction and dispel this illusion, it is urgent to clarify the reality that the language of crisis obscures: high quanta of energy degrade social relations just as inevitably as they destroy the physical milieu.[26]

As Illich explains, the standard account of the energy crisis promoted energy policies that presuppose that "well-being can be identified with high amounts of per capita energy use."[27] Within this account, policies may differ regarding an emphasis on energy management versus an emphasis on technological innovation, but what these positions have in common is a commitment to "huge public expenditures and increased social control."[28] According to the logic of the standard account, any third option goes unnoticed, for, unlike the standard logic that seeks to maximize per capita energy use toward their ecological limits, the third option focuses on "the use of minimum feasible power as the foundation of any of various social orders that would be both modern and desirable."[29] Central to the third option, which Illich advocates, is an insight that the standard account overlooks, that is, "that energy and equity can grow concurrently only to a point."[30]

Thus, Illich's underlying move in "Energy and Equity" is to debunk "the widespread belief that clean and abundant energy is the panacea for social ills" by exposing how this belief operates according to a "political fallacy,"[31] namely, the assumption that "equity and energy

26. Illich, *Toward a History of Needs*, 111.
27. Illich, *Toward a History of Needs*, 112.
28. Illich, *Toward a History of Needs*, 112.
29. Illich, *Toward a History of Needs*, 112.
30. Illich, *Toward a History of Needs*, 112.
31. Illich, *Toward a History of Needs*, 113.

consumption can be indefinitely correlated, at least under some ideal political conditions."[32] To do so, Illich demonstrates that just as "non-metabolic power pollutes," so too, "mechanical power corrupts."[33] Just as there is a threshold for ecological destruction, so too is there one for social disintegration. Equitable social relations and energy consumption are, indeed, related, but they are not identical. In fact, social polarization occurs at a lower threshold than ecological degradation. Thus, even if we could keep our energy consumption from causing biological degradation, it would still be the case that dependence on energy consumption would be socially divisive. This is because "no society can have a population that is hooked on progressively larger numbers of energy slaves and whose members are also autonomously active."[34]

For Illich, then, the energy crisis presents a "political[ly] ambiguous issue."[35] It can lead either to "the search for a postindustrial, labor-intensive, low-energy and high-equity economy," or it can "reinforce the present escalation of capital-intensive institutional growth, and carry us past the last turnoff from a hyperindustrial Armaggeddon."[36] To paraphrase, in the idiom of the contemporary Transition movement, the energy crisis can lead us to embrace an "energy descent"[37] in which we regenerate the conditions for less energy consumption and more equitable social relations, or it can continue along the path of "powering up" and greater social inequities. To return to Illich's fundamental point about energy and equity: one cannot be committed to a high degree of social equity and addicted to high levels of energy consumption at the same time. Beyond a threshold, energy use rises at the expense of equity. The energy crisis cannot, then, be resolved by escalating energy inputs. According to Illich, "it can only be dissolved" in a way that exposes the illusion that "well-being depends on the number of energy slaves a man has at his command."[38]

To expose this illusion, Illich again turns to ritual as an analytic key. In the same way that he analyzed schooling as a paradigmatic ritual of

32. Illich, *Toward a History of Needs*, 113.
33. Illich, *Toward a History of Needs*, 113.
34. Illich, *Toward a History of Needs*, 113.
35. Illich, *Toward a History of Needs*, 115.
36. Illich, *Toward a History of Needs*, 112.
37. See Hopkins, *Transition Handbook*, 50–53.
38. Illich, *Toward a History of Needs*, 116.

progressive/consumer societies, here he examines the industrialization of traffic as what we might call "the ritual of energy consumption." At the level of social analysis, it is clear to Illich that the energy crisis demonstrates the need for limits on energy consumption just as the side effects of obligatory schooling call for limits on "curriculum consumption." Thus, in the same way that Illich focuses on schooling as ritual to expose the gap between our expectations and the realities of schooling, so he focuses on the ritual of energy consumption as an analytical tool that accounts for the gap between what we expect from a high-speed industrialized mode of transport and how that impacts on humanity.

To demystify the "industrialization of traffic" as the "rain-dance of time-consuming acceleration," Illich makes some helpful distinctions. First, traffic refers to "any movement of people from one place to another when they are outside their homes." Thus, traffic is Illich's umbrella term that covers both transit, that which is self-powered by human metabolism, and transport, which is any "mode of movement which relies on other sources of energy."[39] These distinctions are made to enable us to see how all traffic is not the same. By distinguishing between transit and transport, Illich is able to highlight the idea that inside the industrialization of traffic, there is a negative correlation between "social justice and motorized power," namely, how "enforced dependence on auto-mobile machines [ends up] den[ying] a community of self-propelled people just those values supposedly procured by improved transportation."[40] Thus, we expect motorized transport to deliver to us increased freedom of movement and choice: in short, a greater range of mobility and access coupled with reduced time-in-travel. Nonetheless, the industrialization of traffic comes with a cost, something Illich expresses as an overall increase in "life-time" spent within "a ritual of progressively paralyzing speed."[41]

Illich's fundamental argument here is that "total traffic is the result of two profoundly distinct modes of production."[42] Whereas transit is labor-intensive, transport is capital-intensive. Whereas transit occurs through personal activity, which is to say, "natural mobility" and "autonomous outputs" of transients, transport occurs when passengers become

---

39. Illich, *Toward a History of Needs*, 118.
40. Illich, *Toward a History of Needs*, 118.
41. Illich, *Toward a History of Needs*, 136.
42. Illich, *Toward a History of Needs*, 129.

"clients" who consume an "industrial commodity." By definition, the natural mobility of transit has use-value, but unlike transport, it need not have exchange-value. Unlike the means of transit, human metabolism and feet, which are "native to [humanity]" and abundantly available, the means of transport as an industrial product and commodity are, by definition, scarce. Thus, whereas conflict over the means of transport tends to be cast as fundamentally competitive, transit presents "a non-zero sum game."[43]

Illich is concerned with exposing the counterproductive results that occur when the industrial mode displaces the autonomous means. For him, the "industrialization of traffic" results in a radical monopoly "[by] exercis[ing] this kind of deep-seated monopoly [and thereby] becom[ing] the dominant means of satisfying needs that formerly occasioned a personal response."[44] In this way, being "auto-mobile" is displaced by the monopolistic intrusion of motorized automobiles, and we are joined together in ritualized dependence on transportation. Thus, Illich claims that "in this fools' paradise, all passengers would be equal, but they would be just as equally captive consumers of transport,"[45] and therefore, they would certainly be less free.

Writing in the early 1970s, then, Illich's social criticism focused on the way that dominant social institutions ritualized consumption of their products in such a way that dependence increased even as satisfaction waned. While the characteristic mood of the 1960s was increasing frustration directed toward "further technological and bureaucratic escalation," Illich observed that the turn into the 1970s was marked by a cry for "more," and ritual was one of his ways of trying to account for this collective drive for "more":

> Self-defeating escalation of power became the core-ritual practiced in highly industrialized nations. In this context the Vietnam War is both revealing and concealing. It makes this ritual visible for the entire world in a narrow theater of war, yet it also distracts attention from the same ritual being played out in many so-called peaceful arenas. . . . Many Americans argue that the resources squandered on the war in the Far East could be used effectively to overwhelm poverty at home. Others are anxious to use the [war costs] for increasing international

43. Illich, *Toward a History of Needs*, 128–29.
44. Illich, *Toward a History of Needs*, 130.
45. Illich, *Toward a History of Needs*, 132.

development assistance.... They fail to grasp the underlying institutional structure common to a peaceful war on poverty and a bloody war on dissidence. Both escalate what they are meant to eliminate.[46]

A closer examination of this counterproductive escalation of power through dependence on industrial tools takes us to a second aspect of Illich's project of demythologization—his turn to Greek myth.

DEMYTHOLOGIZING THE PROMETHEAN ENTERPRISE

As we have seen, Illich's social criticism entered into its second stage in the early 1970s, at a time when many from the left were questioning the role of dominant institutions in society. In addition to his turn to ritual, what characterized this second stage was the way "[his] rhetoric was inspired by the stories of myth,"[47] as another way of exposing the growing dissonance he observed between (*a*) what we say about and expect from institutions and (*b*) what dominant institutions do to us. Illich diagnosed how we tend to speak of such dominant institutions, like schooling, transportation, or health care, as primary sites of human flourishing or catalysts for social progressivism, when, he argued, careful observation suggests that their *dominance* also makes them crucibles of unprecedented forms of alienation. This is because once they exercise a monopoly, they force "clients" to exchange vital personal activities for dependent consumption of institutional outputs, that is, scarce commodities. Thus, at the heart of Illich's social criticism in the early 1970s lies this claim: dominant institutions call forth our trusting commitment and allegiance while at the same time entrapping or colonizing domains of human activity in novel and fundamentally disabling ways. To explicate his claim, Illich no longer addressed his audience through reason alone; rather, he clothed his argument inside his reappropriation of Greek myth.

In the "Rebirth of Epimethean Man," an essay included as the final chapter of *Deschooling Society*, Illich challenges the certainties and social conditions generated by dominant institutions, interpreting them in the light of Greek epic tragedy. It might be said that Illich reopened Pandora's box, turning to the characters of Prometheus, Epimetheus, and Pandora as a way of "demythologizing" what he describes as the "Promethean

---

46. Illich, *Tools for Conviviality*, 8.
47. Illich and Rahnema, "Twenty-Six Years Later," 107.

enterprise"[48] of contemporary Western society. Illich maps the ancient myth onto contemporary consumer society in this way: "The history of modern man begins with the degradation of Pandora's myth.... It is the history of the Promethean endeavor *to forge institutions in order to corral each of the rampant ills*. It is the history of fading hope and rising expectations."[49]

Marginalizing the Promethean Ethos and the Rebirth of Epimethean Humanity

In ancient Greece the story goes that Pandora, the All-Giver, was sent by the gods to live among humanity. She carried with her a jar containing various social ills that escaped. In her jar, however, she also kept one good gift—the gift of hope.

According to Illich, there is a shift between the original account of Pandora and that of the later, classical Greeks. The former emphasized humanity's incapacity to control or manipulate the cosmos and therefore the importance of living in hope. Within the later view, "classical Greeks began to replace hope with expectations. In their version of Pandora she released both evils and goods."[50] As Illich points out, through subsequent retellings, and with a decidedly misogynous bias, the myth in its classical form did not remember Pandora in the same way and, so Illich claims, not well enough. That is, it remembered her primarily for the ills she brought, while forgetting "that the All-Giver was also the bearer of hope."[51] In Illich's retelling, Prometheus (meaning "foresight") warns his brother Epimetheus (or "hindsight") to stay away from this woman, Pandora. Instead of disregarding Pandora and her box, however, Epimetheus marries her, thereby forging a human alliance with this bearer of hope.

Prometheus, the allegedly foreseeing visionary, perceives a future of new possibilities for humanity. Casting himself in the role of epic hero, Prometheus, in a great act of hubris, or unbounded presumption, tricks the gods with a false offering and steals their fire to fashion new tools of iron. As the one who acts in foresight, Prometheus may have deceived the gods and may even be considered the "god of technologists": the one

48. Illich, *Deschooling Society*, 104.
49. Illich, *Deschooling Society*, 105; italics added.
50. Illich, *Deschooling Society*, 106.
51. Illich, *Deschooling Society*, 106.

who challenged the gods and enabled humanity to overcome the vicissitudes of necessity. Yet, even with so-called foresight, he did not overcome his mortal condition. He remained "wound up in iron chains,"[52] less free than he was before and bound by the work of his own hands.

In Illich's view, Prometheus and Epimetheus represent more than distant figures from Greek mythology; they represent alternative ways of regarding the human condition: two rival versions of approaching human flourishing. Epimetheus lives by embracing the hope that comes through another; Prometheus merely endures by being bound to his expectation. As Illich contends, recovering the art of living depends upon rediscovering the distinction between these two orientations:

> Hope, in its strong sense, means trusting faith in the goodness of nature, while expectation, as I will use it here, means reliance on results which are planned and controlled by man. Hope centers desire on a person from whom we await a gift. Expectation looks forward to satisfaction from a predictable process which will produce what we have the right to claim. The Promethean ethos has now eclipsed hope. Survival of the human race depends on its rediscovery as a social force.[53]

Let me explore this last statement with a brief paraphrase that illumines Illich's use of this myth: Prometheus tried to transcend, or better, to defy, his creatureliness by transgressing a perceived limit; he, a mortal, took what belonged to the gods. As a result of his trangression, he used fire to forge tools of iron. Similarly, we have tried to transcend or defy our own creatureliness by transgressing the perceived limits to what we can have, need, or want. We have done so by forging institutions as our tools of false transcendence. Prometheus's hubris provoked nemesis, or a backlash from the gods; he ended up in iron chains, alienated and held captive by the tools of his own hands. In the same way, our hubris has provoked a new form of nemesis, the backlash of the gods of industrialized progress, who have alienated and captivated us. We have chained ourselves in dependence upon our dominant institutions and, more generally, upon our technological artifacts, whether they be institutions or devices. In this state of dependence, we embody the Promethean ethos. That is, we expect satisfaction from the very conditions that cause our alienation. We live no longer by a sense of trust and surprise that comes

---

52. Illich, *Deschooling Society*, 115.
53. Illich, *Deschooling Society*, 106.

from hope. Within the Promethean ethos, we live by the double-edged sword of entitlement—"we should have X"—and of frustration—"we don't have enough of X." The Promethean ethos, then, is another way of naming a double alienation in consumer society, one that tends to reproduce two kinds of people: "the prisoners of addiction and the prisoners of envy."[54] Either way, we seem to live enclosed by the mirage of Promethean expectation.

The keynote that Illich strikes here is hope, the recovery of hope as an energizing social force. What's more, he suggests that in addition to the "Promethean majority," there is a growing minority who do not cling to the expectations of the Promethean enterprise. There are those, Illich tells us, who do not expect modern institutions to become their "arks of salvation." He describes them in this way:

> We now need a name for those who value hope above expectations. We need a name for those who love people more than products. . . . We need a name for those who love the earth on which each can meet the other. . . . We need a name for those who collaborate with their Promethean brother in the lighting of the fire and the shaping of iron, but who do so to enhance their ability to tend and care and wait upon the other.[55]

In this way, Illich brings into view "a minority [who seek] to formulate its suspicion that our constant deceptions tie us to contemporary institutions as the chains bound Prometheus to his rock."[56] In this way, Illich's prophetic imagination seeks to energize "those who yearned because the old order had failed them or squeezed them out."[57] Illich calls the manifestation of "these hopeful brothers and sisters" the "rebirth of Epimethean [humanity]."[58]

What is important here, according to Illich, is the ability to discriminate between authentic human flourishing and its institutionalized counterfeits. Expectation, Illich says simply, is "counterfeit hope";[59] it offers only a mirage of infinite possibilities instead of a real horizon by which we might shape and limit our action. At stake, for Illich, is the awareness

54. Illich, *Tools for Conviviality*, 47.
55. Illich, *Deschooling Society*, 115–16.
56. Illich, *Deschooling Society*, 114.
57. Brueggemann, *Prophetic Imagination*, 105.
58. Illich, *Deschooling Society*, 116.
59. Illich, *Deschooling Society*, 29.

that the Promethean ideal, while held by a majority of the social elites, operates according to an anthropological fallacy that must be exposed and renounced in favor of the Epimethean alternative.

Exposing the Promethean Fallacy

It should be noted that Illich's reading of contemporary society in the light of this myth coheres within his more general "project of demythologizing"[60] the Promethean ideal. In doing so, Illich diagnoses the symptoms, or better, the consequences of its contemporary nemesis in this way: "Everywhere nature becomes poisonous, society inhumane, and the inner life is invaded and personal vocation smothered."[61] Yet, within the horizon of the Promethean ethos, we cling to rising expectations. Through our hubris, we have transgressed and eroded any perceived limit, the proportion, the fittingness of what is good and what is enough. The result is that our hubris has also provoked a new kind of alienation, something Illich calls the "ethos of non-satiety."[62] For Illich, social inclusion within the institutional landscape of the Promethean enterprise is not the remedy for but rather the root of physical depredation, social polarization, and psychological passivity.[63]

While Illich does indeed highlight the Promethean parallel between "classical" and "contemporary [humanity],"[64] he also draws attention to the way contemporary manifestations of hubris—what he calls industrialized hubris—go beyond the Promethean ideal of the ancient Greeks.

In Illich's view, the ancients recognized that they not only inhabit the world vulnerably, but they also have the capacity actively to shape the world according to their plans. That is, they perceived their capacity "for the casting of the environment into [their] own image."[65] And yet, this perception, Illich observes, was kept in check by the following perspective: "the world was governed by fate, facts, and necessity,"[66] the very conditions that Prometheus disturbed. Thus, while Prometheus led

---

60. Illich, *Deschooling Society*, 38.
61. Illich, *Deschooling Society*, 113.
62. Illich, *Deschooling Society*, 113.
63. Illich, *Deschooling Society*, 113.
64. Illich, *Deschooling Society*, 107.
65. Illich, *Deschooling Society*, 107.
66. Illich, *Deschooling Society*, 107.

humanity into a new era by forging tools of iron, the ancients remained aware of the risk of defying the complex "fate-nature-environment."[67] What distinguished Prometheus from Everyman or "common humanity" is not his use of tools per se but rather the use of *techné* as an expansive grasp of power that transgresses, and even eclipses, a perceived limit upon the range of human action. Thus, "by stealing fire from the gods," Illich tells us, "Prometheus turned facts into problems, called necessity into question, and defied fate."[68]

For Illich, Prometheus represents a particular ethos, or way of being human, a heroic aberration that has now become the new normal within progressive modernity. For the ancients, Prometheus represented the tragically heroic exception to the "human rule"; now he has become the universal ideal of Everyman.[69] Whereas the ancients lived with this double awareness that balanced human potential and risk within the bounds of limits, "contemporary [humanity]" does not:

> Classical man framed a civilized context for human perspective. He was aware that he could defy fate-nature-environment, but only at his own risk. Contemporary man goes further; he attempts to create the world in his image, to build a totally man-made environment, and then discovers that he can do so only on the condition of constantly remaking himself to fit it. We must now face the fact that man himself is at stake.[70]

This raises the critical issue of what has happened to the way in which we imagine human flourishing in the wake, and wane, of the myth of modern progress. For Illich, it has been effectively inscribed and colonized within a particular technological ethos that is perceived as universally valid. This imagination generates the certainty among citizens "that the 'good life' consists in having institutions which define the values that both they and their society need."[71] Within this imagination, human goods come to us primarily as institutional outputs: "Man now defines himself as the furnace which burns up the value produced by his tools. *And there is no limit to his capacity.* His is the act of Prometheus

---

67. Illich, *Deschooling Society*, 107.
68. Illich, *Deschooling Society*, 107.
69. Illich, *Limits to Medicine*, 262–63.
70. Illich, *Deschooling Society*, 107.
71. Illich, *Deschooling Society*, 113.

carried to an extreme."[72] Thus, within this ethos, the "good life" is defined, perhaps, by institutional dependence and unlimited consumption.

What has happened to how we imagine human floursishing? In Illich's view, there has been "a corruption of [humanity]'s self-image." More precisely, this self-image has been refashioned according to the following fallacy:

> [a] conception of [the human being] as an organism dependent not on nature and individuals, but rather on institutions. This institutionalization of substantive values, this belief that a planned process of treatment ultimately gives results desired by the recipient, this consumer ethos, is at the heart of the Promethean fallacy.[73]

In exposing the Promethean fallacy, Illich diagnoses how we have come to imagine dominant institutions as the structural cradles of progressive modernity and human flourishing. As an iconoclast, Illich enters into these temples and tears the mythical veil in two, exposing how they may become the primary crucibles of an unprecedented form of alienation and captivity. He exposes, I suggest, how the dominance of these structures generates disabling institutional dependence while undermining personal relatedness. In short, the Promethean fallacy ends up privileging counterproductive social forms and relations that are fundamentally dehumanizing.

After (the Contemporary) Prometheus?

In his reappropriation of this ancient myth, two aspects of Illich's retelling stand out. First, Illich's commentary on the Greek myth embeds an apparent anomaly: a final allusion to the biblical narrative. As Illich points out, both Deucalion, Prometheus's son, and Noah represent a new beginning for humanity after the destruction of the Flood. It is here, Illich suggests, that "the Greek myth turns into hopeful prophecy."[74]

While Illich's allusion to the scriptural narrative is more suggestive than explicit, the connection warrants at least two comments. Explicitly, it highlights a correlation between the message of the narratives: Pandora's box and Noah's ark represent the presence of those who come

---

72. Illich, *Deschooling Society*, 114; italics mine.
73. Illich, *Deschooling Society*, 114.
74. Illich, *Deschooling Society*, 115.

bearing hope. Implicitly, Illich's turn to Noah, as a representative within the biblical imagination, suggests a compelling, albeit not absolute, convergence between what Greek mythological and biblical narrative offer us: the truth about the dignity of our humanity, as well as the depths to which this dignity can be distorted.

Second, Illich writes to persuade us that not only is the Promethean ethos built upon an anthropological fallacy, but alternatives are at hand. There are those, Illich tells us, who imagine that another way is possible, those who by "hopeful trust and classical irony (*eironeia*) must conspire to expose the Promethean fallacy."[75] Rhetorically, Illich turns to the stories of myth not so much to persuade us to accept prescriptions for human action but to enlarge our imagination about which actions are possible and desirable. The recovery of "hopeful trust" means that we can "love people more than products."[76] The recovery of "classical irony" does not mean, however, that we counter the Promethean ethos with a simplistic anti-institutionalism or overreactive technophobia. It means recovering the fittingness of limits as the condition for, not a challenge or obstacle to, our flourishing. It means that we approach institutions not as "arks of salvation" but as available means "to enhance [our] ability to tend and care and wait upon the other."[77]

In the final chapter of *Limits to Medicine*, for example, Illich frames the question of alternatives by taking a step back in order to revisit the significance of myth for humanity, specifically, the way that "myth has fulfilled the function of setting limits to the materialization of greedy, envious, murderous dreams."[78] Thus, for the Greeks, myth framed hubris as an imaginable yet undesirable act of presumption, a trangression against what humans can "handle." In the same way, I would suggest, industrial hubris destroys the "mythical framework of limits" and enfolds irrational expectations inside an all-encompassing framework of technological rationality and human control; it projects the illusion that through our artifacts, there is no limit to what we can "handle," adapt or overcome. Thus, "unbounded material progress," which should be considered beyond the limit of what humans can need, want, and have,

---

75. Illich, *Deschooling Society*, 114.
76. Illich, *Deschooling Society*, 115.
77. Illich, *Deschooling Society*, 116.
78. Illich, *Limits to Medicine*, 261–62.

"has become Everyman's goal."⁷⁹ Similarly, for the Greeks, *nemesis* named an exceptional condition, a form of punishment or pain reserved for the hero who trespassed into what belonged to the gods; but industrialized *nemesis* is not for the hero, but "for the masses,"⁸⁰ all those who have been included within the Promethean enterprise and, therefore, the "ethos of non-satiety."⁸¹

As others have argued, Illich's social criticism attempted to "remythologize history in order to demythologize contemporary society."⁸² Here, I suggest that we read Illich's turn to myth primarily as an interruptive gesture, within which he attempts to rejuvenate the political process of establishing limits to growth as a response to development mania. For Illich was keenly aware that in their contemporary, industrialized modalities, hubris and nemesis have eroded the perception of limits. "Inherited myths" no longer provide the awareness and embrace of limits by which humanity must live. This is all the more alarming given that "beyond a certain level of industrial hubris, nemesis must set in, because progress, like the broom of the sorcerer's apprentice, can no longer be turned off."⁸³ Thus, Illich argues that reversal of nemesis will not come from merely reclaiming our dependence on "inherited myths" but by recovering "politically established limits."⁸⁴

TOWARD THE POLITICS OF CONVIVIALITY

Whereas Illich's engagement with the myth of Prometheus offers a critique of modern industrial society in terms of the patterns of hubris and nemesis, his constructive engagement with alternatives to "the monopoly of the industrial mode of production"⁸⁵ focuses on the key concept of conviviality. Conviviality, as used here by Illich, refers to "a modern society of responsibly limited tools."⁸⁶ The "convivial reconstruction" of society suggests for Illich an inversion of "the present structure of major

---

79. Illich, *Limits to Medicine*, 263.
80. Illich, *Limits to Medicine*, 263.
81. Illich, *Deschooling Society*, 113.
82. Hulbert, "Don Quixote," 164.
83. Illich, *Limits to Medicine*, 265.
84. Illich, *Limits to Medicine*, 263.
85. Illich, *Tools for Conviviality*, ix.
86. Illich, *Tools for Conviviality*, xii.

institutions"[87] by reconfiguring "the triadic relationship between persons, tools, and a new collectivity."[88] Thus, whereas some writings[89] employ ritual and myth as a way of inspiring the social imagination to move beyond "industrial expectations,"[90] Illich's concept of conviviality lies at the heart of a constructive political proposal, which Illich describes as follows:

> I choose the term "conviviality" to designate the opposite of industrial productivity. I intend it to mean autonomous and creative intercourse among persons, and the intercourse of persons with their environment; and this in contrast with the conditioned response of persons to the demands made upon them by others, and by a man-made environment. I consider conviviality to be individual freedom realized in personal interdependence and, as such, an intrinsic ethical value.[91]

The Institutional Spectrum

To appreciate the tension that Illich discerns between the industrial and the convivial, it is helpful to recall that one of the key Illich strategies in *Deschooling Society* was not to abolish schools but to amplify what he called the institutional spectrum.[92] That Illich was keen to advance a spectrum of institutions should make clear how criticism cannot be reduced to a facile anti-institutionalism; rather, he attempted "to recognize [and promote] those institutions which support personal growth rather than addiction."[93] At one end of the spectrum lie manipulative institutions, generally characterized by "forced commitment or selective service."[94] At the other end of the spectrum lie convivial institutions, such as libraries, which are characterized by the informal and voluntary. In referring to an institutional spectrum, Illich is highlighting the idea that the crisis runs deeper than Marxist insights regarding ownership of the

---

87. Illich, *Tools for Conviviality*, xi.
88. Illich, *Tools for Conviviality*, xii.
89. The three primary books include *Deschooling Society*, *Limits to Medicine*, and *Disabling Professions*.
90. Illich, *Tools for Conviviality*, xi.
91. Illich, *Tools for Conviviality*, 11.
92. See Illich, *Deschooling Society*, chapter 4.
93. Illich, *Deschooling Society*, 53.
94. Illich, *Deschooling Society*, 54.

means of production. For Illich, the crisis lies in the "industrial mode of production itself."[95]

To illustrate the differences at the ends of the spectrum we can turn to another of Illich's distinctions: the distinction between autonomous and heteronomous modes of production. Autonomous production is domestic or community-based; it happens through the direct action of people doing things, such as learning, moving, and caring for themselves and others. This mode of production generates "use-values," such as self-directed learning, self-powered mobility and mutual self-care. Heteronomous production, on the other hand, is industrialized; it happens through "capital-intensive production [in which] services are designed for others, not with others nor for the producer."[96] This mode of production results in a staple of commodities with exchange-values, such as schooling, transportation, or medical treatment. To put it simply, autonomous production refers to a *process* that people do (i.e., action); heteronomous production refers to a *product* that people get (i.e., consumption).

In Illich's view, the point is not to absolutize one mode or the other but to recognize how they can interact negatively or positively. When society is organized to privilege "managed commodity production," the result is a "negative synergy," in which "people are trained for consumption rather than for action, and at the same time their range of action is narrowed."[97] So, schooling is meant to enhance the personal activity of learning; transportation is meant to enable mobility; hospitals and health care systems are meant to promote personal well-being. Yet when these institutions become dominant and monopolize the activity they exist to enhance, then dependence on schooling fosters incompetence; transportation demands more time and more congestion in traffic; and health care systems lead to "pathogenic medicine," or, at least, to conditions in which people find it more difficult to care for one another. These are all examples of what Illich calls "specific counterproductivity," the outcome of "an industrially [i.e., heteronomously] induced paralysis of practical self-governing activity."[98] Toward the manipulative end of the institutional spectrum, dominant institutions monopolize activity, and therefore

---

95. Illich, *Tools for Conviviality*, xi.
96. Illich, *Limits to Medicine*, 214.
97. Illich, *Limits to Medicine*, 216.
98. Illich, *Limits to Medicine*, 213.

heteronomous production hampers or disables the autonomous, resulting in counterproductivity.[99]

There is, however, not only a negative synergy but also an "optimal synergy" between these two modes of production. Illich never imagined or promoted a social order without any schools, highways, or hospitals, but he did imagine a balance, or "optimal synergy," between the heteronomous and the autonomous, between the industrial and the convivial modes of production. With these subtle but enabling distinctions, Illich sought to argue that personal growth is effective when one's schooling does not overprogram or interfere with informal and self-directed inquiry; traffic is effective when transportation does not overcome but instead complements transit, or self-powered mobility; sick-care is effective when medicalization does not atrophy the personal ability to suffer and to care for oneself or another.[100]

Thus, by highlighting the convivial end of the spectrum, Illich does not suggest that we can or should abolish the social forms that are industrial. Rather, he suggests that we aim to recover a balance between the manipulatively industrial and the convivial, the heteronomous and the autonomous modes of production, respectively. Manipulative institutions privilege dependence upon the consumption of commodities by enhancing efficiently organized production.[101] Convivial institutions, by contrast, aim at interdependence by cultivating personal activity. Thus Illich suggests that we must recover ways of inhabiting the convivial end of the spectrum, precisely because "the desirable future depends on our deliberately choosing a life of action over a life of consumption."[102]

It is to be noted that when Illich juxtaposes "compulsory consumption"[103] and "personal autonomy," there is more at stake here than a "lifestyle choice." One of Illich's aims in *Tools for Conviviality* was to expose how industrial development disturbs a "multiple balance,"[104] which has threatening social and environmental consequences. Indeed, Illich's political agenda in the 1970s was to change the terms of debate beyond "the one-dimensional debate [that] . . . somehow human action can be

---

99. Illich, *Limits to Medicine*, 213.
100. Illich, *Limits to Medicine*, 216.
101. Illich, *Deschooling Society*, 62.
102. Illich, *Deschooling Society*, 52.
103. Illich, *Tools for Conviviality*, 53.
104. See Illich, *Tools for Conviviality*, chapter 3.

engineered to fit into the requirements of the world conceived as a technological totality."[105]

Furthermore, by speaking of convivial institutions and convivial tools, Illich was clearly not advocating a reactionary technophobia. Rather, his convivial reconstruction sought to reimagine the relationship between persons and tools in a way that was not captive to either the Promethean illusion that we can and should manage the world as a technical problem or the more general illusion that we can cultivate a convivial way of life while clinging to destructively "great expectations." Illich sought to generate a different set of expectations, not just lower expectations, but rather ones by which we might live well and cultivate a more satisfying "life together." He saw clearly that even in the detours of the industrial wilderness, a path toward convivial reconstruction remained, but that to take this path

> we must radically reduce our expectations that machines will do our work for us or that therapists can make us learned or healthy. The only [response] to the environmental crisis is the shared insight of people that they would be happier if they could work together and *care* for each other.[106]

Beyond the Military-Industrial-Professional Complex

In the last section, I examined the institutional spectrum of how institutional structures can either disable or promote personal activity and interdependence. Here, we examine dominant subjects or roles that are congruent within these structures—that is, the way that dominant, manipulative institutions generate and reproduce the dominance of "disabling professions."[107] In Illich's view, these "new dominant professions"[108] enact a subtle form of imperialism over the satisfaction of human needs, effectively coupling their diagnosis of need to their provision of the remedy. Thus, Illich also observes that convivial reconstruction depends upon the recognition of imperialism, on not one but three levels: "the pernicious spread of one nation beyond its boundaries; the omnipresent influence of multinational corporations; and the mushrooming of

---

105. Illich, *Tools for Conviviality*, 50.
106. Illich, *Tools for Conviviality*, 49–50.
107. See Illich, *Disabling Professions*.
108. Illich, *Disabling Professions*, 16.

professional monopolies over production."¹⁰⁹ He argues that we must reckon with not only the military-industrial complex but also the military-industrial-professional complex.¹¹⁰

Thus, in addition to challenging the radical monopoly of social institutions, Illich also makes clear that convivial reconstruction would entail debunking the "social acceptance of the illusion of professional omniscience and omnipotence."¹¹¹ This illusion results in the technocratic power "to legislate needs," thereby eroding people's competence to discern whose needs are met by whom and by which means.¹¹² The problem, Illich tells us, is not that needs have been politicized, but rather that the politicization of needs has been hijacked by a "professional élite."¹¹³ The way forward comes through a participatory politics "in which needs are defined by general consent,"¹¹⁴ and this means disestablishing the new dominant professions' control over human needs that they alone can satisfy.

As a prime example, we can take Illich's critique of the medical profession. Here, it is crucial to recognize that Illich's critique of medicalization was never leveled against medical treatment per se. Rather, Illich stood against the disabling conditions generated and sustained by this medical monopoly, conditions described in the opening lines to *Limits to Medicine*: "The medical establishment has become a major threat to health. The disabling impact of professional control has reached the proportions of an epidemic."¹¹⁵

Illich wrote *Limits to Medicine* in the mid-1970s, at a time when other critical voices emerged to challenge the so-called medical establishment. Research and public discussion led to a growing awareness of a new kind of medical epidemic, one characterized by *iatrogenesis*.¹¹⁶

---

109. Illich, *Tools for Conviviality*, 43.

110. Here, the phrase "military-industrial-professional" complex is my phrase for capturing the threefold form of imperialism to which Illich refers in the quote above. My phrase appends "professional" to President Eisenhower's reference to the "military-industrial complex" in his 1960 presidential address.

111. Illich, *Disabling Professions*, 11–12.

112. Illich, *Disabling Professions*, 12.

113. Illich, *Disabling Professions*, 15. See also John McKnight's account of "the professional problem," in *Careless Society*, 16–25.

114. Illich, *Disabling Professions*, 15.

115. Illich, *Limits to Medicine*, 3.

116. See Illich, *Limits to Medicine*, 3. Here, Illich employs the term *iatrogenesis*,

In fact, Illich alludes to how "the sick-making power of diagnosis and therapy" led to "a crisis of confidence"[117] in modern medicine. In Illich's view, responding to this crisis meant dealing with the underlying yet unacknowledged illusion of doctors' effectiveness and the "so-called progress of medicine."[118] Summarizing his massive bibliographic research on modern medicine, Illich addressed this illusion, pointing out that "the primary determinant of the state of health of any population" is the environment, not professional medical intervention.[119] Put a bit differently, to say that professional intervention is not the most decisive factor in health care is to say that the pursuit of health is not primarily a technical task, but a collective task, and therefore a political one.[120]

In Illich's view, this political task could not be achieved without moving beyond the illusory grip of "professional power," that is, "a specialized form of the privilege to prescribe."[121] In coining this term, Illich sought to highlight how professionalism enacts a triple authority: "to define a person as a client, to determine that person's need and to hand the person a prescription."[122] For Illich, it is important is to recognize how this authority to impute needs conforms to and reproduces a growth economy, one characterized by market-intense relations, in which human needs become coterminous with either industrialized or professionalized commodities.[123]

Without this awareness, I would suggest, we succumb to a political process that turns citizens into impotent clients who must be contained within the military-industrial-professional complex in order be saved by armies, machines, and experts.[124] Engaging critically with this complex, and more specifically with professional power, entails recognizing how this disabling dominance operates through a series of illusions.

"com[ing] from iatros, from the Greek word for 'physician,' and genesis, meaning 'origin,'" as a concept for discussing "the disease of medical progress."

117. Illich, *Limits to Medicine*, 4.
118. Illich, *Limits to Medicine*, 13.
119. Illich, *Limits to Medicine*, 17.
120. See Russell, "Does More Medicine Make Us Sicker?"
121. Illich, *Limits to Medicine*, 17.
122. Illich, *Limits to Medicine*, 17.
123. Illich, *Disabling Professions*, 22.
124. Illich, *Disabling Professions*, 29.

- The first illusion affirms that "people are born to be consumers and that they can attain any of their goals by purchasing goods and services."[125] This illusion underwrites the way the growth economy discounts use-values and obliterates the distinction between personal action and consumption of industrialized or professionalized "packaged commodities," or between "personal aliveness and engineered provision."[126]

- The second illusion equates technological progress with "more complex and inscrutable" forms of technology, thereby requiring and privileging a special class of licensed operators and trained professionals over ordinary tool users. This concentrates agency in the hands of a new clergy of specialists and professionals[127] who erode the confidence of the layperson.

- The third illusion relates to "the professional dream that good things will be forever replaced by better things,"[128] thereby reinforcing the drive toward professionalization and expertise in the search "for the ultimate bicycle, the supreme windmill, the safe pill, the perfect solar panel."[129]

- The fourth illusion claims that only experts can discern and set appropriate limits, so that "entire populations socialized to need what they are told to need will now be told what they do *not* need."[130]

- The fifth illusion corresponds with "the experts of self-help." This is what Illich calls "the professionalization of laymen,"[131] which demands that ordinary citizens be trained and licensed to help themselves. This means, for example, that the small-scale farmer who has always grown organically must now be certified to do so, if she wants to grow and sell freely and legally.

This emphasis on dominant illusions, or mystifying certainties, brings us full circle in order to review two fundamental, and complementary, aspects of Illich's social criticism:

125. Illich, *Disabling Professions*, 29.
126. Illich, *Disabling Professions*, 32.
127. Illich, *Disabling Professions*, 20–22; *Toward a History of Needs*, 27–28.
128. Illich, *Disabling Professions*, 35.
129. Illich, *Disabling Professions*, 35.
130. Illich, *Disabling Professions*, 35.
131. Illich, *Disabling Professions*, 37.

1) His identification of the "neo-Promethean"[132] contours of consumer society with elaborate rituals of inclusion.[133]

2) His "project of demythologizing,"[134] which culminates in a political proposal, namely, the politics of conviviality.

As we have seen, Illich's politics of conviviality aimed to illumine and promote the desirable balance "between heteronomous management and autonomous action," or, a "life of action" over a "life of consumption." At the center of his politics of conviviality, then, was the commitment to making "*the expansion of freedom*, rather than the growth of services [and proliferation of commodities], the criterion of social progress."[135]

What is often less recognized, however, is how Illich's conception of human flourishing cannot be isolated from his commitment to justice. In Illich's terms, there must be a balance between "distributive justice" and what he called "participatory justice," elaborating the distinction as follows:

> During the last years I have found it necessary to examine again and again the correlation between the nature of tools and the meaning of justice that prevails in the society that uses them. I have had to observe the decline in freedom in societies where rights are shaped by expertise. I have had to weigh the trade-offs between new tools that enhance the production of commodities and those equally modern ones that permit the generation of values in use; between rights to mass-produced commodities and the level of liberty that permits satisfying and creative personal expression.[136]

The crucial point here is that the politics of conviviality entails a robust account of justice, one that goes beyond equality as "equity in the rightful access to consumption," in order to push toward equality as "equity in liberty for action." Thus, Illich writes,

> I am, like those I seek as my readers, so profoundly committed to a radically equitable access to goods, rights, and jobs that I find it almost unnecessary to insist on the struggle for this side of justice. I find it much more important, and difficult, to deal

---

132. Illich, *Disabling Professions*, 12.
133. Illich, *Disabling Professions*, 28.
134. Illich, *Deschooling Society*, 38.
135. Cayley and Illich, *Rivers North of the Future*, 14.
136. Illich, *Toward a History of Needs*, xii.

with its complement: the politics of conviviality. I use the term in the technical sense I gave to it in *Tools for Conviviality*: to designate the struggle for an equitable distribution of the liberty to generate use-values and for the instrumentation of this liberty through the assignment of an absolute priority to the production of those industrial and professional commodities that confer on the least advantaged the greatest power to generate values in use.[137]

This journey into Illich's social criticism brings us back full circle to his claim about development as "the most pernicious of the West's missionary efforts."[138] For with development as a full-blown post-1945 economic and political agenda, the "replacement of convivial means by manipulative industrial ware is truly universal."[139] Within development, social inclusion means "the worldwide acceptance of the Western self-image of *homo oeconomicus* in his most extreme form as *homo industrialis*, with all needs commodity-defined."[140]

Given this history of development, we have seen how Illich's "prophetic imagination" criticizes the false consciousness of this dominant cultural assumption, especially the anthropological fallacy at its heart: "The needs that the rain dance of development kindled not only justified the despoliation and poisoning of the earth; they also acted on a deeper level. They transmogrified human nature. They reshaped the mind and sense of *Homo sapiens* into those of *Homo miserabilis*."[141] In following Illich's criticisms of this dominant consciousness, I recognize that it can be disturbing to face these criticisms, as they relate to the air we are still breathing—whether we live in the suburbs like Naperville or a favela like Vila Andrade. That said, the "prophetic imagination" does not criticize simply in order to dismantle the falsity of the status quo but to energize us to rebuild around the truthfulness of an alternative. And the way Illich criticizes for the sake of a truly *hope*-ful alternative is what makes his imagination prophetic.

Later, in Part Three, I will develop the practical implications of Illich's emphasis on convivial recovery and how it recovers hope as a social force. The next chapter, however, traces Illich's analysis of development as

137. Illich, *Toward a History of Needs*, xii–xiii.
138. Illich, *In the Mirror of the Past*, 95.
139. Illich, *Toward a History of Needs*, 3.
140. Illich, *Toward a History of Needs*, 95.
141. Illich, "Needs," 95.

"Western missionary enterprise" as a theological detour. More specifically, I want to examine how this paradigm of development, with its underlying technological ethos and ideal of Promethean humanity, relates to the Christian social imagination as a corrupted narrative of inclusion that I encountered in Brazil in particular, as well as how it impinges upon the incarnational logic of Christian mission.

6

The Corruption of the Best Is the Worst

Ivan Illich and Christian Mission after (Dis)Order and Progress

My exposure to "To Hell with Good Intentions" and my initial forays into Illich's other writings cast a new light on the Brazilian context and called into question what I thought Christians were *for*. I had not questioned why Christians would not be for "order and progress"—the motto sacralized on the Brazilian flag. I had not questioned what it might mean to speak of needs as "Western," nor had I questioned whether our perception of needs has a history. I was left with the question, While the official motto of Brazil was "order and progress," how exactly did this coupling work together to escalate and normalize conditions of *disorder and progress (desordem e progresso)*? I wondered whether attention to how we perceive our own and others' neediness—and dignity—might be a clue to understanding the transformative possibility of Christian missionary presence as well at its corruption.

I realized that by taking Illich as my guide, I was going to have to question not only my intentions and actions but also the arena in which Christian witness has unfolded in Brazil. By taking Illich as my guide, I realized that I would actually have to question the certainties and assumptions that shape the way Christians imagine their place and role in relation to God's "good intentions" for the whole world.

My turn to Illich did not to lead to immediate answers or facile solutions; it simply led to the further questioning of my own certainties and enabled a return to my initial question, that which operates as the subtext of this book: What makes it possible to enact a distinctly Christian presence in an authentically missionary (open toward others as "good news") manner without resorting to manipulative control or insular disengagement?

In this third and final chapter of Part Two, I want to explore the conditions of "(dis)order and progress" by developing Illich's insight that "so-called development has increasingly turned the world into a man-made thing,"[1] in order to explore how this technological milieu impacts and even distorts the ethos of incarnational mission. In other words, this chapter seeks to show what is at stake and, in fact, what happens when you "drop" Christian mission inside development as a "Western missionary enterprise."

REVISITING THE GOSPEL ACCORDING TO TRUMAN: DEVELOPMENT AS "ECONOMIC PEACE"

In chapter 2, I examined the way Illich questioned "allliances for progress," highlighting how those alliances, in Illich's view, were cloaked in the missionary endeavor of extending the American way of life through the paradigm of development. To further explicate why Illich speaks of development as a missionary effort and why he speaks so vehemently against it, the following exchange between Illich and David Cayley is illuminating:

> CAYLEY: When I first knew you, you were engaged in a crusade against the missionary activity of the Church, if that's a good description of your campaigns of the early and middle 1960s . . .
>
> ILLICH: No, it is not, and I reject your imputation that in the 1960s I took a stand against the missionary activities of the Church. That was the time of development mania—the years of Kennedy's Alliance for Progress. Those were the days of the Peace Corps . . . [and] as a parallel to the secular Peace Corps, an agency called Papal Volunteers for Latin America. And I denounced this . . . as a *corruptio* of the mission given by Jesus to his apostles. This was a mission carried out by a Catholic

---

1. Illich, "Philosophy . . . Artifacts . . . Friendship," 1.

institution imbued with American values which kept the star-spangled banner behind the altar in every Church and justified the do-goodism called development by claiming it as a missionary activity . . . to reinforce American cultural domination in South America and, in this way, lead South Americans to modern values—exactly those values which I believe are a corruption, initiated by the Church itself and later secularized, of Christian mandates to love. . . . Is that clear enough?[2]

For many, Illich's severe critique of the development paradigm will not be clear or obvious, especially those who assume development is a benign concept that remains synonymous with a universalizable direction toward, and commitment to, positive social change. Development, so conceived, stands for desirable social conditions. To develop, so the logic goes, is to grow into a condition that is more mature or better than before. In Illich's view, however, development does not refer to a desirable, universal vision of human flourishing or well-being. To understand why this is the case, we have followed Illich's trail as a historian (as well as the trail left behind by his friends), examining the usage and significance of the concept of development in its historical context, particularly in relation to the invention of a condition called underdevelopment.

In Illich's view, development,[3] as a globalized economic and geopolitical phenomenon, represents a historical break with the past that has a birthday: January 20, 1949. He describes its birthday as follows:

> That day, most of us met the term in its present meaning for the first time when President Truman announced his [Four Point Program]. Until then, we used "development" to refer to species, real estate and moves in chess—only thereafter to people, countries and economic strategies. Since then, we have been flooded by development theories whose concepts are now curiosities

---

2. Cayley and Illich, *Rivers North of the Future*, 194–95.

3. Illich recognizes that development is a "plastic word" whose meaning has been stretched in different directions, yet he also discerns a commonality in usage that he describes as follows: "Fundamentally, [development] implies the replacement of general competence and satisfying subsistence activities by the use and consumption of commodities; the monopoly of wage-labor over all other kinds of work; redefinition of needs in terms of goods and services mass-produced according to expert design; finally, the rearrangement of the environment in such a fashion that space, time and design favor production and consumption while they degrade or paralyze use-value oriented activities that satisfy needs directly. And all such worldwide homogeneous changes and processes are valued as inevitable and good" (*In the Mirror of the Past*, 90).

for collectors—"growth," "catching up," "modernization," "imperialism," "dualism," "dependency," "basic needs," "transfer of technology," "world system."[4]

This is not to say that on this date President Truman coined the term *development*, but rather that he deployed it in his State of the Union address in a novel way, as the stage upon which "we [the developed] hope to create the conditions that will lead eventually to personal freedom and happiness for all mankind."[5]

The heart of Truman's vision comes in "Point Four" of his address:

> Fourth, we must embark on a bold new program for making the benefits of our scientific advances and industrial progress available for the improvement and growth of underdeveloped areas. More than half the people of the world are living in conditions approaching misery. Their food is inadequate. They are victims of disease. Their economic life is primitive and stagnant. Their poverty is a handicap and a threat both to them and to more prosperous areas.... The old imperialism—exploitation for foreign profit—has no place in our plans. We envisage a problem of development based on the concepts of democratic fair-dealing.[6]

Thus, in same way that Pope Alexander VI, in 1493, divided the world between the Spanish and the Portuguese with the papal bull *Inter caetera*,[7] so Truman, on January 20, 1949, divided the whole world into two kinds of people: the developed and the underdeveloped. Development has come to mean many things, but since then it has always meant "at least one thing: to escape from the undignified condition called underdevelopment."[8]

It is difficult to exaggerate just how ambitious Truman's developmentalist vision truly was, but as Arturo Escobar, a Colombian anthropologist and Illichian collaborator, suggests, Truman's speech positioned development as the project of universalizing the American dream: "In Truman's vision, capital, science, and technology were the main ingredients that would make this massive revolution possible. Only in this way

---

4. Illich, *In the Mirror of the Past*, 90
5. Truman, quoted in Rist, *History of Development*, 72.
6. Truman, quoted in Rist, *History of Development*, 71.
7. See Jennings, *Christian Imagination*, 221.
8. Esteva, "Development," 2.

could the American dream of peace and abundance be extended to all the people of the planet."⁹

Once unleashed, the paradigm called development, like "progress" itself, exerted its descriptive and explanatory power with a force that is difficult to exaggerate. As Escobar points out, from Truman's decisive speech in 1949 until the 1970s, the international commitment to development was established as a given, a postwar certainty in the social imagination of the West.¹⁰ Illich, arguably the first post-development thinker, continued to cut against the grain of this dominant certainty, however, convinced that—if unchecked—it offered a false vision of human flourishing, and therefore needed to be subverted.

In fact, Illich's unique contribution to the field of post-development studies lies in the way he entirely reframed the development paradigm, so that it became no longer the golden solution, or the magic pill, but a generative problem itself. Within the development paradigm, two key perceptions were established as social facts: first, the fundamental problem was the condition of underdevelopment, whose essential mark was poverty; second, the solution was to extend the US "war on poverty" from the homeland to neighboring countries in the South through development. Illich began to form different perceptions about what was happening within the development paradigm:

> We have embodied our world-view in our institutions and are now their prisoners. Factories, newsmedia, hospitals, governments and schools produce goods and services packaged to contain our view of the world. We—the rich—conceive of progress as the expansion of these establishments. . . . In less than a hundred years industrial society has moulded patent solutions to basic human needs and converted us to the belief that man's needs were shaped by the Creator as demands for the products that we have invented. This is as true for Russia and Japan as for the North Atlantic community. The consumer is trained for obsolescence, which means continuing loyalty towards the same producers who will give him the same basic packages in different quality or new wrappings.¹¹

Thus, whereas Truman's "Four Point Program" hailed "the benefits of our scientific advances and industrial progress" as the means for

9. Escobar, *Encountering Development*, 4.
10. Escobar, *Encountering Development*, 4.
11. Illich, "Development as Planned Poverty," 95.

"improvement and growth of underdeveloped areas," Illich exposed the darker side of such a commitment to "industrial progress" and "greater production." In doing so, Illich repositioned development no longer as the solution to perceived "Third World" poverty, but rather as a generative force for novel forms of consumption, and new forms of dependence upon industrially produced "packaged solutions."[12]

In fact, much of Illich's early critique of development turned on his diagnosis of the counterproductivity of the industrial mode of production, and more specifically, how industrial dominance generated what Illich called "modernized poverty . . . the new mutant of impoverishment . . . [characterized by] the peculiarly modern inability to use personal endowments, communal life, and environmental resources in an autonomous way."[13] Thus, for Illich, development was not the strategic solution in a "war on poverty." Rather, Illich demystified the benevolent, US-led "war on poverty," showing how development generated the "planned poverty"[14] of underdevelopment, that is, the condition in which "mass needs are converted to the demand for new brands of packaged solutions which are forever beyond the reach of the majority."[15] At one level, then, Illich aimed his critique at the way development problematized poverty as a technical problem, but he also recognized that, as a missionary effort, development promised even more than packaged deals. As an offspring of progress, it also promised to include all people into "economic peace."

Truman's "Four Point Program," then, functioned like a missionary tract—it was proclaimed by Truman as chief evangelist and endorsed by leading political and economic elites around the globe as nothing less than a gospel.[16] As "the gospel according to Truman," development announced and promised to deliver a peace plan for "peace-loving peoples" for the sake of "help[ing] the free people of the world."[17] In Illich's view, development undoubtedly announced a "peace plan," but like a Trojan horse, this gospel came freighted with "bad news" for those awaiting its arrival. The bad news of this gospel, however, was not intrinsically linked to its attempt to extend and universalize a particular conception

---

12. Illich, "Development as Planned Poverty," 97.
13. Illich, *Toward a History of Needs*, vii–viii.
14. Illich, "Development as Planned Poverty," 94.
15. Illich, "Development as Planned Poverty," 97.
16. Gorringe, *Furthering Humanity*, 178.
17. Truman, quoted in Rist, *History of Development*, 71.

of peace. The bad news was that this particular conception of peace, *pax oeconomica*, is ultimately nothing less than a war against "people's peace," which is also to say, it is a "war against subsistence."[18]

To bring to light the destructive fallout of "economic peace," I want to turn to Illich's narration of peace in his 1980 speech "The De-linking of Peace and Development."[19] As a historian addressing researchers in peace studies, Illich highlights the idea that peace is not an abstraction. That is, peace is not a universal condition without variation. Rather, peace is vernacular, like certain kinds of speech. There has always been a diversity of "people's peace," just as there has always been a diversity of languages, and thus "each *ethnos*—people, community, culture—has been mirrored, symbolically expressed and reinforced by its own *ethos*—myth, law, goddess, ideal—of peace."[20]

To illustrate the indelible link between *ethnos* and *ethos*, or, people and peace, Illich distinguished between Jewish *shalom* and Roman *pax*:

> Look at the Jewish patriarch when he raises his arms in blessing over his family and flock. He invokes *shalom*, which we translate as peace. He sees shalom as grace, flowing from heaven, "like oil dripping through the beard of Aaron the forefather." For the Semitic father, peace is the blessing of justice which the one true God pours over the twelve tribes of recently settled shepherds.[21]

Having characterized Jewish *shalom*, Illich draws the contrast between it and Rome's *pax*:

> To the Jew, the angel announces *shalom*, not the Roman *pax*. Roman peace means something utterly different. When the Roman governor raises the ensign of his legion to ram it into the soil of Palestine, he does not look toward heaven. He faces a far-off city; he imposes *its* law and *its* order. There is nothing in common between *shalom* and this *pax romana*, though both exist in the same place and time.[22]

This insight about each *ethnos*, or people, sharing an *ethos* and a particular sense of peace is what sets up Illich's distinction between "people's

---

18. The phrase "The War Against Subsistence" is the title of chapter 3 of Illich's book *Shadow Work*.
19. See Illich, *In the Mirror of the Past*, 15–26.
20. Illich, *In the Mirror of the Past*, 16.
21. Illich, *In the Mirror of the Past*, 16.
22. Illich, *In the Mirror of the Past*, 16.

peace" and "economic peace." People's peace is congruent with a shared sense of limitation in a space shaped by a shared culture. It is the sense of harmony that arises when people live within the proportionality they establish, especially through the nurturing interchange between human beings and their place. In other words, it is their common sense of what is appropriate, fitting, or good.

This shared sense of peace establishes the first person plural; it "places the 'I' within the corresponding 'we.'"[23] Thus, economic peace generates and imposes sameness; it counterfeits "[people's] peace [as] that condition under which each culture flowers in its own incomparable way."[24] And yet, just as forms of vernacular speech have been destroyed by national languages, so too has the diversity of people's peace been destroyed by the monoculture of economic peace.

In 1980, Illich protested against a different kind of war, one that had gone largely unnoticed. He protested by arguing that "under the cover of 'development,' a worldwide war has been waged against people's peace." Today, we might update his claim, inserting neoliberal globalization or Empire[25] as the concepts that name the contemporary war against people's peace. Nonetheless, it is the same war. These all are configurations or variations on the same theme: the advancement of industrial and technical progress that imposes economic peace, that is, "a balance between sovereign, economic powers acting under the assumption of scarcity."[26] For scarcity has become, in Illich's analysis, a dominant assumption about the-world-as-it-is. But in perceiving scarcity as the condition from which we need to be freed and economic growth as the road to freedom, economic peace actually wages a triple threat against people's peace. It does so by its attack

- on popular or vernacular culture, which is condemned and suppressed as "backward";
- against the environment, which is transformed from a commons into a resource; and

---

23. Illich, *In the Mirror of the Past*, 17.
24. Illich, *In the Mirror of the Past*, 17.
25. See Míguez, Rieger, and Mo Sung, *Beyond the Spirit of Empire*.
26. Illich, *In the Mirror of the Past*, 19.

- against women, who are "neutered" and transformed into *homo oeconomicus*, or "universal man."[27]

Illich's fundamental point is that to be for people's peace, we have to be for limits and alternatives to development. This is for two related reasons: development means extending economic peace, and economic peace means war. Of course, it is not always only a visible war of militia, fighter planes, and bombs, but economic peace is always what Illich calls "the war against subsistence"—the war that destroys the conditions for subsistence through consumption.

In *The Subsistence Perspective: Beyond the Globalised Economy*, German feminist scholar-activists Maria Mies and Veronika Bennholdt-Thomsen borrow and extend Illich's insight regarding this kind of war. They, too, suggest that since 1945 the war against subsistence has meant that "everything that is connected with the immediate creation and maintenance of life, and also everything that is not arranged through the production or consumption of commodities, has been devalued."[28] In the aftermath of this war, everyone seems to share a common double fate: to become a wage earner in order to become a consumer, and this so that we can afford to buy the goods and services upon which we have become dependent. As Mies and Bennholdt-Thomsen point out, however, these are recent assumptions based on novel commodity-intensive social conditions. Following Illich, they also recognize that only after World War II did the war against subsistence begin systematically, and that its beginning coincides "with the new paradigm of development."[29]

In their telling of the history of the "subsistence perspective," the decisive issue that they highlight is one that resonates deeply with Illich's historical studies on peace and the novelty of economic peace. They assert that "if life depends, in a material and symbolic sense, on wage labour and the acquisition of money," then an orientation toward subsistence can and should be rejected "as romantic, as backward-looking, or even as the threat of death."[30] If this is so, then Truman was right after all! If this is so, then the development paradigm can and must be embraced for what Truman declared it to be: "a bold new program . . . for the improvement

---

27. Illich, *In the Mirror of the Past*, 23.
28. Mies and Bennholdt-Thomsen, *Subsistence Perspective*, 17.
29. Mies and Bennholdt-Thomsen, *Subsistence Perspective*, 18.
30. Mies and Bennholdt-Thomsen, *Subsistence Perspective*, 17.

and growth of underdeveloped areas."[31] If this is so, then Truman's gospel of economic peace is worth sharing with the rest of the world.

But therein lies the problem. For from the subsistence perspective of Mies and Bennholdt-Thomsen, as well as Illich, the dominance of wage labor and the expansion of consumption within the market economy are not life-giving, but rather fundamentally parasitic on subsistence activities. Thus, like Illich, their understanding does not romanticize the past and the history of subsistence, but rather destigmatizes the subsistence perspective by "emphasis[ing] that it is us, the people, who create and maintain life, not money or [financial] capital. That is subsistence."[32] Echoing Illich, these two contemporary feminists argue that the war against subsistence is

> a war not only to colonise subsistence work but also to colonise language, culture, food, education, thinking, image, symbols. Mono-labour, mono-language, mono-culture, mono-food, mono-thought, mono-medicine, mono-education are supposed to take the place of the manifold and diverse ways of subsistence. A subsistence perspective means resistance against mono-culturisation and putting an end to the war against subsistence.[33]

Thus, in following Illich's method of historicizing peace, it is crucial that we recognize the opposition between (*a*) subsistence as a diverse and culturally imbued set of activities that promote and embody people's peace, and (*b*) development as a geopolitical agenda and global gospel in the post–World War II "war against subsistence." "People's peace," writes Illich, is convivial and lies in "the peaceful enjoyment of that which is not scarce."[34] Truman's development, on the other hand, destroys the means of subsistence and "inevitably means the imposition of *pax oeconomica* at the cost of every form of popular peace."[35]

On this reading, development, as the gospel according to Truman, has enacted an economic mission. It has created a social space that intensifies market dependence and market relations by transforming the means of subsistence into "packaged deals" of goods and services as the solution to "Third World" poverty. In Illich's terms, development names

---

31. Truman, quoted in Rist, *History of Development*, 71.
32. Mies and Bennholdt-Thomsen, *Subsistence Perspective*, 19.
33. Mies and Bennholdt-Thomsen, *Subsistence Perspective*, 19.
34. Illich, *In the Mirror of the Past*, 19.
35. Illich, *In the Mirror of the Past*, 22.

the "replacement of convivial means by manipulative industrial ware,"[36] leading to dependence on a "life of consumption"[37] as the dominant means of needs-satisfaction. And on Illich's reading, the perception of needs, especially the perception of needs of others, is a key conceptual link between development (as the gospel according to Truman) and the Christian gospel—or rather, its corruption.

REVISITING "THE CORRUPTION OF THE BEST IS THE WORST": GOOD AND BAD SAMARITANS

In a Feschtrift entitled *The Challenges of Ivan Illich: A Collective Reflection*, Illich's friend and colleague Carl Mitcham comments that of all the challenges that Illich's thought provokes, at least one of them, his "corruption hypothesis," is clearly a theological issue.[38] Put simply, Illich understands that the unfolding of life in the West is characterized not so much by its rejection of Christianity, but rather by the corruption of Christianity, a perversion of the gospel itself. While Illich's earlier writings consistently evaluated the link between dominant institutions and certainties in relation to themes of the Christian faith,[39] it was only later, in his lecture entitled "Hospitality and Pain," that he began to experiment explicitly with the "corruption hypothesis":

> I want to explore with you a phenomenon that I consider constitutive of the West, of that West which has shaped me, body and soul, flesh and blood. This central reality of the West is marvelously expressed in the old Latin phrase: *Corruptio optimi quae est pessima*—the historical progression in which God's Incarnation is turned topsy-turvy, inside out. I want to speak of the mysterious darkness that envelops our world, the demonic night paradoxically resulting from the world's equally mysterious vocation to glory. My subject is a mystery of faith, a mystery whose depth of evil could not have come to be without the greatness of the truth revealed to us.[40]

---

36. Illich, *Toward a History of Needs*, 3.
37. Illich, *Deschooling Society*, 52.
38. Mitcham, "Challenges of This Collection," 18.
39. See Hoinacki, "The Trajectory of Ivan Illich."
40. Illich, "Hospitality and Pain," quoted in *Rivers North of the Future*, 29.

As Mitcham points out, the force of Illich's so-called corruption hypothesis lies not so much in its originality[41] as in the way in which he deploys it heuristically. Indeed, the way he leans on the corruption hypothesis provides the imaginative impetus for his turning to the Incarnation as the decisive anthropological *horizon* by which to orient our perception of humanity's capacity for the "fullness of life" (John 10:10) as well as humanity's capacity for corruption. In the light of the way in which Illich discerned a tension between incarnation and institutionalization, his corruption hypothesis can be read as an insight for discerning incarnational counterfeits. In sum, Illich's emphasis on *corruptio* presents not a challenge to isolate and retrieve some ideal or "presumed best Christianity," but rather a challenge to cultivate a greater awareness of how social forms, and their corruption, unfolded historically in the West in relation to Christian mission.

For example, in historicizing the new, free relationship that the parable of the Good Samaritan enacts, which we explored in chapter 3, Illich chronicles in great detail how the incarnational threshold mutated into the institutionalization of hospitality, a gradual shift from open Christian households to *xenodocheia* (houses for foreigners) and eventually to hospitals. His assertion in narrating these shifts is that while the parable speaks of a personal response to the presence and call of a neighbor, the corruption of the threshold of personal action and call ultimately transformed the practice of hospitality into an industry of service.[42] And the growth of service systems—for example, in education, transportation, medicine—in turn eclipses and even colonizes the personal freedom and mutual presence that enables being a neighbor. The result is that Christian hospitality mutates into a kind of template for a "modern service society."[43] In such a society, it becomes increasingly difficult to hear, much less be "moved in our gut" by, a neighbor's call (Luke 10:33). Instead, services are provided based on a diagnosis of his needs. In short, whereas relationships within this modern service society tend toward the "impersonal," the "planned," and the "expected," the Samaritan's relationship with the Jew in the ditch is "personal," "gratuitous," and "surprising."[44] With these contrasting strands of adjectives scattered throughout Illich's discourse, a

---

41. For similarities between Illich's notion of "corruption of the best is the worst" and other thinkers, see Mitcham, "Challenges of This Collection," 31–32 n. 22.

42. Cayley and Illich, *Rivers North of the Future*, 55–56.

43. Cayley and Illich, *Rivers North of the Futures*, 56.

44. Cayley and Illich, *Rivers North of the Futures*, 47–58.

thread can be detected that runs throughout his commentary on the Samaritan, something that might be characterized as the dialectical tension between incarnation and institutionalization, or as movements toward incarnation and de-incarnation.

For Illich, this "institutional turn" within Christianity is the key to understanding the rise of Western modernity, whose roots he finds in "the attempts of the churches to institutionalize, legitimize, and manage Christian vocation."[45] Going further still, Illich interprets the "nesting" and "hatching" of this evil within the church in terms of what the New Testament calls the "Anti-Christ" and the *mysterium iniquitatis* (the mystery of evil). He insists that

> the *mysterium iniquitatis* is a *mysterium* because it can be grasped only through the revelation of God in Christ. This must be recognized. But I also believe that the mysterious evil that entered the world with the Incarnation can be investigated historically, and, for this, neither faith nor belief is required but only a certain power of observation.[46]

What Illich seems to grasp, reluctantly yet insistently, is that the history of the West has been, in effect, an unfolding from the institutionalization and therefore the corruption of Christianity. This corruption, this unprecedented evil, emerges within the church, mutates, and reproduces itself through other institutions.

Illich is saying that, through the eyes of faith, one can recognize that the transformation of the Samaritan's free response into hospitalization is not isolated but instead paradigmatic of other corruptions: how "faith is eclipsed by prediction, hope by planning, and charity by the studied knowledge of the other's needs."[47] In the light of the revelation of God in Christ, one may perceive that the freedom that comes from Christ's call to "go and do likewise" (Luke 10:37) has become transmogrified into what Illich sees as the anti-Christic responsibility of trying to save or change or reform the world by attempting to manage the gospel. Put differently, Illich the historian narrates the arena of "(dis)order and progress" that I encountered in Brazil as the unfolding of development (Truman's gospel) less in terms of the rejection of Christianity than its historical mutation and corruption.

---

45. Cayley and Illich, *Rivers North of the Futures*, 48.
46. Cayley and Illich, *Rivers North of the Futures*, 60.
47. Cayley and Illich, *Rivers North of the Future*, 37.

RECONTEXTUALIZING HUMAN DIGNITY

Thus far in this chapter, I have been following Illich's historical criticism of development as itself a missionary enterprise that manifests a parasitic corruption of Christian mission. The question still remains, What does mission after "(dis)order and progress" look like? In Part Three, I develop a response to that questions in terms of a "convivival turn" that enables the incarnational logic of Christian mission. But as bridge that sets up that what is at stake in making that turn, I want to recall the previous account of incarnational mission and the triad of following, participating, and joining.

The Corruption of Following: Pedagogical Imperialism

The first dimension of incarnational mission focuses on discipleship of following Jesus as a pattern for mission. While this mission clearly includes "making disciples" and teaching others (Matt 28:16–20), Willie Jennings stresses that Christianity's "pedagogical vision [lies] inside of its christological horizon and embodiment."[48] By contrast, in the colonialist encounters with new worlds and new peoples, an inversion took place in which

> theology was inverted with pedagogy. Teaching was not envisioned inside of discipleship, but discipleship was envisioned inside teaching. Pedagogical evaluation was normatively exaggerated, expanded evaluation. The inversion of theology with pedagogy meant that . . . the native subject was formed into a deficient barbarian in need of continuous external and internal self-examination and evaluation.[49]

Here, Jennings exposes how the colonialist legacy "produced a reductive theological vision in which the world's people become perpetual students,"[50] an insight that relates directly to development as a (neo)colonial strategy that enacts what Jennings calls "pedagogical imperialism."[51]

As Arturo Escobar points out, development promoted a mode of encountering "Third World" populations through the twin pillars of

---

48. Jennings, *Christian Imagination*, 106.
49. Jennings, *Christian Imagination*, 106.
50. Jennings, *Christian Imagination*, 112.
51. Jennings, *Christian Imagination*, 112.

professionalization and institutionalization.[52] In other words, development enacted "a top-down, ethnocentric, and technocratic approach . . . a system of more or less universally applicable technical interventions intended to deliver some 'badly needed' goods to a 'target population.'"[53] The apparent "success," that is, the explanatory power of development, relied on its capacity to conceive human flourishing "as a technical problem"[54] and to generate a "discursive formation"[55] that linked scientific knowledge to the power of technical application. What is significant here is recognizing the way that "the production of the Third World through the articulation of knowledge and power is essential to the discourse of development."[56]

Escobar's insights shed light on Illich's attempts to expose the shadow side of "the gospel of global Education and Development."[57] The problem, Illich argues, is that there is nothing clean or innocent about this coupling of education and development. Education—once repackaged as an institutional product and subsequently a commodity—has been placed inside the development paradigm that Illich and other post-development thinkers view as a project of recolonization. As part of this project, the coupling of education and development turns on two basic assumptions: (1) that we inhabit an "inner and outer world" that may be isolated one from the other and rendered "subject to management"; and (2) that both worlds "need to be filled with some product which is scarce."[58] As understood by Illich:

> Education names the institutional enterprise which furnishes the pupil's world with skills, competence or attitudes which are both scarce and—in the educator's judgment—socially desirable. Development names the corresponding institutional process by which the outer world, conceived as an environment of scarce resources, is transformed into a social space filled with goods of economic value.[59]

52. Escobar, *Encountering Development*, 44–47.
53. Escobar, *Encountering Development*, 44.
54. Escobar, *Encountering Development*, 52.
55. Escobar, *Encountering Development*, 10.
56. Escobar, *Encountering Development*, 12.
57. Prakash and Stuchul, "Voice in the Wilderness," 511.
58. Illich, "Eco-pedagogics and the Commons," 7.
59. Illich, "Eco-pedagogics and the Commons," 7.

Indeed, Illich refers to education and development as "social construction enterprises" that generate "self-fulfilling prophecies about [humanity]," operating in tandem as "mighty motors to create scarcity, expand the assumption of it, intensify the sense of it and legitimize institutions built around it."[60] By describing them in this way, Illich draws our attention to the way these twin forces construct and usher us into a "commodity-intensive reality" that Illich also refers to as "economic space."[61] Inside the social construction enterprise of education and development, the only space that counts is economic space. This is a space where reality becomes subject to measurement and management, where everything has economic value and, as such, is rendered as a potential commodity destined for consumption. Within this space, scarcity is perceived as a certainty, or a basic human condition. In other words, development extends economic space, while education, as used here by Illich, prepares, conditions, and adapts us for living inside of it.

At one level, what is significant here is recognizing how development promotes what Jennings describes as "pedagogical imperialism."[62] To make the connection with incarnational mission more explicit, however, one can frame this issue theologically in terms of Docetism, not as the explicit "denial of Christ's materiality, or his becoming fully human" but as "faltering in the face of a new materiality,"[63] a failure to discern how new encounters and new spatial logics can be shared incarnationally. As Jennings puts it,

> The point here is the continuation of the logic of the incarnation ... it is the logic of discipleship and mission, the going forth in the triune name. The denial of incarnational practice is precisely the failure to go forward as the Son came forward and wishes to go forward in intimate joining.[64]

The Corruption of Participation

The second dimension of incarnational mission relates to participation in Christ as the power for mission. As Langmead points out, if the first

60. Illich, "Eco-pedagogics and the Commons," 10.
61. Illich, "Eco-pedagogics and the Commons," 11.
62. Jennings, *Christian Imagination*, 112.
63. Jennings, *Christian Imagination*, 112.
64. Jennings, *Christian Imagination*, 113.

dimension, that of following, is isolated from the second, there is the risk of conceiving our role in mission as entirely "extrinsic" to the Incarnation. Thus, one crucial aspect of this second dimension relates to participation in Christ as the empowering source of grace and freedom for incarnational mission.[65] In relation to this second dimension, what Illich highlights is the way that dependence upon technological artifacts and/or institutional mediation can displace interpersonal dependence and the role of Christ as the enfleshed mediator between God and humanity (1 Tim 2:5).

Earlier in this chapter, I focused on the way that Illich's early social criticism diagnosed the industrialized and professionalized forms of hubris in terms of the Promethean "corruption [of humanity's] self-image," namely, "a conception of [humanity] as an organism dependent not on nature and individuals, but rather on institutions."[66] With this in mind, I want to return briefly to Illich's "corruption hypothesis" as a way of expanding this notion and how it impinges upon incarnational mission.

In fact, I want to place everything that Illich says about this Promethean fallacy inside of what he says elsewhere and later about the corruption of Christianity. This is not only because the Promethean ideal and the "corruption hypothesis" both illustrate the rise of the technological ethos and a modern drive toward institutionalization over embodied presence, or, a spirit of control over "a spirit of contingency."[67] It is also because thinking in terms of the "prometheanization" of Christian mission might enable and require us to relate a Christian discernment of contemporary "disorder" to technological artifacts and dominant social institutions—including the church.

Here, it is useful to recall that Christian theology has traditionally located a fittingness between (*a*) our being created "in the image of God" (Gen 1:26–28) and (*b*) the Incarnation as "the image of God" (2 Cor 4:4; Col 1:15), the hypostatic union of the fullness of God as well as the fullness of humanity. Similarly, Christian theology has traditionally interpreted the "fall" in Genesis in relation to human pride, the hubristic aspiration to be "like God" (Gen 3:5), and subsequent disobedience by transgressing the limits and conditions for human flourishing set by

---

65. Langmead, *Word Made Flesh*, 52.
66. Illich, *Deschooling Society*, 114.
67. Schroyer, *Beyond Western Economics*, 64.

the Creator.[68] In *Creation and Fall*, Dietrich Bonhoeffer juxtaposes "humankind-imago-dei" with "humankind-sicut-deus" (i.e., the "like God" humanity). Bonhoeffer writes,

> Imago dei—humankind in the image of God in being for God and the neighbor, in its original creatureliness and limitedness; sicut deus—humankind similar to God in knowing-out-of-itself about good and evil, in having no limit and acting-out-of-its-own-resources. . . . Now [after the fall] humankind stands in the middle, with no limit. Standing in the middle means living from its own resources and no longer from the center. Having no limit means being alone. To be in the center and to be alone means to be sicut deus. . . . Losing the limit Adam has lost creatureliness.[69]

Notice how Bonhoeffer's biblical juxtaposition of two ways of being human resonates deeply with Illich's contrastive reading of Epimethean humanity ("humankind-imago-dei") and Promethean humanity ("humankind-sicut-deus"), respectively. Illich's insights are consistent with both of these traditional understandings, but Illich also brings into focus a distinctively modern twist to the "fall," that is, not just a transgression of limits, but an idolatrous dependence upon institutions as "saving artifacts." Holding the critique of the Promethean ideal and the "corruption hypothesis" together, we are in a position to hear the disquieting question implied by Illich's insights: What if the congruence between being created in the image of God and being conformed to the image of the Son has been intercepted and corrupted by either (*a*) the colonial attempt to re-create others in our own image or (*b*) the neocolonial attempt to create and live through dominant institutions and technological artifacts that, in turn, re-create humanity in their image? This double-question echoes the missiological question that I raised earlier in Part Two: Into whom or what are we being included?

Again, there are connections with Illich to be made regarding (*a*) the Promethean ideal and (*b*) "the corruption of the best is the worst," as an impetus that brings to the surface a difficulty for theology, in general, and incarnational mission in particular. The focus of Illich's work in the late 1960s and through the 1970s raised a question with which contemporary theology has not yet adequately engaged, namely, "the mutual

---

68. Bonhoeffer, *Creation and Fall*, 113.
69. Bonhoeffer, *Creation and Fall*, 113, 115.

definition of man's nature and the nature of modern institutions."[70] At the same time, Illich's coupling of anthropology with institutionalization, specifically, and more generally with technological artifacts, raises another series of questions: Could it be that the mediation between God and humanity that is unique to the Incarnate Savior (1 Tim 2:5) has been displaced and corrupted via the mediation of institutional and technological forms whose rituals of inclusion tempt us toward a "technopelagian" confidence in our own efforts and grasp for power? Could it be that these human creatures whom God fashioned "according to the image of God" (Gen 1:26–28) and who were destined to be conformed to "the image of God's Son" (Rom 8:29) have been lured into trying "to create the world in [their own] image," only to find their image being corrupted according to the image and likeness of their artifacts, the work of their own hands?

These are some of the questions Illich's thought raises because of how Illich juxtaposes a common theological idea, that of humanity created in the image of God, alongside an uncommon one: humanity (re)created in the image of its institutions as saving artifacts. More specifically, Illich invites us to reconsider how incarnational mission not only requires ecclesial embodiment, but also how our ecclesial forms can either distort or enhance our collective capacities to participate in Christ. In this technological milieu, Illich suggests, the ongoing ecclesial task is to cultivate forms of church that challenge us to "deeper poverty instead of security in achievements; personalization of love . . . instead of depersonalization by idolatry; faith in the other rather than prediction."[71]

The Corruption of Joining

The third dimension of incarnational mission deals with God's incarnating dynamic as the encompassing framework for mission. As Langmead suggests, this third dimension also deals with mission as inculturation or contextualization. Paradoxically, Illich points out, "the Church began to define her mission as inculturation in the very decade when all that was left of local folkways had been castrated, becoming raw material for a bureaucratically staged facsimile folklore."[72] In other words, missiology's

---

70. Illich, *Deschooling Society*, 2.
71. Illich, *Celebration of Awareness*, 100.
72. Illich, "Philosophy . . . Artifacts . . . Friendship," 3.

"contextual turn" happened at a historical moment in which the paradigm of development had produced the "measure" for human flourishing.

In order to see how Illich diagnoses and responds to this false universalism of development, I return to his apophaticism as a way of recontextualizing human flourishing in relation to the particularity of the Incarnation. To do so, I consider Linda Woodhead's claim that "one of theology's most important contributions to the anthropological enterprise is to undermine it."[73] This is, no doubt, a provocative claim, but I believe we should not allow Woodhead's boldness to eclipse the subtlety of her position. The paradox of human dignity, she tells us, is that it cannot be isolated "by reference to humanity alone."[74] This is because "our human nature is fulfilled through participation in God, it shares in the mystery of God—and can never be pinned down."[75] Thus, apophaticism does not aim to abolish the anthropological enterprise, but rather it recontextualizes it by "bringing the human into the sphere of the divine."[76]

So, how does this relate to Illich? Hoinacki's observation that at the heart of Illich's theological imagination is an "apophatical theological stance" is helpful here.[77] This insight also complements Eric Fromm's claim that at the heart of Illich's vision is an anthropological core, his "humanistic radicalism."[78] In Fromm's view, Illich's vision is humanistic because what is driving his vision is a concern for "[humanity's] unfolding,"[79] or, to use a term that is more in vogue today: human flourishing. Illich's vision is radical because he continuously questions dominant modern certainties related to human flourishing, for example, progress, development, or consumption. By linking these insights, I want to suggest that not only does Illich's theological imagination revolve around an anthropological core, but also that Illich attends to human flourishing apophatically, not by doctrinally asserting "what the human is" but by historicizing what "being and becoming human" should not be and yet has become.

While Illich's writings do not exhibit a great deal of doctrinal precision, what he ultimately shares in common with the Christian apophatic

---

73. Woodhead, "Apophatic Anthropology," 233.
74. Woodhead, "Apophatic Anthropology," 233.
75. Woodhead, "Apophatic Anthropology," 233.
76. Woodhead, "Apophatic Anthropology," 233.
77. Hoinacki, "Trajectory of Ivan Illich," 384.
78. Fromm, "Introduction," in Illich, *Celebration of Awareness*, 7–10.
79. Fromm, "Introduction," in Illich, *Celebration of Awareness*, 10.

tradition is a crucial methodological insight, namely, that the first move in theological anthropology is not identifying and isolating the properties that "make us human" but rather identifying the One who is "truly human" for our sake.[80] As Bonhoeffer puts it, the "who" proceeds the "what."[81] In other words, the key to theological discernment in the anthropological enterprise is the Incarnation as the decisive "context" for the renewal of our participation in the "divine image,"[82] as well as our joining in God's mission for the world. Thus, the Incarnation is God's flesh coming toward us to give us what we were created for and created to receive: to be joined and enclosed within the circle of life and love that is God (1 John 4:16). The Incarnation is also the human movement toward God with all of its creatureliness. Thus, the Incarnation is both from and toward God, as well as from and toward the world.

To return to Woodhead's claim regarding apophatic anthropology, the theological problem of an anthropology that is decontextualized and severed from the Incarnation is just this: it assumes that humanity can define itself self-referentially.[83] It assumes that humanity is its own measure. The tragic trajectory of this cataphaticism is that "in telling us who we are, it often becomes self-fulfilling, fixing in us the nature it claims to describe."[84]

I want to suggest that Illich's critique of development is most adequately understood in light of this apophatic stance. Illich's early essays in *Celebration of Awareness* advance the basic thesis that life in contemporary Western societies has become based upon certainties that are generated and reproduced by the dominance of historically novel institutions and systems that not only divide the world into over- and underprivileged, but that are fundamentally dehumanizing and, therefore, unsustainable as well. Illich's early writings, then, are manifestos for an alternative path through the detours of development and political revolution alike. In fact, Illich positioned Kennedy and Castro as twin paths inside the same detour, the detour of the narrative of a progressive modernity whose central device is the inclusion and assimilation of the masses into the

---

80. See McFarland, *Difference & Identity*, 14–29; Jennings, "'He Became Truly Human,'" 240–55; Nellas, *Deification in Christ*, 21–104.

81. Bonhoeffer, *Christ the Center*, 37.

82. See McFarland, *The Divine Image*.

83. Woodhead, "Apophatic Anthropology," 233.

84. Woodhead, "Apophatic Anthropology," 243.

expectations of a "better life," which comes from the counterfeit redemptive power of ever-growing industrial productivity.

Seen in this light, the fundamental problem with development is not its inability to close the gap between the rich and poor, nor whether or not it can create better centralized channels by which to counter inequality and grant greater access to scarce resources. Rather, for Illich, the more basic problem is that the development paradigm has projected "a vision of what is desirable and possible" that has "radically distorted our view of what human beings can have and want."[85]

In his later writings, Illich highlights the fallacy of "defining our common humanity by common needs,"[86] a dominant certainty that emerged within the development era. In *Toward a History of Needs* and *The Development Dictionary*, Illich exposes how development discourse about needs presupposes that needs are universal constants, whereas the notion of needs as equivalent to demands for industrialized "package deals" is a fairly recent, post–World War II invention. Moreover, the flaw with this account of humanity is that is distorts creatureliness: human nature is no longer marked by the limits of necessity nor the depth of desire, but rather "by the measure of what we lack and, therefore, need."[87]

However, an appropriately apophatic anthropology, following Woodhead, might undermine the enterprise of defining human nature self-referentially. What Illich offers repeatedly is a critique of development as "the most pernicious of the West's missionary efforts,"[88] which attempts to reproduce "blueprint anthropologies" by defining the needs of others in terms of "Western needs" or commodity dependence.[89] Once naturalized as givens, development becomes the project of meeting these "needs." The flaw with this project is that it is constructed upon a false and overly cataphatic anthropology, that is, the assumption that Western needs are ahistorical constants of a universal humanity. Ultimately, the legacy of needs, as they have functioned within development discourse, has led to a redefinition of humanity in terms of neediness, and specifically, "individual units with input *requirements*."[90] In other words, hu-

---

85. Fromm, "Introduction," in Illich, *Celebration of Awareness*, 181.
86. Illich, "Needs," 106.
87. Illich, "Needs," 97.
88. Illich, *In the Mirror of the Past*, 95.
89. Illich, *In the Mirror of the Past*, 93.
90. Illich, "Needs," 107.

man beings are recast as "institutional avatars," or "cyborgs,"[91] thereby "reshap[ing] the mind and sense of *Homo sapiens* into those of *Homo miserabilis*."[92]

Development, then, operates as an anthropological enterprise that "freezes" a historical moment in which the human condition has already been decontextualized from an integrative account of creation and redemption. Thus, our creatureliness becomes transmogrified into

> limitless dependence, in the sense of accumulating dependent relationships to things, persons, institutions, [which] is something other than the *fundamental* dependence we cannot avoid, dependence on whatever it is that enables our sense of being an agent, a giver.[93]

And so, to speak of Illich's apophatic anthropology demonstrates a way of decentering humanity without deconstructing it. It is created to live from and toward God, to be "alive to God" (Rom 6:11). For Illich, the Christian life is the embrace of life in which we are not the measure of all things. This "not," however, does not mean lack, or *nihil*, but hope in the promise of a gift that we were created to receive and share. The Incarnation confirms and makes possible the creaturely embrace of an apophatic anthropology: an understanding of being human in which humanity is not its own measure, but rather is iconic, looking beyond itself to see itself fully, receiving the fullness of its being from a source that has the power to indwell it, while remaining beyond it. It is neither consigned to the *nihil* of postmodern dissolution nor cast as the "creature-who-plays-God," attempting to re-create itself and others in relation to a false self-image. Thus, the logic of Illich's apophatic anthropology is that the human condition is not adequately conceived in terms of neediness, but rather in terms of a fragile yet promising openness to receive what it does not possess by nature but may receive by grace: to share the life of the One who is "truly human" for our sake.[94]

---

91. Illich, "Needs," 108.
92. Illich, "Needs," 95.
93. Williams, *On Christian Theology*, 70.
94. See Jennings, "'He Became Truly Human.'"

CONCLUSION: WHOSE IMAGE? WHICH FLOURISHING? DISCERNING TWO RIVAL VERSIONS OF INCLUSION

Earlier in Part Two, I referred to Willie Jennings's claim that "Christianity in the Western world lives and moves within a diseased social imagination."[95] Here, in conclusion, I want to return to Jennings's claim by situating Illich's critique of development inside Jennings's call for Christian theology to attend to its ongoing relationship with the "colonial wound." Indeed, Jennings argues that "the colonial wound is real and remains largely untheorized within Western theology."[96] It remains a wound precisely because it impoverishes our capacity to imagine life-giving forms of social inclusion and cultural intimacy into which we are invited to enter *through* "the incarnate life of the Son of God, who took on the life of the creature, a life of joining, belonging, connection, and intimacy."[97] Thus, at the heart of the Christian imagination, there is a renewed and surprising invitation for being joined together with each other and with God. What the metaphor of wound brings into focus is the historical distortions of the Christian relational imagination, or as I have been describing it here, the historical detours or "turnings away" from an original vision. Jennings writes,

> That intimacy [of being joined through the Incarnation] should by now have given Christians a faith that understands its own deep wisdom and power of joining, mixing, merging, and being changed by multiple ways of life to witness a God who surprises us by love of differences and draws us to new capacities to imagine their reconciliation. Instead, the intimacy that marks Christian history is a painful one, one in which the joining often means oppression, violence, and death, if not of bodies then most certainly of ways of life, forms of language, and visions of the word. What happened to the original trajectory of intimacy?[98]

In developing his critical and constructive repair of this "diseased social imagination," Jennings offers three related suggestions that are relevant here. First, to grasp the loss and horror that comes with inclusion within the colonial wound, we have to return to a prior, fundamentally

---

95. Jennings, *Christian Imagination*, 6.
96. Jennings, *Christian Imagination*, 115.
97. Jennings, *Christian Imagination*, 115.
98. Jennings, *Christian Imagination*, 9.

theological error. For Jennings, this is the ecclesial failure of forgetting "Gentile existence,"[99] a loss of memory that effectively effaces the Jewish-Gentile threshold and subsequently the awareness that *goyim*, or Gentiles, are those who were first "outside" before having been brought near (Eph 2:11–22). This means that *goyim* have indeed been included in the promises of God, but it also means that the unfolding of our entrance into the story places us as "outsiders-brought-in" and not as insiders who enfold other people into our own prior forms of belonging and identity. In other words, there is a profound loss of imagination that makes sense of intimacy among those whose lives are marked by cultural, ethnic, or racial difference. The result is at once both a cause and an effect of the colonial wound. The logic of colonial missionary expansion inverts the outside-in into an inside-out. The dominant subjects of this expansion, whether they be white, male, colonial Europeans or "developed" persons, become the measure of whatever "other" they encounter, refashioning them in their own image. In this inversion, there is no room for reception, precisely because of the misperception of the other's dignity—and their own.

Second, in Jennings's account, race displaces place as the determinative marker of identity and difference, and whiteness emerges as the universal or standard by which the fullness of humanity is measured. To the extent that Christian mission operates inside this displacement, it effectively becomes a project of re-creating others, the Many, in relation to the (invisible) image of whiteness, the One. Third, Christian theology now struggles to imagine how the One and the Many might be reconciled in Christ, *the One for the Many*.[100] Therefore, in attending to detours away from "the original trajectory of intimacy," one of the fundamental theological questions that Jennings poses is, "How are the people of God constituted?"[101]

Indeed, Jennings's question is but another way of interrogating the issues of social inclusion, and more precisely incarnational inclusion. In the last chapter, we observed Illich's emphasis on the enfleshed particularity of the Incarnation as the scandalous new possibility and condition for inclusion into a new, unrestricted "we." By the same logic, Jennings

---

99. Jennings, *Christian Imagination*, 25.
100. Jennings, *Christian Imagination*, 259.
101. Jennings, *Christian Imagination*, 250.

affirms the Incarnation as God's gift of "The One for the Many,"[102] and that it is the loss of our awareness of being included through and into this One, who represents Israel, that lies at the heart of the diseased social imagination and the colonial wound. Whereas Jennings takes the eclipse of "Gentile existence"[103] and the dominance of race as the lens to bring the distortions into view, Illich takes the dominance of social institutions and technological artifacts. Indeed, what the racialized humanity and the Promethean/"developed" humanity share in common is a hubristic attempt to assert an idealized humanity, a false universal, that displaces the primacy of the Incarnate One in order to become the "measure" by which the Many can and must be included.

As we saw earlier in this chapter, this notion of an idealized humanity as its own measure characterizes the technological ethos as well as the "technological imperative: all that can be done must be done."[104] As Garrigós also argues, what animates Illich's stance is his desire to respond to contemporary forms of hubris with the recovery of limits:

> Limit has a positive sense in his writings. It is the condition of the possibility of hospitality. In Illich, limit is a threshold and, as such, the boundary that separates inhospitable terrain from the inhabitable, rain and storm from shelter. Without this mark, the gesture that best defines humans would not be possible: [the gesture of] welcoming reception.[105]

Garrigós speaks generally about a "philosophy of hospitality"[106] as an ordering concept for reading Illich. I am concerned here with turning this insight about hospitality specifically toward the practice of Christian mission. Indeed, the colonial wound can also be seen in the way that "Christianity . . . inverted its sense of hospitality . . . claim[ing] to be the host, the owner of the spaces it entered, and demanded native peoples to enter its cultural logics, its ways of being in the world, and its conceptualities."[107] In Garrigós' view, Illich enables us to see not only overt forms of conquest and arrogance but also the subtleties of technological as well as missionary hubris:

---

102. Jennings, *Christian Imagination*, 259.
103. Jennings, *Christian Imagination*, 260.
104. Garrigós, "Hospitality Cannot Be a Challenge," 122.
105. Garrigós, "Hospitality Cannot Be a Challenge," 122.
106. Garrigós, "Hospitality Cannot Be a Challenge," 122.
107. Jennings, *Christian Imagination*, 8.

> Missionaries, experts, planners, promoters of development or democracy, for all their goodwill, are still figures of a perverted charity. Here one sees the terrible danger in every political proposal that promises salvation. Before the arrogance of the technician, Illich counters with the humility of the guest ... [indeed] each of Illich's books may be read as an attempt to recover the blessings of such receptivity in some institutional domain.[108]

Such a posture of receptivity, like the receptivity of Epimetheus, is likely to require nothing less than a "rebirth"[109] of our social imaginations. Translating this insight into a Johannine idiom, Illich invites us to imagine ourselves as Nicodemus before Jesus and to hear once again the invitation to be "born again" so that we may "see the kingdom of God" (John 3:3). This death and rebirth may enable us to evaluate in a new way the dominant institutions that cover the ground upon which we walk and fill the air we breathe in the contemporary technological milieu. Only then, Illich would suggest, might we see the kingdom as the available alternative that Jesus promised it to be (John 3:3).

It is at this point, the question of alternatives, where some of Illich's critics balk: reading his critique of institutionalization as an uncritical anti-institutionalism. As I suggested earlier, however, through Illich's commentary on the Good Samaritan, and through his account of convivial reconstruction, there is another way of reading Illich: namely, as someone who calls us to reimagine and recover structures and modes of collectivity that are fitting for humanity and proportionate with humanity's vocation in the world. Here, it is important to recognize that Illich does not suggest that we can extract personal agency from structures of formation, nor is he suggesting that we can divorce "following the naked Christ" from ecclesial embodiment. Rather, I read Illich as a prophetic voice who "shows how revolutionary a faith Christianity is"[110] and who enables us to overhear the biblical call to repentance—the renewing of our minds (Rom 12:1–2) in a way that does not conform to the dominant script, but rather embraces an alternative one. As a prophetic voice, Illich writes with a twin purpose: to energize us to cling to a "better hope" (Heb 7:19) and to dismantle the false expectations generated by institutional and systemic idols that colonize life—even as they make promises of a "better life" that is to come. This repentance is a matter of discerning

108. Garrigós, "Hospitality Cannot Be a Challenge," 122.
109. Illich, *Deschooling Society*, 105.
110. Cayley, "Introduction," in *Ivan Illich in Conversation*, 54.

between the pattern of incarnational mission, on the one hand, and being conformed to dominant patterns of de-incarnation, on the other.

And this brings us back to Illich's keyword—conviviality. In the light of this sense of hubris that Illich and others have diagnosed as leading to "(dis)order and progress," convivial recovery opens up a way for reimagining the goodness and dignity of being creatures, for embracing limits as a condition for human flourishing. Against the Promethean ideal, he advocates convivial recovery as an alternative pattern of relationship between "persons, tools, and a new collectivity."[111] In this way, convivial recovery is both "fitting" with incarnational mission as well as a practical alternative to the Promethean ideal:

- Instead of the Promethean endeavor that attempts to overcome social ills through enclosure into manipulative institutions, convivial recovery aims to re-embed technological "means" within the limits and "ends" discerned through interpersonal and communal bonds.
- Instead of the Promethean fallacy that assumes humanity is dependent upon institutions (and not other persons and the goodness of nature), convivial recovery aims to regenerate and nurture our collective dependence upon nature (read: creation) and other persons, for the sake of "individual freedom realized in personal interdependence."[112]
- Instead of the "great expectations" of the Promethean ethos as an "ethos of non-satiety"[113] rooted in the perception of scarcity as a basic human condition, convivial recovery aims to cultivate an "ethos of enough-ness," that is, a balance between means and ends that nurtures a common sense of satisfaction and abundance.

In the light of this, it is important to keep in mind that Illich is no more against the appropriate use of technology than he is against authentic missionary encounters. He is against the way the "good intentions" of both can become "distracting from or destructive of personal relatedness."[114] He is against the way the dominance of technological artifacts extends a market-intensive society characterized by disembodied/statistical relations, depersonalized dependence on institutions—primarily the state or

---

111. Illich, *Tools for Conviviality*, xii.
112. Illich, *Tools for Conviviality*, 11.
113. Illich, *Deschooling Society*, 113.
114. Illich, *Tools for Conviviality*, xiii.

market—and false expectations regarding human flourishing. He is for the cultivation of greater awareness in relation to technological innovation and missionary desire alike. Both share "the aim to make life always better . . . ," but the technological has " . . . crippled the search for the appropriate, proportionate, harmonious or simply good life." What Illich promotes is precisely the kind of hope that the Western technological way of life "easily writes off as simplistic or irresponsible."[115]

Illich expressed those hopes in what I call a "convivial turn"—a preferential option for freedom-in-interdependence—which is, in fact, a theological turn. The "convivial turn" is a theological turn because it enables us to reclaim freedom from the false dilemma of either "being in control" through technological artifacts, or from the threat of living in despair. In other words, the cultivation of conviviality enables us to reclaim the freedom of living in hope and of "prolong[ing] the Incarnation."[116]

---

115. Illich, "Philosophy . . . Artifacts . . . Friendship," 3.
116. Cayley and Illich, *Rivers North of the Future*, 207.

Interlude

Overhearing the Gospel according to Samba (Part Two): Missionary Poverty and the "True Welcome"

At the end of Part One, I narrated how the experience of being included in the samba circle (*roda de samba*) became a living parable of the invitation to be included in the "new humanity" that comes into being through the Incarnation (Eph 2:15). In the samba circle, I received and "put on" a new identity as a *brasicano* not by faking or forcing it but by being included and learning to belong to a new "we." In doing so, I overheard a call to what Illich calls missionary adoption: "a rebirth out of love into a new people."[1]

Identities, however, are not static properties; rather, they are formed through encounters, and in a real sense, we become aware of our identities as we enact them through relationships. At the beginning of Part Two, I described how my initial identity and sense of orientation as a missionary-as-*brasicano* clashed with a set of encounters that cast me in the role of missionary-as-professional helper. The initial sense of vulnerability and openness as one who has been *adopted* into a new people slowly and subtly morphed into a sense of being filled with "good intentions." The centrifugal force of these "good intentions" threatened to pull me out of a personal space (of belonging as a *brasicano* inside a convivial "we") and into the professional space of evaluation in which a missionary "us" diagnoses and treats a statistical "them." This question was before me: Which identity would be more determinative for my presence as a missionary?

---

1. Illich, *Church, Change and Development*, 98.

Just as in the samba circle I was able to integrate my initial sense of orientation as an intercultural missionary, so once again, the samba circle became the learning environment through which I was enabled to attend to the rupture of disorientation. The initial orientation that I (re)discovered in the samba circle had to do with internalizing Illich's insight that "the missioner is [one] who leaves his own to bring the Gospel to those who are not his own, thus becoming one of them while continuing to remain what he is."[2] Yet, besides this crucial insight into what Illich calls "missionary adoption," I also overheard an insight into "missionary poverty"—that is, "spiritual poverty [or] detachment which the missioner will have to achieve if he wants to be truly an instrument of the Incarnation rather than an agent of his own culture."[3]

In other words, even as Illich exposed the detours and missionary failures linked to "pedagogical imperialism,"[4] he also cast light on the possibility of a different kind of pedagogical transformation, which one could call "missional cultural submission."[5] For in "The Eloquence of Silence," Illich describes "the spirit of poverty" that is required by missionaries who are fully committed to learning a foreign language by immersion. It is required because "language learning is one of the few occasions in which an adult can go through a deep experience of poverty, of weakness, and of dependence on the good will of another."[6] As Illich describes it, learning the sounds as well as the silences of another language requires an act of love and attention to the one from whom you are learning to hear. I would also say, by analogy, that learning another culture's musical forms requires the same kind of love and attention. For just as we learn to speak language as a flow between words and silence, so too do we learn to play music as a flow between notes and rests. What I discovered in the samba circle was not just the eloquence of silence but also the eloquence of *rhythm*, its power to create belonging. Learning to hear and "keep step" with that eloquence marked the beginning of the healing of the wound that had ruptured not just around me but inside of me as well.

---

2. Illich, *Church, Change and Development*, 113.
3. Illich, *Church, Change and Development*, 116.
4. Jennings, *Christian Imagination*, 112.
5. Jennings, *Christian Imagination*, 148.
6. Illich, *Celebration of Awareness*, 42–43.

O PASSO: LEARNING TO HEAR THE ELOQUENCE OF RHYTHM

My musical journey inside the samba circle (*roda de samba*) goes hand in hand with my study of *O Passo*, the method by which I was initiated into playing with the *bloco*. In fact, the *bloco* incorporated *O Passo*, which is Portuguese for "the step," as its basic methodological approach for dealing directly with two of the challenges that led Lucas Ciavatta to create the method: first, how to develop each musician's perception of the rhythm in relation to the beat; and then, second, how to develop each musician's capacity for playing together as a group.

One of the most striking aspects of this musical apprenticeship was that for the first month we hardly touched our instruments. Or, to be more precise, we used our bodies as our main instruments: stepping in time to sense the beat simply, while clapping and/or saying the musical phrases that we would eventually play on our "proper" instruments. In addition to this form of training using our bodies, we also learned a common musical vocabulary, such as *virada*, *paradinha*, and *convenções*, as well as a simplified system of musical notation using only numbers and letters. Within the first month, we could all find and follow the beat, execute a basic repertoire of traditional phrases, as well as transcribe and read new phrases.

The experience with the samba group also taught me, at times in the most humiliating ways, the truth of our *maestro*'s mantra: "*You can only play what you can hear.*" For just as children do not learn to speak by imitating "adult speech" but by hearing and making "baby sounds" in order to make progress, I learned that I would *not* learn to play Brazilian percussion fluently and with joyful ease simply by trying to imitate Duda playing samba at full speed. Rather, Duda got me to focus on my perception (what I could hear) in order to make "baby sounds" and develop my technique (what I could play). In other words, the fundamental challenge was not how to play faster but to hear the interaction between the beat and "swing" of the rhythm and (then) to be able to play what you hear.

Therein lies one of the paradoxical insights of what learning the "eloquence of rhythm" and learning to be a musician have to do with learning to be an intercultural missionary: namely, right perception of what the other is doing is always a matter of *active reception*—the discipline of learning to *hear* first, then *respond* in a way that is fitting. In this way, musical perception (what you can hear and what the music calls for) precedes musical technique (what you can play). In mission as well as in music, "you can only play what you can hear." So the basic question is not, What should I do (play)? It is, rather, What do I hear through this encounter? And then: What response does that hearing *call forth* in me?

It is significant, however, that the emphasis on musical disciplines and perception is not an end in itself, but rather a means for enhancing group performance. In the context of the group, the musical autonomy of the musician is best understood in terms of another paradox: *relational autonomy*. By putting relational and autonomy together, O Passo seeks to develop a form of interdependence in which the musicians learn to express their bodies and instruments (autonomy) through negotiation with and for the sake of the group and its collective music-making (relationality). "Group," then, names a context in which members experience and practice the difference between just being beside of (*ao lado de*) and being together (*junto*).[7]

This is because one of the most difficult challenges in playing samba in a *bloco* is not executing the notes of the phrases in isolation, or what Ciavatta calls playing "right"; the most difficult bit is executing the notes in full synchronization with the group, playing "together." In O Passo, Ciavatta expands on what is at stake in his distinction between "playing right" (*tocar certo*) and "playing together" (*tocar junto*) in the following way:

> Playing "right"—playing your part—is only the beginning. Invariably, playing "together" is much more complicated than playing "right." This is because in music, in which the "sounded environment" [*ambiente sonoro*] is necessarily shared, "rightness" depends entirely on "togetherness." But "together" does not mean "annulled by the group," "buried," or "protected from the awareness of one's own deficiencies." "Together" means this: playing your part as a creative individual in order to strengthen and be strengthened by the group that builds up and enriches you even while demanding your contribution and helping you in the process of achievement.[8]

---

7. Ciavatta, *O Passo*, 144.
8. Ciavatta, *O Passo*, 37–38.

THE PEDAGOGY OF THE *RODA*:
ENACTING THE "TRUE WELCOME"

At end of Part One, I juxtaposed the samba circle with the image of a circle from Dorotheos of Gaza, to illustrate the relationship between the love of God (as the center point of the circle) and the love of neighbor (as the points along the circumference of the circle). In Dorotheos's teaching, the image of the circle displays the inseparability of the double commandment to love God and neighbor, showing how the closer one moves toward the center point, the closer the distance becomes between any other two points, as well. Dorotheos's teaching around the circle also displays how the corruption or distortion of love operates oppositionally, or centrifugally, as well:

> The diagram works in reverse as well. If you follow a single line from the center out to the edge again, you notice that all the lines become farther apart as they go away from the center. . . . We cannot love God and hate or even be indifferent to our neighbor. Growth in the love of God also has to include love of those images of God with whom we share the world.[9]

What I experienced in the samba circle was a kind of musical choreography that drew our attention centripetally to the center (toward the *maestro*) and to one another at the same time. At the same time, I experienced a new awareness of how the presence and movement of the body in samba echoes Illich's emphasis on *embodiment* as a precondition for Christian life and mission.[10] To put in bluntly, we neither "samba" (*sambar*) nor "follow" without our bodies encountering and becoming interdependent with other bodies to "keep step" and follow the rhythm together.

What I also experienced in the samba circle was the way the instruments created a vast range of pitch and volume (when played together) while being quite limited when played in isolation. Unlike the range of a piano keyboard that spans multiple octaves and can be played as a solo instrument, a cowbell (*agogô*) usually has two (sometime four) pitches, always in the treble range. Most of the other percussion instruments in the

---

9. Bondi, *To Pray and to Love*, 31–32.

10. As David Cayley points out, one of Illich's key insights was his diagnosis of contemporary forms of "disembodiment, the loss of the inhabited and personally experienced body. . . . This replacement of the dense, concretely situated flesh by an abstract construction was a horror for Illich because, from the perspective of his Incarnational Christianity, it is as a *body* that the truth confronts us, and only through the body that we come to know it" (*Rivers North of the Future*, 40–41).

bloco do not have defined pitches and only resonate for short durations. But it is precisely the way the instruments are limited and complementary that creates the conditions for interdependence, as the *surdo* and the *agogô* need each other for the call-and-response of bass and treble to happen.

Related to the convivial interplay between percussionists and instruments is the refrain that that I often heard in the samba circle: less is more (*menos é mais*). In samba, therefore, the phrase "less is more" is a way of highlighting how the constraints that particularize and limit one's participation in the ensemble can and must be approached as a "liberating constraint."[11] In fact, theologian/musician Jeremy Begbie illustrates how "liberating constraint" relates both to musical improvisation as well as to participation in the body of Christ:

> All the skills which promote reciprocal "undistorted communication"—which should characterize the Church as persons-in-communion—are present in a very heightened form [in musical improvisation]: for example, giving "space" to the other through alert attentiveness, listening in patient silence, contributing to the growth of others by "making the best" of what is received from them . . . in a process of concentrated dialogical action, where the constraint of [ourselves and] others is experienced not as essentially oppressive but as conferring and confirming an inalienable particularity and uniqueness.[12]

Therefore, the samba circle represents a convivial space in which the tools (read: instruments) actually enable human activity and in which "individual freedom [is] realized in personal interdependence."[13] In this way, the sense of limits that are present in the samba circle are "liberating constraints" because they manifest (musical) freedom in the "triadic relationship between person, tools, and a new collectivity."[14]

In undergoing these constraints, I began to sense the difference between the "pedagogical imperialism"[15] that exalts evaluation over belonging and a different pedagogy that privileges belonging as the primary condition for learning. What I learned in "crossing over" into the samba circle—and through Illich—is that there is a massive difference between having a vocation as a missionary (as one "being sent") and becoming

11. See Begbie, *Theology, Music and Time*, chapter 8.
12. Begbie, *Theology, Music and Time*, 206.
13. Illich, *Tools for Conviviality*, 11.
14. Illich, *Tools for Conviviality*, xii.
15. Jennings, *Christian Imagination*, 112.

someone who has embraced what Illich calls "missionary poverty." It is the difference between asserting oneself in the role of host by acting out of "good intentions" and accepting the role of guest by becoming detached from a sense of entitlement to one's own ways for the sake of being receptive to the ways of those to whom one is sent. It is also the difference between merely *trying* to play samba like Brazilians and *learning* to use their instruments and to "swing" in the samba circle with them.

The question that the samba circle raised for me was not, Is it possible to engage in intercultural encounters that are life-giving for host and guest, for the giver and the receiver? The question was, Are we willing to submit to those encounters as guests? Missionary poverty names the disposition of being a guest who arrives open to receive, not assuming the position of the host and giver. If the "colonial wound" names the way the mission in the West has assumed an inverted sense of hospitality that imposed its so-called gifts with "good intentions," then perhaps the healing of that wound begins by exchanging missionary hubris with the "humility of the guest."[16]

As a *gringo* in the *roda de samba*, it was obvious that I was not in a position to lead or even to serve. I was there to learn. I was there as welcomed guest, the one invited to cross the threshold. I was being included in the samba circle. It was obvious that if I were going to learn to play samba, then I would have to submit to the *bloco* and their ways. In the same way that I was included by Mount Level to cross the color line, in Brazil I was included by the *bloco* to "cross over" in the land of samba as a guest.

As I mentioned before, I joined the samba circle because of a friend's invitation. After that initial connection I became an apprentice with the *bloco* because I was drawn into a musical universe that was as captivating as it was demanding. The experience of crossing the threshold into immersion in the world of samba reminds me of a scene in Ken Burns's documentary *Jazz*, in which he describes how Benny Goodman, one of the first white jazz musicians, found himself being drawn into Harlem to learn jazz from African-American musicians.[17] Burns narrates Goodman's immersion into jazz by saying that Goodman was able to "cross over" because jazz made it easy to "cross over." In the same way, I "crossed over" because—as demanding as it was to learn—samba made it easy.

---

16. Garrigós, "Hospitality Cannot Be a Challenge," 122.
17. See Burns, *Jazz*, Episode 4, "The True Welcome."

PART 3—RE-TURN

Taking the Convivial Turn

VIRADA (PART THREE): BEING TURNED BY FRIENDSHIP

IN PART ONE, I began with a *virada* that began to frame a geographical journey in Brazil as an intercultural missionary inside the theological journey of discipleship, summarized by Illich's phrase "following the naked Christ." In Part Two, I continued to narrate that learning journey as a kind of rupture, a wound that opened up from an initial sense of orientation leading to a sense of disorientation. That sense of disorientation came from trying to enact Christian mission in Brazil without grasping the historical contours and expectations shaped by "(dis)order and progress" in Brazil. By following Illich (in conversation with other theologians and storytellers) as a guide for navigating "(dis)order and progress," I began to sense the shift from "imagining mission as 'expansion' to understanding and imagining mission as a genuine and deep 'encounter.'"[1]

Here, in Part Three, I continue to narrate my *itinerarium*, or journey in Brazil, by turning to a set of experiences that constellated into a third *virada*—this time, a turning point from disorientation to a new orientation. As result of this *virada*, I began to discern the difference between two ways of engaging in mission: either as a technical problem to be solved or "fixed" or as a relational possibility to be shared. In terms of Christian discipleship and mission, I discovered the possibility of making what I would call a "convivial turn"—a preferential option for freedom in interdependence. I discovered that this so-called convivial turn is also a theological turn. This is because a convivial turn enables us to reclaim freedom from the false dilemma of either (*a*) "being in control" through technological artifacts or social institutions, or (*b*) the threat of living in despair. In other words, I discovered that the cultivation of conviviality

---

1. Bevans and Schroeder, "We Were Gentle among You," 2.

enables us to reclaim the freedom of living in hope and of authentic missionary encounters. And in the most Illichian of ways, I discovered this through friendship.

To describe the journey as a new orientation is not to say I stopped questioning. My experience in serving and leading at Igreja Batista Catuaí included a steep learning curve resulting in pastoral skills, experience, and insights for which I remain grateful. That said, by 2009 that learning curve had given way to a steep *questioning curve* as well.

Put simply, I was questioning our entire model of church. For although we did not use the label "attractional church," that is what we were effectively doing. To be clear, we were not doing "attractional church" based on gimmicky, manipulative techniques; we were doing it out of the conviction that inviting people into services, events, and programs offered by the church was the best way to fulfill the Great Commission as well as our tagline: "Lead to the Way those who are on the way" (*Levar para o Caminho os que estão a caminho*).

Meanwhile, I found myself being pulled in two directions. On the one hand, I was busy going to church to lead services and deliver programs; on the other hand, I was increasingly active in my neighborhood doing urban agriculture with Catholic nuns and neighbors. Over time, I was overcome by the irrepressible urge to question two things:

- the lack of significance that I experienced in what we were doing when we gathered as church; and
- the growing awareness that my sense of vocation and mission was unfolding outside the walls of "gathered church."

In 2009, on a Skype conversation with Claudio Oliver, I unleashed my frustration about feeling divided between a professional/formal role at a church and a deprofessionalized/informal role in my neighbourhood, saying in effect,

> When I gather for church on Sunday morning, everything we do is ostensibly for God's service, yet most of it doesn't make much sense, plus I don't feel alive; when I am in the neighborhood the rest of the week and around the garden with the nuns, my neighbors, and my kids, everything I do makes sense, and I find myself alive to God. But . . . how do I put this—is it ministry? Is it mission?

As I reflect back on that conversation, I now sense that the answer I was looking for was in the very question I was asking. But I didn't hear it that way at the time, and it would take a series of encounters for the shift in mindset to happen. What follows here are three flashbacks that offer snapshots that—when framed together—compose the *virada* of being turned by friendship to receive a new orientation for mission.

SNAPSHOT #1: CLAUDIO'S WORMERY

What I remember from the first time that I met Claudio was being introduced through him to the thought of Ivan Illich—particularly Illich's talk "To Hell with Good Intentions." What I remember from the second time I went to visit Claudio was meeting his worms! When I say worms, I mean red wigglers, or *Eisenia fetida*, if you prefer the Latin taxonomical name. The visit occurred in 2008, at a time when Claudio and his family were still living in the center of Curitiba, on the fifth floor of an apartment building. I noticed that Claudio kept making short visits to his balcony. When I asked him about what he was doing, he called me to his balcony and showed me his wormery and his vertical garden: varieties of lettuce as well as root crops growing inside recycled two liter bottles. These were filled with the rich compost taken from his wormery. In response to my questions, Claudio explained to me how it worked: instead of treating all of his food waste as garbage (*lixo*), he fed it to his worms, which then turned what used to be garbage into rich soil.

As he tended his wormery and the garden that was growing around it, Claudio told me some of the backstory of what led me to this scene on his balcony. He explained that he grew up on the edge of a *favela* in Niterói, Rio de Janeiro. He had also wanted to work the land and work with animals, but as a first-generation university student, there was the pressure (both internal and external) to have a professional career. So, he ended up training to become a dentist. Now, more than twenty years later, he explained that he was working his way back to the earth, back to the soil that he longed to care for. "I am on the fifth floor, but you can only start from where you are," he said.

While I was fascinated by his description of how this fifth-floor garden worked, what impressed me most were the reasons for which he was doing this. Claudio explained that his little balcony garden was an experiment in finding responses for treating creation as creation, and not as garbage, for honoring the Creator as Creator, and for offering signs of hope and life in the midst of so much waste. When I mentioned wanting to do this from my fourth-floor balcony, instead giving me a pep talk, he gave me a warning instead: "Of course, you can do a wormery from your balcony, and you should. But I have to warn you that if you do, it is the most subversive thing that you can do inside your house." I must have looked perplexed, so to give me a visual prop, Claudio picked up a decomposing banana peel out of his wormery to make the point: "In the beginning, God created and said, 'It is good.' This banana peel that I am holding is 'good.' When God sees it, God says, 'It is good.' And if God says it is 'good,' then who gave us the right to call it garbage [*lixo*]? By whose authority do we get to call this banana peel *lixo* and treat it like *lixo*?" Here Claudio paused for a while, then said, "The truth is we are not authorized to treat it like *lixo*. And if you begin to handle your own food discards—like this banana peel—as creation instead of *lixo*, then it will never be *lixo* again. You will see it as creation, and you will rethink what *lixo* is and what we are called to do with creation. So, man, it is subversive because composting food waste is about learning to repent and rethink how we treat God's good creation."

SNAPSHOT #2: THE SISTERS' NURSERY GARDEN

Over the next few months, I discovered how right Claudio was. If what happened around the wormery on his balcony was my "come to Jesus" moment in terms of creation care, then what happened around the wormery on my balcony was the beginning of a journey back toward creation. I began to see not just banana peels but all of what God created as good and worthy of my attention. Becoming "evangelical" about this new ritual of transforming what was *lixo* into soil, I connected with a few of my neighbors who decided that they wanted to get involved. We set up a community wormery on the ground-level bike shed, and ground-level neighbors started offering their small plots as community grow sites. From the fourth floor, I was gradually making my way back to the soil of the earth—one wormery and one square meter at a time.

During those initial months of reconnecting with the soil, I also got to know the Claretian sisters who ran a nursery only three blocks away. In fact, Sister Francisca, who was director of the nursery at the time, would also become my spiritual director. After sharing with her about my newfound connection to the soil, she lit up and without missing a beat proceeded to show me a vacant area behind the nursery and next to the orchard. She explained, "The sisters have always wanted to have a community garden to tend with the children of the nursery and to supply the kitchen. We have the land here, and we have the tools. What we need is someone to get it going and coordinate it. Could that be you?"

I was not about to say no to Sister Francisca, and that is how I soon found myself in a green space the size of a football pitch working with a team of volunteers and neighbors to transform the tall grass and weeds into a garden. I was no longer confined to a few pots on my balcony or a few small plots in our apartment complex. I was back in the garden, and from there my imagination turned back to the story of God creating us and placing in a garden to care for it (Gen 2:15). I was back in the garden, and from there I began to realize that just as God came to meet God's human partners and walk with them in garden, so too I was meeting God there. In fact, on one particular workday, it happened that no one showed up. I was there by myself for several hours getting on with the work in the garden. I realized that I was not upset or even disappointed that I was there by myself. Then, with my knees on the ground and with my hands in the soil transplanting seedlings from the greenhouse, a phrase came to mind from St. Irenaeus: "The glory of God is the human person fully alive." It was as if God whispered to me that phrase—which I heard so often quoted in seminary some ten years before—so that I would hear it afresh and see what was happening around me. What was happening? In the garden, I was discovering a way to become alive to God. I was discovering that the garden was not an ideal place to "get back to," as if nostalgically returning to a lost paradise. I was discovering the garden as a demonstration plot for finding and sharing the fullness of life that begins in a garden (Gen 1–2) and ends in a garden city (Rev 22). In doing so, I rediscovered the invitation to bring the garden with us—wherever we are.

SNAPSHOT #3: DONA RAQUEL'S *QUINTAL*

One of the things that I learned from keeping a wormery is that not everything goes in a wormery. For example, worms do not thrive with acidic foods, so I quickly learned to bury our discards of citrus fruit instead of giving them to the worms. But what about those times when you have too much leftover bread, or potatoes, or rice? When I went back to Claudio with this question, he said that if you cannot keep bread and starches in the human food chain, then the best option is to give it to animals. He encouraged me to find someone in the neighborhood with chickens and to suggest a swap: free food scraps for some occasional eggs.

It did not take long to find chickens, once I knew that I was looking for them. Soon after the conversation with Claudio, I was cycling in an unpaved area less than two blocks from our apartment when I heard a rooster. I followed the sound and was led to a simple *chacara*, an old-style farmhouse that would have been common before the waves of urbanization turned most of the area into apartments and high-rise buildings. Arriving at the *chacara*, I found the rooster and a flock of two dozen hens. With them, in the *quintal* (yard), I found the chicken-keeping neighbor that I was looking for: her name was Dona Raquel.

Dona Raquel was as enthusiastic about showing me her hens as she was about making fun of my Portuguese accent. She was not used to hearing *gringos* speak Portuguese with an American accent, but once she got over the novelty of hearing my Portuguese, she was all ears. When I suggested that we begin a little neighborly experiment in bartering food scraps for produce, she was all in. From that day on, I would collect and deliver food discards that her chickens could eat, and occasionally, she would give us some of her urban free-range eggs.

A few months into our experiment, I noticed that Dona Raquel's *quintal* was getting increasingly untidy with litter. She did not seem to be bothered that her chickens' living conditions were not in order, but I was bothered. Eventually I brought it up: "Dona Raquel, I have noticed that there is a lot more garbage in your *quintal* than before. Would you like me to help you to tidy it up?" Whether she was surprised or confused by my offer, I honestly do not remember. I just remember that she said yes.

I organized a workday that coincided with a visit from Claudio to Londrina, in part because I wanted Dona Raquel to meet the Brazilian friend who had inspired me. On the day of the litter pick (trash collection), however, I felt less than inspired. For several hours Claudio and I picked up litter from Dona Raquel's *quintal*. Not only did we end up doing it *for* her, we ended up doing it *without* her. She was not even in the yard while we were there. At one point, she called out to say that she needed to run an errand and that she would return after a while.

In the midst of what began to feel like a neighborly misfire, I began to ask the why questions: Why were we doing this? Why, exactly, had I offered to help? In my mind's eye, Claudio and I had come there to litter pick *with* Dona Raquel. In her mind, I had offered to help, and she clearly understood that as an offer to do it *for* her. As I began to process this out loud with Claudio, I began to question my own motives: "Maybe we are here today not because Dona Raquel needed us to do a litter pick, but because I needed to be needed. Maybe it is because I could not help that I offered to help in the first place. Maybe my default setting is still dialed to 'good intentions,' and that is the reason we are standing here picking up her litter..."

I suppose I expected Claudio to say something like, "You are being harsh on yourself.... It was a nice gesture..." But knowing Claudio, I expected he would not say something nice; he would say something true. Which is exactly what happened: "What if we are not here because of her need or your mixed-up motives—whatever they may be? Sure, you could ask, Does Dona Raquel need us to do this for her? You could ask, Did you offer to help out impulsively, from 'good intentions,' and because you see yourself as Mr. Helper? But I have a better question: Even if we knew that Dona Raquel—or any other neighbor—did not need our *help*, would we still treat them as a neighbor? Even if we knew that this little corner of creation would carry on just fine without us, would we still treat it in a way that honors God as creator? Let me suggest an answer to the question 'Why are we here?' that does not depend on your diagnosis of her needs. Let's just say we are here to make an offering to God—to worship God by caring for this little bit of God's creation. If we can do something because it honors God—whether or not it meets someone else's needs—then that is a better why. So if you are feeling strangled by the cord of 'good intentions,' then cut the cord! Ask what honors God, and do that. How did Illich put it... 'to hell with good intentions'? But just remember: the way to cut the cord of 'good intentions' is not by doing nothing, but by doing what is good in and of itself."

As we continued as our litter pick in Dona Raquel's *quintal*, I found myself flashing back to my first encounter with Claudio and how he introduced me to Illich's 1968 talk "To Hell with Good Intentions." That is when I began to understand what Illich was getting at when he challenged US "do-gooderism" (as he called it) and called on short-term missionaries to renounce their "good intentions." Now, with Claudio's reframe in Dona Raquel's *quintal*, I was beginning to grasp not just what Illich asked them to renounce, but also what he wanted them to embrace: Illich called it gratuity.

> Is there another word for the nonpurposeful action which is only performed because it's beautiful, it's good, it's fitting, and not because it's meant to achieve, to construct, to change, to manage? ... The Samaritan acts because his action is good, not because this man can be saved or not saved, not because this man needs medical attention, or needs food, but because, imagining that I am the Samaritan, he needs me. What the beaten-up Jew's presence evokes in the Samaritan's belly is a response which is not purposeful but gratuitous and good. And I claim that the recovery of this possibility is the basic issue ... the possibility that a beautiful and good life is primarily a life of gratuity, and that gratuity is not something which can flow out of me unless it is opened and challenged through you.[2]

In Illich's lexicon of concepts, gratuity names that kind of action that is good, right or fitting (whether it is empirically useful or not). It was precisely the gratuitous act that Claudio was inviting me to embrace in Dona Raquel's *quintal*. The sense of the "coin dropping" on that day—of knowing the difference between "good intentions" and gratuitous action—was a moment of insight that crystallized nearly two years of conversations with Claudio. In the most Illichian of ways, then, I discovered the answers that I was seeking through friendship as the "source, condition, and context for the possible coming about of commitment and like-mindeness."[3] In reflecting on my friendship with Claudio and how that has shaped me, the point is not that our friendship binds us together because we think and act the same. Rather, it is because of the bond of friendship that we are both willing to be transformed into new ways of thinking and acting.

As a case in point—which may even sound a bit trivial—Claudio and I both have a bumper sticker that reads, "Treat the earth as if your life depends on it—Gen. 2:15."[4] Over time, I decided to turn that bumper sticker into a laptop sticker to serve as a daily reminder of a few insights that have come to me through friendship with Claudio. First, it expresses

2. Cayley and Illich, *Rivers North of the Future*, 226–27.
3. Cayley and Illich, *Rivers North of the Future*, 147.
4. See www.restoringeden.org.

the theological impact of Gen 2:15—the inextricable connection between humanity and soil (*humus*), expressed originally through a play on words between *adam* (literally, the "earth creature") and *adamah* (the fertile soil from which God created *adam*). Second, I display it because it so concisely paraphrases the first biblical "job description" given to humans—namely, to observe and serve *adamah* (Gen 2:15). Third, I want to have a regular reminder that caring directly for *adamah* is a way of connecting deeply with creation and aligning my action with the promise "See, I am making all things new" (Rev 21:5).

Given my ecclesial background and formation, I had a long way to go to understand "treat[ing] the earth as if your life depends on it" as an expression of my decision to "accept Jesus as my personal Lord and Savior." In fact, I had to undergo what Pope Francis has called an "ecological conversion."[5] In my twenties and thirties, I studied academic theology; I could analyze the anatomy of theological systems; and I could even recite key facets of a Christian doctrine of creation. But did I actively treat the earth as if my life depends on it? Probably not. The turning point for my "ecological conversion" did not come in a classroom, or through a book. It happened in the most unlikely of places: by a wormery on the fifth floor of an apartment building through words spoken by a friend.

I say "turning point" because for the last ten years I have been trying to live more deeply into the ongoing "ecological conversion" that was triggered on Claudio's balcony. A basic insight to which I keep returning is this: by going back to that first "job description" given to humans—observing and serving *adamah* (Gen 2:15)—I discovered that there is a way to share life, ministry, and even mission from the ground up. I am not saying it is the only way, but I am saying that it is the way I discovered to cut the cord of "good intentions" and align with God's good intentions for the world.

---

5. See Pope Francis, *Laudato Si'*, 102–4.

7

Back to the Future
Or, the Re-turn of Hope as a Social Force

WHEN ILLICH WROTE ABOUT "the recovery of hope as a social force" in *Deschooling Society*, he wrote during a time when hope was a revolutionary watchword and key to the thinking of the first-generation Latin American liberation theologians. These liberation theologians, no doubt, shared Illich's concern about the recovery of hope as a social force, as well as Illich's sense that hope is not a function of human planning and power, but rather that hope finds its source in God's promise and gift.[1]

The twist in Illich's conception of hope, however, is a twist that contrasts the dominance of the Promethean stance with the rebirth of an Epimethean one. As we saw earlier, Promethean means "foresight," and writing in 1971, it seems clear that Illich was at pains to show how Promethean foresight did not translate into or cohere with the liberationist emphasis on revolutionary witness grounded in walking together in solidarity toward God's promised future. The Promethean way of looking ahead meant and still means the techno-economic rationality by which we plan, engineer, and attempt to control the future, doing so in order to maintain a way of life centered around addictive and unsustainable patterns of consumption. To be conformed to the Promethean ethos, which Illich also calls "an ethos of non-satiety,"[2] is not compatible with the future promised by Christian hope. In Illich's lexicon, the Promethean

---

1. Illich, *Deschooling Society*, 105.
2. Illich, *Deschooling Society*, 113.

ethos "counterfeits" hope by transmogrifying a posture of anticipation into one of Promethean expectation. Here, expectation names a posture of entitlement and possessiveness that tries to secure an outcome, when the future can only be anticipated by trusting in a promised gift.[3]

In Illich's terms, then, one simply cannot be Promethean and live in hope. Restated in more explicitly theological terms: Promethean humanity cannot embrace the dignity of creatureliness and attempts to transcend it by trying to live in Act 5, or in a one-act play, assuming, either way, that humanity must write and complete the ending to the drama. Epimethean humanity embraces both the fragility and goodness of its creatureliness, recognizing that it lives in "hopeful trust"[4] of a good Giver, and therefore lives now (in Act 4) in the light of its trusting hope for a good end (Act 5).

In returning to Illich's call for the recovery of hope and its difference from its Promethean counterfeit, it is also important to recognize what has changed since 1971. "Rising expectations"[5] accurately described the dominant mood of post–World War II industrialization and economic booms. That period was still arguably the last years of the golden age of the development decades. It was before the landmark publication of *The Limits to Growth*, which presented the urgency of searching for alternatives to the twin forces of ecological degradation and economic growth. That period was also before the 1973 economic recession that, among other things, exposed the fragility of linking economic growth to foreign oil dependency. It was a time before the effects of industrialized hubris, more commonly known now as the economic and ecological crises, became mainstream concerns.

Some forty years after Illich's first published indictment of the Promethean ethos, there are still rising expectations, but the difference is that the fragility of the Promethean enterprise and the side effects of the Promethean ethos have been exposed. Some still cling to "rising expectations," but there is a growing sense that there is no abiding hope in "expecting" to reform dominant social institutions, be it the nation-state or the market. There is a growing sense that neither the nation-state nor the market can solve all social ills, a sense that things are not generally improving, but possibly getting worse. For this reason, I would suggest

---

3. Illich, *Deschooling Society*, 105.
4. Illich, *Deschooling Society*, 114.
5. Illich, *Deschooling Society*, 105.

that returning to Illich's distinction between Promethean expectation and the rediscovery of hope is all the more relevant and urgent today, and to do so, I want to situate Illich once more in relation to voices from the "two tables" that I introduced in Part Two.

THE AMBIGUITY OF *ESPERANDO*: ON WAITING AND HOPING

At Table Two, I turn to Portuguese sociologist Boaventura de Sousa Santos, a scholar-activist whose recent work has focused on new social movements (NSMs), specifically on the World Social Forum.[6] Through his engagement with the World Social Forum, Santos's research highlights "the re-emergence of a critical utopia, that is to say a radical critique of present-day reality and the aspiration to a better society."[7] Santos juxtaposes critical utopia with the dominant conservative utopia of neoliberal globalization and the way that market dominance and its laws offer only "a closed horizon, an end to history."[8] Santos suggests that this conservative utopia has established global monocultures, thereby resulting in "the waste of experience."[9] He goes on to link the recovery of critical utopia with a "turning back" to the past in order to reincorporate social experiences that have been eclipsed. He does so for the sake of recovering conceptions of human flourishing that are possible alternatives to the global monocultures produced within the conservative utopia.

I turn to Santos here not only because he approaches the question of utopia or hope in a way that resonates with Illich's stance of thinking "in the mirror of the past" but also because he is a voice from the table of "other storytellers" (Table Two) who has mingled directly with the table of the theologians (Table One). In 2005, on the margins of the Third-World Social Forum, Santos was invited to address the First-World Forum for Liberation and Theology. His topic was the role of religion and theology in the contemporary world, an appropriate request given that two-thirds of the delegates at the WSF identified themselves as "religious." In his address to this largely religious audience, then, Santos's basic point is that critical theory (his area of expertise) and theology can and should

---

6. See Santos, *The Rise of the Global Left*.
7. Santos, *Rise of the Global Left*, 11.
8. Santos, *Rise of the Global Left*, 11.
9. Santos, *Rise of the Global Left*, 31.

work in tandem. In other words, as a neo-Marxist sociologist, Santos is quite happy to tell theologians that theology, like critical theory, is not just about understanding the world as it is but also about this world's transformation. On this basis Santos believes theology has a part to play. To do so, he insists, it must grasp the growing discrepancy "between current [social] experience and expectations of a better world."[10]

Santos suggests that through the revolutionary impulse of the late 1960s, the call for reform meant change "for the better." A radical shift in the meaning of reform, however, means this concept is no longer synonymous with "positive social change." Calls for reform abound, and yet, argues Santos, the gap between negative social experience and expectations seems to be ever-widening: "Today, when we see a reform, we know or we have the expectation that it will lead to something worse, not better."[11]

The result is a growing shift toward what Santos calls an "uncivil society."[12] By "uncivil," Santos is suggesting the way in which reform has given rise to the apparent spread of political democracy, defined as electoral representation, coupled with increasing signs of social fascism, something he sees manifested through regimes of heightened surveillance, control, and "security." Within this inversion of reform, he argues, the freedom of citizens atrophies into the freedom of consumer choice. Thus, the agency of citizens, or, at least, their sense of their own capacity to accomplish things by direct action, becomes more and more circumscribed within the tyranny of consumerism and consumption. Beyond the sphere of consumption, a conglomerate of social and economic powers and institutions extends its reach into the overall shape of lives. This controlling reach, he argues, is symptomatic of an "uncivil society,"[13] a society in crisis and on the edge of chaos. Santos captures the existential pressure of coping with such incivility with a wordplay on the verb *esperar*, which means either "to wait" or "to hope." He claims that in contemporary conditions of incivility, we live "*em espera, mas sem esperança*"—that is, "in waiting, but without hope."[14]

Santos recognizes that theology, in its colonizing and extremist manifestations, has played a significant role in the shaping of incivility.

---

10. Quoted in Peixoto, "Boaventura: 'Não faz sentido,'" 1.
11. Quoted in Peixoto, "Boaventura: 'Não faz sentido,'" 1.
12. Quoted in Peixoto, "Boaventura: 'Não faz sentido,'" 2.
13. Quoted in Peixoto, "Boaventura: 'Não faz sentido,'" 2.
14. Quoted in Peixoto, "Boaventura: 'Não faz sentido,'" 1.

Nonetheless, he also affirms that theology has a crucial role to play in the necessary transition from "just waiting" to the recovery of hope—not just the recovery of hope as a concept, but, as Illich puts it, "the rediscovery of hope as a social force."[15] Santos concludes his challenge to theologians in this way: "It makes total sense that salvation exists in another world; what doesn't make any sense is the notion that salvation doesn't exist in this one."[16]

Some might argue that invoking salvation is a curious trope from Santos, the sociologist. In fact, it is wholly congruent with his insight regarding the critical function of theology. For Santos, if theology is going to remain critical of the dominant social forces that reduce social experience to "just waiting," and if theology is going to celebrate hope in the midst of this waiting, then it must give an account of its hope (1 Pet 3:15b), the hope in which we have been saved (Rom 8:24).

I read Santos here as a critical friend who wants to know if theology can face "incivility" and chaos without flinching and without projecting an illusion of control. Can theology be radical without resorting to manipulative forms of witness that displace others through fundamentalism and violence, or more subtly through captivity to the cultural logic of neoliberal globalization and a global economy? Can it offer "signs of salvation" that transform "just waiting" into hope in action? In effect, Santos is asking, Can theology speak into the reality of threatening disorder to resist it and embody a "living hope" (1 Pet 1:3) through a promise regarding not only an "afterlife" but "life otherwise," that is, another way of life together?

THE LONG REVOLUTION

At Table One, I turn to Tim Gorringe as one of the theologians who has taken seriously Santos's line of questioning. In his theology of culture, *Furthering Humanity*, Gorringe explores, among other things, how Christian theology is capable of engaging "the continuing fallout of modernity"[17] and the signs of contemporary incivility, especially the coupling of a hegemonic global economy with the threat of ecological collapse.[18] Gor-

---

15. Illich, *Deschooling Society*, 106.
16. Quoted in Peixoto, "Boaventura: 'Não faz sentido,'" 3.
17. Gorringe, *Furthering Humanity*, 262.
18. Gorringe, *Furthering Humanity*, 262.

ringe reads the postmodern turn critically, alongside Frederick Jameson, in terms of "the logic of the market," "the captivity of consumer choice," and, therefore, "the absolutization of individualism."[19] Like Santos, Gorringe is against the waste of past social experience, and he believes that the way forward lies with recovery and the reincorporation of religious/theological experience:

> Doubtless we are in a new situation.... If it is true that human beings are *homo orans*, creatures which pray and contemplate, at least as deeply as they are *homo sapiens*, and if, therefore, the idea that the great religions would all disappear was a rationalist pipe dream, then these religions will have to build on the new situation and not repress it. At the same time, if there is anything to be learned from the sum of human experience so far, it is that no society can be structured around the principle that "anything goes." Limits are vital not just to ecological but to cultural and spiritual life. They represent guidelines for the long revolution, the process by which we become and remain truly human.[20]

Here, I cannot do justice to the nuance and complexity of Gorringe's extensive treatment of culture, power, and mission; rather, I want to highlight how he gestures toward reincorporation of past theological experience in order to envision a "third way" between cultural imperialism and cultural relativism. For Gorringe, this third way entails a double-awareness. First, the church must recognize its complicity in the religious imperialism that refashions the other in its own image and renounces this as a way of negotiating difference. Second, the church must not capitulate and retreat into a "benevolent relativism."[21] Neither is necessary; neither is possible as a way of continuing faithful Christian witness. What is necessary and possible, Gorringe argues, is "rethinking mission and evangelism."[22] Thus, in a situation "characterized by the imperialism of the market and the—postmodern—disintegration which follows from that,"[23] Gorringe asks two related questions: Where does the church stand? And what does the church offer to the ongoing task of "the long revolution"?[24]

19. Gorringe, *Furthering Humanity*, 262.
20. Gorringe, *Furthering Humanity*, 262.
21. Gorringe, *Furthering Humanity*, 262.
22. Gorringe, *Furthering Humanity*, 262.
23. Gorringe, *Furthering Humanity*, 262.
24. Gorringe, *Furthering Humanity*, 262.

What I find striking about his approach to "the long revolution" is the way Gorringe turns back toward the past in order to attend to clues for enacting a renewal in the present. What is more, he makes two moves that resonate deeply with an Illichian perspective. First, like Santos, he seeks to rehabilitate the significance of "a 'residual' form of culture."[25] By residual, Gorringe does not mean backward or "out of date."[26] Rather, the residual "can represent a challenge to the present which effectively shapes the future."[27] In Santos's terms, the residual makes visible forms of social experience that are yet available but that the monoculture of linear time tries to eclipse. This is why Gorringe insists that the church must respond to the hegemony of the market and cannot flee to the past. In other words, it does not reincorporate the residual by "a regress to a pre-modern fantasy world" but by "an appeal to the wisdom of the past."[28] This "turning back" to reincorporate a treasury of wisdom represents the church's way of making social experience of the past available in the present. Ultimately, this turning back "represents, as it has always done, a call to metanoia, repentance and a new way of doing things."[29]

Second, this metanoia, or renewing of the mind (Rom 12:2), does not culminate in passive or detached reflection but rather in renewed action. Reincorporating the prophetic wisdom of Isaiah, Gorringe insists that this will lead to "action for justice, action for liberation and action for peace for both people and planet."[30] Extending the logic of Isaiah, this will be action that refuses "to accept capitalism as the narrative of the world,"[31] action that brings forth "a new kind of economy, an economy for life,"[32] while enacting "*a change in cultural attitudes* [which] *is essential to that.*"[33] This action is grounded in the reality of the Incarnation and resurrection, and so it will necessarily challenge dominant assumptions about what is possible. It will be action taken in hope, by taking

---

25. Gorringe, *Furthering Humanity*, 263.
26. Gorringe, *Furthering Humanity*, 263.
27. Gorringe, *Furthering Humanity*, 263.
28. Gorringe, *Furthering Humanity*, 263.
29. Gorringe, *Furthering Humanity*, 263.
30. Gorringe, *Furthering Humanity*, 263.
31. Gorringe, *Furthering Humanity*, 263.
32. Gorringe, *Furthering Humanity*, 263–64.
33. Gorringe, *Furthering Humanity*, 264.

for granted "that history under God both can be and is full of surprises because it exists within the field of force of God's kingdom."[34]

In the light of these two voices who advocate a "turning back" in order to rediscover hope, it is important to highlight that while turning back could be enacted as a nostalgic flight into the past, it does not have to be that. Indeed, these voices resonate with Illich's stance of viewing the present "in the mirror of the past," not as a nostalgic return to the past itself but as a call to enact hope in the present.

REIMAGINING RESPONSE-ABILITY: ACCOUNTING FOR THE HOPE WITHIN US

In the last section, I highlighted the significance of hope in Illich's theological imagination, specifically his emphasis on hope as a way of return, a way of turning back, from an illusion of control over the future. For Promethean expectation "tries to compel tomorrow," whereas "hope enlarges the present."[35] Indeed, the following quotation from Lee Hoinacki captures the sense in which Illich's stance embodies "living hope" (1 Pet 1:3):

> Because of his rootedness in his own tradition, Illich knows that no word or action is complete on its own. The current running through everything that Illich writes or does is an anticipatory belief in his action's ultimate eschatological consummation. The power of his practice—in life and art—derives from his recognition that he faces a crisis, that is, a crossroad. There are only two choices for him: Either he follows the contemporary world in its postmodern *acedia*, or spineless boredom, sauntering toward nihilism, or he lives in hope, eyes fixed on a future eschaton.[36]

To unpack that quotation, I want to link the Illichian theme of hope to the closely related theme of responsibility, doing so once again by situating Illich in relation to two other voices.

In her work entitled *Dreamworld and Catastrophe: The Passing of Mass Utopia in East and West*, Susan Buck-Morss offers a narration of the history of the twentieth century as the dreamlike "construction of mass

---

34. Gorringe, *Furthering Humanity*, 264.
35. Cayley, "Preface," in Cayley and Illich, *Rivers North of the Future*, xix.
36. Hoinacki, "Reading Ivan Illich," 6.

utopia."[37] What makes her narrative so compelling is the way that she shows how both the capitalist and socialist visions have been, in fact, two variations on the common theme of mass utopia. Buck-Morss argues that this form of utopia is nothing other than the common vision of an industrialized modernity in which technological progress promises, packages, and delivers the "good life" to the masses, whether through privatized accumulation of capital or through state-driven collectivization.

The problem, she tells us, is that this "dream" is transitory, and with its abandonment the political landscape has become a truncated vision of personal, or individualized, utopia, coupled with collective political cynicism. Neither of these stances offers a constructive way forward, and, as she explains, we need to gain a different perspective on our entrenchment in the present historical moment:

> "History" has failed us. . . . There is real tragedy in the shattering of the dreams of modernity—of social utopia, historical progress, and material plenty for all. But to submit to melancholy at this point would be to confer on the past a wholeness that never did exist, confusing the loss of the dream with the loss of the dream's realization. The alternative of political cynicism is equally problematic, however, because in denying the possibilities for change it prevents them; anticipating defeat, it brings defeat into being. Rather than taking a self-ironizing distance from history's failure, we—the "we" who may have nothing more nor less in common than sharing *this* time—would do well to bring the ruins up close and work our way through the rubble in order to rescue the utopian hopes that modernity engendered, because we cannot afford to let them disappear.[38]

Buck-Morss wants to renew a political sensibility of the collective, one that is forged out of contemporary fragments. To do so, she argues that we must "come to terms with the mass dreamworlds at the moment of their passing."[39] This, she insists, is the first step toward illuminating the terrain of the contemporary political landscape, thereby navigating between the extremes of nostalgically clinging to a passing dreamworld, on the one hand, and cynically waiting around for an imminent catastrophe, on the other.

---

37. Buck-Morss, *Dreamworld and Catastrophe*, x.
38. Buck-Morss, *Dreamworld and Catastrophe*, 68.
39. Buck-Morss, *Dreamworld and Catastrophe*, x.

Even though she does not use the dramatic categories of "epic" and "lyric," introduced in earlier chapters, Buck-Morss clearly sees how the passing of the dreamworld of mass utopia results in a tragic fracturing of both the epic and lyric dimensions of human existence. As she sees it, an epic (comprehensive) account of catastrophe has replaced the narrative of mass utopia, and the lyric (personal) dimension has atrophied into a privatized utopia.

What I find most striking about Buck-Morss's account here is not the content of the hope, a revitalized leftist vision of cosmopolitan democracy, but the orientation toward the past as the way of locating "our" hope. As she puts it, we must "bring the ruins up close and work our way through the rubble" because we cannot afford not to do so. Still, Buck-Morss's hope is a not an eschatological hope but a modern hope, and the urgent task, she tells us, is to "rescue the utopian hopes that modernity engendered." While I appreciate the urgency of Buck-Morss's proposal to move beyond postmodern fragmentation and the individualism of privatized utopias, I also wonder whether that urgency renders our responsibility for a collective utopia inside or outside the Promethean shadow. In other words, I wonder whether the collective utopia she imagines is reducible to "results which are planned and controlled by [humanity]."[40]

To further emphasize the importance of relating hope to human responsibility, I turn to Dietrich Bonhoeffer's 1932 lectures, later published as *Creation and Fall: A Theological Exposition of Genesis 1–3*. The methodological insight that shapes these lectures is that theology is always an exercise in "beginning from the middle."[41] Two aspects of this seem most significant for my work. First, we—as creatures—live and think "in the middle." We live embedded in history and without direct knowledge of history's beginning or end. To illustrate this, Bonhoeffer describes our condition as living within history as within "a circle."[42] His argument highlights the creaturely limits of thought and knowledge. Thus, he suggests, not only does our thinking necessarily originate and remain conditioned by our access to knowledge within the circle of history, but also, Bonhoeffer contends, against the Hegelian idealism of his time, that we cannot think our way outside of the circle. The Bible, however, begins by speaking of the beginning in which God created the heavens and

---

40. Illich, *Deschooling Society*, 105.
41. Bonhoeffer, *Creation and Fall*, 28.
42. Bonhoeffer, *Creation and Fall*, 26

the earth (Gen 1:1), a claim that poses the following question: Who can speak of the beginning? Bonhoeffer's answer is that there are two and only two possibilities:

- either a claim from someone who has been a liar from the beginning (John 8:44);
- or a claim from someone who truly was with God "in the beginning" (John 1:1–2) and whose Word comes to us "in the middle."[43]

Bonhoeffer's theological exposition relies on the insight that the key to understanding our beginning and our end, and therefore how we "account for the hope that is in [us]" (1 Pet 3:15b), is our access to and trust in the witness of another. This, Bonhoeffer argues, means that the witness of the Incarnate Word is the key not only to reading the world as creation but also to the methodological dynamic commonly described as contextualization. Thus, following Bonhoeffer, I want to suggest that for theological inquiry to be adequately contextual, it must always be an exercise in recontextualization, the repositioning of our own knowledge and witness in and through the witness of the Incarnation.

As I read Bonhoeffer, then, for theology to "begin in the middle," it must share Buck-Morss's urgency for recovering an awareness of our own historical locatedness. Yet, as an act of hope, it also has to remain open and alert to the revelation of God in Christ, or the Word, as the Christian source of hope—which is also the alternative to conceding history's "failure."

In this way, I believe, Illich's understanding of the Incarnation exemplifies Bonhoeffer's axiom about beginning from the middle, a methodological awareness of both the fragility of Christian witness as well as its foolishness. This awareness eventually led Illich to the conclusion that "one of the ways of understanding the history of Western Christianity is as a progressive loss of the sense that the freedom for which Christ is our model and our witness is *folly*."[44] This echoes a Pauline sense of foolishness (1 Cor 1:25) and freedom:

> That God could be man can be explained only by love. Logically, it's a contradiction. The ability to understand it depends on what my tradition calls faith, but that too is something which contemporary people have trouble grasping. Faith is a mode of

---

43. Bonhoeffer, *Creation and Fall*, 28–29.
44. Cayley and Illich, *Rivers North of the Future*, 58, emphasis mine.

> knowledge which does not base itself on either my worldly experiences or the resources of my intelligence. It founds certainty on *the word of someone whom I trust* and makes this knowledge which is based on trust more fundamental than anything I can know by reason. This, of course, is a possibility only when I believe that God's word can reach me. It makes sense only if the One whom I trust is God.[45]

Thus Illich's understanding of history resonates with and yet differs significantly from the Buck-Morss position outlined earlier. Both thinkers are acutely aware of our ineradicable situatedness in the middle of history, the sense in which we have been "placed." Yet unlike Buck-Morss, the source of Illich's hope is not "the utopian hopes that modernity engendered," but rather a hope that "centers desire on a person from whom we await a gift."[46] Thus, like Bonhoeffer, Illich locates the source of hope by returning to the difference the Incarnation makes, as the Word made flesh (John 1:14), and as the renewed anthropological horizon that may be prolonged as a movement within history, a movement that works through and not above the rubble and ruins of history. In other words, Illich shows us a theological way of beginning again in the middle, a return to the difference the Incarnation makes.

Illich's comments also resonate with Bonhoeffer's idea that the revelatory character of the Word makes possible something we would not have imagined or done otherwise, as it comes to us in a fallen or "broken middle."[47] That is, it comes to us as a source of hope precisely "as we bring the ruins up close."[48] Illich also reminds us that what the act of God's revelation makes possible is not an escape but an encounter, not so much a way out as a way through. This enables us to renew our awareness of how to find our way amidst the ruins. Or better, it is to sense the fundamental difference between the despair of being trapped under the rubble and ruins and the hope of being turned toward a face, and knowing that God is coming toward us, even through the face of the closest Samaritan. The real question, therefore, that Illich's stance poses for Christian mission is not whether God's Word can reach us but whether we are willing to embrace response-ability, that is, to live by responding to the call of

---

45. Cayley and Illich, *Rivers North of the Future*, 57; emphasis mine.
46. Illich, *Deschooling Society*, 105.
47. See Rose, *The Broken Middle*.
48. Buck-Morss, *Dreamworld and Catastrophe*, 68.

"Another," to live in trust and hope before the face of the One who speaks, even in the middle of history's rubble and ruins.

To put the matter in this way is to recognize how Illich provokes us to discern between different conceptions of responsibility. From an Illichian perspective, to claim responsibility from within Prometheus's shadow would mean to live and act from the illusion that the future is in our hands, and therefore we can control and direct it to the shape of our desires. Such "foresight" leads to the hubristic conclusion that there is no such thing as "too much" or "too far." This temptation, Illich tells us, is not a responsible solution to a problem, but rather an illusion that must be renounced.

Indeed, as one of the contributors to *The Post Carbon Reader* makes clear, regarding multiple sustainability crises, we are not dealing with problems that correspond with isolatable, one-off solutions; we are dealing with predicaments.[49] Nevertheless, while predicaments are undesirable, persistent, and seemingly insurmountable, there is no reason to treat them as absolute or final. Predicaments are conditions that bear a sense of urgency, and it is an urgency that is not overcome by one-off solutions; rather, predicaments elicit a range of responses.

Illich's critique of Promethean responsibility and his call for the "rebirth of Epimethean humanity,"[50] however, is not for the sake of abdicating human responsibility but ultimately for the sake of amplifying our range of possible and desirable responses. Moreover, in terms of Christian mission, Illich enables us to reimagine our responsibility to become response-able to God's Word that comes to us "in the middle." As a response that reframes mission in terms of our response-ability to God's Word, I turn again to Claudio Oliver and a speech given at the People's Summit for Rio +20, on the theme of "Christianity and the Environmental Crisis: The Church's Role in Sustainability."[51]

> [We are considering] the embrace of responsibility for the planet as an expression of our relationship with God.

---

49. Miller, "Foreword," in Heinberg and Lerch, *Post Carbon Reader*, xvi.
50. Illich, *Deschooling Society*, 105–16.
51. Oliver, "Crise ambiental e cristianismo," 1.

> This possibility, however, implies a risk—that, even without realizing it, we might continue to allow the narrative which drives and informs the agenda and the action of the church to be imposed from the outside, from the center and logic of the present system and of the empire.
>
> [Here's a different center and a different logic.] The relationship between human beings and the earth opens and closes the biblical narrative. We are creatures formed from the fertile soil [in Hebrew, *adamah*]. . . . We are beings of the . . . soil. *Adamah* is the raw material from which *Adam*, or the earth-creature, is made. Or, if you prefer the Latin version, it is *humus*, this fertile matrix of soil, that gives rise to *humanity* as well as *humility*—the virtuous posture or disposition that is fitting with this relationship.[52]

Here, Claudio's argument involves reframing a missional account of responsibility in terms of response-ability to God, and this, he insists, happens by returning to the biblical narrative in order to "remember once more in whose image we were created."[53] Cultivating response-ability, then, is a matter of "allow[ing] God's image in us to determine the shape of our lives."[54] As an alternative to the dominant self-image of human beings as consumers, then, Claudio describes the biblical alternative as follows:

> The first statement of the Bible is that we are created in the image and likeness of a God who is generous, creative, kind and attentive to the details of life. This God puts us in a garden to observe it (*shamar*) and to serve (*avad*) it (Gen 2:15). Looking at the earth as our origin and home and reimagining our primary identity as "people of the soil" is to reclaim vital principles for taking a stand in the midst of a world that is suffering the pains of childbirth and is awaiting the manifestation of those who call themselves "children of God."[55]

The last line of Claudio's speech reflects on creation as suffering the pains of childbirth and the role of those who attend to this pain and suffering. It is a biblical allusion that evokes Illich's metaphor of mission as

---

52. Oliver, "Crise ambiental e cristianismo," 1.
53. Oliver, "Crise ambiental e cristianismo," 4.
54. Oliver, "Crise ambiental e cristianismo," 4.
55. Oliver, "Crise ambiental e cristianismo," 4.

midwifery.⁵⁶ In Romans 8:19, Paul writes, "For the creation waits with eager longing for the revealing of the children of God." He continues by connecting the revealing of "the freedom of the glory of the children of God" (Rom 8:21) with the virtue of hope: "For in hope were saved. Now hope that is seen is not hope. For who hopes for what is seen? But if we hope for what we do not see, we wait for it with patience" (Rom 8:24–25).

I hear a deep resonance between the Pauline passage and what Illich suggests in "The Rebirth of Epimethean Man," namely, that the rediscovery of hope is the key to the rediscovery of human flourishing. Illich's insight makes clear that living in hope in 1971 and, by implication, in 2019 means being freed from living with either rising Promethean expectations or despair. Perhaps the freedom from either assuming a position of control, or the freedom from the fear of not being in control at all, is what it means for us to reveal "the freedom of the glory of the children of God" (Rom 8:21). What the metaphor of midwifery suggests is a mode of incarnational response-ability that exchanges the hubris of being "like God" (Gen 3:5) and "playing God" for the humility of being "in the image of God" (Gen 1:26–28) and "playing creature" once again. To "play creature" means (among other things) to enact hope as a social force in the present, by becoming response-able to the Word while also becoming aware that "it is not the church's task to engineer [the future's] shape. She must resist the temptation. . . . Otherwise she cannot celebrate the wondrous surprise of the coming, the advent."⁵⁷

---

56. Illich, *Church, Change and Development*, 105.
57. Illich, *Celebration of Awareness*, 100.

8

Convivial Recovery as Improvisation

AT THE END OF Part One, I introduced the notion of Christian theodrama as a way of undergirding Illich's theological imagination, particularly his attention to the way the Incarnation enables us to inhabit Act 4 by "reading" our historical moment between the decisive climax of Act 3 and the theodrama's consummation in Act 5. In Part 2, I considered the technological issue of the ethos of progress and development as a Promethean attempt to secure and inhabit Act 5. Here, I want to extend this theodramatic approach by turning to Wells's account of theatrical improvisation as a way of reimagining how convivial recovery enables us to delink human action from the "great expectations" of the Promethean ethos in order to unleash hope as a social force.

REIMAGINING MISSION AS IMPROVISATION

In developing his account of the Christian life "as faithfully improvising on the Christian tradition,"[1] Wells identifies an intrinsic similarity between theatrical improvisation and participation in the body of Christ. He describes this similarity as follows:

> Improvisation in the theatre is a practice through which actors seek to develop trust in themselves and one another that they

---
1. Wells, *Improvisation*, 11.

may conduct unscripted dramas without fear. [Wells's book] is a study of how the church may become a community of trust in order that it may faithfully encounter the unknown of the future without fear. It is a treatment of how the story and practices of the church shape and empower Christians with the uninhibited freedom sometimes experienced by theatrical improvisers.[2]

I do not offer exhaustive coverage of Wells's account of improvisation here; rather, I draw on Wells simply as a heuristic strategy for illuminating how the practical implications of Illich's insights are best approached in terms of improvisational responses to the fundamentally "anti-improvisational" character of Promethean "foresight"—that is, the ethos of planning and control.[3]

As used by Wells, improvisation does not connote a way of acting haphazardly or without intentionality. Rather, improvisation points to the fact that the Christian life is more than "performing a script"; it also provides a way of "describ[ing] the desire to cherish a tradition without being locked in the past."[4] For Wells, then, improvisation names "that process of corporate discernment and embodiment [that is] central to the mission and worship of the church."[5] As such, improvisation is at once inevitable, scriptural, and ecclesial.[6]

Wells's account of improvisation includes an array of practices, but he lists two practices as fundamental for Christian ethics, precisely because they correspond to "God's two primary ways of working." He writes,

> In the incarnation [God] overwhelms humanity with the abundance of his grace. And in the resurrection he uses what humanity has rejected to save humanity. The first [way] describes what ... I call overaccepting. The second [way] describes what I call reincorporation.... If they are the way God works in his gospel, should they not be the principal ways in which the church seeks to imitate him?[7]

---

2. Wells, *Improvisation*, 11.
3. Illich, *Deschooling Society*, 105.
4. Wells, *Improvisation*, 66.
5. Wells, *Improvisation*, 18.
6. Wells, *Improvisation*, 65–66.
7. Wells, *Improvisation*, 20.

Understood in more general terms, overaccepting names the practice "in which a community fits a new action or concept into a larger narrative."[8] To overaccept means to find a "third way" between either merely accepting a state of conditions as they are or trying to deny or block them. Once again, overaccepting names a way of mirroring a divine pattern that occurs throughout the scriptural narrative, and of which the Incarnation offers the definitive embodiment:

> In the annunciation and the nativity, God overaccepts human life. He does not reject his people, nor does he simply accept them: instead he comes among them as a Jew. If the gospel story begins with God in Jesus overaccepting life, it ends with God in Jesus overaccepting death. Jesus does not avoid the cross, nor is the cross the end of the story. In the resurrection, God shows that even the worst offer, the execution of the Son of God, can be overaccepted—even death and its causes can become part of the story.[9]

By "reincorporation," Wells means the way in which Christians draw upon discarded yet vital elements of the past as resources for improvising on the Christian story, in anticipation of its eschatological fulfillment in Act 5. To stay within Wells's thinking, reincorporation is a vital practice for living improvisationally within a theodramatic perspective. This is because "Christian ethics is about learning to take the right things for granted."[10] Christians learn to take the right things for granted precisely by seeing, describing, and acting in the light of the particularities of the Christian story, itself a theodrama. Conversely, taking the wrong things for granted is, more often than not, a matter of the church "mis-placing" itself or finding itself "mis-placed" in the wrong act: "It is not the church's vocation to create (Act One) or to conclude (Act Five) the story. The Messiah has come (Act Three), and it is the church's role to follow in Christ's footsteps (Act Four), not to act as if the fullness of God were yet to be revealed (Act Two)."[11] Indeed, my account of the Promethean enterprise or ethos in chapter 5 amplifies the sense in which the church in the contemporary West has struggled to find its place—how it has both shaped and been shaped by a "diseased social imagination" that takes the wrong

---

8. Wells, *Improvisation*, 13.
9. Wells, *Improvisation*, 135.
10. Wells, *Improvisation*, 143.
11. Wells, *Improvisation*, 143.

things for granted, such as the assumption of scarcity and the imputation of "needs" as the unlimited desire for commodities.

To assert that the practice of reincorporation is congruent with a theodramatic perspective is to argue that "the Christian story is larger and greater in depth and scope than the smaller stories that present themselves."[12] In the light of this assumption, Wells also assumes that reincorporating elements of the past makes it possible and desirable for the church to engage in two crucial improvisational strategies. First, the church is enabled to renarrate "smaller stories," such as the rise of the technological or Promethean ethos, in the light of the "larger story." Second, the church is enabled to address evil, "both in the contemporary world and in the church's own history."[13] Thus, reincorporation names an alternative to trying to escape adverse conditions or merely being overwhelmed by them.

To explore the significance of the past for Christian ethics, Wells suggests that we think of church history as a road "stretching from the past into the future."[14] Of course, roads are paths for embarking and continuing on journeys that take time, but roads themselves also offer distractions, which may divert the pilgrim from the true path. In addition, Wells suggests the pursuit of particular routes may leave behind debris or "discards." This is the point Wells wants to highlight:

> The revelation brought by the liberation movement in the church in the last thirty years is that the earth cast aside in making the road is at least as much a part of Act Four as the road itself. . . . It is now much easier to see, for poor and rich alike, that the losers [the discarded] whose voice has not been heard, are at least as much a part of Act Four as those winners who have written the history. . . . By working with and being with the poor, the excluded, the discarded "earth" . . . and in some circumstances being the poor, the church faithfully follows Act Three and anticipates Act Five. The closer the church is to the poor in Act Four, the more prepared it will be to come face to face with God in Act Five.[15]

Reincorporation, then, is a vital practice, but it is also paradoxical, precisely because it allows us to move toward a *telos*, an end that

---

12. Wells, *Improvisation*, 143.
13. Wells, *Improvisation*, 144.
14. Wells, *Improvisation*, 144.
15. Wells, *Improvisation*, 144–45.

is discernible but not yet realized. The task of the church is to re-turn, or "turn back," to draw on what has already happened in the story. On Wells's reading, the paradox is not merely a phenomenon common to theatre or storytelling. In fact, it operates throughout the New Testament itself: from Mary's *Magnificat* as a reincorporative improvisation on Hannah's song (Luke 1:46–55), to the Gospels' portrayal of Jesus's ministry that recapitulates the roles of prophet, priest, and king in Israel, to St. Paul's passionate meditations on God's ingathering of the Gentiles into a Jewish hope, to other "echoes of scripture" in the New Testament. The lesson that Wells draws from this pattern of reincorporation is that "the key to improvising on the Christian story is not being clever or original, but in being so steeped in the discarded elements of the story that one can draw on them when the vital moment comes."[16] For Wells, what matters more than originality is memory. A church that does not practice reincorporation is a church that has lost its memory, and it is therefore a church "mis-placed" and misled into imagining that it can or must plan its future. Moreover, because "the future is formed out of the past," we are called, paradoxically, to improvise by "walking backwards" into the future:

> The improviser has to be like a man walking backwards. He sees where he has been, but he pays no attention to the future. His story can take him anywhere, but he must still "balance" it, and give it shape, by remembering incidents that have been shelved and reincorporating them.[17]

To employ improvisation as a heuristic strategy for understanding the task of incarnational mission is to take forward a fundamental direction of Illich: namely, that the conditions for "prolong[ing] the Incarnation" arise "out of sharing the good of convivial life."[18] In other words, the cultivation of conviviality enables incarnational mission. In order to develop what Illich calls convivial recovery, I return to his writings of the 1970s and explore them in the context of the twenty-first century.

---

16. Wells, *Improvisation*, 146.
17. Johnstone, quoted in Wells, *Improvisation*, 146.
18. Illich and Rahnema, "Twenty-Six Years Later," 106.

ILLICH ON CONVIVIAL RECOVERY

Writing in the early 1970s, just following *Deschooling Society*, in which he initiated his "project of demythologization" of the consumer society, Illich observed and outlined a response to a crisis. While many, particularly from the left, identified the crisis as "the capitalist control of industrial production," Illich struggled to analyze something that these critics did not see: "the crisis in the industrial mode of production itself."[19]

In chapter 5, I discussed Illich's analysis of the "rituals" of schools as dominant institutions and energy consumption—linked to the private automobile, as a dominant example of radical monopolies. I described how the dominance or monopoly of the industrial mode of production generated an enclosure, inside which personal activities are transmogrified into "needs" that are met by the consumption of "institutional outputs." It was in the light of this imbalance and the false dependency on industrialized modes of production and their products or staples that Illich called for the rebirth of "Epimethean humanity," those who love "people more than products."[20]

In *Tools for Conviviality*, Illich translates his call for the "rebirth of Epimethean humanity" into counter-research on the "convivial reconstruction" of society, "a modern society of responsibly limited tools."[21] Such a reconstruction, Illich argued, entails an inversion of the Promethean ethos permeating "the present structure of major institutions,"[22] thereby reconfiguring "the triadic relationship between persons, tools, and a new collectivity."[23] Illich describes the difficulty as well as the possibility of convivial alternatives to the "the crisis in the industrial mode of production" as follows:

> It is now difficult to imagine a modern society in which industrial growth is balanced and kept in check by several complementary, distinct, and equally scientific modes of production. Our vision of the possible and the feasible is so restricted by industrial expectations that any alternative to more mass production sounds like a return to past oppression or like a Utopian design for noble savages. In fact, however, the vision of new

19. Illich, *Tools for Conviviality*, xi.
20. Illich, *Deschooling Society*, 115.
21. Illich, *Tools for Conviviality*, xii.
22. Illich, *Tools for Conviviality*, xii.
23. Illich, *Tools for Conviviality*, xi.

possibilities requires only the recognition that scientific discoveries can be used in at least two opposite ways. The first leads to specialization of functions, institutionalization of values and centralization of power and turns people into the accessories of bureaucracies or machines. The second enlarges the range of each person's *competence, control, and initiative*, limited only by other individuals' claims to an equal range of power and freedom.[24]

Finding alternatives, Illich tells us, is a matter of convivial recovery. By this he means a way of diagnosing and responding creatively to dominant forms of social addictions generated within the Promethean ethos—that is, our dependence upon institutional outputs that we equate with our "needs." As "addicts of consumption," we find ourselves "having come to demand what institutions can produce, [and] we soon believe that we cannot do without it."[25] Illich also observes a connection between a "life of consumption," as a social addiction, and the common experience of "psychological resistance. . . . Like heroin addiction, the habit [of institutional dependence] distorts basic value judgments. Addicts of any kind are willing to pay increasing amounts for declining satisfactions."[26] As frustrations grow deeper, Illich argues, so too does the sense that there is more to be gained from any given habit. From the perspective of the addict, any available alternative to remaining an addict appears as no real choice at all. The choice seems to be either to say yes to the current condition of dependence or to say yes to the pain of withdrawal and the undesirability of the unknown.

Illich wants us, however, to reframe the "addict's excuse" as a false dilemma. He does not deny that "withdrawal from growth mania [as a symptom of addiction] will be painful."[27] Indeed, he recognizes that this withdrawal will be especially painful "for members of the generation which has to experience the transition and above all for those most disabled by consumption."[28] Illich also recognizes that the alternative that recovery poses is, indeed, a risky one. There is no guarantee of recovery, but he knows that recovery is not just a matter of quitting our addictive

24. Illich, *Tools for Conviviality*, xii, italics mine.
25. Illich, *Tools for Conviviality*, 18.
26. Illich, *Tools for Conviviality*, 82.
27. Illich, *Tools for Conviviality*, 83.
28. Illich, *Tools for Conviviality*, 83.

habits and simply enduring the withdrawal symptoms. Rather, recovery entails a path, a way of return, for those who are willing to take it.

In the early 1970s, Illich described three primary obstacles to this path of re-turning as "the idolatry of science, the corruption of ordinary language, and the loss of respect for the formal process by which social decisions are made."[29] Thus, embarking on the path of convivial recovery meant that:

- in relation to the professional power of the culture of experts who delimit and determine how to focus and apply "scientific knowledge" to "knowledge-consumers," we must demythologize science by the recovery of common sense and the direct sharing of knowledge by citizens;

- in relation to the industrialized monopoly over basic personal activities, and subsequently, "the functional shift from verb to noun" (for example, "I want to walk" becomes "I need transport"), we must recover verbs as a way of designating ourselves as "actors" instead of "consumers";[30]

- in relation to the cynicism and sense of impotence surrounding partisan politics and the dominance of representative democracy, we must recover more radically democratic forms of "social process," "due procedure" and conflict resolution in relation to the "upper limits of productivity, privilege, professional monopoly, or efficiency."[31]

Here, Illich employs the trope of addiction and recovery as a way of diagnosing our disabling social conditioning. From this perspective, there is also no guarantee of full recovery, but the recovering addict knows that embarking on the path toward full recovery is worth the risk, because she has experienced a new sense of freedom.

Convivial recovery, then, is a matter of reclaiming the collective discipline by which we (re)discover the "competence, control and initiative" through which we experience and expand "individual freedom realized in personal interdependence."[32] We become, then, not just "mere consumers" or addicts of consumption, but *recovering* addicts of consumption.

29. Illich, *Tools for Conviviality*, 83.
30. Illich, *Tools for Conviviality*, 85.
31. Illich, *Tools for Conviviality*, 94–95.
32. Illich, *Tools for Conviviality*, 11.

LESSONS FROM NEW SOCIAL MOVEMENTS TAKING THE CONVIVIAL TURN

Illich wrote *Tools for Conviviality* before most of the so-called developing countries of the world had embarked decisively on the path of full and rapid industrialization. Nearly twenty years after its publication, Illich reflected back on that moment of crisis and the possibility of a political inversion in the following way:

> It happened in a way I had not anticipated. In the last words of [*Tools for Conviviality*] I said that I know in which direction things would happen but not what would bring them to that point. At that time I believed in some big, symbolic event, in something similar to the Wall Street crash. Instead of that, it is hundreds of millions of people just using their brains and trusting their senses. We now live in a world in which people misuse most of those things that industry and government do for their own purposes.[33]

More recently, a number of contemporary thinkers and activists, many either close friends of Illich or those inspired by him, have confirmed Illich's insights about "people just using their brains and trusting their senses." In effect, these intellectuals and storytellers have updated and elaborated Illich's insights regarding convivial recovery, casting a vision for and narration of new social movements taking a "convivial turn." I want to attend to those storytellers, whose vision for, and narration of, new social movements (hereafter NSMs) indicates a convivial turn, as a way of shedding light on what it means to think with and after Illich.

In *Grassroots Post-modernism: Remaking the Soil of Cultures*, Gustavo Esteva and Madhu Suri Prakash narrate how NSMs are finding ways of going beyond the options of modernity's Promethean enterprise of social inclusion into either the nation-state or market. For Esteva and Prakash, both close friends of Illich, "grassroots post-modernism" names "a wide collection of culturally diverse initiatives and struggles of the so-called illiterate and uneducated non-modern 'masses,' pioneering radical post-modern paths out of the morass of modern life."[34] It is post-modernism because it seeks to go beyond the certainties of modernity; yet it is grassroots because it derives from "the people" and their autonomous initiatives and ingenuity, realities that do not always reach the

---

33. Cayley and Illich, *Ivan Illich in Conversation*, 117.
34. Esteva and Prakash, *Grassroots Post-modernism*, 3.

consciousness of academic postmodernism's field of engagement. Rather, they argue that a critical narration of modernity needs to be developed in order to move beyond modernity. For the "Two-thirds World," or the "social majorities,"[35] modernity names five centuries of the death of local cultures and the enclosure of common land by the "social minorities." The result is that the "social majorities" have been stripped of traditional and communal strategies and, therefore, have been dehumanized into a condition known as underdevelopment.

Going beyond modernity, then, entails the autonomous survival and flourishing or well-being of local communities through "the creation and regeneration of post-modern spaces."[36] This, in turn, means (*a*) recognizing that modernity offers two great Promethean expectations, the market and the nation-state; and (*b*) reading the signs of modernity's breakdown: perpetual violence in the name of the state, as well as the consequence of collapsing markets. Esteva and Prakash, attempt to chronicle an array of social movements, from the Zapatistas in Mexico to Gandhi-inspired social movements in India, that "are not entering the trap of modern expectations: to count upon the market or the state."[37]

According to Esteva and Prakash, the movement beyond modernity has already begun and is well underway: at the grassroots, social movements and collectives may be marked by an Illichian celebration of awareness and an interdependent creativity, which already charts their own paths to resistance and liberation. In telling the stories of these people and their movements, Esteva and Prakash neither romanticize nor underestimate their efforts, but rather seek to make visible how these grassroots initiatives have discovered that another way is possible and to share inspiration for taking the path toward convivial recovery. Esteva and Prakash state their intention as follows:

> We seek to learn from their communal ingenuity and cultural arts for escaping or going beyond the monoculturalism of the modern world. In exploring their brands of post-modernism, we explicitly resist the urge of all modern experts: "helping" or "educating" the masses to join the mainstream minority march,

35. The terms "Two-thirds World," "social majorities," and "social minorities" are used interchangeably throughout the work of Esteva and Prakash. Because they are used so extensively in their work, I have placed them in quotation marks, but I have not included direct references on every occasion I cite them.

36. Esteva and Prakash, *Grassroots Post-modernism*, 4.

37. Esteva and Prakash, *Grassroots Post-modernism*, 4.

headed onward and forward, towards global progress and development.[38]

In a similar way, Esteva's collaboration in a more recent post-development manifesto, *The Future of Development: A Radical Manifesto*, offers another attempt at narrating this array of NSMs and their efforts at "re-organizing society from the bottom up."[39] Without attempting to homogenize these movements, like Via Campesina, Occupy, and Transition, or underestimate the differences between them, the authors recognize the following "family resemblances":

- they prioritize "community over the individual as the unit of human welfare," thereby advocating communitarianism as an alternative to individualism and/or socialist collectivism;
- they advocate collective action that challenges "the individual's right to consume and the market's right to produce," doing so out of an awareness of the twin threats of the economic and environmental crises;
- they are deeply rooted in traditional wisdom and local culture;
- they do not seek to return nostalgically to a "golden age," but instead "they are dissolving the historical break—the rupture with the past—imposed by modernity";
- they seek to reimagine and enact *buen vivir*, that is, "what living well is in local, rooted terms";
- they represent a range of initiatives seeking to restrict "the sphere of the global market" as "a common enemy"; and
- they compose an ongoing insurrection, "entirely evident but at the same time invisible," precisely because it is a reorganization of society from the bottom up.[40]

According to these storytellers, there is a common denominator that links these NSMs to Illich's vision for convivial recovery. That link is the recovery of *verbs*:

> People are substituting verbs such as learning and healing for nouns such as education and health. The latter define "needs"

38. Esteva and Prakash, *Grassroots Post-modernism*, 5.
39. Esteva, Barbones, and Babcicky, *Future of Development*, 99.
40. See Esteva, Barbones, and Babcicky, *Future of Development*, 99–102.

whose satisfaction depends on public or private entities that are increasingly incapable of satisfying them. The former express the recovery of personal and collective agency towards autonomous paths of social transformation.[41]

Here, the authors highlight this shift from nouns to verbs, from the consumption of heteronomously produced commodities to the recovery of culturally autonomous activities, as follows:

- from food consumption to "eating";
- from education to "learning";
- from health care to "healing";
- from housing development to "settling" or "dwelling"; and
- from market relations to "exchanging."[42]

Two observations follow from the contemporary reading of Illich's notion of "the recovery of verbs." First, these are social movements characterized by improvisation. This means the awareness of contingencies, readiness for surprises, and collective ingenuity that create possibilities that are not captive to the "planning" orchestrated by "monolithic institutions: the nation-state, multinational corporations as well as national or international institutions."[43] Improvisation, then, does not mean attempting to live by sheer spontaneity, doing things "willy-nilly," or "making it up as you go along," but rather by an intentionality "where people refuse to be seduced and controlled by economic laws."[44] "The challenge of the 'social majorities is to continue improvising creative transitions from an imposed universe to the regeneration of their more familiar pluriverse."[45] The primary way they do so is by drawing on available "social experience," wisdom, and cultural practices of the past, and reincorporating them into the present. In doing so, they are creating spaces that do not take the logic/assumption of scarcity for granted.

---

41. Esteva, Barbones, and Babcicky, *Future of Development*, 101.

42. For a more expansive account of this shift from nouns to verbs, see Esteva, Barbones, and Babcicky, *Future of Development*, 101–12.

43. Esteva and Prakash, *Grassroots Post-modernism*, 5.

44. Esteva and Prakash, *Grassroots Post-modernism*, 194.

45. Esteva and Prakash, *Grassroots Post-modernism*, 198.

Second, these are social movements that do not cling to a Promethean sense of expectation; rather, they "shelter" an Epimethean sense of hope. As Prakash and Esteva describe it,

> To express having hope, in Spanish, one can say: "*Abrigo esperanzas.*" *Abrigar* is to shelter, to protect, to keep warm, to entertain, to cherish, to nurse. People at the grassroots have few expectations, if any. But they are continually nourishing their hopes, protecting them, keeping them warm to avoid their freezing in heartless, hostile environments.[46]

Through this chapter, I have been exploring ways of thinking "after Illich." I have explored how convivial recovery relates to, or enacts, reincorporation as a practice of improvisation in relation to contemporary social movements. If, in showing that social movements have been taking up Illichian insights and improvising creatively on them, then the question still remains: What kind of imagination and action would be fitting for inhabiting Act 4? What might a "convivial turn" look like in an ecclesial context? In this next and final chapter I will respond to those questions by developing the congruence between convivial recovery and incarnational mission, turning from "grassroots postmodernism" to a grassroots ecclesial community—Casa da Videira.

---

46. Esteva and Prakash, *Grassroots Post-modernism*, 106.

9

Another World Happens— a View from Casa da Videira

IN THE LAST CHAPTER, I began to explore ways of thinking "after Illich" in relation to contemporary social movements. In this chapter, I want discuss Illich's concern for convivial recovery specifically in relation to incarnational mission. To do so, I turn to Casa da Videira as a way of showing how Illich's insights have inspired a Christian community to "become a community of trust in order that it may faithfully encounter the unknown of the future without fear," doing so as a collective attempt at "faithfully improvising on the Christian tradition."[1]

A PREFERENTIAL OPTION FOR THE POSSIBLE

In 2003, inspired by the horticultural metaphor of Jesus as the Vine (John 15), Igreja do Caminho (Church of the Way) launched Casa da Videira (The Vine's House; CdV hereafter) as both a Christian charity and a missional incubator. As founding pastor, Claudio Oliver originally envisioned CdV as a platform for facilitating the outreach initiatives of the local church (such as urban agriculture, street ministry with homeless people, neighborhood-based community organizing, carpentry, as well as cultural and film productions). While CdV has always focused on relationally based alternatives to program-based forms of mission, over the last ten to fifteen years it has evolved from hosting a range of

---

1. Wells, *Improvisation*, 11.

missional initiatives to operating as a "grassroots ecclesial community."[2] A community member of CdV describes the ethos that has permeated CdV as follows:

> Casa da Videira is a collective of friends and families who have decided to turn their lives, skills and homes into flourishing spaces for balanced, relational and abundant life. It is an expression of a way of life where community, simplicity, tradition, discipline and limits guide its members' lives in consonance with their faith and loyalty in following the steps of Jesus.[3]

To explore how improvisation is a useful term for describing Claudio and his community in Brazil, it is worth recalling Wells's description of the two primary practices for improvisation. First, overaccepting involves situating a present action or concept into a larger narrative framework. Second, reincorporation involves reclaiming ways of acting and thinking from the past and bringing them into the present. Both overaccepting and reincorporation name postures designed to enlarge a range of responses, ways of "getting unstuck" that are faithful to the Christian narrative.

In a real sense, the story of CdV needs to be told within a narrative that goes back at least a decade before the beginning of CdV. That story has to do with the formation of a community that actually began through another act of improvisation—a collective act of overaccepting. That is, the community that birthed CdV began in November 1993, shortly after Claudio and his wife, Kátia, lost their first son. In Claudio's telling of the story, he was incapable of dealing with the pain of that loss. In addition, Claudio's local church had divided over leadership issues, and while Claudio was not the pastor of this church, the confused and disenchanted young people looked to him for a way forward. Instead of trying merely to accept his grief or block the pain, Claudio found another way to respond: by taking care of the teenage youth group of his local church. As Claudio describes it, the only way he could respond to the loss of his own child was to find joy in taking care of others' children as if they were his own, and "leaving the pain of his own loss with God."[4]

---

2. I borrow this phrase from Guillermo Cook's treatment of Latin American base communities from a Protestant perspective. See especially chapter 8 in Cook, *The Expectation of the Poor*.

3. René Seifert, email, January 7, 2014.

4. Oliver, email, April 27, 2010.

Effectively becoming the pastor of the youth group, Claudio began to engage with their questions and their desire to put Jesus's words into practice: "For I was hungry and you gave me food, I was thirsty and you gave me something to drink, I was a stranger and you welcomed me" (Matt 25:35). Thus, soon after having lost a child, Claudio *overaccepted* this loss by caring for "a group of tots," as he describes them, and taking them to the streets of Curitiba with six liters of milk and three dozen bread rolls in order to meet and serve Jesus. From that initial response of overaccepting, a vision of relational ministry and incarnational mission emerged, a vision that the group distilled into the tagline of their incipient expression of church: serving our generation with faithfulness (*servir nossa geraçao com fidelidade*). That phrase points to the coherence that exists between a range of improvisations on the theme of faithful service: from going to the streets with milk and bread, to starting a vertical garden on a balcony, to an urban homestead that has transformed two hundred tons of organic "waste" into soil and conditions for sharing life. In fact, the creative reception of "waste" as unused gift serves as a bridge between overaccepting and the second fundamental practice of improvisation, reincorporation.

If taking bread and coffee to the homeless on the streets was the way that CdV began to improvise, one of the ways that Claudio and his community continued to improvise was by caring for creation, literally by collecting and returning organic waste to the soils of their gardens as a profoundly symbolic example of reincorporation. Indeed, as Claudio points out, the practice of taking bread and coffee to the streets, and the practice of reincorporating tons of organic waste on an urban homestead, share the same desire to serve and the same motivation: namely, that "the best way to be Good News to the friends we meet on the way"[5] is by cultivating and sharing abundant life (*vida em abundância*).[6]

This shift from experimenting with faithful improvisations on the street and to the soil (as well) takes the story of CdV to 2008. For by this time, the members of CdV became increasingly concerned about the widening gap between Curitiba's alleged reputation as one of the greenest or ecologically progressive cities in Latin America and the twin issues of urban waste management and food security. Based on reflections

---

5. Oliver, *Relationality*, 25.
6. Oliver, email, April 27, 2010.

around the triad of "scripture, culture, and agriculture,"[7] CdV launched Quinta da Videira (The Vine's Homestead) as their collective response. In this new configuration, three families relocated within walking distance of each other right on the edge between sprawling gentrification and the long-term residents marginalized and threatened by municipal re-urbanization.

Through its urban homestead, the members of CdV began to experiment with the obstacles and possibilities of engaging the problems of urban waste and food security. They soon made a discovery: the recovery of a sustainable mode of food production in urban spaces lies precisely in the recovery of the biological nutrient cycle—what they call the "cycle of life" (*cíclo da vida*). As a way of subverting the dominant waste management mindset of diverting nutrients into landfills, CdV began to treat their own food discards and others people's "waste" not as a problem "to get rid of" but as a vital asset. In fact, the basic activity of their homestead was, in effect, an urban waste rescue mission:

- vegetable and fruit discards from local farmers' markets and shops become the primary food source for livestock (e.g., chickens, goats, and rabbits);
- wood shavings from the local carpentry shop become a ready supply of carbon-rich bedding for animal excreta;
- bedding mixed with used coffee grounds from McDonald's locks up ammonia to cut the pungent smell of animal urine, while also adding a vital source of nitrogen;
- cultivating an army of earthworms generates rich compost from the animal manure that becomes the basis for a year-round rotation scheme of raised no-till vegetable beds;
- the worms, in turn, are fed to the chickens as a primary protein source and an alternative to dependence upon monoculture-based animal feeds (e.g., soy and corn).

In a real sense, the vision began on the fifth floor of an apartment building by making a "preferential option for the possible." By referring to Claudio's stance in this way, I mean the way his activism operates through a commitment to doing what is *possible* instead of clinging to an *ideal* scenario. In the case of living in the apartment building, opting

---

7. The triad comes Davis, *Scripture, Culture, and Agriculture*.

for the possible meant establishing a worm bin and a vertical garden of lettuce and root crops growing inside recycled bottles. From there Claudio started to experiment in finding a response for treating creation as creation and not as garbage. From there Claudio began to remake soil and grow food not as someone who was looking for a one-off solution to the issues of waste management and food security, but rather as someone who was prepared to sow seeds of possibility and co-inspiration.

Looking back to 2008, Claudio would be the first person to acknowledge his surprise at how those seeds, like the mustard seeds in Jesus's parable of the kingdom (Mark 4:30–32), grew and the impact they have had. Later, he would describe the sowing of those seeds as follows:

> It has been a long road since the day . . . I decided to be a good steward of my little balcony garden, 0.60 square meters, and committed myself to not complaining for what I didn't have but for caring for what was possible. I shared with our team by that time that we were called to do the best with what we had and not dream about ideal conditions. Our role was to be faithful and trust.
>
> From there, we went to our church's parking lot, transforming it into a garden; then to my personal backyard, transforming it into a food garden; then to an urban homestead [of 300 square meters], with chicken coops, urban goats, volunteers, friends, inspiration, lives changed, neighborhood transformation. . . .
>
> Everything we do, no matter how good it is, is only a station, a moment, in our journey. . . . We will call it "experimental," hoping that the people that will come will find a place to experiment and experience LIFE, the abundant kind of life with which we believe God provides us.[8]

What Claudio narrates here is the fruit of this community's capacity to be inspired by a vision without clinging to an "ideal," the willingness to risk and take the next possible step, and then take the next one after that: from 0.6 square meters, to 300 square meters, to the next possible expression. What may be less obvious about Claudio's description is the way this community's journey can be understood as an experiment in incarnational mission that is a creative response to "non-incarnational"

---

8. Oliver, email correspondence, April 2, 2014. Note that in Portuguese the verb *experimentar* can mean to experiment or to experience, a wonderful ambiguity that Claudio is playing on in the original Portuguese.

forms of mission that offer "merely *professional and program-oriented* mission at the expense of relationship and whole-of-life involvement."[9]

As Claudio states in his booklet *Relationality*, the most important issue for Christian mission is not how, but whom:

> What is new and transformational in Jesus' proposal are the questions he raised and the answers he lived out: Who will we include in our relationships? To whom will we extend our embrace? Whom will we receive into our hearts? With whom will we build commonality and conviviality? And . . . to whom will we give access to what the Lord has given us?[10]

From this insight, CdV's vision of community living has emerged as an alternative to the "statistical 'we'" that comes from "being made subject to the same technical management process."[11] Rather, CdV seeks to live out a new "we" that is "born out of sharing the good of convivial life."[12] As Claudio makes clear, their community is a convivial "we" centered on the Incarnation:

> We have been created as local people, in local environments, in a pluriverse of possibilities and expressions, instead of a universe where a unique version of reality offers "once [sic] size fits all" solutions. To arrive in our local contexts, or to move to a different one, requires the same basic attitude that was in Jesus (Phil 2:5–11): to arrive with a willingness to self-empty, in an attitude of service, being available to incarnate, enjoy and interact with the flavors, limits, smells and tastes that are local and from where we can become capable of finding the best way to be Good News to the friends we meet on the way.[13]

What I find striking about Claudio's description of mission is not only his confidence in the power of friendship and his emphasis upon the particularity of the Incarnation as the basis for "re-turning," or the renewal of our "basic attitude" (Phil 2:5–11), but also how his account fits with Illich's emphasis on conviviality, which, in turn, corresponds with his call for the rebirth of Epimethean humanity.[14] For while the

9. Langmead, *Word Made Flesh*, 218.
10. Oliver, *Relationality*, 21.
11. Illich and Mahnema, "Twenty-Six Years Later," 106.
12. Illich and Mahnema, "Twenty-Six Years Later," 106.
13. Oliver, *Relationality*, 25.
14. See Illich, *Deschooling Society*, chapter 6.

Promethean ethos centers on technical or institutional control, planning, and predictability, the Epimethean alternative recognizes that the "good life" cannot be controlled and delivered according to Promethean expectations. Rather, the convivial "good life," toward which Claudio's description points, can only be cultivated and shared by those who are willing to relinquish the Promethean illusion of being "in control" in order to "tend and care and wait upon the other."[15]

By making this link between the incarnational and the Epimethean, then, I want to weave together two threads that run throughout this chapter and to make some points of clarification. First, holding the incarnational logic of the gospel and the Epimethean together is not to equate them, but rather to highlight the idea that there is no "antithesis between the glorification of God and the search for a truly human life on earth."[16] Second, the link between the incarnational mindset and the Epimethean embrace of contingency by living in hope, both described by Claudio above, is another way of saying that the Christian life in general, and Christian mission in particular, are not a matter of technique or control but of presence, faithfulness, and "hopeful trust."[17] In other words, in a technological society, "the fidelity of the Christian community increasingly depends on its competence to express the faith . . . and live in a situation never before interpreted in the light of the gospel."[18] In the next two sections, I want to focus on how the witness of CdV weaves together two complementary strands that run through Illich's thought: namely, how convivial recovery enables vital expressions of incarnational mission.

VIDA PARAOIKIANA[19] (1): "SUBVERSIVE HABITATION" AND THE REINCORPORATION OF "LIFE AROUND HOMES"

In November 2011, a Brazilian national newspaper, *O Estado de São Paulo*, produced a feature article on CdV, describing how three families decided

---

15. Illich, *Deschooling Society*, 116.
16. Bosch, *Transforming Mission*, 426.
17. Illich, *Deschooling Society*, 114.
18. Illich, *Celebration of Awareness*, 93.
19. The phrase "vida paraoikiana" is a fusion of Portuguese and Greek in which the Portuguese word *vida* (life) is modified with the Portuguese adjectival form tacked onto the Greek word *paraoikia*. Around 2009, we coined the term to describe and make sense of the fundamental ecology of relationships that enable life to flourish in

to make an experiment in community living in a *bairro* (residential neighborhood) in Curitiba, Parana. Their community life focused around urban agriculture and sustainable food production. Claudio was quoted in the article confirming that they were "ordinary people" and that the odd thing was how three families growing food together had seemingly become exceptional, and therefore newsworthy:

> We are normal, just as enslaved as everybody else, but we decided to begin to untie the small knots.... Community is the word.... There is no way to think about another way of life thinking that you can do everything by yourself [*sozinho*]. Here we are completely dependent upon personal relations [*relacoes humanas*].... Seriously, I don't know why you are interviewing me. I only do 50% of what our great-grandparents did. Doing half of what they did makes the news. Just imagine if someone were to interview them?[20]

Here, I want to uncover what was not reported in that feature article: namely, why CdV took a turn toward becoming a "grassroots ecclesial community." To do so, I turn to one of Claudio's pastoral letters from 2009. In this letter, Claudio begins to cast a theological vision and rationale for the home-based agricultural and communal regeneration featured in the newspaper article. The background to that letter included collective reflections and dialogues on "grassroots postmodernism," Illich, and biblical reflections on the obstacles and possibilities of moving beyond "going to church" for the sake of being church. That pastoral letter was Claudio's attempt at distilling previous questions, elaborating further questions, and proposing a possible way forward. The letter began with one of Claudio's favorite questions: not *how*, but *is it possible*?

> Is it possible to live out an experience that is genuinely communitarian, biblically faithful, and genuinely spiritual and that can be established as an experience at a human scale? What are the forms of human gathering that can be identified and that might serve as inspiration for such an initiative? If such a proposal is possible, what are the possibilities? If it is impossible, what are

---

a given place. In English, this phrase could be translated "parish life," but we prefer to leave it untranslated. This is because it has resonance not only with the Portuguese term for parish, *paróquia*, but also with Portuguese equivalents for neighborhood, *bairro* and *vizinhança*.

20. Santos, "Agricultores, pecuaristas—e pós-graduados," 5.

the obstacles? Is it possible to overcome them? What and whose interests are engaged [*atingidos*] when this path is chosen?[21]

Claudio continues by pointing out two trajectories that run throughout human history. On the one hand, different cultures have experimented with sustainable social forms of dwelling, such as clans, tribes, villages, *kibbutzim*, ashrams, *faxinais*, *quilombos*, doing so in order to find a balance between human interaction with one another and with the surrounding habitat. On the other hand, different cultures, most especially empires, have repeatedly reproduced an imbalance through forms of social organization that are not sustainable, thereby leading to collapse. After framing their contemporary context in the light of similarities and differences with previous empires and collapses, Claudio highlights the gap that he perceives between the response at the grassroots and the Brazilian evangelical church's (lack of) response to this historical moment:

> The clamor for solutions is coming from the grassroots [*de base social traditional*], and the growing number of news features and publications confirms that each day more and more people are finding ways of experimenting and committing themselves to more communitarian and sustainable ways of life.[22]

Again, the fundamental question that Claudio is asking is this: "Is it possible to live out an experience [of 'being church'] that is genuinely communitarian, biblically faithful, and genuinely spiritual, and that can be established as an experience at a human scale?"[23]

The letter develops a response to that question by raising three further questions. The first is, "In the midst of this, what is the good news that we receive and share?"[24] Claudio's response begins by returning to Jesus's message recorded at the beginning of Mark's Gospel: "The kingdom of God has come near; repent, and believe in the good news" (1:15).

> This [biblical] text . . . suffers an apocalyptic deformation [when it] places the good news out of reach and distant in time. My paraphrase of this verse—which attempts to reclaim the original force of Jesus' message of good news—would be this: "*The absolute dominion/reign of God is within reach; therefore, change*

21. Oliver, "Será possível a igreja?," 1.
22. Oliver, "Será possível a igreja?," 3.
23. Oliver, "Será possível a igreja?," 1.
24. Oliver, "Será possível a igreja?," 4.

> *your whole way of thinking and believe that this is good news."* This means believing that mercy, service, solidarity, love, humility, self-emptying, nonviolence, submission, sacrifice, strength of character, receiving insults . . . mourning, sharing one's possessions, renunciation, depending on others, being hospitable, losing and nonresistance are all "good news." To believe is to trust [in this way of life], which is a difficult step—as well as the fundamental step toward entering and enjoying life under God's reign.[25]

The second question returns to that of social forms, asking whether the basic embodiment of this good news is primarily individual or collective and asserting that is it the latter. This leads to a third question: How might the collective dimension of faith, the *ekklesia*, be expressed? Based on the study of and reflection on the Bible as well as church history, Claudio offers the following insight(s) regarding the form of the *ekklesia*:

> The church, even in its "proto-stage" experienced around Jesus, happens around the home (*kat'oikon*) and the family well before becoming a local church (*kath' hole*) or the church of a city (*hole te ekklesia*), retaining, even with these wider dimensions, the prevalence of the homes and families that served as "ecclesial hosts." It is from this dimension of the home and the family that the church unfolds and develops. One can observe this phenomenon for the initial expansion of Christianity, which took place in homes—both as a structure for receiving and as a support base for the announcing. Not only in the Pauline expansion, but also with Jesus' sending of the seventy, we find the focus on the *home* as the structure which offers shelter and support for those who depend totally on the hospitality being offered.[26]

To be clear, Claudio is not arguing that the "primitive," home-based form of the *ekklesia* is its only valid expression; rather, in this letter he is attempting to recover a discarded ecclesial form. Or, to return to Wells's language of improvisation, his is an attempt to reincorporate a collective expression of the *ekklesia* that has been discarded along the road of church history. The rest of the letter explores this possibility of reincorporation, reading the early church's domestic improvisations, in the midst of an empire, as inspiration for contemporary ones:

25. Oliver, "Será possível a igreja?," 4.
26. Oliver, "Será possível a igreja?," 5.

> The "church-that-gathers-around-homes" (*syn te kay oikon auton ekklesia*) is the base from which an alternative to the empire begins: the humanization of relations, respect for women, the valorization of children, frugality in eating [*alimentação*], the interruption of an economic system based upon slavery and castes, simplicity in lifestyle, non-monetized relationships. Above all, it is in the dimensions of the home that the greatest danger [*perigo*] to the empire gathers: that is, an assembly in search of solutions to problems they confront (the original meaning of *ekklesia*), the flagrant negation of hope in any administration of centralized solution that rests in the hands of rulers, princes, or emperors. The backbone [*espina dorsal*] of the system is broken from inside the home. My hunch is that this possibility was as real yesterday as it could be today.[27]

> [Thus] this domestic form [*organização caseira*] gains its importance to the extent that it does not gather an "affinity group" or out of geographical ease, but sees itself as an assembly called in order to come up with solutions, to deal with problems, to come up with another locus for action, sharing, prayer, spirituality, belonging and loyalty. In this way, it becomes a threat to the status quo, a chink in the system [*um desagregador dos sistema*] and a pathology to be removed [*estirpada*] at all costs.[28]

Claudio concludes the letter as follows:

> We stand before a world that is falling apart through its own certainties, that fragments itself while struggling to hold itself together, unaltered before the imminence of chaos. I close by restating my initial questions: What "good news" can be given to those around us? Is it more institutions, more programs, new and better methodologies, more costs? Is it possible for another way of life to emerge that establishes alternatives to either (*a*) submission to the system and its improvement or (*b*) a negating escape plan [*escapismo negador*] from reality? Would these alternatives waiting to be created come from some kind of genius? Or are they available through the attentive and respectful observation of the past and the grassroots initiatives [*bases sociais*] that have come before us?[29]

---

27. Oliver, "Será possível a igreja?," 5–6.
28. Oliver, "Será possível a igreja?," 6–7.
29. Oliver, "Será possível a igreja?," 7.

Claudio's letter, then, is a pastoral exercise in reincorporating Christian wisdom and the practices of a "domestic church," and in dialogue with contemporary grassroots initiatives and their myriad attempts to reincorporate cultural or "residual" wisdom and the arts of living from the past. It articulates the deep questioning and sense of experimentation at CdV, an attempt at faithful improvisation in recovering a sustainable social form, which offers a missional response to unsustainable social structures and related crises.

In a later document circulated among us in 2012,[30] the shape of this "home-based" ecclesial improvisation gained a conceptual focus around the notion of *paróquia*, the Portuguese equivalent of the English word "parish." In fact, the term *paróquia* comes from the Greek, *paraoikia*, which translates as "around the home" or "life around homes." In that document, Claudio describes *paraoikia* as follows:

> The importance of the term lies in the way it reveals the tension between the immediate surroundings of one's home in relation to the wider social, political and economic context. The home (*oikos*) is inserted [in that wider context] without being totally submitted—the relation the pilgrim has with and in a foreign land. In this sense, the term connotes a sense of movement, pilgrimage and of knowing oneself to be taking a direction toward an alternative that is "established." Here, there is a sense of utopia, not in the pejorative sense of a "non-place," but as a place of coming-to-be, or becoming [*devir*]. The point of reference, then, is the sovereignty of the home over its surroundings, the home as a sign of hope and resistance.[31]

To be clear, the reincorporation of *paraoikia*, or home-based ecclesial life, is not an attempt to immunize the church from its wider surrounding. On the contrary, *paraoikia* names an attempt to regenerate the conditions for convivial interdependence, an alternative "security system" (for example, Mark 10:29–31) to the illusion of independence, or the threat of alienating dependences, in a global economy.

As contemporary US theologian Eleazar Fernandez puts the matter, "Global capitalism is a pervasive phenomenon. There is no place to

---

30. Oliver, "Quinta da Videira." Note that in Portuguese, *quinta* may refer to one's "backyard," or more generally to the area surrounding one's home or dwelling. As used here by Claudio, a functional equivalent for *quinta* might be "urban homestead."

31. Oliver, "Quinta da Videira," 1.

hide outside of the reach and influence of the global market."³² In the light of that description of contemporary imperial or market forces, the *paraoikia* of CdV names an attempt to improvise "ways of faithfulness and resistance while living in the space occupied by global capitalism."³³ For, as Fernandez insists, this vision of the church as household offers a third way between the strategies of escape or conquest, proffering instead a distinct identity defined as a stance of "subversive cohabitation":

> A New Testament concept that corresponds to the posture of subversive cohabitation is *paraoikoi* ("resident aliens"). The New Testament Christians adopted the term *paraoikoi* to speak of their identity in relation to the world (Acts 7:6; 1 Pet. 2:11). As resident aliens, they not only have a specific identity, task and burden, but also a specific promise and destiny. They are expected to behave in accordance with their identity. Following the Johannine reading of the otherworldly identity of Jesus ("not of this world"), resident aliens know that they are "in" the world, but not "of" this world. They do not escape from this world but affirm both being in the world and not letting the world define them.³⁴

The search described in Claudio's letter, then, is not a search for an "ideal" church but a possible way of being church that dwells within the tension of being a countercultural community without becoming a disengaged ghetto, an ecclesial retreat from the world. In dialogue with the voices and examples of "grassroots postmodernism," CdV could be described as an experiment at regeneration, at grassroots ecclesial community, a way of regenerating a new *inside* even "while living in the space occupied by global capitalism."³⁵ Thus, CdV represents an attempt at offering "subversive cohabitation," a way of "dwelling" together for the sake of seeking the kingdom (Matt 6:33), in order to receive, experience, and share good news, the good news of "abundant life" (John 10:10). This might include

- the reincorporation of waste and discarded ways of living in community;
- interdependence through the recovery of verbs—for example, eating together, learning, caring for one another, sharing, exchanging;

---

32. Fernandez, "Church as a Household of Life Abundant," 177.
33. Fernandez, "Church as a Household of Life Abundant," 176.
34. Fernandez, "Church as a Household of Life Abundant," 177–78.
35. Fernandez, "Church as a Household of Life Abundant," 177.

- envisioning the home not as a ghetto or a place of retreat but as a strategic site for the regeneration of people's space, establishing the recovery of dwelling as a verb that makes possible "subversive cohabitation."[36]

VIDA PARAOIKIANA (2): RE-INHABITING THE "PARISH" AS A DEMONSTRATION PLOT FOR ABUNDANT LIFE

In the last section, I focused on CdV's search to imagine and become a "grassroots ecclesial community," a search for recovering or reincorporating *paraoikia*, or what Fernandez calls "subversive cohabitation." Here, I want to explore more clearly what *paraoikia* enables: not only what it is against or seeks to resist but what it is for. I turn, therefore, to Fernandez's metaphor of "the church as a household of life abundant."[37] CdV's turn toward *paraoikia* cannot be understood apart from the intention of establishing a demonstration plot for "life abundant," a place where people can "come and see" (John 1:46).

As a way of reiterating and summarizing the issues raised in Claudio's pastoral letter, the following questions from Eleazar Fernandez are significant:

> How do we imagine the church in the face of today's ecological and economic challenges? What image of the church would be adequate and responsive to our globalized context? What would discipleship and ministry look like in an age of predatory global capitalism that destroys both human beings and the ecosystem?[38]

---

36. It is worth highlighting how Claudio's use of the term *paraoikia* as well as Fernandez's notion of "subversive cohabitation" both resonate with Illich's notion of the vernacular, as a way of specifying how people act and interact within a shared sense of space. Illich describes as the vernacular follows: "*Vernacular* comes from an Indo-Germanic root that implies 'rootedness' and 'abode.' *Vernaculum* as a Latin word was used for whatever was homebred, homespun, homegrown, homemade, as opposed to what was obtained in formal exchange.... We need a simple, straightforward word to designate ... autonomous, non-market related actions through which people satisfy everyday needs—the actions that by their own true nature escape bureaucratic control, satisfying needs to which, in the very process, they give specific shape. Vernacular seems a good old word for this purpose" (*Shadow Work*, 57–58).

37. Fernandez, "Church as a Household of Life Abundant," 172.

38. Fernandez, "Church as a Household of Life Abundant," 172.

Fernandez makes clear that while the church does not act in isolation from other social actors, it plays a crucial role "in reenvisioning an alternative economic paradigm," a role that requires embodying "in its own life and ministries the new economic paradigm . . . an economy of life abundant for all members of God's household."[39] CdV also cannot be understood apart from the process of turning from the illusions and false abundance of the dominant economic paradigm and toward seeking the reality of the "abundant kingdom" through the practices of regenerative, home-based agriculture.

Highlighting the link between this false abundance of the global economy and agricultural practices, Fred Bahnson, permaculture gardener and food activist from the US, makes a vital distinction between the "abundant mirage" and God's "abundant kingdom."[40] The market-based food system that resonates with the global economy, he argues, projects an "abundant mirage," inside which we are conditioned to see a bountiful supply of cheap, convenient food. To call it a mirage is to highlight the falsity of this perception: how the heavily mechanized and oil-based forms of modern agriculture depend upon unsustainable levels of energy consumption; how centralized production and distribution escalates dependence upon a food system in which greater numbers are left either "stuffed or starved";[41] how the simultaneous rise in obesity and world hunger are two sides of the same coin. The task is to see this as a "mirage" and not a reality that we are called to embrace:

> To boast of one hundred bushels-an-acre of wheat while our fields erode into the sea, and to proclaim that by 2050 the world's farmers must double production to feed a growing population while we waste as much food as it would take to feed those people: by such acts, we speak a lie. . . . Our food system is one of the powers and principalities, fallen and in need of redemption. Perhaps the way out of such a system is not to keep shoring up the old system or try to be reconciled to it, but to step around it and create something new. To create what might look less like a *system* and more like *a way of life*. . . . Something that might even begin to resemble the kingdom of God.[42]

---

39. Fernandez, "Church as a Household of Life Abundant," 172.
40. See Bahnson and Wirzba, *Making Peace with the Land*, chapter 4.
41. See Patel, *Stuffed and Starved*.
42. Bahnson and Wirzba, *Making Peace with the Land*, 90–91.

As Bahnson makes clear, the "abundant kingdom" is precisely that alternative reality that we are called to embrace. To seek and enter that alternative is to take seriously Jesus's claim to be the source of "life abundant" as well as the church's vocation to be "a household of life abundant."[43] One way of responding begins by raising the question, "What kind of agriculture would make space for the abundant kingdom of God to take root and flourish among us"?[44]

At a practical level, Bahnson clarifies how taking seriously our allegiance to Jesus and the kingdom does not mean turning to Jesus as an agricultural expert or to the Bible as an agricultural "manual." Rather, it means recognizing agricultural and eating practices as part of the kingdom that we are encouraged to seek first (Matt 6:33). It means repenting of the technological ethos, the illusion that we can and should exercise absolute control over the cosmos, much less absolute control over our food. To return to Illich's distinction between Promethean expectation and Epimethean hope, I would argue, with Bahnson, that in the abundant kingdom, the alternative to this false expectation of the abundant mirage is hopeful trust that "centers desire on a person from whom we await a gift."[45] In Bahnson's words,

> Jesus' admonishment is simply a call to give up control over our daily sustenance. Food is not a product. It is not "fuel for the machine." It is not a commodity or a reflection of our technological ingenuity. It is before everything else an unearned gift from God, manna from heaven, a blessing. As eaters in the abundant mirage, which offers the illusion of control and limitless bounty, we need to learn how to receive food as a gift and not a given. Perhaps a more kingdom-centered approach to eating begins with the radical trust that God's abundance is enough.[46]

More specifically, this sense of trust beckons us to recover and reincorporate agricultural practices that are congruent with and serve the reality of the "abundant kingdom," the practices of regenerative agriculture. Whereas modern agriculture depends heavily on fossil fuels and capital-intensive machinery, regenerative agriculture depends on sunlight and labor-intensive care that enhances the quality of the soil base instead of

---

43. Fernandez, "Church as a Household of Life Abundant," 172.
44. Bahnson and Wirzba, *Making Peace with the Land*, 92.
45. Illich, *Deschooling Society*, 105.
46. Bahnson and Wirzba, *Making Peace with the Land*, 94.

depleting it. By respecting the natural patterns and cycles of the earth, as well as trusting in the abundance of creation, regenerative agriculture can serve as "a means by which we can seek first the kingdom of God."[47] This brings us back to the way that CdV reincorporates the practices of regenerative agriculture in order to "seek first the kingdom."

Their urban agriculture initiative is an experiment organized around two foci: (1) reincorporating organic waste in the cycle of life, and (2) family or home-based food sovereignty (*agricultura familiar*). It may be noted that these regenerative practices not only address the problem of organic and food waste but also promote a form of more sustainable and convivial production by making it possible to reweave the social bond inside the work itself by

> allowing a substantial aspect of one's survival—food—to be under one's control, instead of in the hands of innumerable intermediaries such as the "boss," the market or one's seller. These intermediaries all stimulate/oblige/promote the cultivation of monocultures all the way to the kitchen door by convincing growers that they will generate a sufficient income to buy what goods they need, when in fact, turning over the area around the home into monocultures would only serve to acquire a fraction of the quantity and quality that could be produced in one's backyard or garden [*quintal*]. . . .
>
> The practice of vegetable and animal production around the home [*na quinta*] demonstrates that, even in the face of crisis situations—from debased price quotes or environmental difficulties—it is possible to cultivate a space that guarantees that one can cope with outside pressures on the home and to do so with dignity. . . .
>
> By forming a cycle, both animals and plant are integrated, problems are faced and resolved. . . . Eggs, meats and milk are provided, as well as traditional fruits and vegetables. . . . In addition to this, the soil is regenerated . . . the environment [*ambiente*] becomes more diverse, the social bond is strengthened and dependence upon money as the sole Mediator and the market as the sole Provider is questioned—and sometimes even overcome [*vencida*].[48]

Closely related to Claudio's description of the practices of regenerative agriculture is his description of how they have recovered the verb

---

47. Bahnson and Wirzba, *Making Peace with the Land*, 101.
48. Oliver, "Quinta da Videira," 1–2.

of "eating together." Here, Claudio makes use of Esteva and Prakash's *comida/alimento* distinction. His description also holds together the disciplined enjoyment of the *convivium* within a larger sense of "eucharistic table manners":[49]

> [A]limento is what McDonald's and nutritionism gives to you, *comida* is what your mum makes for you. . . . It's a family together, people talking, warm fresh veggies, sweet potatoes with brown sugar and cinnamon in the morning (for Southerners in your country), corn bread, laughing, crying, prayer, thanksgiving, culture, old histories, yesterday morning histories, little ones learning who we are through food, love, fights, reconciliation, dating, a baby's first meal, planning next lunch or tomorrow's dinner. This one hour of *life* is about remembering who and *whose* we are, from where we come, memories to help us cross difficult times with hope . . . well . . . this is *comida*.[50]

This is a description of the *cotidiano* (everyday life), and yet this description makes profound connections between the recovery of verbs, such as "eating," and the recovery of conditions for sharing abundance. This glimpse into life together at CdV also points to the way one community has entered and shared the common struggle toward convivial recovery with other grassroots initiatives and NSMs in order to regenerate a convivial way of life. At the same time, the fundamental motivation behind what CdV does together is the desire to receive and share the abundant life that comes to us through the person of Jesus Christ. Thus, the recovery of verbs as a means of recovering abundance remains centered on a promise: "I came that they may have life, and have it abundantly" (John 10:10). Claudio elaborates the link between their work and that promise with a riff (or "practical exegesis") on the Greek word *zoe*:

> *Zoe* is what it's like to feel alive. So we understand that what Jesus offers for us is this sensation of being alive, enjoying life, living abundantly. All this starts when we look to those pieces of life, sent to die as garbage, and reintroduce them into the cycle of life, respecting them as part of creation. It's a process that begins in the soil and ends at our tables. We harvest our veggies from this cycle, we breed our animals inside of it. . . . Where the world

---

49. See Wirzba, *Food and Faith*, chapter 5.
50. Oliver, quoted in Bahnson and Wirzba, *Making Peace with the Land*, 106.

sees garbage, we see nourishment; where the world sees death, we see life; in a world of loneliness, we discover community.[51]

Thus, one could understand this community as a grassroots initiative seeking, as Claudio puts it, to reclaim the home as a center of production and not merely a center of consumption, thereby challenging unbridled dependence upon commodities and the cash-nexus. But I would also argue that in the fullest sense CdV is a "grassroots ecclesial community" whose vision of "abundant kingdom homesteading"[52] represents a form of "subversive cohabitation."[53] In a space of about three hundred square meters, one community has shown that it is possible to produce enough food for three families, as well as providing for neighbors, thereby cultivating a demonstration plot for abundant life.

Another way of saying that CdV has been experimenting with faithful improvisation on weaving together incarnational mission and convivial recovery is that CdV's journey has been a consequence of a permanent cycle of observing, questioning, and responding to each moment or context, or as they like to say, "the embrace and celebration of contingencies." This sensibility arises out of the understanding of the Christian life as a journey where the most important thing is not knowing where are we going but knowing with Whom, trusting in God's promise to be with us and recognizing that very often "the sign of God is that we will be led where we did not plan to go."[54]

In June 2014, at the invitation of Mennonite friends, the members of CdV discerned a call to relocate and expand its operation, moving from an urban homestead (of three hundred square meters) to twenty-nine acres in a rural context, just outside Curitiba, in the neighboring town of Palmeira, Paraná. While CdV catalyzed a number of initiatives related to *agricultura domiciliar* (home-based agriculture) over that three-year period, one of the things that CdV discerned is that land-based activism is not their *raison d'etrê*, but rather the communal and practical expression of their Christian faith. Inspired by radical Christian movements (especially

51. Oliver, quoted in Bahnson and Wirzba, *Making Peace with the Land*, 106–7.
52. Bahnson and Wirzba, *Making Peace with the Land*, 104.
53. Fernandez, "Church as a Household of Life Abundant," 177.
54. A phrase that Claudio Oliver attributes to Mennonite origin.

the Bruderhof), they seek to live out the gospel in community, and the range of initiatives they develop around the food cycle are expressions that flow out of their daily reading of Scripture and their commitment to live in community. A second thing that CdV discerned from 2014 to 2017 is its vocation to work with young people. As one member put it, their charism is working with a growing number of young people who "know what they don't want, but don't know what they do want." These young people are not finding a sense of purpose in just having a career; they are switched on about harsh economic realities and making a living while responding to climate change and living sustainably within limits. They know that they don't want to settle for what they see as the status quo and business as usual, but they struggle to find an alternative.

At the end of 2017 the community decided to move back into the city to respond to the demand, converting an underutilized Carmelite convent into a cohousing, coworking live-in Christian community and social enterprise incubator. What they are discovering afresh in the urban context is that the change that they seek in the world cannot be predicted or legislated into existence, but it can be found by embracing contingencies with hope and the sense of anticipation that "another world happens."[55]

Of course, this community's way is not the only way to respond to the economic and ecological crises generated by the predatory nature of global capitalism. The collective witness of this community does not offer an "ideal" way or model to be reproduced. Rather, by its demonstration plot, it offers a possibility and a sign of hope. This is a sign, as Claudio prefers to say, that another world is possible, necessary, and is happening. In Fernandez's terms, it takes seriously the ecclesial vocation to enact its faithfulness through "subversive cohabitation." Yet, it does so without the ecclesial hubris of expecting that the church should exercise control over social issues in order to be effective. In Bahnson's terms, it takes seriously the importance of "creating infrastructures of holiness,"[56] which enable us to see and seek the abundant kingdom as an available alternative. As signs of the kingdom, these structures do not circumscribe our action or range of influence, but rather offer a place to dwell, a place to take a stand.

As an alternative to the Promethean endeavor that expects a better life through the escalation of technical, institutional, and professional

---

55. "Another world happens" is the literal translation of CdV's motto: *Um outro mundo acontece.*

56. Bahnson and Wirzba, *Making Peace with the Land*, 107.

control over the environment (in general) and food production (in particular), CdV offers a witness that wagers its hope upon a promise, upon the conviction that "Jesus is the incarnation of the most frequent promise in the Bible: God with us."[57] As such, CdV's experiments of weaving together conviviality and incarnational mission are thoroughly imbued with Illichian inspiration. And yet, it would be a very un-Illichian move to assert that there is but one way to express "faith seeking conviviality." For convivial recovery makes possible a range of faithful response, as "there is a dimension of the Christian life that requires more than repetition.... That dimension, the key to abiding faithfulness, is improvisation."[58] CdV is one community's attempt to improvise, one community's attempt to receive, cultivate, and share the promise of life together that comes to us through the Incarnation (John 10:10).

---

57. Oliver, *Relationality*, 20.
58. Wells, *Improvisation*, 65.

Interlude

Overhearing the Gospel according to Samba (Part Three): Becoming Alive and the Abundant Community

Just as Part One and Part Two conclude with a reflection on the samba circle, so too does Part Three conclude by returning to the samba circle as a primary context for the renewal of my imagination as a missionary (Rom 12:2). In the other two interludes, I also connected the samba circle with two other circular images: a biblical image of disciples encircling the Risen Christ to receive and share his peace (John 20) and Dorotheos of Gaza's image of a circle that displays the inseparability of the love of God (represented by the center point) and the love of neighbor (represented by the points along the circumference). Here, in this third reflection, I want to focus on the space between the points, that is, the atmosphere or ethos that is shared between them. In this way, I want to juxtapose two contrasting social spaces: one that generates the perception of scarcity and another (characterized by convivial relations) that manifests abundance.

MANIFESTING ABUNDANCE

In chapter 3, I explored the way that Illich discerned "detours" away from human flourishing as happening inside a social wound that might be described as a techno-colonial wound. I also explored how inside this wound, "economic peace" has emerged as a counterfeit panacea. Within this wound, I suggest now, we are conditioned to "see" scarcity as natural. In other words, we are conditioned to perceive the human condition as rooted in an original insufficiency or lack that we must overcome by what Illich calls "economic peace."

As the shadow cast within the myth of progress and the rise of development, this perception of scarcity seems to have replaced, eclipsed, or obscured an earlier perception of an ordered creation that is "good" and abundant and to which we relate in care and with limits (Gen 2:15). To this way of thinking, if scarcity is a basic condition, then creation itself is not only finite but also defective. If scarcity is a basic condition of creation, then God cannot say "good" over it. Indeed, it would call into question the goodness of the Creator. Living with the perception of scarcity tempts us, also, to imagine ourselves as either "like God" (Gen 3:5) or "less than human"—that is, nothing except what we manage to consume. In other words, it turns us away from the humility and dignity of being creatures who bear God's image, in a cosmos God created out of love and deemed good.

We find ourselves, therefore, in a vicious cycle in the consumer economy, "the world where the good life is measured and defined by the sum of goods and services."[1] Modern industrial progress makes possible more efficient production of goods and services and so a greater capacity for consumption. On the one hand, we perceive this apparent abundance of commodities and imagine that the good life consists in having them. Yet, the threat of scarcity grows ever more menacing, precisely because the social space of consumer society conditions us to expect that our flourishing depends upon those institutions, systems, operators, and experts who alone can provide what we need.

The paradox is that by assuming that we can overcome scarcity by consuming our way out of it, we end up escalating the conditions that give rise to the problem, a social imbalance between means and ends, a widening gap between our needs and desires and our capacity to satisfy them.[2] Thus, within the social space of consumer society, we no longer perceive a world that is created good and with abundance. We no longer perceive a world of proportions, of action that is determined by what is good, fitting, and enough. We find ourselves in a world in which the means for enjoying what we need to flourish are not just limited but scarce.

What I learned in the samba circle, however, is that the means for creating a shared sense of abundance are limited but never scarce. From inside the samba circle, I began to imagine anew how communities might

---

1. McKnight and Block, *Abundant Community*, 16.
2. Leiss, *Limits to Satisfaction*, 38–42.

dispel the false perception of scarcity as a basic condition by creating a shared sense of abundance through "the invisible structures of an abundant community."[3] As a way of illuminating these invisible structures of community, the following description of playing jazz may be an apt description of the playing of samba as well:

> Think of an after-hours jazz club, where musicians gather because they want to play their music together. . . . They start playing something. It sounds wonderful, and even though they may not have ever seen each other before and have spoken only a few words, wonderful music emerges. To an outsider it is magical.
>
> What is operating is a clear structure, but if you are not part of the jazz culture, the rules and customs that make the music possible are invisible. Similarly, the properties of gifts, associations, and hospitality are the hidden structure of [abundant] community life. . . .
>
> . . . The jazz way is the community way of playing. The invisible structures of gifts, association, and hospitality create the possibility and are the rules of a competent community. They are always available and essential.[4]

Like the jazz way, the samba circle is a community way of playing. It is a social space in which people share their gifts, associate for a common purpose, and extend hospitality. Furthermore, in the samba circle the means for creating and sharing abundance are always available and therefore never scarce. This leads me to imagine that the same could be true inside the body of Christ (1 Cor 12).

CULTIVATING CONSPIRACY

In order to explore further this connection between the samba circle and the body of Christ as a social space gathered around the risen Christ, I want to return to the ritual action of the *conspiratio* that, as I observed in chapter 2, lies at the origin of the peace Illich sought to cultivate and share. In the essay "The Cultivation of Conspiracy," and in his other comments about the eucharistic gathering, Illich highlights the new "we" and the "almost unimaginable intimacy" of the *conspiratio*, the shared peace

---

3. McKnight and Block, *Abundant Community*, 81.
4. McKnight and Block, *Abundant Community*, 82.

made possible by the ritual inclusion in the "'I' of the Incarnation"[5] and that enables us to prolong the Incarnation.

Although Illich does not refer to the Gospel of John directly, the sending narrative dramatizes the incarnational interruption of the *con-spiratio* and the new "we," the new inside, that arises around the risen Christ:

> When it was evening on that day, the first day of the week, and the doors of the house where the disciples had met were locked for fear of the Jews, Jesus came and stood among them, and said, "Peace be with you." After he said this, he showed them his hands and his side. Then the disciples rejoiced when they saw the Lord. Jesus said to them again, "Peace be with you. As the Father has sent me, so I send you." When he had said this, he breathed on them [*con-spiratio*] and said to them, "Receive the Holy Spirit." (John 20:19–23)

Here, the peace of Christ is shared as an intensification of the Jewish *shalom*. As *shalom*, the peace of Christ is still shared life and harmony under God's blessing, but now it can be shared among the community that arises around the risen Christ himself, the One who inspires us with his breath and words, the One calling us into an intimacy that makes it possible for our lives to share his word of peace and to breathe his Spirit upon one another.

Indeed, what we find in this text is not only a sending narrative but also a re-creation narrative.[6] Whereas God began creation on the first day (Gen 1:5), John 20:19 states that it was "the first day of the week," a Johannine reference to "resurrection day" as the beginning of a new creation. In the original creation narrative, God came to walk with Adam and Eve in the garden, but they hid from God out of fear. In the Johannine text, the disciples were hiding out of fear, but, like God searching out Adam and Eve in the garden, "Jesus came and stood among them" (John 20:26). Just as God originally breathed into the nostrils of *adam*, the earth-creature (Gen 2:7), here in John 20 the risen Christ breathes God's Spirit (back) into his disciples. Thus, God's "original peace"[7] has been unleashed into the world through this small circle gathered around Israel's Messiah to receive and share his peace.

---

5. Illich, "Cultivation of Conspiracy," 240.
6. I owe this insight to a conversation and email correspondence with James Alison.
7. See Burrell and Malits, *Original Peace*.

Of course, from a Promethean perspective, we would have expected something bigger, grander, and more systemic than a "conspiracy" of peace as an interruption of "economic peace." But, as Illich insists, "criticism of the established order of our modern, technogene, information-centered society can only grow out of a milieu of intense hospitality."[8]

As we have seen, Illich elaborated the hospitable alternative to alienation within the technological milieu and economic peace in terms of the recovery of conviviality. *Conviviality* is his term for the cultivation of the intense hospitality that is necessary to dispel the perception of scarcity. As such, conviviality is always personal, but never individualistic. Rather, it is "individual freedom realized in personal interdependence."[9] It refers to a quality of freedom that comes from being included within a "we" that is not the statistical "we" of market relations that compete for economic peace. As such, cultivating a convivial way of life enables us to conspire—that is, to share and to receive—the peace of Christ relationally.

To recognize, then, that conviviality enables "courageous, disciplined, self-critical renunciation accomplished in community"[10] is to recognize a basic Illichian point about Christian peacemaking in a consumer society. For Illich, even as we attend to the presence of the Incarnate One in our midst, we cannot forget to attend to the alienation this One has come to suture.

Illich argues that alienation conditions us into being one of two kinds of slaves: "prisoners of addiction or prisoners of envy."[11] Thus, Illich reminds us that in a consumer society we might not all be cash-poor, but all of us are impoverished, because the "ethos of non-satiety"[12] threatens "to steal, kill, and destroy" (John 10:10) the "abundant life" we were created to receive.

On my reading, then, Illich's emphasis on convivial recovery and his insights about peace represent a way of living by the promise and gift of peace without denying our impoverishment. That is, Illich will not allow us to turn peacemaking into a defensive strategy for insulating ourselves from the suffering and alienation that is in us and between us. He makes us attend to the wound, but he also encourages us to do so with a sense

---

8. Illich, "Cultivation of Conspiracy," 241–42.
9. Illich, *Tools for Conviviality*, 11.
10. Cayley, "Introduction," in Cayley and Illich, *Rivers North of the Future*, 44.
11. Illich, *Tools for Conviviality*, 47.
12. Illich, *Deschooling Society*, 113.

of hope. Thus, Illich invites us to cultivate a disposition of gratuity, which does not demand results that we can control but instead "centers desire on a person from whom we await a gift."[13]

In Illich's view the Incarnation is "a surprise, remains a surprise, and could not exist as anything else."[14] It follows, therefore, that a disposition of gratuity means that we are called to embrace the paradox of preparing ourselves to be surprised. For even within the social space of economic peace in which the threat of scarcity leads us into an escalating and competitive sense of fear, the Incarnation extends to us and through us, creating a new "inside" in which we do not have to be afraid. The first disciples did not know in advance how they could possibly live beyond those locked doors without being afraid, but they found a way. We do not have to know in advance exactly how to regenerate a convivial life of action and interdependence or how to delink "seek[ing] first the kingdom of God" (Matt 6:33) from the manipulative and disabling life of consumption. We could, however, begin to prepare ourselves to be surprised by becoming fully alive as a response to Christ's gift of peace.

This emphasis on gratuity and becoming alive leads back to what I encountered in the samba circle. To be clear, I do not intend to collapse or equate being incorporated into the *roda* with the fullness of being incorporated into the body of Christ. But I do want to maintain the parable. For if I had to pick one word to sum up the experience of being in the *roda*, I would pick one of the Illichian keywords that I have come to cherish: *aliveness*.

Toward the end of his life, Illich had this to say about the condition of "being alive":

> So I say let's be alive and let's celebrate—really celebrate—enjoy consciously, ritually, openly, the permission to be alive at this moment, with all our pains and with all our miseries. It seems to me an antidote to despair or religiosity—religiosity of that very evil kind.[15]

For Illich, aliveness arises from an awareness of our vocation to live between the false dilemma of clinging to the illusion of human control and falling under the temptation to despair. In other words, aliveness arises

---

13. Illich, *Deschooling Society*, 105.
14. Cayley and Illich, *Rivers North of the Future*, 48.
15. Cayley and Illich, *Ivan Illich in Conversation*, 284.

from an awareness of both the humility and dignity intrinsic to the human vocation of being creatures.

Similarly, the pulsating swing of samba gestures toward this sense of aliveness, Indeed, once a year at carnival, "the mystery of samba"[16] becomes a privileged expression for dramatizing and celebrating an interruption of time and space, an inversion in which, at least for a few days every year, the old social order dies and something else comes alive. Of course, after carnival, the old returns. But nonetheless, the music and the mysterious experience of samba can be a parable of the aliveness that Christians are called to celebrate with their lives. It gestures incompletely but compellingly toward an aliveness that Christians celebrate—that in the life, death, and resurrection of one person, a different kind of interruption and inversion has taken place, that the world has been reconciled to God, so that "in Christ, there is a new creation: everything old has passed away; see, everything has become new!" (2 Cor 5:17). So, finally, the sense of gratuity embodied in the samba circle points beyond itself to the gratuity of creaturely existence itself, the gift not only of being, but also the gift of vocation to enter a way of life through which we are being made alive, of being included in the life of the Son, of prolonging the Incarnation, *so that we might live through him*" (1 John 4:9).

---

16. See Vianna, *O mistério do samba* [*The Mystery of Samba*].

Conclusion

Beginning Again in the Middle—
Doing Theology from Someone Else's Garden

IN THE INTRODUCTION, I described these reflections as doing theology with and after Ivan Illich. Because of the way that I was "introduced" to Illich and because of Illich's own insights, it is worth reiterating that these reflections are a way of doing theology that arose out of friendship. As Illich himself once alluded to in a conversation, the most significant turning points in our lives are often a matter of being befriended by the right people at the right time.[1] From 2007 to 2010, I had the privilege of being befriended by and becoming friends with the community of Casa da Videira (CdV). Through this community, I was inspired not only to do theology with and after Illich but also to live out the vision that captured me and that I came to describe as "faith seeking conviviality."

In 2010, when our family moved to the UK for me to do doctoral research on these themes, I was sent not just as a PhD student but also as Casa da Videira's first "reverse missionary." They explained that they had seen a number of US missionaries come through Brazil, but, to quote Claudio, I was "the best failure of a US missionary that they had ever met"! This was said to me during a simple commissioning service, and in the light of who said it, I received it as the ultimate compliment and benediction.

We found inspiration in the idea of "reverse missionary" from Henri Nouwen, who—without using that exact term—describes a similar vocation in his Latin American journal, ¡Gracias!: "If I have any vocation

---

1. See conversation with David Cayley, *Ivan Illich in Conversation*, 61.

in Latin America, it is the vocation to receive from the people the gifts they have to offer us and to bring these gifts back up north for our own conversion and healing."[2] Ever since leaving Brazil, I have remained one of CdV's conspirators on "reverse mission"—someone who has returned from the so-called mission field of the Global South in order to enact "faith seeking conviviality" with other conspirators in the North.

This notion of "reverse mission" brings me back to a methodological thread that runs throughout this book: "The theologian is always beginning in the middle of things."[3] As I say in the introduction and repeat here, the "middle" refers to the way we are always already placed in history, and we do theology with an awareness of the sense of placed-ness and the stories that make us who we are. My experience suggests that, in the deepest sense, we do not actually get to choose the stories that most shape our convictions and sense of identity. I did not choose to be born white, male, and North American, and those three characteristics will always mark my identity and shape my story. Yet one of the things that my experience as an intercultural missionary in Brazil taught me is this: while I will never be *less than* white, male, and American, I am called to *more*. Because I have been befriended and chosen by Jesus (John 15:16), I am called to become *more* than the identity with which I was born. Because I have been baptized into body of Christ—in which "there is no longer Jew or Greek, slave or free, male and female" (Gal 3:28)—white, male, and American are identity markers that I must acknowledge and yet hold lightly. Even becoming immersed in intercultural relationships and becoming *brasicano* is not a matter of getting a new identity badge, but a token of the "more than" that comes with becoming joined to the "new humanity" (Eph 2:15). This book—as an exercise in "beginning in the middle"—emerged out of the desire to reflect on and live out that "more than" and the promise of life together we receive through the Messiah Jesus.

By way of conclusion, I would like to begin *again* in the middle, reflecting on how doing theology with and after Illich has continued to renew my imagination and practice of mission—even beyond Brazil. "Conclusion" does not mean a "pull-off-the-shelf" model to be applied. It is more of a narration of a discovery that might serve as (co)inspiration for others on a similar journey. As Illich himself makes clear,

2. Nouwen, ¡Gracias!, 188.
3. Williams, *On Christian Theology*, xii.

> We can only live these changes: we cannot think our way to humanity. Every one of us, and every group with which we live and work, must become the model of the era which we desire to create. The many models which will develop should give each one of us an environment in which we can celebrate our potential—and discover the way into a more humane world.[4]

Therefore, instead of a ready-made model, I conclude with an image for intercultural mission that is not originally mine, but with which I fully resonate and make my own—the image of "entering into someone else's garden."[5]

For me, this convergence between doing theology and gardening happens in the context of developing what Stephen Bevans calls a "mission spirituality."[6] We can speak generally of spiritualities as personal expressions of "the way persons cope with life," and in this sense, everybody has a spirituality. But mission spirituality refers to

> a spirituality for women and men who want to grow and thrive in their identity as people who consciously participate in the mission of the triune God, particularly insofar as such participation involves moving beyond their own zones of security in terms of culture, social status, language, and location.[7]

Therefore, while every mission spirituality entails a number of core components, or constants,[8] every mission spirituality must always be contextualized and personalized. In what follows, I want to highlight some aspects of my own emerging mission spirituality expressed through the phrase "faith seeking conviviality." And in the spirit of doing theology like a gardener, I will do so through the scriptural (and convivial) themes of gardening and food as well as through the lens of the image of "entering someone else's garden."

---

4. Illich, *Celebration of Awareness*, 15.
5. See Bevans and Schroeder, *Prophetic Dialogue*, 72–87.
6. See Bevans, "Towards a Mission Spirituality."
7. Bevans, "Towards a Mission Spirituality," 1.
8. For a developed account of the six constants of mission, see Bevans and Schroeder, *Constants in Context: A Theology of Mission for Today*.

WHY ARE YOU ENTERING SOMEONE ELSE'S GARDEN? *FAITH* SEEKING CONVIVIALITY

"Faith seeking conviviality" refers to the way that I have found to integrate my concerns with my knowledge of God's concerns. It has become my shorthand reminder for remembering my *why*, *how*, and *what* of mission spirituality. I begin by exploring why through the first word of that phrase: *faith* seeking conviviality.

In Part One, I framed the journey into the "garden" of Brazil as a narrative of being joined and sent. In the same way that Jesus joined his first disciples around him and sent them out with his peace (John 20), so too were we gathered to receive the peace of Christ at Mount Level Missionary Baptist Church and sent out to share that same peace as missionaries in Brazil. The experience has everything to do with my *why*.

If you were to ask me, "Why would a historically African-American congregation founded in 1864 by emancipated slaves in North Durham, North Carolina, not only receive but love a white couple in their midst?" the best answer I can think of is: because of their faith in Jesus. They did not have to, and given the history of race and violence in Durham, they had good reasons not to. But because they can trust Jesus to overcome the hostility of race, they shared the peace of Christ with us. What's more, they commissioned us to share that same peace in Latin America. Therefore, the best answer that I have for why I would even enter someone else's garden as a missionary has everything to do with the reason we were received and commissioned by Mount Level: faith in Jesus.

The question can still be asked: What does faith in Jesus have to do with gardening and sharing food as an expression of mission spirituality? As a response to that question, I connect the themes of gardens and food (which are common in Scripture) with a less obvious image: the image of Jesus as New Gardener who comes manifesting "abundant life" (John 10:10).

In the prologue to the Gospel of John, the ministry of Jesus Christ is identified with bringing "life" into the world (John 1:4; 10:10)—the very life of God, full of boundless energy, love, and communion. That the incarnate Christ is the human bearer of this life means that the "work of Christ . . . is not so much about the salvation of individual souls but about leading people into true, abundant, eternal, resurrection life."[9] Thus, the Johannine Christ is not a gnostic bridge-figure to a divine realm of

---

9. Wirzba, *Food and Faith*, xviii.

fullness that lies inaccessibly beyond our material order of food, water, plants and bodies. Rather, as "living water," "bread of life," and the "true vine" (John 4:14; 6:35; 15:1), the work of Christ manifests the divine life through the material order so that God's glory might be known on earth as it is in heaven.

As recent scholarship on the link between theology and food has emphasized, Jesus's ministry clearly shows us how central the sharing of food and table fellowship is to God's purposes to heal the world.[10] What is perhaps less obvious but no less vital is the connection between how we produce and access food as a means for receiving and sharing abundant life. In order to develop the linkage between the ministry of Christ and the work of food production, I want to develop the notion of Jesus Christ as the New Gardener—the one who "came to cultivate the gardens of this earth and our lives."[11]

Imagining Christ as the New Gardener brings together two complementary insights about gardening as an expression of mission. First, to speak of Jesus Christ as the New Gardener is to refer back to God as the first, or prototypical, gardener—"the Lord God . . . planted a garden in . . . Eden" (Gen 2:8–9)—and to remember God-as-Gardener places us as creatures who live in the hope that "the wilderness [of our world] is made to be what it both should and will be: paradise, God's garden."[12] Second, to imagine Christ as the New Gardener is to recall the basic human vocation to join with God's gardening in the world—the vocation to enact what Norman Wirzba calls "Godly gardening."[13]

Gardening is more than the physical activities of weeding, watering, sowing, tending, and harvest; it is a way of enacting our membership in creation and, as Wirzba contends, to do so in a distinct way: "to develop into Godly gardeners . . . who work harmoniously among the processes of life and death, and in their work witness to the life-creating presence of God in the world."[14] Put a bit differently, "Godly gardening" always involves two cultivations, or two "crops": what we grow from the soil and

---

10. Besides Wirzba's recent work, some recent contributions to the "food and faith" conversation include Jennifer Ayres, *Good Food*; Fred Bahnson, *Soil and Sacrament*; and Méndez-Montoya, *The Theology of Food*.

11. Wirzba, *Food and Faith*, 62.

12. Lash, *Believing Three Ways in One God*, 121–22.

13. Wirzba, *Food and Faith*, 61–70.

14. Wirzba, *Food and Faith*, 61.

how we grow from being with the soil—in other words, *what* we produce through gardening and *who* we become as we are "gardened."

It is no mere coincidence that upon Christ's resurrection in the garden of Gethsemane (a new Eden), John recounts that Mary mistakes him for a gardener (John 20:15).[15] Just as Adam's call was to steward creation in dependence on God, so we now see the New Adam, the One who has inaugurated the resurrection of humankind, fully respond to the call of God to steward creation in the light of the coming resurrection of all creation. Seen in this light, we discover afresh that "God's garden, made 'in the beginning,' does not lie behind us, but ahead of us, in hope, and, in the meantime, all around us as our place of work."[16]

To borrow a classical distinction that goes back to St. Augustine, faith carries a double meaning. For there is the "faith which is believed" (*fides quae creditur*), such as scriptural and doctrinal formulations as found in the Apostles' or Nicene Creed. Here, faith refers to an objective content: "I believe in Jesus Christ, [God's] only Son, our Lord." There is also the "faith by which it is believed" (*fides qua creditur*), by which we personally assent and act in *trust*. In mission spirituality, both senses of faith are at work. It is faith in the first sense of "belief" that enables us to acknowledge the reality and "the mission of the triune God"; it is faith in the second sense, as an act of trust, that enables us to participate in that mission by "moving beyond [our] own zones of security in terms of culture, social status, language, and location."[17]

HOW DO YOU ENTER SOMEONE ELSE'S GARDEN? FAITH *SEEKING* CONVIVIALITY

In Part Two, I narrated the journey into Brazil as a complex negotiation of entering into a garden mixed with cultural "seeds" and "weeds."[18] On the one hand, I encountered people filled with "justice, joy, and peace" (Rom 14:17) who were signs of continuity with the gospel of God's kingdom. But I also discovered how the "seeds" could be choked out by the "weeds"—that is, institutional realities and certainties that produced habits of dis-encounter (*desencontro*) and lack of dialogue in direct

---

15. Wright, *John for Everyone, Part 2*, 146.
16. Lash, *Believing Three Ways in One God*, 124.
17. Bevans, "Towards a Mission Spirituality," 1–2.
18. Bevans and Schroeder, *Prophetic Dialogue*, 74.

discontinuity with the logic of sharing the peace of Christ. In other words, I discovered the "seeds" of incarnational presence getting choked out by the "weeds" in the same garden.

Just as a gardener in a new habitat has to learn which plants come from good seed and which are weeds, my formation as a missionary had everything to do with learning to tell the difference between the two. Knowing the difference between "seeds" and "weeds" and knowing how to interact with them is a matter of "prophetic dialogue."[19] Engaging in prophetic dialogue, in the first instance, is about *how* one enters another's "garden" without *assuming* that one knows how to identify all plants and how they should be treated:

> One then approaches the "other" with an initial attitude of discerning how God is already present (dialogue) and then eventually, together *with* the people, after developing respectful and mutual relationships, confronts the "weeds" with the "good news" (prophecy). Underlying this approach is a radical trust and belief in the power of God's Spirit at work in the lives and cultures of people—people who are different from oneself. . . . Finally, one's own Christian faith and experience of the "good news" is the primary motivation and source behind one's commitment to and identity in mission/ministry. At the same time this faith and "good news" is shared in word and deed in a dialogical manner.[20]

In saying that prophetic dialogue has to do with *how* I enter someone's garden, I am also saying it has to do with how I enact my *seeking*, the second word in the phrase: faith *seeking* conviviality. The inspiration that I found in Brazil (through Casa da Videira) and beyond as their "reverse missionary" has lead me to seek "prophetic dialogue" primarily by beginning with practices related to the food cycle (e.g., composting, growing and sharing food).

At a basic level, food matters to us all for the simple reason that we are all eaters. Because we need food to live, our common dependence upon the food cycle has a leveling effect—with no exceptions. In the words of one community-based local food network, "If you eat, you're in!"[21] In this basic sense, we're all "in."

---

19. Bevans and Schroeder, *Prophetic Dialogue*.
20. Bevans and Schroeder, *Prophetic Dialogue*, 75.
21. The slogan "If you eat, you're in!" is associated with Incredible Edible, a local food movement based in Todmorden, UK. See https://www.incredible-edible-todmorden.

But at a deeper level, what I am coming to appreciate is that *food is never just about food*—never just about calories or something reducible to a nutritional profile. Rather, food connects us to a way of living. Food connects us "vertically," toward God; horizontally, toward our neighbors; and downward, as *human* beings rooted in the *humus* of the earth. As practical theologian Jennifer Ayres puts it in *Good Food*,

> In the food itself, the earth that yields it, the labor that prepares it, and the social relationships formed around it, Christians are confronted with both God's presence and God's demand. It is an embodied confrontation, with multiple layers of meaning, and it refuses both theological abstraction and simplistic responses. Instead what is needed is a grounded practical theology of food.[22]

Therefore, food offers a lens for understanding flourishing human community (in general) and a vibrant mission spirituality (in particular). By attending to the food cycle, we also find ourselves attending to questions such as, Where does our food come from? Why do some people have too much and others not enough? What do we do with what is left over or considered waste? With whom are we willing to break bread? In asking these questions, we discover that food is never simply about food! Food matters for mission spirituality, then, because food-related practices are more than mere basic human activities; they are also vital spiritual practices that are part and parcel of (*a*) our membership in "the community of creation,"[23] and (*b*) the focal concerns expressed by the Great Commandments: to love God and to love neighbor.

One of the reasons that food matters to me is because the food cycle has become a generative theme for mission and ministry as a "reverse missionary." In August 2015, after nearly five years of living in student housing at Queen's Foundation[24] while doing the PhD, our family made the transition with another family to live intentionally in a neighborhood—also known as the parish of Summerfield, where Ladywood

---

co.uk/.

22. Ayres, *Good Food*, 4.

23. See Bauckham, *Bible and Ecology: Rediscovering the Community of Creation*.

24. The Queen's Foundation for Ecumenical Theological Education is a residential theological college and research community based in Birmingham, UK. From 2011 to 2015, I was afforded the unique opportunity to experiment with and work out my approach to "faith seeking conviviality" while writing a PhD on the same theme. See http://www.queens.ac.uk/.

and Soho come together along the Dudley Road in Birmingham, UK. Together our two households along with other near neighbors form an expression of place-based Christian community called Companions for Hope. The tagline for Companions is "cultivating abundant community from the ground up."

Having lived in this place for more than three years now—an inner-city area that is marginalized and badged as deprived—I have discovered this: the conditions of poverty and social exclusion run much deeper than whether someone is "cash-poor." I have discovered that transformative responses to poverty must address not only financial or material poverty but also poverty of identity and relational poverty.[25] In fact, what I have discovered is quite simple: place-based transformation begins to happen when people find something meaningful to do and someone to do it with![26]

As I have been working to enter the "garden" of Summerfield, I have noticed its jagged beauty as well as its brokenness. I have seen some extravagant acts of sharing and neighborliness. Mixed in with these "seeds," I have also become more aware of the "weeds" and the extent to which human relationships and our relationships with the food cycle are open wounds that cry out for healing. Paradoxically, it has been through the embodied knowing of a particular place and its people that I have come to perceive the brokenness of the "global food system"—the disconnection between the four P's of people, place, planet, and policies.[27] As a symptom of that brokenness, consider that between 30 and 50 percent of all food produced in the global food chain is wasted, ending up in a bin rather than a belly.[28]

Approaching mission spirituality through the food cycle provides a focal lens for responding to the growing reality of food poverty: by uprooting the unjust "weeds" and false promises of capitalist food systems and by sowing "seeds" of an alternate theological vision centered around

25. For more on the "Web of Poverty" as a framework for grasping the multidimensional aspects of poverty, see Church Urban Fund at https://www.cuf.org.uk/learn-about/web-of-poverty.

26. While it is beyond the scope of this book to develop fully how local communties enact convivial recovery in the UK context (where I currently live) in a way that utilizes the structures of the welfare state without becoming *dependent* on them, for an insightful examination of what that might look like, see Cottam, *Radical Help*.

27. See Ayres, *Good Food*, 13–52.

28. See "Almost Half of the World's Food Thrown Away, Report Finds," available at https://www.theguardian.com/environment/2013/jan/10/half-world-food-waste.

"membership (digging, planting, growing, nurturing, respecting) and fellowship (hospitality, neighborliness, communalism, being with)."[29]

Through the lens of food, "prophetic dialogue" means engaging broken food systems as well as food poverty from a missiological standpoint. Seen in this light, gardens offer more than food; they also offer strategic sites of formation that enable us to discern the difference between illusion and reality, between the "abundant mirage" and the "abundant kingdom." Through the practices of regenerative agriculure, we come to deepen our relationship with the soil, with neighbors and fellow gardeners, and cultivate an abiding relationship with the Creator as the source of every good gift (Jas 1:17). Through gardening, we see food poverty as a symptom of brokenness and dis-ease that spreads inside the distorted contours of "abundant mirage," and therefore we see the issue of food production as a site of missional engagement and as one way of seeking God's abundant kingdom (Matt 6:33).

WHAT DO YOU DO IN SOMEONE ELSE'S GARDEN? FAITH SEEKING *CONVIVIALITY*

At the beginning of Part Three, I described a scenario of entering into Dona Raquel's backyard and garden, and how that experience led me to question why I had entered into her garden in the first place. In reflecting on the experience, it occurs to me that I was not even really aware of my *why*—and the extent to which "good intentions" were a driving factor. In reflecting on that experience with Claudio, I also discovered a why beyond and better than "good intentions." I was learning to attend to creation not as a problem to be fixed or a need to be met but as a garden to be tended.

I entered Dona Raquel's garden to help her remove things that I did not think belonged there. To me, it was obvious what I would do if this were my garden, but less obvious was how I should enter into her garden in the first place. Reflecting back on how I entered her garden, what I find unsettling and embarrassing is not trying to help per se but *assuming* that I knew how to tend her garden without even asking her in the first place.

While that moment in Dona Raquel's garden was more of a missionary miscue than a massive cultural blunder, it was enough to provoke a moment of insight. Like the moment in which an addict has a

---

29. Allen, "Food Poverty and Christianity," 20.

wake-up call and thinks, "I've had enough!," then embarks on a journey of recovery, that was the moment I thought, "I'm tired of being addicted to 'good intentions,' and I want to go into recovery. From now on I intend to become a *recovering* do-gooder."

Like many journeys of recovery, mine has not been a straight line of growth, but more like a spiral of discernment focused around key moments of encounter. Many of those moments have been the turning points (*viradas*) that happened in Brazil. Others took place as a PhD student at the University of Birmingham while living at Queen's Foundation and becoming a part of the residential community there. Initially, we landed at Queen's because we needed student housing as a family coming from overseas. But Queen's became so much more than what Americans would call a "dorm." At Queen's, we founds friends with whom we could share life by eating together, praying together, taking care of each other's children, planting a garden, keeping chickens, forming a band for the occasional social—as well as just hanging out. In effect, Queen's was the village that welcomed us when we moved to the UK in 2011.

Yet at a level deeper than welcome, the community of friends that embraced us at Queen's also enabled my "recovery journey" not only by supporting me through the PhD but also by being the living example that led me to join the dots that I had seen in Casa da Videira in Brazil. If my journey was in large part about healing the separation of discipleship, community, and mission by bringing them together in a place,[30] then Queen's was a kind of field hospital on the way. I say "on the way" because as significant as the time at Queen's was, it was still temporary student housing. By 2015, our days at Queen's were coming to an end. In August of that year, I moved with my family from Queen's not only with my PhD completed and defended, but with a renewed vision and passion for the next season of life. What if we imagined the work of entering into another "garden" not by planting another church (as in Brazil) but by *cultivating abundant community from the ground up*?

My phrasing of the question is intentional because it illustrates again how gardening (in particular) and the food cycle (in general) had become generative themes for mission and ministry as a "reverse missionary." This was the beginning of Companions for Hope and our

---

30. I owe this way of putting the matter directly to the wisdom offered in *The New Parish*, as well as friendship with the authors: Paul Sparks, Tim Soerens, and Dwight Friesen.

call to cultivate abundant community from the ground up by being neighbors on purpose.

Over the last three years, the spiral of discernment has continued around our desire to live out and integrate three core commitments or practices:

- *discipleship*: being and making disciples—apprentices of Jesus's way of life together in the kingdom of God;
- *friendship*: being and making friends—knowing and being known, that is, relating to others as *com-panions* (literally, those with whom one breaks bread); and
- *hospitality*: being included guests and inclusive hosts—enacting welcome and care in ways that enable a culture of grace and truth to flourish.

We all have a strong sense of being sent and called to this place, and we do not actually spend a lot of time talking about mission. Rather, mission is the overflow of these three core practices that are being defined and refined together: discipleship, friendship, and hospitality in a place.

Practically, we are involved in a range of local initiatives: community gardens, prison/community resettlement, community meals and social events, Place of Welcome,[31] social enterprise incubators, discipleship groups, and neighborhood prayer meetings. That said, connecting with the food cycle has become my primary way of "enacting hope"[32] with others in our parish and answering the missiological question, What do you do in someone else's garden? This is because engaging in the convivial practices of growing and sharing food is the best way that we have found for sharing with others what we have received: the way of life, friendship, and hospitality that comes from sharing the peace of Christ (John 20). In this way, we understand mission in Summerfield not as a set of techniques or programs for treating or "fixing" others but as a relational possibility among friends and neighbors who experiment with being neighbors on purpose.

Our parish of Summerfield is known for its great diversity. When we moved here and our youngest child switched primary schools, we were

31. See https://www.placesofwelcome.org.uk/.
32. See Morisy, *Bothered & Bewildered*, 16.

astonished to learn that at her new primary school (Oasis Academy Foundry) of just over two hundred students, forty-four languages were spoken! At the school gate, I was more likely to hear Polish, Romanian, or an African language than English. Also, the second largest men's prison in Engand, HMP Birmingham, is located just on the edge of our parish, and as a remand prison, many prisoners are released to resettle in the local community. These are just two examples of the social and cultural diversity in and around Summerfield. Here, variety and difference run rampant—and sometimes, unfortunately, that diversity suffers from lack of dialogue and division.

Soon after relocating to Summerfield, another event took place whose effects were felt not only in our neighborhood but also throughout the nation and across the world: the United Kingdom European Union membership referendum that would kickstart the process known as Brexit. One of the side effects of the "Brexit vote" was bringing to the surface the resentment and even hate toward immigrants and foreigners—two people groups that Summerfield has in abundance! As foreigners and recent relocaters ourselves, we began to share meals with neighbors and have conversations with local people about life in the neighborhood. We soon realized that you do not just drift into being neighbors in a place as diverse as Summerfield. It requires intentionality to make the shift from "accidentally" living on the same street to being neighbors on purpose.

So, with the support of Rabiyah Latif at Near Neighbours[33] and in partnership with the local parish church (Christ Church Summerfield), Summerfield Residents Association, and The Real Junk Food Project Birmingham, we hatched a plan called "Neighbour Nights." The concept of Neighbour Nights was simple and twofold: to connect people around (1) food and (2) how their passions connect with the local community. On the first Wednesday of every month, we invite neighbors to share

- food that they are willing to bring and share; and also
- anything they can offer that will contribute to the well-being of the local community.

In this way, instead of taking an issue-based approach to community organizing that starts with a litany of problems, we take an asset-based approach. By bringing together and actively involving the diversity of the

---

33. For more information on Near Neighbours, see https://www.near-neighbours.org.uk/about.

neighborhood, the primary function of Neighbour Nights is to "detect and connect" what we have together.

Why? Because when you try to create common ground by focusing on common problems, it is easy to get stuck asking questions about what's wrong with your neighborhood.

- Why are the queues at the local doctors' office taking so long?
- When is the council ever going to sort garbage collection and the chronic litter problem?

While we recognize that these questions do require solutions, our experience also tells us that at the grassroots/neighborhood level, it is more transformational to begin by asking other questions, such as:

- What are you passionate about?
- What would you like to see happen in this place?
- What are you willing to contribute to the well-being of this local community?

In other words, we want to start with what is strong instead of with what is wrong. Or even better: we want to come together to respond to what's wrong by starting with what's strong—which is asset-based community development in a nutshell.[34]

Detecting and Connecting Gifts: From "Problem Solvers" to "Treasure Seekers"

One of the core principles of asset-based community development (ABCD) is to focus on the assets—the gifts of a local community. It's worth repeating that from an ABCD perspective, focusing on gifts in the community does not mean repressing or ignoring present problems or issues. In other words, it is about addressing the needs of the local community by first detecting and connecting the gifts at hand.

---

34. It would not be an exaggeration to say that in North America and Europe Illich's legacy (both intellectually and practically) finds an enduring home within the asset-based community development (ABCD) movement. For more on ABCD, I would recommend starting with two websites: in the UK/Europe, see http://www.nurturedevelopment.org; and in the US, see http://www.abundantcommunity.com/.

One of the most precious gifts that we have found in the last year has been getting to know Ewa. In fact, meeting Ewa was one of those serendipitous encounters that I can only describe as a gift in itself.

Flashback to August 2017: I was walking our dog, Rio, by the Edgbaston Reservoir, when suddenly Rio spotted Ewa, who by first impressions was clearly a dog-lover as well as a keen forager. After just a few minutes of chatting with Ewa, I found out that

- she is Polish;
- she has lived locally for the last twelve years;
- she was trained as a chef; and
- she has been looking for a place to connect and use her passionate gift for cooking.

September 2017: I invited Ewa to Place of Welcome, a weekly neighborhood drop-in coffee morning, in order to introduce her to a few neighbors, including our neighborhood super-connector, Ann. I knew that Ann was looking for cooks at The Real Junk Food Project Birmingham.[35] Watching the sparks fly between Ewa and Ann, I knew that I would soon be looking at the next cook on the rota at TRJFP Birmingham!

October 2017: Ewa helped us kick off our first Neighbour Nights monthly gathering as lead chef (and she has not missed one yet)! Six months in, Ewa has not only become lead chef, she has also "detected and connected" others from the local Polish community to join in Neighbour Nights, as well as other neighborhood activities. By being connected to a community of neighbors and friends, Ewa has shown herself to be a skilled community-based chef who has a real gift for bringing people together around food.

Today: when I see Ewa bringing "her game" to the neighborhood, I now see her as more than a chef. In fact, she has become a key character in the story of our neighborhood, someone who is weaving the fabric of care and love one meal at time.

Which makes me think: could it be that neighborhoods like Summerfield are filled with Ewas who have not met each other yet? If this is so, then paradoxically, the most creative way to address issues such as community cohesion and social isolation is not by assuming the role of "problem solver," but rather by growing into the role of "treasure seeker."

---

35. See https://trjfpbrum.com/.

If this is so, then the work of network weaving at the neighborhood level is primarily the work of *detecting and connecting the gifts of Ewas with the gifts of other Ewas*.

When we started Neighbour Nights in October 2017, we began with a simple question: Instead of taking an issue-based approach to community organizing, which starts with neighborhood problems, what might happen by bringing neighbors together around food to talk about their gifts and how to share them? Another term for what happens by "bringing neighbors together around their gifts" is the power of associating.

As Companions, we have focused on gifts and the importance of *gift-mindedness* as a posture for cultivating a sense of abundant community. If we think of gifts as the raw material for cultivating community, associations are the ways those gifts get exchanged.

In fact, the power of associational life lies in its simplicity. In *The Abundant Community*, John McKnight and Peter Block describe it this way:

> An association is fundamentally a group of people who have a shared affinity. Associational life begins with a group of people who are drawn together for some reason, and that reason is what makes it work. Say they all like dogs, so they have a dog club. Or they all like reading fiction, so they have a book club. An association is often a fulfillment of one's individual likes and purposes. It is a place for having something in common, standing on common ground.[36]

In other words, whether by common location, common function or common interest, associations are vital to neighborhood life because they are the primary social process by which gifts get expressed in community.

As a once-a-month repeatable gathering, Neighbour Nights has become such an association in Summerfield. In fact, in addition to creating a context where individual residents can share their gifts, it has become a kind of association of associations. And herein lies the paradox of community organizing toward associational life in the neighborhood: some organization is necessary in order to associate and to create the environment for gift sharing and getting things done, yet too much organization ends up destroying the social fabric of associations!

---

36. McKnight and Block, *Abundant Community*, 71.

After eighteen months of Neighbour Nights, we recognize that there is a balancing act in this kind of community organizing. On the one hand, we know that just living in proximity is not enough. Proximity might make us neighbors in a formal, sociological sense, but by itself, proximity does not create associational life. Associational life must be convened, literally "called to come together." On the other hand, we could try to move beyond convening to managing the relationships and outcomes between these associations. The temptation is to make all the exchanges predictable and more "efficient" in a managerial sense. But predictability and efficiency come with the cost of losing neighborliness, and we are committed not to being managers on task, but rather to being neighbors on purpose.

For Companions for Hope, "being neighbors on purpose" is shorthand for intentionally designing just enough structure to become "an organizing agent rather than a service-providing system."[37] Why? Because we believe that service provision does not satisfy the core longings of living with dignity and community. We believe that beyond service provision (as important as it is), there are the gifts of the people and the power of association to make those gifts sharable.

Therefore, I see the associations that come together through Neighbour Nights as a form of community gardening in both senses of the term: gardening in the community as well as gardening of the community. The gifts of people such as Ewa are like seeds, powerful yet dormant unless exposed to the right conditions; the associations are the "microclimates" that provide these seeds with enough soil, water, warmth, and light to grow.

This portrait of Neighbour Nights and encountering neighbors such as Ewa is by itself an incomplete picture of engaging in mission by "entering someone else's garden." By itself it does not capture the variety of interactions (e.g, listening, waiting, connecting, cooking together, exchanging words of encouragement and prayers) that go into the "microclimate" of trust and friendship with Ewa and with others. But the portrait of Neighbour Nights does show and tell one way we have learned to "garden together" with our neighbors.

---

37. McKnight and Block, *Abundant Community*, 109.

WHAT HAPPENS IN YOUR OWN GARDEN? CULTIVATING THE EDGES

One of the advantages of approaching mission in terms of gardening is the way the metaphor portrays one's neighborhood (or parish, to use a more common term in the UK) in terms of an *ecology* of relationships. For gardeners know that plants do not flourish in isolation from their environment; rather, they flourish because of it. Therefore, to enable plant growth gardeners will often focus not on the plant itself but on the quality of the soil, light, and water around it. Similarly, gardeners will often design "companion planting" or guilds to create symbiotic exchanges between plants. In effect, gardening is the art of creating and facilitating beneficial interactions in an ecology of relationships; I would argue that the same could be said about intercultural mission.

As I have come to appreciate the notion of mission as gardening, I actually find myself going back to my first degree (biology) and the biological phenomenon known as the "edge effect." In ecological systems, an edge is the frontier between two systems and ecological habitats. For example, the shoreline is the frontier, or edge, between a pond (aquatic habitat) and a field (land habitat). As the interface between two systems, edges characteristically exhibit more biodiversity that single systems alone. Therefore, the "edge effect" is a biological phenomenon, and good gardeners mimic the principle by working with and designing edges that will enhance biodiversity and beneficial interactions.

We can also observe the "edge effect" in terms of interactions between people and habitats. Especially in cities like Birmingham, the diversity and density of the population plus the impact of the built environment means that contact with cultural diversity is an everyday, sometimes intense, reality. The main street in our neighborhood, the Dudley Road, is lined with bus stops, shops, restaurants (mostly takeout!), churches, mosques, and even a hospital. That environment creates a lot of edges and places of contact with human diversity. Whereas in biological systems the "edge effect" naturally tends toward greater biodiversity and resilience, in human ecology, encounters and interactions at these edges may be beneficial or harmful, even violent.

Given that the "edge effect" in human ecology must be tended in order to be beneficial, a practical question that we (as Companions for Hope) have asked is, What would it look like to tend and cultivate these edges so that the "edge effect" would be beneficial instead of divisive?

Neighbour Nights is one answer that we have found. In addition to Neighbour Nights, over the last three years we have experimented with or supported a number of other set pieces: a pop-up café at a bus stop by a school that brings together regular commuters and local parents who see each other every day and are looking for an "excuse" to meet; a community garden outside of a prison that has brought together the local community and resettled prisoners; a drop-in coffee morning in a parish church hall that brings together church members and local residents. What these all have in common is the intention to value the edges in the local ecology of relationships instead of seeing the edges as places of dangerous encounters or "no-go zones," approaching them as privileged sites for missional engagement with others with whom we share the same "garden."

Another insight that comes from observing the "edge effect" is that edges not only offer sites where bio- and human diversity can flourish, edges also create unique microhabitats where "niche species" flourish. Amphibians, such as frogs, are an example of a niche species that has adapted to flourish at the edge between water and land. They can live in water and on land, but their "niche" is in the intersection between the two habitats. By analogy, we are seeking to discover what it means to become "amphibious" in our approach to mission—adapting in order to flourish at the edge of two habitats as as "niche species." This means attending to the edge—or creative difference—between our garden and others. This means persistently asking the question, What is beneficial (or not) about the relationship between what we do in our own garden (as Christian community) and what we do when find ourselves in someone else's garden?

Living here has led to other questions: as relative newcomers to this place, how could we not be perceived and treated as an invasive species that competes with existing plants? In the same way that the presence of bees enhances diversity through cross-pollination, we wanted to connect with existing forms of church and community in order to activate and release the gifts already present in the body of Christ as well as those from other traditions and faiths in the neighborhood.

Companions is not a full-fledged congregation belonging to one denomination. Its unique and primary function is as a "niche species" in the local ecology to serve and to cultivate the edge between "the gathered/ institutional church" habitat and the "neighborhood" habitat. Most active participants in Companions are members of (or at least worship regularly with) other expressions of gathered/institutional church in the area. In this way, Companions seeks to connect with and express ecumenical unity across diverse expressions of institutional church. Whereas many missional communities end up trying to establish their own habitat, our intention is not to abandon the institutional church habitat but to inhabit it in a way that different forms of churches in our neighborhood can see and relate to each other as members of the same body of Christ. Also, through our roots, rhythms, and relationships, we seek to be immersed in the "neighborhood" habitat not as professionals who deliver services but as Christians who share salt and light (Matt 5) by "being neighbors on purpose."

To borrow a phrase common to Brazilian liberation theology, perhaps Companions is best described as an ecumenical *base Christian community*. Describing it in this way makes clear that it is small; it functions as a part of and not in isolation from the rest of the body; it works from the "ground up" or grassroots of society; and last but not least, it seeks to activate all the baptized (laity) as the base of the church.[38]

Without a two-way flow between the institutional church and the neighborhood, institutional forms of church can become counterproductively preoccupied with maintenance of institutional forms and techniques for getting people to become consumers of institutional programs and services. As a base Christian community, our first question is not, "How do we re-*form* the church as institution?" but "What might it look like to re-*function* the way the body of Christ inhabits its place in the world as those who are sent there?"[39]

To put it in Illichian terms, we are concerned with convivial recovery in and of the church as well, which (like the samba circle mentioned earlier) requires and makes possible the exercise of personal gifts and the expansion of freedom in interdependence. This is not an anti-institutional stance but one that prioritizes the recovery of verbs that enables authentic missionary presence. In our case: we *gather* in each others' homes; we *eat* together; we *pray* together; we *read* Scripture together; we *intercede for* and *prayer-walk* our patch; we *support* one another prayerfully and, when necessary, financially; we *learn from* and *celebrate* the difference of each other's Christian traditions and those of our neighbors. These are a

---

38. See Hebblethwaite, *Base Communities*.

39. This distinction between re-forming and re-functioning the church (in particular) is my riff on the distinction that Cormac Russell makes regarding institutions (in general).

few of the verbs that enable us to tend our own garden, while also seeking the peace of the city where God has sent us (Jer 29:7) and tending the "garden" of our neighborhood as well. The recovery of verbs as a base Christian community does not exclude gathering with and participating in established institutional forms of church. As a base Christian community, church attendance or "going to church" is not a substitute for other verbs intrinsic to discipleship and mission, but rather is an aspect in the movement of becoming "a church that goes forth."[40]

———

I began the learning journey that has led to this book by asking two questions. First, given the history of Christian missionary expansion in its colonial and neocolonial forms, on what *basis* do we go on fulfilling the "Great Commission" (Matt 28:16–20) as Christ's disciples? A second question, intimately related to the first, is this: What makes it possible to embody a distinctively Christian presence that is *missionary* without being *manipulative*? The journey is ongoing, but what I have discovered so far is that we find the answers to those questions less by seeking a *strategy* to implement and more by embracing a *spirituality* to live out.[41]

The shift from mission strategy to mission spirituality can be a subtle one, but it operates according to a distinct logic. As I have described it here, "faith seeking conviviality" is an expression that does not begin with asking how or what, but why. Put slightly differently, it does not begin with mission, or with church as such, but with God. More specifically, it begins with Christ as God-with-us, so that we may approach mission as a *response* to the call to "follow the naked Christ" in faith, hope, and love. The good news is that in recovering this fundamental sense of responseability (i.e., the ability to respond to the call of Another), the church might also rediscover what it means to live as an abundant community.

Paradoxically, I am learning that in "throwaway culture,"[42] where places and people are constantly being discarded, cultivating abundant community also begins with *a preferential option for the discarded*. It begins by observing what or who is being discarded and what would it take to reincorporate them as gifts. It is paradoxical to suggest that God's

---

40. See Pope Francis, *The Name of God Is Mercy*.
41. See Bevans and Schroeder, *Prophetic Dialogue*, 2.
42. Pope Francis, *Laudato Si'*, 16–18.

abundance is manifest most clearly where the symptoms of the "scarcity mindset" are most visible. On the other hand, this paradox should be strangely familiar to followers of the "King of the discarded"—the One who was "rejected [and *discarded*] by mortals yet chosen and precious in God's sight" (1 Pet 2:4).

Recovering response-ability also means that the church does not have to propose one-off solutions (which is often a Promethean temptation anyway) but rather to amplify the range of faithful responses. Through the direct action of activities like gardening and food production, the church is offering (or being offered) demonstration plots of abundant life: sites where even in the margins, we—and our non-Christian neighbors—might meet one another, tend the earth, and "taste and see that the Lord is good" (Ps 34:8).

It is worth reiterating that I am not peddling these particular areas of engagement as a panacea for all social ills in marginalized urban communities like the one where I live. In fact, I am suggesting that the search for panaceas is part of the problem. What is at stake is the cultivation of community-based places where an alternative imagination awakens—places where neighbors can stand, care, and work together in ways that demonstrate that the means for manifesting abundance are also abundant.

In doing so, we can stand against the forces that try to steal, kill, and destroy the abundant life for which we were created. In doing so, we can offer a counter-sign of peace. These counter-signs should neither be romanticized nor underestimated. Rather, we should receive them as tokens of God's in-breaking economy of abundance. At the level of imagination, these tokens offer holy interruptions that disrupt our "default settings" regarding what is possible and desirable.

"Faith seeking conviviality" expresses a concern for the "dignity of each [person] and each human relationship"[43] as well as the integrity of our ecological relationships as members of "the community of creation,"[44] but it is not reducible to mere humanism or ecological concern. Rather, as an expression of practical theology, it offers "a *response* to the call of God in which we come to realize that our purpose for 'being in the world' is to respond to the 'purposes of God.'"[45]

---

43. Illlich, *Celebration of Awareness*, 18.
44. See Bauckham, *Bible and Ecology*.
45. Veling, *Practical Theology*, 12.

True, the imbalances that have led to social polarization, biological degradation, and economic disparity are all very much the work of our human hands. While healing those wounds will require our best efforts, it is equally necessary to say that what most determines the shape and impact of our practical action is not, in fact, our technique and human capacity to control outcomes but (paradoxically) our capacity to trust and to show fidelity to the promise of abundant life together (John 10:10). Hearing and responding in fidelity to such a promise is the antidote to the hubris and sense of despair that come with the presumption that we must control all outcomes. In terms of mission, then, the fundamental issue is not between action and passivity, but rather in discerning which human actions fit with our place in the "garden." The most promising ways, Illich suggests, do not lie in "powering up" and escalating our impact on the world but in recalibrating it. It depends upon a "poverty of spirit" that trusts "the word in its weakness"[46]—a word that invites us to wager upon the availability of a different kind of power (Rom 1:16) and a different way of life (Eph 2:10).

---

46. Illich, *Tools for Conviviality*, 110.

Bibliography

Allen, Chris. "Food Poverty and Christianity in Britain: A Theological Re-assessment." *Political Theology* 17 (2016) 361–77.
Alves, Rubem A. *Protestantism and Repression: A Brazilian Case Study*. Translated by John Drury. London: SCM, 1985.
Ayres, Jennifer. *Good Food: Grounded Practical Theology*. Waco: Baylor University Press, 2013.
Bahnson, Fred. *Soil and Sacrament: A Spiritual Memoir of Food and Faith*. New York: Simon & Schuster, 2013.
Bahnson, Fred, and Norman Wirzba. *Making Peace with the Land: God's Call to Reconcile with Creation*. Downers Grove: IVP, 2012.
Barreto, Raimundo. "Facing the Poor in Brazil: Towards an Evangélico Progressive Social Ethics." PhD diss., Princeton Theological Seminary, 2006.
Bauckham, Richard. *Bible and Ecology: Rediscovering the Community of Creation*. Waco: Baylor University Press, 2010.
Bedford, Nancy. "To Speak of God from More than One Place: Theological Reflections from the Experience of Migration." In *Latin American Liberation Theology: The Next Generation*, edited by Ivan Petrella, 95–118. Maryknoll, NY: Orbis, 2005.
Begbie, Jeremy. *Theology, Music and Time*. Cambridge: Cambridge University Press, 2000.
Bevans, Stephen. *Prophetic Dialogue: Reflections on Christian Mission Today*. Maryknoll, NY: Orbis, 2011.
———. "Towards a Mission Spirituality." Unpublished paper. https://www.cppsmissionaries.org/download/mission/TOWARDS_A_MISSION_SPIRITUALITY_Bevans.pdf.
Bevans, Stephen B., and Roger P. Schroeder. *Constants in Context: A Theology of Mission for Today*. Maryknoll, NY: Orbis, 2004.
———. "'We Were Gentle among You': Christian Mission as Dialogue." *Australian eJournal of Theology* 7 (June 2006) 1–17.
Bieler, Andrea, and Luise Schottroff. *The Eucharist: Bodies, Bread, & Resurrection*. Minneapolis: Fortress, 2007.
Bingemer, Maria Clara, and Peter Casarella, eds. *Witnessing: Prophecy, Politics, and Wisdom*. Maryknoll, NY: Orbis, 2014.
Bondi, Roberta C. *To Pray and to Love: Conversations on Prayer with the Early Church*. Minneapolis: Fortress, 1991.

Bonhoeffer, Dietrich. *Christ the Center*. Translated by E. H. Robertson. New York: Harper & Row, 1960.

———. *Creation and Fall: A Theological Exposition of Genesis 1–3*. Translated by Douglas Stephen Bax. Edited by John W. de Gruchy. Dietrich Bonhoeffer Works 3. Minneapolis: Fortress, 1996.

———. *Life Together; Prayerbook of the Bible*. Translated by James H. Burtness and Donald W. Bloesch. Edited by Geffrey B. Kelley. Dietrich Bonhoeffer Works 5. Minneapolis: Fortress, 1997.

Bosch, David. *Transforming Mission: Paradigm Shifts in Theology of Mission*. Maryknoll, NY: Orbis, 1991.

Bouma-Prediger, Steve. *For the Beauty of the Earth: A Christian Vision for Creation Care*. Grand Rapids: Baker Academic, 2001.

Brock, Brian. *Christian Ethics in a Technological Age*. Grand Rapids: Eerdmans, 2010.

Brother John of Taizé. *Friends in Christ: Paths to a New Understanding of Church*. Maryknoll, NY: Orbis, 2012.

Brueggemann, Walter. *The Prophetic Imagination*. Philadelphia: Fortress, 1978.

Buck-Morss, Susan. *Dreamworld and Catastrophe: The Passing of Mass Utopia in East and West*. Cambridge: MIT Press, 2002.

Burns, Ken, dir. *Jazz*. PBS Documentary, 2001.

Burrell, David. *Freedom and Creation in Three Traditions*. Notre Dame: University of Notre Dame Press, 1993.

———. *Friendship and Ways to Truth*. Notre Dame: University of Notre Dame Press, 2000.

———. "Incarnation and Creation: The Hidden Dimension." *Modern Theology* 12 (1996) 211–20.

Burrell, David, and Elena Malits. *Original Peace: Restoring God's Creation*. New York: Paulist, 1997.

Cavanagh, John, and Jerry Mander, eds. *Alternatives to Economic Globalization: A Better World Is Possible*. 2nd ed. San Francisco: Berrett-Koehler, 2004.

Cavanaugh, William T. *Being Consumed: Economics and Christian Desire*. Grand Rapids: Eerdmans, 2008.

Cayley, David, and Ivan Illich. *Ivan Illich in Conversation*. Concord, ON: House of Anansi, 1992.

———. *The Rivers North of the Future: The Testament of Ivan Illich, as Told to David Cayley*. Toronto: House of Anansi, 2005.

CIA, Directorate of Intelligence. "The Committed Church and Change in Latin America." Reference Title: ESAU XLIII/69, 10 September 1969. Declassified May 2007.

Ciavatta, Lucas. *O passo: A pulsação e o ensino-aprendizagem de ritmos*. Rio de Janeiro: L. Ciavatta, 2003.

Cloke, Paul, and Mike Pears, eds. *Mission in Marginal Places: The Praxis*. Milton Keynes: Paternoster, 2016.

Cook, Guillermo. *The Expectation of the Poor: Latin American Base Ecclesial Communities in Protestant Perspective*. Maryknoll, NY: Orbis, 1985.

Corbett, Steve, and Brian Fikkert. *When Helping Hurts: How to Alleviate Poverty without Hurting the Poor . . . and Yourself*. Chicago: Moody, 2014.

Costas, Orlando. *Christ Outside the Gate: Mission beyond Christendom*. 1982. Reprint, Eugene, OR: Wipf & Stock, 2005.

Cottam, Hilary. *Radical Help: How We Can Remake the Relationships between Us and Revolutionise the Welfare State*. London: Virago, 2018.
Cyprian. "Letter 69, 1–5." In *Documents in Early Christian Thought*, edited by Maurice Wiles and Mark Santer, 160–62. Cambridge: Cambridge University Press, 1977.
DaMatta, Roberto. *Carnivals, Rogues, and Heroes: An Interpretation of the Brazilian Dilemma*. Translated by John Drury. Notre Dame: University of Notre Dame Press, 1991.
———. *O que faz o brasil, Brasil?* Rio de Janeiro: Rocco, 1984.
Davis, Ellen. *Scripture, Culture, and Agriculture: An Agrarian Reading of the Bible*. New York: Cambridge University Press, 2009.
Dawn, Marva. *Powers, Weakness, and the Tabernacling of God*. Grand Rapids: Eerdmans, 2001.
Ellul, Jacques. *On Freedom, Love, and Power*. Edited by W. H. Vanderburg. Toronto: University of Toronto Press, 2010.
Escobar, Arturo. *Encountering Development: The Making and Unmaking of the Third World*. Princeton: Princeton University Press, 1995.
Esteva, Gustavo. "Back from the Future." Unpublished notes from Schooling and Education: A Symposium with Friends of Ivan Illich, TALC New Vision, Milwaukee, 2004.
———."Development." In *The Development Dictionary: A Guide to Knowledge as Power*, edited by Wolfgang Sachs, 1–23. 2nd ed. London: Zed, 2010.
———. "Más allá del desarrollo: La buena vida." *Revista América Latina en movimiento*, No. 445 (2009) 1–5.
———, ed. *Repensar el mundo con Iván Illich*. Guadalajara: Taller Editorial la Casa del Mago, 2012.
Esteva, Gustavo, and Madhu Suri Prakash. *Grassroots Post-Modernism: Remaking the Soil of Cultures*. London: Zed, 1998.
Esteva, Gustavo, Salvatore Babones, and Philipp Babcicky. *The Future of Development: A Radical Manifesto*. Bristol, UK: Policy Press, 2013.
Ewell, Samuel. *Building Up the Church: Live Experiments in Faith, Hope, and Love*. Eugene, OR: Wipf & Stock, 2008.
———. "Resenha: Rostos do protestantismo latino-americano, de José Míguez Bonino." *Práxis evangélica: Revista de teologia prática latino-americana* 9 (2006) 209–16.
Ewell, Samuel, and Claudio Oliver. "Are We Response-able?" *The New Urban World Journal* 2 (2013) 82–84.
Farias, Domenico. "In the Shadow of Jerome." In *The Challenges of Ivan Illich: A Collective Reflection*, edited by Lee Hoinacki and Carl Mitcham, 59–70. Albany: State University of New York Press, 2002.
Fernandez, Eleazar S. "The Church as a Household of Life Abundant: Reimagining the Church in the Context of Global Economics." In *Theology That Matters: Ecology, Economy and God*, edited by Darby Kathleen Ray, 172–88. Minneapolis: Fortress, 2006.
Ford, David, ed. *The Modern Theologians: An Introduction to Christian Theology in the Twentieth Century*. 2nd ed. Cambridge, MA: Blackwell, 1997.
Francis, Pope. *The Joy of the Gospel = Evangelii Gaudium*. New York: Image, 2014.
———. *Laudato Si': On Care for Our Common Home*. London: Catholic Truth Society, 2015.

———. *The Name of God Is Mercy*. Translated by Oonagh Stransky. New York: Random House, 2016.

Gabbard, David A. *Silencing Ivan Illich: A Foucauldian Analysis of Intellectual Exclusion*. San Francisco: Austin & Winfield, 1993.

Galeano, Eduardo. *Open Veins of Latin America: Five Centuries of the Pillage of a Continent*. Translated by Cedric Belfrage. 25th anniversary ed. New York: Monthly Review, 1997.

Garrigós, Alfons. "Hospitality Cannot Be a Challenge." In *The Challenges of Ivan Illich: A Collective Reflection*, edited by Lee Hoinacki and Carl Mitcham, 113–26. Albany: State University of New York Press, 2002.

Gorringe, Timothy. *Furthering Humanity: A Theology of Culture*. Aldershot, UK: Ashgate, 2004.

Gray, Francine du Plessex. *Divine Disobedience: Profiles in Catholic Radicalism*. New York: Knopf, 1970.

Groome, Thomas. *Sharing Faith: A Comprehensive Approach to Religious Education and Pastoral Ministry; The Way of Shared Praxis*. San Francisco: HarperSanFrancisco, 1991.

Gutiérrez, Gustavo. *We Drink from Our Own Wells: The Spiritual Journey of a People*. Translated by Matthew O'Connell. Maryknoll, NY: Orbis, 1984.

Hartch, Todd. *The Prophet of Cuernavaca: Ivan Illich and the Crisis of the West*. New York: Oxford University Press, 2015.

Hauerwas, Stanley. *War and the American Difference: Theological Reflections on Violence and National Identity*. Grand Rapids: Baker Academic, 2011.

Hauerwas, Stanley, and Sam Wells, eds. *The Blackwell Companion to Christian Ethics*. Malden, MA: Blackwell, 2006.

Healy, Nicholas. *Church, World, and the Christian Life: Practical-Prophetic Ecclesiology*. Cambridge: Cambridge University Press, 2000.

Hebblethwaite, Margaret. *Base Communities: An Introduction*. London: G. Chapman, 1993.

Heinberg, Richard, and Daniel Lerch, eds. *The Post Carbon Reader: Managing the 21st Century's Sustainability Crises*. Healdsburg, CA: Watershed Media, 2010.

Hiebert, Paul. "The Missionary as Mediator of Global Theologizing." In *Globalizing Theology: Belief and Practice in an Era of World Christianity*, edited by Craig Ott and Harold A. Netland, 288–308. Grand Rapids: Baker Academic, 2006.

Hoinacki, Lee. *Dying Is Not Death*. Eugene, OR: Resource Publications, 2006.

———. "Reading Ivan Illich." In *The Challenges of Ivan Illich: A Collective Reflection*, edited by Lee Hoinacki and Carl Mitcham, 1–7. Albany: State University of New York Press, 2002.

———. *Stumbling toward Justice: Stories of Place*. University Park, PA: Pennsylvania State University Press, 1999.

———. "The Trajectory of Ivan Illich." *Bulletin of Science, Technology & Society* 23 (2003) 382–89.

Hoinacki, Lee, and Carl Mitcham, eds. *The Challenges of Ivan Illich: A Collective Reflection*. Albany: State University of New York Press, 2002.

Hopkins, Rob. *The Transition Handbook: From Oil Dependency to Local Resilience*. Totnes, UK: Green Books, 2008.

Hudson, Trevor. *A Mile in My Shoes: Cultivating Compassion*. Nashville: Upper Room, 2005.

Hulbert, Alastair. "Don Quixote in Contemporary Global Tragicomedy." In *The Challenges of Ivan Illich: A Collective Reflection*, edited by Lee Hoinacki and Carl Mitcham, 163–74. Albany: State University of New York Press, 2002.

Illich, Ivan. *Beyond Economics and Ecology: The Radical Thought of Ivan Illich*. Edited by Samuel Sajay. New York: Marion Boyars, 2013.

———. *Celebration of Awareness: A Call for Institutional Revolution*. Garden City, NY: Doubleday, 1970.

———. *The Church, Change and Development*. Chicago: Urban Training Center, 1970.

———. "The Cultivation of Conspiracy." In *The Challenges of Ivan Illich: A Collective Reflection*, edited by Lee Hoinacki and Carl Mitcham, 233–42. Albany: State University of New York Press, 2002.

———. "The De-linking of Peace and Development." Opening address on the occasion of the first meeting of the Asian Peace Research Association, Yokohama, 1 December 1980. In *In the Mirror of the Past: Lectures and Addresses, 1978–1990*, 15–26. London: Marion Boyars, 1992.

———. *Deschooling Society*. London: Marion Boyars, 1971.

———. "Development as Planned Poverty." In *The Post-Development Reader*, edited by Majid Rahnema and Victoria Bawtree, 94–101. London: Zed, 1997.

———. "Disabling Professions." In *Disabling Professions*, edited by Ivan Illich et al., 1–40. London: Marion Boyars, 2010.

———. "Eco-pedagogics and the Commons." *International Foundation for Development Alternatives* Dossier 37 (October 1983) 3–11.

———. *Gender*. Berkeley, CA: Heyday, 1982.

———. *H2O and the Waters of Forgetfulness*. London: Marion Boyars, 1986.

———. "Hospitality and Pain." Unpublished address, 1987. http://www.davidtinapple.com/illich/1987_hospitality_and_pain.PDF.

———. *In the Mirror of the Past: Lectures and Addresses, 1978–1990*. New York: Marion Boyars, 1992.

———. *In the Vineyard of the Text: A Commentary to Hugh's Didascalicon*. Chicago: University of Chicago Press, 1996.

———. *Limits to Medicine: Medical Nemesis; The Expropriation of Health*. Enlarged ed. London: Marion Boyars, 1995.

———. "Needs." In *The Development Dictionary: A Guide to Knowledge as Power*, edited by Wolfgang Sachs, 95–110. 2nd ed. London: Zed, 2010.

———. "Philosophy . . . Artifacts . . . Friendship." Unpublished address, 1996. http://www.davidtinapple.com/illich/1996_philo_arti_friends.PDF.

———. *The Right to Useful Unemployment and Its Professional Enemies*. London: Marion Boyars, 2009.

———. "The Shadow That the Future Throws." Unpublished address, 1989. http://www.davidtinapple.com/illich/1989_shadow_future.PDF.

———. *Shadow Work*. London: Marion Boyars, 1981.

———. "The Social Construction of Energy." *New Geographies* 2 (2009) 11–22.

———. "To Hell with Good Intentions." Address to the Conference on InterAmerican Student Projects, Cuernavaca, Mexico, April 20, 1968. http://www.davidtinapple.com/illich/1968_cuernavaca.html.

———. "To Honor Jacques Ellul." Based on an address given at Bordeaux, November 13, 1993. http://www.davidtinapple.com/illich/1993_honor_ellul.PDF.

———. *Tools for Conviviality*. London: Marion Boyars, 2009.

———. *Toward a History of Needs*. Berkley, CA: Heyday, 1977.
Illich, Ivan, and Majid Rahnema. "Twenty-Six Years Later: Ivan Illich in Conversation." In *The Post-Development Reader*, edited by Majid Rahnema and Victoria Bawtree, 103–10. London: Zed, 1997.
Illich, Ivan, et al. "Declaration on Soil." A joint statement, drafted in Hebenshausen, Germany, December 6, 1990. http://www.davidtinapple.com/illich/1990_declaraion_soil.PDF.
Inchausti, Robert. *Subversive Orthodoxy: Outlaws, Revolutionaries, and Other Christians in Disguise*. Grand Rapids: Brazos, 2005.
Jacobson, Matthew Frye. *Whiteness of a Different Color: European Immigrants and the Alchemy of Race*. Cambridge: Harvard University Press, 1999.
Jennings, Willie James. *The Christian Imagination: Theology and the Origins of Race*. New Haven: Yale University Press, 2010.
———. "'He Became Truly Human': Incarnation, Emancipation, and Authentic Humanity." *Modern Theology* 12 (1996) 239–55.
Kahn, Richard. "The Committed Church and Change in Latin America." *The International Journal of Illich Studies* 2 (2010) 1–56.
Katangole, Emmanuel. "A Different World Right Here, a World Being Gestated in the Deeds of the Everyday." *Missionalia* 30 (2002) 206–34.
Kinsler, Ross, and Gloria Kinsler. *The Biblical Jubilee and the Struggle for Life: An Invitation to Personal, Ecclesial, and Social Transformation*. Maryknoll, NY: Orbis, 1999.
Langmead, Ross. *The Word Made Flesh: Towards an Incarnational Missiology*. Lanham, MD: University Press of America, 2004.
Lash, Nicholas. *Believing Three Ways in One God: A Reading of the Apostles' Creed*. Notre Dame: University of Notre Dame Press, 1993.
Latouche, Serge. *Farewell to Growth*. Translated by David Macey. Cambridge: Polity, 2009.
———. *The Westernization of the World: The Significance, Scope and Limits of the Drive towards Global Uniformity*. Translated by Rosemary Morris. Cambridge: Polity, 1996.
Leiss, William. *The Limits to Satisfaction: On Needs and Commodities*. London: Marion Boyars, 1978.
Libânio, João Batista and Alberto Antoniazzi. *Vinte anos de teologia na América Latina e no Brasil*. Rio de Janeiro: Vozes, 1994.
Lohfink, Gerhard. *Jesus and Community: The Social Dimension of Christian Faith*. Translated by John P. Galvin. Philadelphia: Fortress, 1984.
Longuini Neto, L. *O novo rosto da missão: Os movimiento ecumênico e evangelical no protestantismo latino-americano*. Viçosa, Brazil: Editora Ultimato, 2002.
Lupton, Robert. *Toxic Charity: How the Church and Charities Hurt Those They Help (and How to Reverse It)*. New York: HarperOne, 2011.
McClendon, James W., Jr. *Biography as Theology: How Life Stories Can Remake Today's Theology*. Nashville: Abingdon, 1974.
———. *Systematic Theology*. Vol. 3, *Witness*. Nashville: Abingdon, 2000.
McFarland, Ian. *Difference & Identity: A Theological Anthropology*. Cleveland: Pilgrim, 2001.
———. *The Divine Image: Envisioning the Invisible God*. Minneapolis: Fortress, 2005.

McIntosh, Alastair. *Rekindling Community: Connecting People, Environment and Spirituality*. Totnes, UK: Green Books, 2008.
McIntosh, Mark. *Mystical Theology: The Integrity of Spirituality and Theology*. Malden, MA: Blackwell, 1998.
McKnight, John. *The Careless Society: Community and Its Counterfeits*. New York: Basic Books, 1995.
McKnight, John, and Peter Block. *The Abundant Community: Awakening the Power of Families and Neighborhoods*. San Francisco, CA: Berrett-Koehler, 2010.
Méndez-Montoya, Ángel. *The Theology of Food: Eating and the Eucharist*. Oxford: Wiley-Blackwell, 2012.
Mies, Maria, and Veronika Bennholdt-Thomsen. *The Subsistence Perspective: Beyond the Globalized Economy*. Translated by Patrick Camiller et al. New York: Zed, 1999.
Mignolo, Walter D. *The Idea of Latin America*. Malden, MA: Blackwell, 2005.
Míguez, Néstor, Joerg Rieger, and Jung Mo Sung. *Beyond the Spirit of Empire: Theology and Politics in a New Key*. London: SCM, 2009.
Míguez Bonino, José. *Faces of Latin American Protestantism: 1993 Carnahan Lectures*. Translated by Eugene L. Stockwell. Grand Rapids: Eerdmans, 1997.
Mitcham, Carl. "The Challenges of This Collection." In *The Challenges of Ivan Illich: A Collective Reflection*, edited by Lee Hoinacki and Carl Mitcham, 9–19. Albany: State University of New York Press, 2002.
Morisy, Ann. *Bothered & Bewildered: Enacting Hope in Troubled Times*. London: Continuum, 2009.
Myers, Ched. "Between the Seminary, the Sanctuary, and the Streets: Reflections on Alternative Theological Education." *Ministerial Formation* 94 – World Council of Churches Education and Ecumenical Formation (2001) 49–52.
Nellas, Panayiotis. *Deification in Christ: Orthodox Perspectives on the Nature of the Human Person*. Translated by Norma Russell. Crestwood, NY: St. Vladimir's Seminary Press, 1987.
Nouwen, Henri. *Gracias! A Latin American Journal*. Maryknoll, NY: Orbis, 1993.
Oliver, Claudio. "Crise ambiental e cristianismo: o papel da igreja na sustentabilidade." Round table dialogue with Marina Silva, Michelon e Dellambre during the People's Summit/Rio +20. Unpublished address, 2012.
———. "Quinta da Videira, a casa como espaço de viver." Unpublished letter, 2012.
———. *Relationality*. Philadelphia: Relational Tithe, 2010.
———. "Será possível a igreja?" Unpublished letter, 2010.
Oliver, Claudio, and Samuel Ewell. "Salt & Light: The Art of Proportion." *The New Urban World Journal* 1 (2012) 76–78.
Ott, Craig, and Harold A. Netland, eds. *Globalizing Theology: Belief and Practice in an Era of World Christianity*. Grand Rapids: Baker Academic, 2006.
Patel, Raj. *Stuffed and Starved: From Farm to Fork, the Hidden Battle for the World Food System*. Rev. ed. London: Portobello, 2013.
Peixoto, Katarina. "Boaventura: 'Não faz sentido que salvação não seja neste mundo.'" *Carta Maior* (2005). http://www.cartamaior.com.br/?/Editoria/Movimentos-Sociais/Boaventura-e 145-Nao-faz-sentido-que-salvacao-nao-seja-neste-mundoe 145-/2/2909.
Petrella, Ivan. *Beyond Liberation Theology: A Polemic*. London: SCM, 2008.
———. *The Future of Liberation Theology: An Argument and Manifesto*. London: SCM, 2006.

———, ed. *Latin American Liberation Theology: The Next Generation*. Maryknoll, NY: Orbis, 2005.
Phillips, Elizabeth. *Political Theology: A Guide for the Perplexed*. London: T&T Clark International, 2012.
Prakash, Madhu, and Dana Stuchul. "A Voice in the Wilderness: Ivan Illich's Era Dawns." In *Handbook of Public Pedagogy: Education and Learning beyond Schooling*, edited by J. A. Sandlin, Brian D. Schultz, and Jake Burdick, 511–23. New York: Routledge, 2010.
Quash, Ben. *Theology and the Drama of History*. Cambridge: Cambridge University Press, 2005.
Rahnema, Majid. "Towards Post-Development: Searching for Signposts, a New Language and New Paradigms." In *The Post-Development Reader*, edited by Majid Rahnema and Victoria Bawtree, 377–403. London: Zed, 1997.
Ribeiro, Darcy. *O povo brasileiro: A formação e o sentido do Brasil*. São Paulo: Companhia de Bolso, 2007.
Rist, Gilbert. *The History of Development: From Western Origins to Global Faith*. 3rd ed. London: Zed, 2008.
Rose, Gillian. *The Broken Middle: Out of Our Ancient Society*. Oxford: Blackwell, 1992.
Ruddick, Anna. "From the Ground Up: Creating Community through Incarnational Mission." William Temple Foundation. *Temple Tracts* 3:1, Book 12 (2017).
Russell, Cormac. "Does More Medicine Make Us Sicker? Ivan Illich Revisited." *Gaceta Sanitaria* (2019). Article in press.
Sachs, Wolfgang. "One World." In *The Development Dictionary: A Guide to Knowledge as Power*, edited by Wolfgang Sachs, 111–26. 2nd ed. London: Zed, 2010.
Samuel, Sajay. "In Defense of Vernacular Ways." *Viewpoint Magazine*, Issue 2: Theory and Practice (2012). https://www.viewpointmag.com/2012/09/12/in-defense-of-vernacular-ways/.
Sandroni, Carlos. *Feitiço decente: Transformações do samba no Rio de Janeiro (1917–1933)*. Rio de Janeiro: Jorge Zahar Editor, 2001.
Santos, Boaventura de Sousa. *The Rise of the Global Left: The World Social Forum and Beyond*. London: Zed, 2006.
Santos, Valterci. "Agricultores, pecuaristas—e pós-graduados." *O Estado de S. Paulo*, November 2011, 17–23.
Sbert, José. *Epimeteo, Iván Illich y el sendero de la sabiduría*. Edited by Jorge Márquez Muñoz. México, DF: Ediciones Sin Nombre, 2009.
———. "Progress." In *The Development Dictionary: A Guide to Knowledge as Power*, edited by Wolfgang Sachs, 212–27. 2nd ed. London: Zed, 2010.
Scharen, Christian, and Aana M. Vigen, eds. *Ethnography as Christian Theology and Ethics*. London: Continuum, 2001.
Schroyer, Trent. *Beyond Western Economics: Remembering Other Economic Cultures*. New York: Routledge, 2009.
———. "Review Essay: The Rivers North of the Future: The Testament of Ivan Illich, as Told to David Cayley." *Philosophy & Social Criticism* 35 (2009) 483–92.
Schumacher, E. F. *A Guide for the Perplexed*. New York: HarperPerennial, 2004.
———. *Small Is Beautiful: A Study of Economics as If People Mattered*. London: Vintage, 1993.
Schwartz, David. *Who Cares? Rediscovering Community*. Boulder, CO: Westview, 1997.

Schwartz, Roberto. *Misplaced Ideas: Essays on Brazilian Culture.* Edited by John Gledson. New York: Verso, 1992.
Scott, Peter, and William T. Cavanaugh, eds. *The Blackwell Companion to Political Theology.* Malden, MA: Blackwell, 2007.
Sedlacek, Tomas. *Economics of Good and Evil: The Quest for Economic Meaning from Gilgamesh to Wall Street.* New York: Oxford University Press, 2011.
Shanin, Teodor. "The Idea of Progress." In *The Post-Development Reader*, edited by Majid Rahnema and Victoria Bawtree, 65–72. London: Zed, 1997.
Shannon, Christopher. "Ivan Illich's Politics of Carnival." *The House Blog*, February 28, 2013. http://solidarityhall.org/ivan-illichs-politics-of-carnival/.
Soulen, R. Kendall, and Linda Woodhead, eds. *God and Human Dignity.* Grand Rapids: Eerdmans, 2006.
Sparks, Paul, Tim Soerens, and Dwight J. Friesen. *The New Parish: How Neighborhood Churches Are Transforming Mission, Discipleship and Community.* Downers Grove: IVP, 2014.
Utne, Eric. "Contents." *Utne Reader*, January–February 1995.
Veling, Terry A. *Practical Theology: On Earth as It Is in Heaven.* Maryknoll, NY: Orbis, 2005.
Vianna, Hermano. *O mistério do samba.* Rio de Janeiro: Jorge Zahar Editor, 2002.
Ward, Geoffrey, and Ken Burns. *The War: An Intimate History, 1941–1945.* New York: Knopf, 2007.
Waters, Brent. *From Human to Posthuman: Christian Theology and Technology in a Postmodern World.* Aldershot, UK: Ashgate, 2006.
Wells, Samuel. *God's Companions: Reimagining Christian Ethics.* Malden, MA: Blackwell, 2006.
———. *Improvisation: The Drama of Christian Ethics.* Grand Rapids: Brazos, 2004.
———. *A Nazareth Manifesto: Being with God.* Chichester, UK: Wiley, 2015.
Willard, Dallas. *The Divine Conspiracy: Rediscovering Our Hidden Life in God.* San Francisco: HarperSanFrancisco, 1998.
Williams, Rowan. *On Christian Theology.* Oxford: Blackwell, 2000.
Wirzba, Norman. *Food and Faith: A Theology of Eating.* New York: Cambridge University Press, 2011.
Woodhead. Linda. "Apophatic Anthropology." In *God and Human Dignity*, edited by R. Kendall Soulen and Linda Woodhead, 233–46. Grand Rapids: Eerdmans, 2006.
Wright, Tom. *John for Everyone, Part 2: Chapters 11–21.* 2nd ed. Louisville: Westminster John Knox, 2004.
Xenos, Nicholas. *Scarcity and Modernity.* London: Routledge, 1989.
Zalvidar, Jorge I., and Patrícia Q. Uceda. "Ivan Illich and the Conflict with the Vatican (1966–1969)." *The International Journal of Illich Studies* 2 (2011) 1–12.

Name/Subject Index

ABCD (Asset-Based Community Development), 277
abundance, manifesting, xvii, 257, 285
abundant
    community, xvii, 257–63, 274–75, 279, 280, 284, 293
    kingdom, 250–51, 254–55, 273
    life, xvii, 25, 237–38, 248, 249–56, 267, 268, 285–86
    mirage, 250–51, 273
    spirituality, iii
adamah, 207, 221
agogô, 84–87, 194–95
    agogô-ness of the, 86
agriculture, 251, 289
    domiciliar (home-based), 252, 254
    modern, 250–51
    regenerative, 251–52
    urban, 200, 236, 243, 252
aliveness, 157, 262–63
amateur, 2–3
    distinction between professional and, 2–3
    theologian, 2–3
American way of life, 15, 17, 53, 126, 162
Americanization, xv, 43–44, 46–50, 58, 60
apophaticism, 180
    apophatic anthropology, 62, 180–83, 295
    apophatic theology, 62–63

assimilation, xv, 15, 42–44, 57, 60, 181
Bahnson, Fred, 250–55, 268, 287
beginning in the middle, xv, 1, 18–19, 265
Berry, Wendell, 2
Bevans, Stephen, i, 266, 269,
Bevans, Stephen, and Roger Schroeder, 24, 37, 199, 266, 269–70, 284, 287
Bible
    as a five-act play, 64–65
    as theodrama, 64–65
Bingemer, Maria Clara, 13–14, 287
biography, 5, 37
    as theology, xv, 38–41, 72, 292
Block, Peter, 258–59, 279–80, 293
Bonhoeffer, Dietrich, 18, 52, 178, 181, 217–19, 288
brasicano, xv, 32, 42, 86–87, 91–92, 103, 190, 265
Brueggemann, Walter, 132–33, 145, 288
Buck-Morss, Susan, 215–19, 288
Casa da Videira (CdV), xvii, xxi, 236–56, 264, 274
Casarella, Peter, 13–14, 287
Catholic Church, xxi, 15, 35–36, 49, 51, 53, 70, 72–73, 75
Cayley, David, 20 36–37, 40–43, 59–61, 63–68, 71–73, 76–77, 87, 111, 113, 118–19, 137, 158, 162–63, 172–73, 187, 189, 194, 206, 215, 218–19, 231, 261–62, 264, 288

NAME/SUBJECT INDEX

charity, xv, 16, 53–54, 173, 187, 236, 292
church (*ecclesia*)
    as base Christian community, 283
    as body of Christ, 23, 74–75, 84, 87, 195, 223, 259, 262, 265, 282, 283
    as God's *roda*, 86
    as grassroots ecclesial community, 235, 237, 243, 248–49, 254
    as household of life abundant, 248–51, 254, 289
    and/as parish/*paraoikia*, xviii, 242, 247–49
    Mount Level Missionary Baptist, 29–31, 86, 196, 267
CIDOC, 51–52, 69–70
colonial wound, iv, 119, 184–86, 196, 257
color line, 57
    crossing the, 29, 86, 196
come and see, 101, 249
comida, distinction between *alimento* and, 253
commodities, 134, 142, 152–53, 156–59, 163, 169, 226, 234, 254, 258, 292
Companions for Hope, xxi, 272, 274, 280–81
conspiracy
    cultivation of, xvii, 76–77, 83, 259–61, 291
    divine, 83, 295
consumption
    addicts of, 229–30
    ritualizing, xvi, 133–42
conviviality, 24–25
    faith seeking, i, iii, v, ix, xi, xii, xviii, 25, 256, 264–86
    Illich's definition of, 85
    politics of, xvi, 150, 158–59
    convivial institutions, 151, 153, 154
    convivial reconstruction, 150, 154–55

convivial recovery, 188, 223–35, 236, 242, 253–56, 261, 272
convivial turn, xvii, 22, 189, 199, 231, 235
corruption of the best is the worst, xvi, 67, 161–95
Costas, Orlando, 109–10, 288
counterproductivity, 152–52, 166
creation, 63–64
    and contingency, 118, 177, 242
    and creatureliness, 144, 178, 181–83, 209
    and fall, 18, 178, 217–18, 288
    and incarnation, 78
    and re-creation, 260
    and redemption, 79–80, 183, goodness of, 79
    treating creation as, 201–5
creatures, being, 78, 85, 179, 188, 213, 217, 221, 258, 263, 268
DaMatta, Roberto, 32–33
Davis, Ellen, 239–89
development, 161–89
    "birthday" of, 163
    as corruption of Christian mission, 174
    as economic peace, xvi, 162–70, 257, 261–62
    as missionary enterprise, 160–74
    as planned poverty, 165–66, 291
difference,
    ecclesial, 112
    incarnational, 39, 66
    Jewish-Gentile, 66
dignity, human, xvi, 21, 105, 113–20, 149, 161, 174, 180, 185, 188, 209, 252, 258, 263, 280, 285, 295
disciple(ship), 85–86, 103, 106, 136, 174, 176, 199, 249, 257, 260, 262, 267, 274, 275, 284, 295
Dorotheos of Gaza, 85, 194, 257
"ecological conversion," 207
ecology, 271, 285, 289, 291
    of relationships, 242, 281, 282
edge effect, 281–82
edges, iv, xviii, 281–82

encounter(s), i–ii, iv, vii, 4–5, 7, 10, 12–14, 18, 32, 35, 37, 42, 46, 57, 67, 81, 87, 92, 104, 106, 108, 117, 120, 122, 126, 131–32, 160, 165, 173–76, 185, 188, 190, 193–94, 196, 199–201, 205, 219, 224, 236, 262, 269, 274, 278, 280–82, 289
energy
  consumption, 51, 137–40, 228, 250
  and equity, 137–39
Epimetheus, 142–44
  Epimethean humanity, 143, 178, 209, 220, 228, 241
  receptivity of, 187
epistemological rupture(s), 9, 12, 18, 92, 94, 103
eschatology, 60, 100
Esteva, Gustavo, and Madhu Prakash, 111–13, 231–35, 253
ethnography, 7, 11, 19, 294
ethnos
  distinction between *ethos* and, 65–67, 77, 167
Ewell, Rosalee Velloso, xxi, 4, 29–31
experience, i–ii, vi–vii, 1, 3–10, 12–14, 19–20, 22, 35, 43, 45, 46, 49, 57, 62, 67, 79, 81, 83–87, 91–92, 94, 97–98, 102–3, 110, 120, 122, 190–96, 199–200, 210–14, 229–30, 240, 243–45, 248, 262–63, 265, 267, 270, 273, 287
faith, xix, 22, 44, 61, 63, 171, 173, 218, 245, 253, 267, 284, 289
  fides quae creditur, 269
  fides qua creditur, 269
Farias, Domenico, 61–63, 289
favela, 97–98, 100, 159, 201
flourish(ing), iii, xvi, 21, 84, 105, 127, 142, 144–49, 158, 163, 165, 175, 177, 180, 184, 188–89, 210, 222, 232, 237, 242, 251, 257–58, 271, 275, 281–82

following the naked Christ, xv, 58–87, 187, 199
food
  cycle, 255, 270–75
  poverty, 272–73, 287
  system(s), 250, 272–73
formation
  intercultural, 51, 84
  theological, 51
Freire, Paulo, 14, 69
friendship, i, ii, iv, xiii, xvii, xxi, 14, 39, 61, 63, 70, 77, 92, 101, 106, 162, 179, 189, 199–201, 206, 241, 264, 274–75, 280, 288, 291
garden(s), ii, iii, 130, 200–203, 221, 238–40, 252, 260
  entering someone else's, xviii, 264–82
  gardening, ii, 266–69, 273–74, 280, 281, 285
gifts, 84, 86, 196, 259, 265, 277–84
good intentions, 15–17, 42, 56–57, 104, 131, 161, 188, 190, 201, 205–7, 273, 291
(Good) Samaritan, xvi, 65–68, 77, 104, 130, 171–73, 187, 206, 219
Gorringe, Tim, 212–15, 290
grassroots post-modernism, 235, 243, 248
gratuity, v, 206, 262–63
Great Commission, 200, 284
gringo, 31, 33, 83, 86–87, 196, 204
Gutiérrez, Gustavo, 7–8, 69, 290
Hauerwas, Stanley, 92–93, 108, 112, 290
Hoinacki, Lee, 36, 39, 59, 63, 73, 171, 180, 215, 290, 291, 293
hope
  accounting for, 218
  as a social force, xvii, 159, 208, 212, 222–23
  distinction between expectation and, 144
  enacting, 275, 293
  living, 4, 212, 215

NAME/SUBJECT INDEX

hospitality, ii, 106, 113, 116–18, 171–72, 186–87, 196, 245, 259, 261, 273, 275, 290–91
Hudson, Trevor, 1, 3, 4, 7, 290
humanity
   homo industrialis, 129
   homo miserabilis, 159, 183
   homo oeconomicus, 159
   homo orans, 213
   homo sapiens, 159, 183, 213
humility, 221, 222, 258, 263
   of the guest, 187, 196
identity, iv, 7, 9, 33, 41, 44, 47–48, 63, 82, 87, 91–92, 103, 107–8, 110, 112, 181, 185, 190, 221, 248, 265, 270, 272, 290, 292
   as becoming "more than," 64, 87, 265
   as being an outsider-insider, iii, 19, 33–35
   as belonging-with-difference, 82
   as in-between-ness, 34, 82
image
   of God, 63–64, 114–15, 177–79
   human, 115
   re-creating others in one's own, 185
improvisation, xvii, 64–65, 68, 107–8, 195, 223–38, 245, 247, 254, 256, 295
   as convivial recovery, 223–35
   as mission, 223–27
Incarnation, vi, xv, 20, 22–24, 37–39, 43, 57–59, 61, 64–68, 74, 77–79, 86–87, 102, 109–10, 181, 184, 186, 190, 191, 218, 219, 222–25, 256, 260, 262, 288, 292
   as basis for inculturation, 79
   as basis for "returning," 241
   as scandal, 185
   and institutionalization, 172
   and resurrection, 214
   de-incarnation(al), 42, 57, 173, 188
   experience of the, 110
   particularity of the, 180
   prolong(ing) the, i–iii, xv, 21–23, 27, 37, 67–68, 81, 87, 91, 189, 219, 227, 260, 263
   witness of the, 218
incarnational, ii, 20, 21, 80, 242, 292,
   Christianity, vi, 194
   counterfeits, 172
   and Epimethean, 242
   inclusion, 185
   interruption, 260
   logic of (discipleship and) mission, 84, 131, 160, 174
   (pattern of) mission, iii, 20, 21, 49, 74–75, 77, 105, 162, 174, 176–79, 186, 227, 235–36, 238, 242, 254, 294
   presence, ii, xix-xx, 16–17, 20, 44, 46–47, 51–52, 54, 56, 70, 74, 77–78, 83, 101–4, 106, 110, 111, 128, 131, 148, 161–62, 172, 177, 190, 194, 206, 242, 261, 268, 270, 271, 282–84
inculturation, 79, 179
institutional spectrum, 151, 154
institutionalization, 42, 66–67, 134, 136, 148, 172–73, 175, 177, 179, 187, 229
itinerarium, 21, 37, 39, 74, 105, 199
jazz, 73, 196, 259, 288
Jennings, Willie, xi, xv, xx, 188, 63, 105, 112, 162, 174, 176, 181, 183–86, 191, 195, 292
journey, i, ii, iv–vii, xv, xx, 3–4, 6–10, 13, 18, 19–22, 24, 29, 35, 37, 39, 42, 44, 49, 56–61, 64, 68, 74, 80–81, 91–92, 105, 126, 159, 192, 199–200, 202, 226, 240, 252, 265, 267, 269, 274, 284, 290
justice, v, 13, 36, 55, 137, 140, 158, 167, 213–14, 269, 290
   distributive, 158
   (in)justice, iii, vi, 133
   participatory, 158

language, learning, 18, 32, 44, 45, 48, 51–52, 81, 92–93, 123, 170, 184, 191, 230, 266, 276
liberation theology, 69, 93, 108, 283, 287, 293–94
limits, 138, 140, 144, 147, 149–53, 155–57, 169, 177–78, 182, 186, 188, 195, 209, 213, 217, 230, 237, 241, 255, 258, 291–92
McClendon, James, 38–39, 62, 292
McClintock Fulkerson, Mary, 10–11
McKnight, John, 155, 258–59, 279–80, 293
Mignolo, Walter, 119, 293
military-industrial-professional complex, 154–60
missão integral, 93–94
mission (*see also* incarnational mission)
    as midwifery, 222
    intercultural, 10, 22, 42, 87, 266, 281
missionary
    intercultural, 10, 51–52, 57, 91, 191–92, 199, 265
    reverse, xxi, 264–65, 270–71, 274
missionary adoption, xvi, 81, 87, 91, 190–91
missionary poverty, xvii, 190, 196
Myers, Ched, 92, 293
myth(s), vi, xvi, 122, 136–37, 142–44, 146–51, 158, 167, 228, 230, 258
needs, 98, 127, 134, 141, 155, 159, 164–66, 171, 173, 182–83, 206, 233, 249, 277, 291–92
    commodity-defined, 129, 156, 159, 163, 229
    diagnosing, 101, 172, 205
    distinction between desires and, 258
    history of, 138–41, 157–59, 161, 166, 292
    imputation of, 128, 226
    meeting, 57, 98, 101, 120
    satisfaction of human, 154
    Western, 127, 161
neighbor(hood), ii, xxi, 3, 11, 24, 43, 50, 66–67, 74, 85, 101–3, 106, 130, 165, 172, 178, 194, 200, 202–5, 236, 240, 243, 254, 257, 271–73, 275–85, 293, 295
Neighbour Nights, 276–80, 282
new humanity, 23, 66, 75, 77, 86–87, 91, 125, 190, 265
New Social Movements (NSMs), xvii, 210, 231, 233, 253
Nisbet, Robert, 120–21
Nouwen, Henri, 8, 264–65, 293
Oliver, Claudio, xiii, xvii, 14–15, 129–31, 200–202, 204–7, 220–21, 236–49, 252–55, 264, 273, 289, 293
participation, 24, 39, 75, 77, 83, 134, 176, 180–81, 195, 223
peace
    of Christ, 25, 102, 260–61, 267, 270, 275
    economic, xvi, 162, 167–70, 257, 261–62
    people's, 76, 167–70
    pax Americana, 16
    pax romana, 167
pedagogical imperialism, 174, 176, 191, 195
pedagogy
    of Pain and Hope, 3–4, 7
    of the *roda*, 194–96
pilgrimage, i, 21, 247
    Christian life as, 74
    of Ivan Illich, xv, 40–42, 49, 56, 60, 74
    of Pain and Hope, 3–7, 99
Pope Francis, 11, 24, 207, 284
poverty, xvii, 15, 49–51, 93, 103–4, 108–9, 130–31, 141–42, 165–66, 170, 179, 190, 191, 196, 272–73, 286–88, 291
    food, 272–73, 287
    missionary, xvii, 190, 196
    modernized, 166
    web of, 272

NAME/SUBJECT INDEX

practical theology, iv–v, 1–3, 271, 285, 287, 295
preferential option
    for the discarded, v, 226–27, 284–85
    for the possible, xii, xvii, 236, 239
presence, iii, xix–xx, 16–17, 20, 44, 46–47, 51–52, 54, 56, 70, 74, 77, 78, 83, 101–4, 106, 110–11, 128, 131, 148, 161–62, 172, 177, 190, 194, 206, 242, 261, 268, 270–71, 282–84
production
    autonomous, 139, 142, 151–53, 158, 232, 234, 249
    capital-intensive, 139–40, 152
    convivial mode(s) of, 153
    heteronomous, 152–53, 158, 234
    industrial mode of, 138, 150, 152, 228
    labor-intensive, 140, 251
    theological, 102
professional(s), xx, 1, 2, 3, 4, 6, 22, 130–31, 133, 154–59, 175, 177, 190, 200–201, 230, 241, 255, 283, 291
professional power, 156, 230
professionalization, 157, 175
progress
    (Des)Ordem e Progresso, 127, 161
    ritualization of, 76, 134, 136, 137
Prometheus, 142–48, 150, 220
    Promethean enterprise, xvi, 142, 145, 150, 209, 225, 231
    Promethean ethos, 143–49, 188, 208–9, 226, 229, 242
    Promethean expectation(s), 145, 209–10, 215, 232, 251
    Promethean fallacy, 146, 148–49, 188
    Promethean humanity, 160–78
    prometheanization of Christian mission, 177
    Neo-Promethean, 158
prophetic dialogue, 24, 37, 266, 270, 273, 284, 287

prophetic imagination, xvi, 132–33, 135, 137, 139, 141, 145, 147, 149, 149, 151, 153, 155, 157, 159, 288
radical monopoly, 138, 141, 155
receptivity, v, 48, 84, 187
research(er), ii, 4–7, 10, 13–14, 18–19, 36, 51, 66, 106, 155–56, 167, 210, 228, 264, 271, 291
response-ability, xvii, 215, 219–22, 285
roda
    de samba(samba circle), 82, 84, 86, 190, 192, 196
    God's, 86
    pedagogy of the, xvii, 194–96
Sachs, Wolfgang, 123–25, 289, 291, 294
samba
    as *bloco*, 82–83, 85, 192–93, 195–96
    as parable of ecclesial belonging, 84
    the gospel according to, xvi, xvii, 81, 81, 86, 162, 166, 170–71, 190, 257
    the mystery of, 263
Santos, Boaventura de Sousa, 111, 210–14, 243, 294
Sbert, José, 58, 125, 294
scarcity, 168, 176, 188, 226, 234, 257–59, 261–62, 285, 295
shalom, 167, 260
Shanin, Teodor, 121–23, 125, 295
subsistence perspective, 169–70, 293
technique, xx, 199, 25, 131, 192–93, 200, 242, 275, 286
technological ethos, xvi, 21, 106, 113, 116–19, 147, 160, 186, 251
technology, xx, 40, 116, 157, 164, 188, 290, 295
theodrama, xv, 59–60, 64–65, 80, 223, 225–26
throwaway culture, iv
Truman, Harry, xvi, 130–31, 162–66, 169–71, 173
use-value(s), 157, 159, 163

distinction between exchange-
value(s) and, 141, 152
Veling, Terry, 1–2, 270, 285, 295
verbs, recovery of, 230, 233–34, 248,
253, 283–84
vernacular, 167, 249
culture, 168
ways, 294
virada(s), vi, xv–xvii, 12–13, 29, 31,
33, 35, 42, 56, 81, 91, 93, 95,
97, 99, 101, 103, 106, 120,
126, 192, 199, 201, 203, 205,
207, 274
"war against subsistence," 167,
169–70
"war on poverty," 15, 50, 142, 166

Wells, Sam, ii, 5, 7, 8, 21, 64, 65, 68,
107–9, 223–27, 236–37, 245,
248, 256, 290
Williams, Rowan, 18, 183, 265, 295
Wirzba, Norman, 250–55, 267–68,
287, 295
witness, iii, xv, xx, 13–14, 17–18, 21,
37–40, 48, 52, 57–59, 61–62,
68, 70, 72–74, 80, 82, 105,
161, 184, 208, 212–13, 218,
242, 255–56, 268, 287, 292
wormery, i, vii, 201–3, 207
worms, 201, 203, 239
wounds, 8, 10–12, 272, 286

Scripture Index

OLD TESTAMENT

Genesis
1	114, 218
2	100, 203, 207, 221, 258, 260, 268
3	177, 222, 258
12	63

Psalms
34:8	285

Jeremiah
6:16	73
29:7	284

NEW TESTAMENT

Matthew
5	71, 283
6:33	248, 251, 262, 273
7:13–14	126
10:16	14
15:22	66
22:37–39	85
25:35	238
28:16–20	20, 174, 284

Mark
1	244
4:30–32	240
10:29–31	247

Luke
1:46–55	227
10:30–37	104, 172, 173

John
1	11, 23, 66, 87, 101, 219, 249, 267
3	24, 187
4	268
6	268
8	218
10	25, 172, 248, 253, 256, 261, 267
15	236, 265, 268
17	87
20	30, 81, 85, 86, 102, 257, 260, 267, 269

Acts
7:6	248
17:28	62
10–11	66

Romans
1:16	75, 286
6	31, 183

12:1–2	18, 22, 187, 214, 257

2 Corinthians

4:4	64, 177

Ephesians

2	23, 66, 75, 77, 86, 87, 92, 125, 185, 190, 265, 286
4	18

Colossians

1	32, 64, 68, 177
3	64

Hebrews

1:3	109
7:19	133, 187
11:13–16	41
12:1	14, 38

1 Peter

1:3	212, 215
2:4	285
2:11	248
3:15b	212, 218

1 John

4:9	59, 61, 75, 263
4:16	181

Revelation

3	29
22	100, 203

www.ingramcontent.com/pod-product-compliance
Lightning Source LLC
Chambersburg PA
CBHW021344300426
44114CB00012B/1075

A critical need for all of us currently involved in mission is for conversation partners who bring fresh language and renewed imagination. Sam Ewell is proving to be one such companion. Here, Ewell brings alive the incarnational theology of Ivan Illich by setting his insights alongside some of the most challenging struggles of mission in the twenty-first century. The book will be greatly appreciated by thinking practitioners, students, and academics alike.

—MIKE PEARS
Director, International Baptist Theological Seminary Centre

Organized around the immensely generative concept of conviviality, guided by the writings of Ivan Illich, and provoked by the author's journeying to and from Brazil as a missionary, this is a book that overflows with wisdom. Drinking from the deep well of the Christian tradition at its best, Samuel E. Ewell has written an extraordinary theology that fuses spirituality with social analysis, story with doctrine, ethics with friendship, experience with scholarship, wormeries with mission, the personal with the prophetic. The result: a theology that dares to imagine what it means to "prolong the incarnation"— and that means living a life together in a wounded world.

—ASHLEY COCKSWORTH
Senior Lecturer in Theology and Practice, University of Roehampton

An extraordinary journey of faith and life! In *Faith Seeking Conviviality* Sam Ewell has used the metaphor of *samba* to walk us through the struggle to live with integrity in the hard places. In this pilgrimage the little-heard voice of Latin American theologian and educator Ivan Illich provides guidance and wisdom. If you are serious about discovering a deeper intersection between faith and life this book is a must-read.

—PERRY SHAW, author of *Transforming Theological Education*

Seemingly overwhelming global issues such as contemporary individualism present us with enormous challenges. In the face of this, Sam Ewell's book comes as a pleasant surprise among recent theological publications, inviting us to open our inner garden and broaden our experiences (provoked by encounter) in order to break with the isolationist logic that separates life from theology.

Sam's empathy with Ivan Illich's thinking is evident as a way of valuing the empirical nature of his research and his unique way of doing theology—theology that is born and reborn in the embodied life of one's neighbor.

Here is a book that challenges us to redefine what we understand about discipleship, friendship, and hospitality, and teaches us that "prolonging the incarnation of Christ" is nothing more than an attempt to build new pathways toward a more humane world!

> —Vanessa Carvalho de Mello
> Professor, South American Theological Seminary, Paraná, Brazil
> Coordinator at the Evangelical Women's Collective for Gender Equality (EWGE), Paraná, Brazil

Illich was a prophet of our present moment whose visionary pronouncements, theological imagination and incarnational practice mark him out as a unique light—a man of grief and hope, wisdom and wit. Sam Ewell's brilliant book holds together the life and thought of Illich, painting a picture of both wry nuance and singular vision. A wonderful book.

> —David Benjamin Blower, *Nomad* Podcast

Sam Ewell says, "I realized that I could not afford not to do theology if I wanted to integrate and give voice to my experience." He goes on to describe his work as "an extended testimony that is at the same time an exercise in doing theology with and after Ivan Illich." These twin themes of voice and testimony, integration and theology coruscate throughout the book, leaving the reader absorbed, challenged, and reenergized by the Spirit.

> —Rev. Dr. Sam Wells
> Vicar, St. Martin-in-the-Fields

"Your Handbook for Not Giving Up!" That is how I would like to subtitle this astonishing book when I hand it out to my Christian friends and co-conspirators in the "Western world." While we are in the midst of a massive awakening to the social and ecological crisis our way of life has perpetuated around the globe, we cannot find a way forward that does not perpetuate the very injustices that caused the crisis to begin with. *Faith Seeking Conviviality* is a stunning and prescient contribution on the life and work of Ivan Illich.